Reinventing Local Media

*Ideas for Thriving
in a Postmodern World*

Volume I

Reinventing Local Media

*Ideas for Thriving
in a Postmodern World*

Volume I

Terry Heaton

*Senior Vice President
Audience Research & Development*

For Allie

Table of Contents

Categories

The Essays

Acknowledgments

As in any publishing endeavor, there are many people to thank. I've been around this business for a long time, and every person I've encountered has helped form my beliefs. This includes members of my self-selected tribe, people like Jeff Jarvis, Doc Searls, David Weinberger, Jay Rosen, Umair Haque, Chris Anderson, Michael Rosenblum, J. D. Lasica, Diane Mermigas and Dan Gillmor.

Thoughts don't originate in a vacuum, and there are many beyond these who've helped me. I'm honored to have had so many friends.

I work with the best and brightest and wish to acknowledge my comrades-in-arms, Jerry Gumbert and Steve Safran. Jerry keeps pushing me to state my lofty thoughts in ways that modernist business people can understand, while Steve inspires me with his mind and keeps me in stitches with his self-effacing humor.

But more than anyone else, I wish to thank my friend Holly Hunter, who has been my editor since I began writing these essays. Despite her youth, she has taught me much, and I'm fortunate to know her. When my Allie passed away suddenly in 2006, Holly was there for me through it all, and I will never be able to repay her for her kindness. Holly, thank you for being you.

I also wish to acknowledge all of those who will read my essays in this form. Your attention blesses me, and I only hope that the words contained herein will challenge you, inspire you and help you think for yourself. To thine own self be true.

Foreword

We live in a time of great uncertainty and great change, much of it driven by the gradual enlightenment of people with limitless knowledge at their fingertips. This Cultural Revolution will eventually challenge every institution of humankind, but in the early 21st century, its primary target is traditional media — the way we inform ourselves about important issues and events.

The market for news and information has never been stronger, but the market for traditional approaches to news is rapidly shrinking. The only choice we have is one of reinvention. Those within the institution blame technology, but technology is only the means; the real problem for media companies is that the energy for all the changes they see is coming from people — the "people formerly known as the audience," as Jay Rosen first noted in his blog, Pressthink. This is why we must study culture if we wish to do business when the dust settles, as it certainly will.

But when we study culture, we do so largely from a foundation of assumptions, beliefs so deep and so basic that we never question them. If we ask ourselves, for example, why we're drifting into moral decay, we'll examine Hollywood, the breakdown of the family, religious factionalism, and so forth. But the question begins with the assumption that morality is already a defined, known and agreed upon set of principles. We don't question those principles, because each leads to further examination, the end result of which, we fear, will be chaos.

Eastern Europe went through a remarkably similar era when movable type was invented and the Bible was printed for the first time. Culture was dominated at the time by the Roman Catholic Church, the "authorized" keepers of the holy book of knowledge. The hierarchical church dictated everything, but their authority was seriously challenged when people outside their immediate control were able to print the text. The church's first response was to brand the printers as heretics, followed by attempts to license printing presses. These were necessary steps, because the church was trying to protect that which gave it its authority — access to knowledge.

So it is today that institutions whose authority flows from protected knowledge are threatened when that knowledge becomes widely disseminated. We have only just begun.

And so I have chosen in my work to examine change from the context of a significant cultural shift. In the decades and centuries to come, scholars will view these times with the same astonishment as we do in considering 15th-century Europe. My reference is Postmodernism, although from a highly pragmatic perspective. I find the term descriptive and appropriate and not nearly as frightening as those who use it, for example, from the pulpit of various places of worship. It is not evil personified. It simply is what it is.

Premodernism: I worship and believe, therefore I understand.

Modernism: I think and reason, therefore I understand.

Postmodernism: I participate and experience, therefore I understand.

The future existence of contemporary traditional media is itself at stake. It's not simply a matter of which will outlast the other, for that prize is similar to being the last buggy whip manufacturer. The future demands something much more radical, something that "fits" the postmodern culture in a way that a hierarchical, top-down press simply cannot.

Opening the newsgathering process to everyone is an excellent first step. Another is acceptance of the right of anyone to be a media company. The definition of what it means to be a journalist is also on the table, for modernism's view (the professional) may not be Postmodernism's.

This is the most exciting time in the history of communications, a land grab not unlike the gold rush days of the 19th century. But it's vital that we realize it's also a time of much bigger change, for the culture itself is shifting. As human beings, what will we do when we're all connected, when the knowledge that drives the institutions of law, medicine, finance, government and others is at our fingertips? What will these institutions do, and how will we respond? What will we do with foreign (strange) cultures when we understand their beliefs and knowledge? How will be buy and sell? How will we advertise? Will we only go to war when everyone approves? What will we do with love and identity and copyright and ourselves?

The disruption that is dismantling the business of media can't be "fixed" by any form of multi-platform distribution model or other logical formula, because at core, it's far deeper than fragmentation, disintermediation or "content." We need to reinvent what it means to be "media." People are running from traditional media, and rather than chasing after them, it would be vastly more productive to understand the reasons why they're running.

It is my hope that this book will serve to enable that understanding.

— **Terry Heaton**
Grapevine, Texas
February 2008

Note: A few of the essays here are several years old, and the technology referenced has advanced — in some cases, dramatically. I've included them, however, because they help lay the foundation for subsequent thought paths and reveal how far we've come in such a short time.   —T. H.

The Triumph of Personal Media Over Mass Media

Personal media — and the disruptive innovations brought about by the revolution — has forever changed how we meet our information and entertainment needs. The essays in this section explore how (and more importantly, why) the people formerly known as the audience came to begin making their own media. Local media companies who intend to survive cannot afford to deny the triumph of the personal over our old paradigm. The title of this section is taken from the book *An Army of Davids*, by blogger Glenn Reynolds.

The essay entitled "The Real Threat to Local Broadcasters" is still something that most traditional media people either don't see or are unable to act upon. There's currently a continuing effort by some traditionalists to vilify bloggers and thereby dismiss personal media as a threat to "real" journalism, which is like saying an automobile isn't a horse. Who knew?

THE PUBLIC JOURNAL

January 29, 2008

Slowly but surely, the path that leads to journalism's future is increasingly one of participation by the people formerly known as the audience. The extent to which the public will be a part of journalism tomorrow is often missed by those who continue the fight to maintain the status quo, but as as Sony CEO Howard Stringer said recently, "When you defend the status quo when the quo has lost its status, you're in trouble." (1)

Traditional journalists try to separate themselves from the rise of personal media by pejoratively referring to "them" as amateurs. "User-generated content" is a convenient but terribly misleading moniker that is used to perpetuate the myth that journalists are somehow special people and that this is what gives us our place in the culture.

This is unfortunate, for what's taking place in front of us is nothing less than a breathtaking reinvention of how we inform each other as a people, and journalists — those normally curious researchers of everything from perps to pets — are missing it almost entirely. As Upton Sinclair wrote many years ago, "It is difficult to get a man to understand something when his salary depends upon his not understanding it."

Since the earliest of times, the journal in journalism was the thing, a neatly bound expression of the writer's stories or the stories of many writers. Regardless, people stood in line to obtain the journal and, sooner or later, the publishers discovered that people would actually pay for it, whether directly through subscriptions or indirectly through advertising. A business model was born, and along with it, the drift away from the journal and towards the "ism" — what 12-step groups refer to as "I, self, me."

Media advisor, analyst, academician and author Robert Picard wrote in 2004 of how commercialization had impacted the soul of the journal.

> This situation has promoted self-interested behavior aimed at exploiting market potential, and there is a growing conflict between the role of newspapers as servants of readers and the exploitation of readers to seek additional commercial gain. It should not be surprising that the public increasingly sees the press as just another business that is more concerned with its own economic interests than with the broader interests of those it purports to serve. (2)

Media evolved in terms of the method and means of delivering the journal, but the essence of the journal itself remained constant — the output of the writer.

In its earliest iterations, blogging was also about the journal. One of the earliest players in the game is actually named "Live Journal," a site where teens could share their thoughts with themselves and their friends. There were the occasional posts by other, more — cough, cough — esteemed bloggers suggesting that Live Journal wasn't blogging at all, but that self-serving argument was put to rest when MySpace started calling such journals "blogs." A blog is a blog. Period.

So now, everybody writes, and everybody publishes. Flickr is a repository of millions of photographs. YouTube is a repository of millions of videos. Facebook and MySpace are home to the journals of millions. Twitter follows the movements of millions. The open source software movement has placed powerful — and free — content management systems in the hands of millions, including advertisers. Aggregators of any form of information stream are also available anywhere and are today even woven into the fabric of browsers. And all of it shows no signs of slowing down.

In 2004, Simon Bucks, Associate Editor of *SkyNews* in London, made news when he was asked about citizen journalism and replied "How about citizen heart surgeons?" In a remarkable recantation of that last year, Bucks noted that the new stars of journalism may be on Facebook or MySpace.

> The cultural issue is altogether tougher, not just for Sky News, but for all news organisations. Most journalists have grown up with the idea that we tell people the news which we think they should be told.
>
> Confession time: I was guilty too. I once argued that you wouldn't trust a citizen journalist any more than a citizen heart surgeon. It was a paternalistic and sermonising approach that most of us shared, but it won't do any more.
>
> Web 2.0 (the generic name for the interactive Internet) is giving the media to the people. On-demand news means that people can choose the news they want, when they want it. And they can interact with it, rant about it, and contribute to it. The coming generation of news-users, the 16- to 24-year-olds, have grown up with this concept, and expect nothing less. (3)

But even more significant than the reality that everybody is a reporter — that citizen "journalism" is here to stay — is what's happening to the journal itself.

Not only is it no longer the realm of the few; its very nature is changing. The journal is a constant now, ever morphing from one form to another and making sense only in the moment it is consumed. No entry is complete unto itself, for all are influenced by what was before and all lead to the next. The journal has become one continuous flow of raw information that serves the moment, and this is the paradigm of journalism for tomorrow.

It is the news gathering process that is tomorrow's journal. If the finished products of our efforts are no longer a sustainable model, then we must let people into — and participate with — the process of gathering the news and let that become our primary model.

And it will come with new guidelines and principles. At one point in its ongoing coverage of the death of actor Heath Ledger, the gossip/entertainment site TMZ.com reported that Ledger had died in the apartment of Mary Kate Olsen, which was incorrect. The *New York Times* "City Room" blog also got it wrong.

Both corrected the mistake as soon as it was known and moved on, and the *Los Angeles Times* later provided a fascinating glimpse into the unedited world of continuous news:

> But here's the problem: Stories have never arrived to the world fully formed or vetted. Journalists have generally had hours — not minutes or seconds — to craft a story from the blast wave of facts and factoids that comes in the wake of a bombshell.
>
> What people are seeing now is an old-fashioned process — reporting — as it unfolds in real time. If the public wants its information as raw and immediate as possible, it'll have to get used to a few missteps along the way, and maybe even approach breaking stories with a bit of skepticism, like a good reporter would. (4)

So a part of this "process" of news is mistakes, and the ethical question is does it matter in a world of raw and unedited news-as-a-process? This is just one of the many issues with which we'll have to grapple in the years to come, for mistakes are a part of everyday life in the professional newsgathering process. They are corrected as stories advance, and nobody thinks anything about it, because for us, the journal is the thing.

So in a world where that newsgathering process is also the product, we have to assume that mistakes and errors will be a part of the stream. We'll correct them when they happen and move on, just like we do today in the process of gathering the news. The legal world will have to make adjustments, too. An error, for example, published in the "unerasable" world of finished-product news, for example, carries a different kind of authoritative weight than one that can be altered within minutes, especially if it's couched in language that doesn't express finality.

These are the types of things that our culture will have to work out as the journal evolves into a continuous, public stream.

Technology is the servant of the public journal, and that is going to continue to shape the degree to which it is truly public. Nobody understands this better than Robert Scoble, the blogging pioneer who is beginning a new job with Fast Company. Scoble got a lot of attention from the blogosphere for live streaming recently from the World Economic Forum in Davos, Switzerland — mostly for his comments that it takes fewer clicks to stream live video than it does to make a phone call.

But the more profound disruption that Scoble is discovering was revealed in an interview with Jeff Jarvis:

> When I turn on my cellphone, it tells Twitter that I'm now streaming, and an audience shows up pretty quickly. I find that even having a small audience makes the interaction more interesting, because people will help me interview whoever I'm aiming the camera at. An audience can now participate in something live and influence the interactions that I'm having with somebody in front of the camera. (5)

Scoble is a guy who's at the cutting edge of the cutting edge, and his experiences will be repeated by many others in the years ahead. This ability to include the people formerly known as the audience in the creation of the product — as it's being created — has staggering ramifications for the news business and the public journal.

Business viability for media in this new world will be driven by many of the same attributes that separate news organizations in the world of the private journal, including the editorial process, the arguments and opinions of those filtering the inbound streams, convenience and habit. The only downside for media companies is the refusal to participate, because the journal that increasingly matters is now written by everyone.

This is the ultimate "new" in new media.

THE ON-DEMAND TRAP

May 24, 2006

L et's pay a visit to the home of Mr. and Mrs. Media and their spoiled two-year-old, Demand. This day is like most other days in the Media home with little Demand wanting what he wants when he wants it. In stereotypical parenting fashion, Mr. Media does the manly things, including spending time in the workshop crafting new toys for his son. It makes him feel so good to be able to do this, and he thanks God every day for the gifts and skills (and tools) he possesses in order to make his son feel happy.

It also offsets his role as disciplinarian.

Mrs. Media, on the other hand, is charged with the up-close and personal responsibilities of catering to Demand's wants and needs. She feeds him, clothes him, and comforts him when he's feeling down. She assesses his toy desires and relays them to her husband. When Mr. Media finishes a new toy, he gives it to her to pass along to his son. This is the way it's done in the Media home. Demand doesn't want his father to give him the toys; he wants his mother to do that, and, after all, he is the demanding one in the household.

As the boy grows, who do you think will have the most value to him, his father or his mother? It's not the maker of the toy who

7

holds the affinity position but the one who gives it to him, and this is the problem with the whole on-demand media frenzy currently underway. This may seem a silly analogy, but is it really?

Did the users of YouTube give their loyalty (and eyeballs) to YouTube or NBC during and after the whole "Lazy Sunday" fiasco? Do users of iTunes give their attention to ABC or iTunes (or their iPod) when they download the latest episode of "Lost?" When users add an RSS feed to their favorite customizable start page, they may be thankful for the feed, but where are they enjoying its contents?

Local television stations used to enjoy the affinity position with people in their communities, and that was no small part of their status and success. Many old-timers will relate to an angry viewer who was upset because something interfered with "his" or "her" station. This love affair was similar to what certain — and very smart — Web applications are experiencing today, and this is a big problem for local broadcasters. When young people run to Google or Yahoo or MySpace and can't name the four networks, well, that doesn't seem too hopeful for the future of broadcasting.

For decades, the networks have been in the content-providing business, so it doesn't matter to them (or it shouldn't) if their programs go one way or another in the future. But not so with network affiliates, because their core competency is built on this idea of the Mrs. Media position. This is why it is so terribly dangerous for local broadcasters to get caught up in the on-demand frenzy and attempt to seize the Mr. Media position as their only hope for the future.

Clearly, it's smart strategy to offer content in an unbundled fashion. There's money to be made and multiple platforms to explore. But it is foolish strategy to assume that such a position is all that's required for local stations (local media in general) to survive online in the long term. There are three profoundly important reasons for this.

The personal media revolution

The disruptive innovation that poses the biggest threat to local media companies isn't multiple platforms for content distribution; it's the triumph of personal technology over mass technology. In this light, betting the ranch on an on-demand strategy is a pure and insane form of denial. It *is* a revolution, and guess who they're revolting against?

A whole new world is growing up around us that doesn't give a hoot about us or our dilemmas. Energized by discontent with institutional media, very low barriers to entry, the simple joy of creating media, a profound sense of community, a deep weariness with hyperbole, and many other forces, people are taking matters into their own hands and having a ball doing it. The younger people are, the more they're involved in this.

As Gordon Borrell says, "The deer now have guns," and *this* is the essential problem for traditional media. It is foolish indeed to invest all resources in an on-demand strategy in the face of this disruption, especially when there are unlimited opportunities *within* the disruption.

A social phenomenon

Doug Rushkoff argues effectively that the Web is a social phenomenon, not a media phenomenon or a technological phenomenon. This makes traditional media people uncomfortable, because it demands a response other than the content-provider safe haven. For all the hype about "on your side" or "CBS cares" or "coverage you can count on," the truth is these are just one-way marketing slogans — words that mean nothing compared to actual behavior that insults people and pushes them away. You can't talk your way out of something you hyped/behaved your way into.

Involving yourself with real people in a real online community setting takes a skillset and values that most broadcasters don't seem to possess.

If, as the *Cluetrain* crowd asserts, markets are conversations, then the Web is the new marketplace and all "content" is commoditized to a point where it's a conversation starter at best or merely a diversion at worst. Either way, the "content" concept is far down the priority list of the marketplace, and interactivity with human beings is number one. According to the Pew Internet Research team, more than half of all Internet users say that the Internet has helped bring significant improvements in communicating with their friends and family, and email is still the number one use of the Web across all demographic groups.

Moreover, to paraphrase one of the *Cluetrain* authors, Doc Searls, the whole notion of media as an "object" that passes through "pipes" on its way to a "destination" is very industrial age and railroadesque. "Consumers" of media are not people at the end of the pipe — mouths opened wide — who are swallowing content and crapping cash. The rules here are different — and threatening to those who don't know how to play nice.

The value of the edge

New media economics guru Umair Haque has coined many new terms in his efforts to help people understand the economic forces of the new world. One of his most important concepts is that of "the edge" — the place at the end of one's "reach" where new media meets end user. Where one's core competency is failing, Haque teaches, one must explore edge competencies and opportunities.

This is another profoundly important reason why a strategy that involves only the providing of on-demand content is foolish and dangerous. If the greatest value is at the point of use, then distancing oneself from that point by becoming only a content provider reduces one's value. This is why Jeff Jarvis can make the statement, "…the future of media is not distribution, it's aggregation." (1)

Media consultant and strategist, John Hagel, writes that media companies will have to make a decision if they want to be in the product business or the relationship business:

> Of course, media companies have elements of both embedded in their companies today, but their hearts and minds are firmly in the product business. Here's the test: how open is the media company to providing access to third party content on behalf of their audiences? If the answer is not very open, the company is primarily a product business. If the answer is very open, then the company is primarily an audience relationship business.
>
> ...one of the consequences of the growing relative scarcity of attention (is that) anyone who can help audiences connect with the most relevant and engaging content will be richly rewarded. (2)

Not only does the "product business," as Hagel calls it, have limited ability to sustain serious long-term revenue, it's also at the most expensive end of the content/delivery model. Why paint yourself into that corner voluntarily?

Few people understand disruptive technologies and innovations like Harvard Business School professor Clayton Christensen. Christensen's 1997 book, *The Innovator's Dilemma: When New Technologies Cause Great Firms to Fail*, is a seminal work in the field of business disruptions and is even more appropriate today than it was when it was written.

In a 2001 interview with *CIO Magazine*, Christensen noted that those who survive business disruptions are those who view the disruption as an opportunity for growth. This advice strikes at the heart of the issue of Mainstream Media and the Personal Media Revolution, and it's something local media companies would do well to consider.

> If you look back in history, the disruptees always viewed new technology as a threat. In reality, they were all poised on the brink of a big growth opportunity. But because the way they reacted was first to discount this innovation as meaningful and second to frame

it as a threat, they ended up getting killed. So the first thing is to look at disruptive technology as a growth opportunity and not as a threat.

...One of the litmus tests is that, in almost every case, a disruptive technology enables a larger population of less skilled people to do things that historically only an expert could do. And to do it in a more convenient setting. In hundreds of industries, this is a very common characteristic. So whenever CIOs are looking at an investment, they just need to remember that sometime in the future, somebody is going to figure out a way for an even less skilled population of people to do the job that now more skilled people have to do. (3)

This is precisely the issue with the triumph of personal technology over mass technology, and it offers amazing opportunities for local media companies. If you're a local station, for example, pick a local information niche and go after it as if you weren't a TV station (or radio station or newspaper). What would you do and what would you build that would meet that need effectively and efficiently? I promise you it won't be an on-demand piece of content.

Because here's the deal: the tools available to everyday people that are turning the media world on its head are also available to professional organizations. You don't have to approach everything with a $100,000 solution when $10,000 will do just fine. If aggregation is where it's at (and I believe that it is), then build aggregators. Let other people be the content creators and move yourself to the edge. Not only is it fun there, but that's where the profitability is going to be downstream.

The affinity position of Mrs. Media is smart strategy.

THE REAL THREAT TO
LOCAL BROADCASTERS

April 24, 2006

Fresh from an encouraging meeting of the Television Bureau of Advertising in New York, it's pretty clear that broadcasters are increasingly beginning to see the light about some of the disruptions that are destroying their business model. In session after session, attendees heard stories of a multi-platform universe, along with a host of warnings about the future.

Beth Comstock, president for digital media and market development at NBC Universal, told the group that conventional wisdom is broadcasting's enemy right now, and she urged attendees to start breaking a few rules. "This isn't just about driving growth," she added. "It's about staying in business."

Multi-platform disruptions are a tip of the iceberg. But embracing the multi-platform universe is only a small part of staying in business in the years to come. It's the metaphorical tip of the iceberg for two reasons. One, the biggest business disruption isn't coming from multiple platforms; it's the drift from mass media to personal media. And, two, if multi-platform is a broadcaster's only strategy, he or she is assigning him or herself to the content-provider (only)

13

space for the future. The real opportunities are on the aggregation side (think Topix.net), not just in making content available everywhere.

However, the biggest threat to local television isn't DVRs or VOD. It isn't audience fragmentation, the decline of the 30-second spot or bad programming. It certainly isn't the Internet or the difficulty of finding that killer online application to support an old business model. And it isn't being cut out of the network supply chain by direct-to-consumer distribution.

The biggest threat to local TV is outside technology companies moving into the local entertainment and information space unchallenged by existing local media. This is a very deadly part of the iceberg, because local media companies either don't see it coming or believe they are immune to such competition.

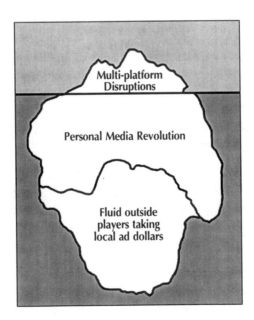

Ball State University's Bob Papper noted at a conference last year in Muncie that television didn't hurt magazines by taking away their readers; they hurt magazines by taking away their advertising. This is the real danger to all local media companies, because local advertising money that used to go — or could go — to local companies is already moving outside the market.

While there's a lot of excitement about revenue growth among local media companies, the reality is that more local online ad money goes to companies outside the market than media companies within the market, and this shows no sign of letting up.

Gordon Borrell, whose company studies local online revenue patterns, recently released his Fourth Annual Benchmarking Report on what local Web sites earn. This graph tells the story. The "Outside Marketing" line represents money from local advertisers that goes outside the market. It is greater than newspapers, TV stations and radio stations combined.

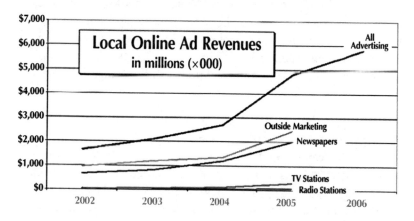

Money going outside the market outpaces money spent within.

Borrell has been telling this story for several years, and he finds the general response from media companies troubling.

> I am very worried when I hear someone say that their trusted local brand is what consumers and advertisers will fall back on. Advertisers don't give a rip about a trusted local brand that's been around for 50 or even 100 years if it doesn't give them what they need. They want something that works. If a young brand with no local representation (and even a ridiculous sounding name) can't compete with WBIG or *The Daily Plutocrat*, then I have to ask how Google and Yahoo were able to suck more than $8 billion out of U.S. advertising budgets last year. (1)

The astonishment expressed by local media salespeople when he pulls out the numbers is understandable, given the historical need for local advertisers to connect physically with a media presence. The Internet, Borrell says, draws dollars out of the marketplace without little more than a phone call — if that.

> That's why it's often so hard for local media to believe how much money is being spent on Internet advertising. The salespeople competing with them don't attend Ad Club or Toastmaster's meetings. They aren't in the Rotary Club or attend the same church or bump into them in a restaurant. Yet they sell local advertising just the same. And it not only works, but it also has a better ROI than direct mail, newspaper classifieds or radio advertising in many cases. (2)

There are a lot of smart people with deep technology roots and connections who understand this phenomenon and are moving with speed to tap into the spigot of local ad dollars. Google and Yahoo! continue to add and tweak local offerings, but the new kids in town are going after the biggest prize of all — local information.

The newest entry into this space is offered by none other than Weblogs, Inc. founder, Jason Calacanis. After selling his company to AOL, Calacanis now finds himself with AOL's brand and resources and has launched "the first" of what he hopes will be a series of local/regional group blogs, Blogging Ohio. He's already purchased domain names for other locations and clearly has plans to build a network. The Blogging Ohio site isn't much just yet, but that's not the point. Calacanis is after local money, and he'll get it. Moreover, the cost of entry into the space is so small that he can afford to wait for it to work.

Here are some quotes from his Website about the project. Pay attention to his focus on the bottom line:

> We needed to get into the game and start learning. We really don't have a detailed plan beyond constant refinement of the product.
> There are two types of advertisers in this space: local businesses and national businesses looking for local reach. So, you might have a local phone store advertise on one local blog while

having Verizon advertise on 15 local blogs where they offer their service. I'm sure we'll have a mix.

My guess is these blogs will lose money for at least a year before they hit profitability.

I would say making it work would be some combination of

a) hitting 50 cities
b) hitting 30M pages a month
c) hitting $3M a year in revenue

Hitting those three milestones would be a sign that this was a scalable business in my mind. (3)

Calacanis isn't alone in building what some are calling Blog Farms. Backfence recently took over operation of Dan Gillmor's Bayosphere and now has a presence on the West Coast. Backfence's business model is built on the creation of hyper-local information sites with content generated by its users. Readers can promote events, rate and review local businesses, create photo galleries and post free classifieds listings. Until the Bayosphere acquisition, Backfence sites have been concentrated around the suburbs of the nation's capital, Backfence CEO Susan DiFife told ClickZ that they'll put the hyper-local on top of Bayosphere. Once again, this is about making money, local money.

"Advertisers are clamoring for the most local customers, particularly the small and medium sized businesses," suggests DeFife. "They're looking for the best way to target that local customer." (4)

According to the ClickZ article, the *Washington Post* is about to launch a hyper-local site. The *New York Times'* About.com operates 40 local blog sites, and there are others.

When broadcasting executives gather this week in Las Vegas for the annual conference of the National Association of Broadcasters, they'll express excitement over multi-platform options available to them. Experts will sit at conference tables facing the audience and pronounce relief from new media threats and encourage broadcasters to make their content available everywhere.

Radio and Television News Directors will also gather and talk about the usual topics of story telling and making nice newscasts.

There will be sessions on making their Websites slick and user-friendly, and they'll hear about podcasts and making their content available everywhere.

But no one — not one speaker — will address the real threat to the industry, and that is the shame of these associations who claim to exist on behalf of the best interests of their members. They are all in the denial of which Gordon Borrell spoke above. They believe these little start-ups are meaningless pests to be squashed by the fly swatters of their brands.

At the risk of sounding like a broken record, it is not enough for local broadcasters to simply drag their brands to the multiple platforms made available by the Internet. Standing by and doing nothing while over half of all the local ad money spent online goes to outside companies is corporate malfeasance gone to seed, and these executives will get what's coming to them in the end.

The foundational understanding that broadcasters *must* get their arms around is this: Revenue isn't the problem; audience is the problem. Fix the problem.

STATIONS MUST EMBRACE
PERSONAL MEDIA TOOLS

May 30, 2005

J.D. Lasica, author of *Darknet: Hollywood's War Against the Digital Generation*, calls the citizens media movement the "personal media revolution." (1) I've adopted the term, because I think it's more fitting as regards what's happening in our culture today. Besides, "citizens media" sounds like it was coined by the Bolsheviks.

I also like it because putting the personal against the professional helps shine a light on one of the great mysteries of our time — why professional media people are so completely ignoring the technologies and concepts that are driving the revolution.

The answer is likely that the great strength — and great weakness — of any profession is specialization. As a class, professionals who view themselves as specialists, easily accept the specialization process and the splitting of tasks and missions. The thinking is that task accomplishment is often better and always safer, if handled by multiple specialists than if one person attempts to do everything alone. This is a strength, because the concept is able to safely climb the mountain of quality. But a system that is designed primarily to protect against error is a weakness in that it is expensive and easily institutionalized.

19

I do this. You do that. And together we can do great things. This is true until technology becomes one or more of the specialists. Then I'm confronted with a choice that I cannot ignore, especially if others around me are making friends with these new specialists.

Can any human being compete with a calculator?

Consider how this has evolved in the television newsgathering process. Modeled after the only thing available, Hollywood's single camera film style, early TV crews included a specialist reporter, a specialist field producer, a specialist camera operator, a specialist sound operator, and any other specialist that was required. While technology is now able to take the place of nearly every specialist, the industry still hasn't fully accepted the disruptive innovations.

This is because institutionalized professionalism cannot tolerate the notion that if technology can eliminate one specialist, what's to keep it from eliminating everybody? It produces a defensive response, which is really a dangerous place to be, because it induces occupational paralysis.

But the picture goes beyond simply gathering news for television. It includes the newsgathering and publishing process altogether. In our new convergence world, specialization is a net liability, and this is where the professional news industry is losing ground every day. Workers must be able to multitask, and not just because it's possible. The most important reason is that you can do amazing things with this technology. Others "out there" are doing it already, and one day they will be our competitors.

In the past year, we've witnessed numerous journalistic scoops compliments of a world that professional journalists abhor — the blogosphere. The more famous cases involved the exploding of certain visible news pedestals, such as the one formerly assigned to Dan Rather, but throughout the land, thousands of local issues and stories are being covered by communities springing up within the world of the blog. This is due to Lasica's "personal media revolution," and professional news organizations need to do more than simply pay attention. We need to embrace and master the technologies they're using.

Web researcher Gordon Borrell says, "The deer now have guns," and he's right. With a PC, a $100 Web camera, a $200 piece of real-time TV production software that includes a teleprompter, free blog software, FTP access to a server, a small digital camera, editing software, and an imagination, anybody can be a TV station, a newspaper or a multimedia news operation. In order to do so, however, the person running the enterprise needs to know how to do everything.

And here's the amazing thing about that. Those who are learning all these new tools and languages, including simple HTML and CSS, are able to go beyond what specialized professionals can do. In an institutionalized specialization paradigm, the only way to compete with these citizen pioneers is to add more specialists to handle the flexibility that technology has given them. This is the conundrum for the mainstream media.

The "quality" argument pales in comparison with a creative mind at the helm of a control panel like this.

And nowhere is this truer than in the world of television stations and the Web. As long as a station is content to allow third-party companies (specialists) to handle their Internet activities, there is no incentive to leave professional ruts and experiment with the same disruptive technologies that everyday people in their communities are using. This is a grave tactical error, in my judgment, because it limits business opportunities driven by innovation.

Let's examine, for example, the process of building and maintaining a content-rich Website, something every TV station must have. Movable Type is one of the more popular pieces of blog software (there are many), and you can actually get a copy of it free. A licensed version will cost $100. This software — out of the box — can do the following: create dynamic pages, store them in a database for easy retrieval, categorize them, broadcast to the Internet that they are available, deliver them to users via RSS, upload images and pictures, and allow complete customization via stylesheets and templates.

Most television stations have a professional third-party company do this for them, and the pricetag isn't cheap. These companies make compelling arguments about ad networks, reliability, convergence ad packages, and content management, but the truth is these are all things that can be done by the stations themselves. Those who don't at least dabble in this are sitting by as a world they can't even imagine is exploding all around them. This is a real tragedy, for how can an organization that's bound by the rules of professionalism possibly compete with individuals and companies who can do the same job at a fraction of the cost? This is the reality local television will be facing in the not-too-distant-future, unless they choose to explore the brave new world for themselves.

One week with Movable Type, and you'll be asking yourself why you're paying another company $10,000 a month to do this for you.

The technological revolution goes beyond the media and strikes at the heart of all of our professional institutions. Not too many years ago, for example, the number of eyes watching the far heavens were limited to the professionals fortunate enough to work in one of the earth's observatories or a few scattered amateurs with telescopes. Today, nearly all of the significant astronomical discoveries being made include amateurs, because technology has advanced to the point where anybody can probe the far reaches of the universe. The recent discovery of a planet circling a star 15,000 light years away from earth, for example, included two avid amateurs in New Zealand using backyard 14-inch and 10-inch telescopes. This is no longer the exception in a world formerly limited to the few. It is now the norm.

"Amateurs" are making their own commercials, writing their own encyclopedia, making their own music and films, and taking on every institution that calls itself "professional." Along the way, they're building their own communities, all thanks to the technologies that take the place of specialists. This is no insignificant thing.

It's time our engineering departments included Internet program-ming, XML and RSS, and for our news departments to employ a few nerds. Better yet, I believe everybody needs a little basic HTML and CSS knowledge, so that the tools available right now don't seem so intimidating. Smart stations will bring in experts and teachers to help give their people a competitive edge, because the stations down-the-street might be even deeper into professional ruts than they are. Not to do so runs the very real risk of turning the video news niche over to independent groups of highly flex-ible journalists who can do anything.

The personal media revolution is a serious threat to the status quo, and it is no respecter of persons. If they can swallow their pride, even professionals can get onboard.

CHAOS AT THE DOOR

June 22, 2005

When historian Henry Adams attended the Paris Exposition in 1900, he had an epiphany that struck his midsection like a body blow from a heavyweight boxer. He suddenly realized that all his background and training hadn't prepared him for the shift from an agricultural age to one birthed in technology. At the age of 62, life had passed him by, and so he wrote the lament, "The law of nature is change (chaos), while the dream of man is order."

If anybody should have seen it coming, it was Adams. His great-grandfather was President John Adams; his grandfather was President John Quincy Adams. He was part of the elite culture — people in the know — and yet there he was, admitting he felt completely lost. Or was it, perhaps, because he was a part of the hierarchical "order" that he missed what was going on beneath him? Regardless, it was likely a horrifying realization.

He later wrote, "Chaos often breeds life when order breeds habit," and this is a great lesson for us as we confront, once again, the pain of change. Chaos is stirring, and new ideas are bubbling up from the bottom, while the ordered, top-down culture we've created is hanging on for dear life. Nowhere is this more evident than in the world of journalism, where mid-career workers are beginning to share Adams' gut-wrenching revelation.

It can be seen in the halls of journalism education. Several institutions are exploring new ways of teaching journalism in an attempt to save the profession — including a group that met last week on the campus of Ball State University in Muncie, Indiana. But in some ways, these are the last people who should be exploring what to do, because a part of their reason for being is maintaining their "habits" of order. And that's a bigger problem than it appears.

Near the end of the Ball State think tank, an idea was considered that involved inviting mid-career journalists to the University for mentor/protégé sessions where students would be the mentors. It was felt that this might be a good way to bring experienced journalists out of the Adams' quandary.

A very bright student that was present raised his hand and asked, "Why would I want to do that, when I'm essentially competing with these people for jobs?" In a blog comment later, the student, Adam Cairns, wrote:

> The larger problem at issue is the number of mid-career journalists in decision-making positions who haven't maintained their tech skills and haven't kept up with Internet trends. Asking a student to give them the Cliffs Notes version of what has been happening in the world the past 10-15 years is sad. Rather than wasting time training editors and publishers about the benefits of the Internet, mid-career journalists should start listening to their younger colleagues or interns and acting upon their youthful recommendations. Then maybe newspapers would be closer to where they should be by now. (1)

While that's not likely to happen, it's hard to argue with Adam, because in the time it will take to re-equip everybody, new business models will already be thriving in the hands of people who do possess the knowledge. Venture capitalists know this and are beginning to provide funding for start-ups that one day may become the new mainstream in terms of both revenue and jobs.

So let's take a moment to examine what's happening at street level, where the personal media revolution is taking place. Web and politics pioneer, Joe Trippi, made an important observation about it last year:

> If information is power, then the Internet, which distributes information democratically to anyone who has access to it, is no longer distributing just information — it's distributing power.
>
> And in a top-down society, it's empowering the bottom. Put more simply— in America, it's empowering the American people. (2)

And the paradox of power is that discontent increases with opportunities for acting on it. The more the bottom is given the tools to make and distribute their own media, the greater their power; the greater their power, the greater their discontent and, along with it, the opportunity for acting on that discontent. This bubbling caldron of energy is profoundly anti-elitist and anti-institution, because the more the bottom surveys the landscape these days, the more they realize that our culture has failed them, and this energy is palpable in the halls of power.

Demograher Hazel Reinhardt presented the Ball State group with evidence of what she calls a "Perfect Storm" of demographic and technological changes impacting the culture. Four demographic shifts will have a profound influence on the media.

- The aging of the population
- Growing racial and ethnic diversity
- The continuing and growing gap between the rich and poor
- Metropolitanization/Regionalization

She offered one slide of Census Bureau numbers that is the source of much discontent.

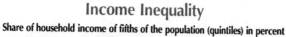

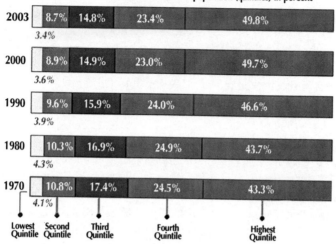

Nearly half the income in the U.S. now goes to just twenty percent of the population. Sixty percent of the population gets less than thirty percent of the nation's income. And what is it that sustains this disparity? The order of a modernist way of life. To the institutions go the wealth, one of the most visible being the media.

Ms. Reinhardt pulls no punches in describing her "Perfect Storm."

> What does the future hold? Change. The status quo can't be the way forward, for the coming together of profound demographic and technological changes will restructure the media, and we are at the beginning of it. This will be geometrically larger than the advent of television in 1950. (3)

The extent to which the public — in the form of citizens media — can undercut the revenue bases of professional journalism will determine how well institutional media will withstand the onslaught. Since media revenue is audience-driven, however, this is one institution that's headed for the tar pits, because — at core — the advertising industry doesn't really care about things like tradition and history. Where that wealth gets redistributed in the economy is anybody's guess, and that's why the entry of Venture Capitalists into the citizens media game is so significant.

There is one group who could slow this down, of course. They are the keepers of the status quo — the lawyers of the land. And given that institutional lawmakers are mostly lawyers too, well you get the idea. In the end, one has to believe that the people will win, even if it means voting every lawyer out of office.

Revolution is like that.

As Ms. Reinhardt noted, no one can really stop the perfect storm. That's why it's important for mid-career journalists to get their hands dirty in using the technology of the personal media revolution instead of thinking about how and where to learn about it. Become a "doer" of the word instead of a "hearer" only. Learning is always accelerated by experience, so those who feel their careers slipping away need to get involved. Start a blog. Build a Web page. Pick up a camera. Play a video game. Get close to young people who are comfortable using technology, and ask questions. Read a book, or better yet, go online and look around for tutorials. They're everywhere. Most of all, don't let fear get in the way. It's only technology. *Do* something!

Henry Adams would be amazed if he could see what's happened a hundred years after Paris, but he would certainly understand the feelings of mid-career journalists. Perhaps a hundred years from now, when some writer is trying to explain the inevitable shift from holograms to worm holes, he'll come across quotes from those lamenting the loss of order, circa 2005.

THE LIVE COVERAGE REVOLUTION

November 7, 2003

Of all the technologies that have changed the presentation of television news, none have made a greater impact than those that bring a live signal from outside a TV studio to the viewers' homes. Moreover, live coverage has not only changed the way news is presented but also what's covered. For example, nobody would bother with a high-speed chase, if the helicopter couldn't beam a live picture back to the studio, and wall-to-wall coverage of major events is made possible by live pictures. Every day, producers build live shots into their newscasts, whether there's anything going on at the scene or not. Live, after all, brings a sense of urgency and drama to a newscast, which can make for compelling TV. Granted, it's gotten out of hand, but TV news will always have live elements, because human nature yearns to take part in history. We want to know how it's going to come out, and we want to know at the same time everybody else does.

In the days before microwave trucks, if we wanted to get a live signal from across town, we called the phone company. And back then, there was only one phone company, so we paid a premium for those hard lines, to say nothing of the waiting time it took to get one installed. I remember one election night in Milwaukee during the early 70s. We had two phone lines to cover the mayor's race, and we all thought we'd died and gone to heaven. Imagine that — a party over two live signals! Of course, the phone company was using microwave equipment to accomplish the task, and we eventually figured out it would be cheaper to have our own than to keep lining Ma Bell's pockets. But even when we got into the microwave business, it was hard to believe you could actually transmit a video signal "through the air."

There are two technologies in the pipeline today that will play significant, live-newsgathering roles for TV news in a Postmodern world. The first is that little device nearly everybody carries these days, the cellular phone. With a little engineering, the output of some new phones can produce a television picture.

The BBC is far ahead of its U.S. counterparts in applying New Media to television news. They were the first to adopt the VJ concept of newsgathering, whereby everybody in the newsroom is a video journalist. Now, they're experimenting with cell phones, specifically 3G (3rd-generation) video mobile phones as cameras. "It's almost like having a satellite truck in your pocket," says Dave Harvey of BBC Bristol. Well, not exactly. The phones produce a fuzzy and distorted picture when blown up from its original size, but Harvey says this is actually an advantage. "For younger viewers who are interested in new technologies and use them all the time, there's something edgy in seeing this sort of image on BBC television. It could make us seem less remote, make us more credible with that age group."

BBC Bristol is using the 3G phones in special reports on underage drinking, with teenage recruits reporting on how easy it is for them to buy liquor. The phones have generated considerable buzz among those who see possible applications, such as reporters "going live" from breaking news before the satellite or microwave truck gets there. There are also predictions of these opening up entirely new avenues of coverage, because their portability and reach allow for coverage from places where conventional technology isn't allowed or those it can't easily access.

These phones will have a place in the new world of television news, although picture quality may limit their use. The U.S. is also far behind other countries in the deployment of 3G, although Ted Friedrichs of Qualcomm's 3G Today says things are moving forward. "We're just waiting for the 3G operators (e.g., Sprint PCS, Verizon Wireless) to accept compelling video-enabled devices from the Asian vendors (e.g., Samsung, LG, Pantech&Curitel, Sanyo, Toshiba, Hitachi, etc.) and start hosting downloaded or streamed video content. He adds that Verizon Wireless already offers broadband wireless service in Washington, D.C., and San Diego and is expected to roll out 20 of their top markets next year. What it means, he says, is that "high speed wireless streaming video is coming to a Verizon cell phone near you." Friedrichs predicts it'll be a reality within six to eight months.

Meanwhile, another technology that is showing dramatic results in the U.S. is Wi-Fi, and I think this may become the most dramatic breakthrough in the video news business since the invention of video tape. It also poses a significant threat to broadcasters, because it's just another one of the tools available to anybody who wants to make their own newscasts. That includes the local newspaper or anyone with a broadband Internet connection.

Wi-Fi is short for "wireless fidelity." It's the popular term for a high-frequency wireless local area network (WLAN). These networks are showing up all over the place, but it is the spreading public (free) Wi-Fi's that make this such a compelling opportunity.

In New York, Drazen Pantic is quietly conducting experiments that are resulting in near broadcast-quality, 320x240-pixel live pictures using a combination of consumer cameras, laptops with opensource software, and public wireless networks. Earlier this year, Pantic produced a one-hour call-in show from the roof of an apartment building using hardware and software that anybody can easily and cheaply acquire. The program was carried on a local cable access channel. The video was transmitted at 15 frames per second (FPS), which is about all the human eye needs to recognize fluid motion. In further tests, his team has transmitted video at the rate 20-25 FPS, very close to the standard videotape broadcast rate of 30 (in my old news film days, the rate was 24 FPS).

Pantic is an interesting fellow with a background in accomplishing great tasks from the bottom up. He was born in Belgrade in 1956 and has a Ph.D. in mathematics with a specialty in probability and random processes. He is the founder of OpenNet, the Internet department of the pioneering independent media organization Radio B92 in Belgrade and the first Internet service provider in Serbia. Some believe he almost single-handedly undermined the Milosevic regime. For his work with New Media technologies as a force to counter political repression in Yugoslavia, he was granted the Electronic Frontier Foundation's Pioneer Award in 1999. He is driven to help the little guy everywhere, and right now he's at the forefront in furthering the Internet as a medium of many voices. Along the way, Pantic is putting pieces of the future puzzle together.

He's stayed with open-source software, because he wants anybody to be able to do this. Among other things, he wants to make impromptu news anchors out of anyone on the street by giving them a 1-2-3 solution, probably in the form of a CD. Boot the computer. Plug in the CD. Click on the broadcast button. Presto, you're on the air. "We just have to make it pain-free," he said.

> "My vision is that very soon (within a year or two) we will see more and more hybrid systems, sitting in the intersection of Internet broadcasting, ITV and conventional cable networks. The key factor will be the ability to transmit and broadcast unmediated hi-quality material from any place towards TV distribution channels that will then filter and select interesting material and package it into sellable units (shows) or offer unmediated access to the raw material. So, to a large extent the production side will be translocated towards the direct actants in the events."

This is pure Postmodernism and ever so close to the OhMyNews! concept of "Every citizen is a reporter."

> "By 'unmediated'," Pantic says, "I mean 'free of spin', not necessarily unfiltered. What we see now with mainstream media is

constant spin, changing focus and relativizing the facts according to some undefined rule of how news sells.

"Audiences have been cultivated and irreversibly changed by the vast amount of information available on the Internet. Many people have seen (especially after 9/11 and the Iraq war) that they can find so much more unmediated information on the Internet than on TV news channels.

"But, on the other side, the majority cannot afford to invest that much energy and time in searching for relevant information. So I think that 'consumers' will demand more and more direct and unmediated reporting from credible sources or direct participants in the events. The role of journalists will be to certify authenticity of the material and make a selection that will maintain a certain level of quality."

While TV news departments doing conventional news can certainly benefit from the technology that Pantic and his colleagues are developing, the energy that's driving it is intended to undermine the status quo. Pantic wants anybody to be able to do TV. That won't sit well with those who already do so, and it doesn't make him very popular with those in charge. I can tell you this. He doesn't care. He's already lived with (and beaten) armed totalitarianism. The truly smart news organizations of today will grasp the significance of all of this and work to position themselves as credible translators of all this "unmediated" information. That's very different than standing on the crumbling pedestal of objectivity and asserting that only those already onboard are permitted to play the game for real.

Postmodernism is the Age of Participation. The need to learn has been replaced by the need to apply, and that means all of the rules of our culture are being rewritten, including those for television news. Postmoderns (Pomos) trust their experiences, and if they've not experienced it, they want to hear it from somebody who has. This means information that is up close and personal and that includes many perspectives, not that which is provided by arms-length experts or delivered in some hyped manner that's a mile wide and an inch deep. Pomos also don't want their information sanitized, because they don't trust the sanitation workers. Part of that distrust is based on Postmodernism's rejection of hierarchy and elitism and a desire for control over their own lives.

Pomos also want to talk to each other and share the "news" that's relevant to them, and this is already occurring on the Internet through blogs and social networking. In the expanding circles of what's important to me, that which is closest and those who are closest are most relevant. The Net facilitates that need like nothing since the telephone. Who would argue that the news of my loved ones is more important to me than the news of my nation?

In the end, we'll see that the whole top-down media culture, whereby information is trickled down to the masses through institutional channels, is replaced by one that is much more user-centric and connected. Involvement in all of life at the local level will increase, including participation in the political process.

These are, indeed, exciting times.

THE DEVALUATION OF INFORMATION

February 22, 2005

In another life, I worked for a company that studied how things work in various cities and regions of the world. Corporate America pays a lot of money for this kind of information, and the job taught me much about, well, how things work — especially beneath the surface. On one of these projects in a midwestern state, I met an old labor guy with a great deal of wisdom. He said something that stuck with me. "The simple truth," he said, "is that resources are always limited, and progress always means whacking somebody else's fatted calf."

The fatted calf of the mainstream media is under a severe whack attack these days. The battlefield is the World Wide Web, and beneath the surface, it's producing an ongoing economic drama of biblical proportions.

In discussing issues relative to the communications revolution that was taking place on his watch, FCC Chairman Michael Powell made this remarkable statement: "I have no problem if a venerable institution disappears tomorrow, as long as that value is distributed elsewhere in the economy."

The idea of value being distributed elsewhere is the whacking stick in today's media revolution, and it's something that should be of

35

concern to everybody. The value of information is the issue, because that value is being redistributed away from media companies and back into the pockets of people who used to spend it on books, newspapers, magazines, Internet subscriptions, cable and many forms of self help and education. Institutional, top-down media had their cake and could eat it too in a passive, mass marketing world. That's gone forever, and, as *Sports Illustrated* President John Squires told newspaper and magazine circulation types last fall, "Get over it."

Subscriber models aren't the only ones affected. Information is further devalued when advertisers refuse to pay existing rates for shrinking audiences, and that trend line continues to drift downward.

So if information has no value, then people shouldn't have to pay for it, right? This argument is as old as the Web, and it's being renewed in many circles in the wake of "long tail" theories about the value of permanent links to online content and even in discussions about *New York Times* purchase of About.com. If better than half the people who ever read an article do so through search engines, the argument goes, then companies like the *Times*, where archives are stored behind paid walls, are shooting themselves in the foot. This is a vastly complex matter, and one for which there are no easy answers.

In an Online Journalism Review essay, Mark Glaser wrote

> Information wants to be free — as long as you don't have to pay the people who dug up that information. While the Net has long been associated with free things — free e-mail, free personal Web pages, free searches — the news business has been repulsed by the notion that their hard-won scoops and journalism should be given away for free. (1)

The Internet — with its Postmodern, deconstructionist architecture — makes it seem that all knowledge is "public" knowledge and all information is "public" information. It was built without a centralized command and control mechanism, and, therefore, the ability to tap unlimited databases is available to everybody. This

is what makes Google so powerful. Absent any top-down structure, Google (anybody) is able to search and retrieve from those
databases at any level, which, among other things, renders the
portal Website concept irrelevant. It also makes attempts to block
it appear odd and out-of-place.

The demand for this is significant. People who couldn't afford to
pay for an education now find they're able to access for free the
hidden knowledge that has helped others rise above them on the
food chain, and the race is on to see who can move from have-
not to have status faster. Human nature craves knowledge and information, so the wellspring for this energy is infinite.

Where knowledge and information isn't "public," people are stepping in to provide substitutes. Blogs are the best example of this.
Craigslist is another, and so are a host of Wikis that are building
a free database of knowledge. Even the copyright debates involving music, films and other forms of entertainment flow from
this issue.

Everything's fine until we start talking about business and the idea
of making money from knowledge and information. If a business
is based on online knowledge and information, it's increasingly
difficult to protect that knowledge and information, so that people
will continue to pay for it. Attempts to do so have a way of back-
firing in this era of breaking down the walls instead of going
through the gates, because even if one is successful, the door is
immediately opened for criticism and competition.

One part of the value argument is that institutional media forms
want readers/users to visit their Web properties only in the form they
were designed. Users are expected to follow the yellow brick road
of Website navigation: home page/section/story/page2 of story, etc.
Websites make money based on page views, and some people see
deep links as a threat to their business model. Carolyn Little, editor of the *Washington Post* online says, "Coming in through the
home page is an old model and coming in sideways is the new
method of arrival for most users."

In Oklahoma, the Tulsa World is threatening legal action against blogger Michael Bates for the sin of quoting the paper's articles and linking to them in his blog. The newspaper knows that Bates has every right to do so under the fair use exception of copyright law, but it's going ahead with the threats anyway, prompting Dan Gillmor to write, "Earth to Tulsa World: Stop being so arrogant, and get a clue."

In the summer of 2004, Patrick Kenealy, the CEO of publisher IDG, got into a tiff with technology writers and bloggers over the issue of deep linking. IDG publishes InfoWorld, an important "voice" in the tech publishing world, and Kenealy didn't like it that writers — specifically those who were making money through advertising or subscriptions — were taking ideas from InfoWorld and linking to its articles. Kenealy felt the company should be compensated for that, so he used software from a company called eMeta to block inbound links. He was immediately vilified. The move ignited a firestorm of controversy from those who not only wanted access to his information but felt Kenealy was cutting off his nose to spite his face.

But Kenealy still defends the action, and says it's a matter of fairness. He notes that when IDG sought online rights from its providers, they boosted compensation by 25%. "We're both producers and consumers of content," he said, "and we want to be fair wherever we are on the value chain." Those linking to his content, he believes, don't have the same ethics.

"We've done everything," he says, "from taking our sites off search engines, to putting them behind walls, to putting some content behind payment walls." He has no intention of changing his mind, and he predicts he'll be justified by the future. "There's already a differentiation," he adds, "between branded and non-branded content." He predicts search engines will one day be based on specialities, and that Google won't be alone.

David Ades, Director of Strategic Initiatives with eMeta, says the line between giving away content for free and making it all paid or restricted is very broad, gray and blurry. He says eMeta is filling an important niche in the online publishing world, because "nobody else focuses on the complexities of monetizing content."

"If you lock down all of your content," he says, "you'll lose all of your users. However, if you start taking action to understand your users and give your users value in exchange for information they're giving you, you're not going to lose your users, because you're giving them something they want."

In today's contextual advertising world, users can add value to content by providing demographic information that publishers can use to serve targeted advertising. Where publishers want further tightening, Ades recommends doing it slowly. "The term 'lock down' brings to mind jail cells slamming," he notes. "It's more a decision to slowly tighten the leash on your content, to bring it closer to you and to understand your users. You only lock down the gold nuggets and the diamonds in the content, and for the gold dust, you measure it out. And you ask for something in exchange."

Ades adds that an important online metric is "value per user," but determining it is a vastly complex matter and different for each publisher.

If, for example, the penultimate value is influence, it would be wise to make the content free and permanent. *Vanity Fair* columnist Michael Wolfed noted in a speech at the 2005 SIIA Information Industry Summit in New York City that the *Wall Street Journal* has lost its position as *the* major voice of influence, because it charges for online content.

> I think the *Journal* felt that it was powerful enough to charge, and for a long time everyone regarded the Journal's activities online as the ultimate. They had unlocked the puzzle. In fact, I don't think they did. I think they locked themselves into a puzzle.
>
> While the *New York Times* on the other hand became this ubiquitous information brand. It became finally the national information brand. And it did this, I think, because it was free.

There's a lot of talk these days about the *Times* charging for premium content and archives, and if that happens, we're likely to see another shift. Jay Rosen of PressThink recently noted that "if that happens and the *Washington Post* remains free, the paths of those two great news organizations will, I believe, diverge."

One of the most visible warriors in this free/paid debate has been the *Encyclopaedia Britannica*. During the Internet bubble days of 1999, the Britannica got a ton of recognition for the bold move of making its pages free to consumers online and adopting an advertising model. Tom Panelas, Director of Corporate Communications for Britannica, says they bought into the free information argument.

"The theory behind the model was traffic," he remembers. "If you could get enough traffic, you could make it work. We did that. We had 8–10 million unique visitors a month. We were doing all the things right, and it seemed to be working."

Then in 2000, the bottom dropped out of the market. Ad rates plummeted, and the *Britannica*'s experiment stopped working. "Of the different aspects of our revenue model," Panelas says, "advertising was the most important ingredient, so when rates fell, it broke the model."

The company did extensive research and concluded that the advertising model wasn't sustainable, and that belief remains today. Panelas adds, "We believe that good quality, reliable information that is well-edited is somewhat rare and therefore valuable. People should be willing to pay for that."

The *Britannica* online boasts a couple of hundred thousand subscribers, according to Panelas, many of them coming through third-party bundling of products and services, something he believes we'll see a lot more of in the future.

The *Britannica* has weathered many storms in the last 15 years, as technology has rewritten their business. Even now, the online "Wikipedia" — which is written and edited by the public — poses a new threat, but the company has faith in its model. "This stuff is constantly changing," Panelas admits, "and the way customers understand this is changing all the time."

He's quick to add, however, that "we live in a society that's too sophisticated to completely abandon empirical and rational thinking."

In a Postmodern world, such assumptions can be dangerous, and this is what's at the heart of the free-versus-paid argument. The rational Modernist world is the one with the institutional doorways and permission gates, but that world is fading, and our culture is rapidly moving in a different direction. It's a "new wine" thing, and it requires new wineskins.

We're at a point in history where media companies must rethink basic assumptions and assign new values to everything. Top-down business models have served us well, but the market is now bottom-up. How can our value assumptions today be altered to meet the bottom line of tomorrow?

For example, if a broadcaster is getting a $200 CPM for a 30-second spot, it might be wise to ask if that 30 second spot would have more value to the company if it was used otherwise — perhaps promoting another profit-making business owned by the station (or the station's owner). Our obsession with the formulas of the past blind us to the possibilities of the future.

Time has value, and it's high on the list for Postmoderns (Pomos). They don't want to give it away like they were forced to do in a media world of passive participation. If they don't want to give us their time, what *will* they give us? We ought to ask them.

The revenue models of tomorrow will likely be quite different from they are today, and nobody has all the answers just yet. Value is value, however, and we ought to be spending more time studying what people are prepared to give us, as we attempt to meet their information and entertainment needs, rather than working overtime to raise old revenue models from the dead.

The fatted calf of today is tomorrow's steak and french fries. Let's shift our thinking and enjoy the meal.

CHAOS IN THE FEEDBACK LOOP

November 25, 2003

When the voice of God (at least we hope it was God) spoke — "If you build it, they will come" — in Field of Dreams, Kevin Costner's character created a baseball diamond amidst the corn on his Iowa farm so the Ghosts of Baseball Past could play their night games. He built it. They came. They played.

The slogan became the mantra of the Internet boom of the late 20th century and proved to be a better movie fantasy than business axiom. We built it. They came. They played. And we had such grandiose thoughts! We knew this Internet thing was something huge, but it just refused to perform the way we felt it should. The early failure of most Web businesses was due, I think, to the fact that we missed the cultural change that came with the technology, and we made a fundamental mistake in our business assumptions. We thought the Internet was just another business tool for Modern times. It's not. It's the lifeblood of Postmodern times, where Modernist business rules don't apply.

As a TV guy, my first view of the Internet was that a computer screen was just another TV set, albeit interactive. This, it turns out, was hopelessly naïve. Like everybody else, my business model for the Web was a one-way street — what could I, as a Web publisher, bring to you, the Web audience? This is Modernist thinking all-the-way, because it's top-down, one-directional. What makes the Internet different is that it is a two-way street. In this sense, it's more an innovative extension of the telephone than the television set.

The first breakthrough to genuinely take advantage of this two-way street for the news business — this feedback loop — is the Weblog. Blogs are redefining contemporary journalism in ways that threaten traditional news people. Andrew Nachison, Director of The Media Center at the American Press Institute, writes:

> To some, blogs represent a degradation, if not a downright blight, on real journalism. One author said in a post to the ONA discussion forum, "Anyone can 'publish' their stuff. Drivel is passed off as journalism. The ramblings of someone somewhere are passed off as news. The result is acres and acres of terrible reporting. Incoherent ramblings and notes-to-myself that are published in public space."
>
> It's a sentiment I encounter often with newspaper editors and other "seasoned" journalists who have been there and done that and believe that journalism is best handled by trained professionals. (1)

Nachison says the information dialog of the future may not resemble what we have known from the past, and that "the emphasis now is on the word relationship — implying a two-way conversation."

Former *TV Guide* and *People* TV critic, Jeff Jarvis, is a prolific Postmodern blogger and another proponent of the idea that relationship is the central component of the Internet. His BuzzMachine blog is a nifty blend of media, pop culture and politics, and Jeff is a highly respected member of the Weblog community.

> This medium is about relationships and the audience wants (desperately) to relate to media (or at least news media) as more than just an audience. They want a conversation. They want influence.

> They want power. No, we want all those things. That is the real
> guiding principle for the future of media: relationships.

This is absolutely true and the key reason most news people want
to run and hide from the medium. Relationships? With the audience? Yes, and it means giving up command and control and the
air of elitism that the press wears so well. It means tossing aside
Walter Lippmann's great social engineering experiment of the last
century — the belief that the people are incompetent to govern
(and inform) themselves and need a group of educated and, therefore, objective elites to do the job for them. It means arguing our
points of view instead of pretending we have none. It means listening instead of just telling. It means actually engaging with the
people we're trying to inform.

It is the chaos of the feedback loop that Modernist news people
fear the most, because it defies their logic and undercuts the core
belief that only someone trained to do so can be a journalist, a folly
that's being exposed every day.

For TV news people, the sense of journalistic protected status is
further heightened by knowledge of "how to do TV." It's one thing
to be able to write, the thinking goes, but it's quite another to use
pictures and words to tell a story. This argument is also falling
apart as the technological revolution is bringing shortcuts and sim-
plicity to the consumer video market. The truth is that a small investment puts anybody in the video news business today, so the
feedback loop is no longer limited to just text and/or still pictures.

This is extremely significant in my view of TV news in a Postmodern world, for it opens the door to an entirely new paradigm
in the world of video news. If, in fact, anybody can be a video
journalist, then the only structural barrier in moving the idea to a
viable business concept is a delivery system. Once again, the Internet is where and how this will happen, and there are two important, on-going developments to watch in order to determine
how soon.

AOL bought a little search company called SingingFish last week. Instead of searching for text-based Web pages, SingingFish's technology searches for multimedia, specifically audio, video and Flash (rich media) clips. Observers believe AOL bought the company not only to enrich their own content offerings but to temporarily block Yahoo and Google from getting into the multimedia search game. SingingFish is the lead player, but others will come along, because the Internet is evolving, from a medium that serves only text and pictures to one that serves other forms of communication as well. This is being made possible by the dramatic growth of broadband connectivity.

Ultimately, if I'm an independent video journalist, I'm going to need a way for people to "find" my products. Multimedia search technology is a key component of this. One day, video news on demand (VNOD) portal companies will offer an organized form of multimedia news clips produced by a variety of journalists, similar to what Google News offers via its computerized text editorial system. The business model will be advertising, and independent VJs will get paid based on the number of times their work is viewed.

The second development to watch is a move by broadband providers to increase upstream speeds instead of just downstream. Currently, there is a dramatic difference in the speed with which I receive (downstream) and send (upstream) a data stream to and from the Web. Playing a video stream from a Website also involves sending packets of data back to the source, and the speed with which this happens can influence the quality of viewing. Upstream speed, therefore, can be a critical element in an Internet-based, video on demand (VOD) world. Moreover, as noted above, the key difference between the Internet and other communications' media is that it is two-way. The degree to which the speed of upstreaming is increased will determine the potential for business opportunities coming from consumers to the Web. Voice over IP, video conferencing, Webcams, and many other applications and potential applications are affected by slow upstream speeds.

A recent reader survey by BroadbandReports.com found increases in upstream speeds to be second only to lower pricing in what users want from their broadband providers. Readers of BroadbandReports.com may not be typical consumers, but among them are highly tech-savvy people who lead the way in Web development and expansion by pushing the creative envelope. The site predicts some areas of the country will see Time Warner Cable upstream speed experiments of 512kbs by Christmas, but that's still just one-sixth of the download speed offered by Time Warner.

These developments also have implications for broadcasting, because even now, TV stations use photographs provided by viewers during emergencies and spot news. When Hurricane Isabel pounded the east coast in September, stations used Webcams and viewer pictures to help tell the story. In the future, citizen reporters will do likewise with digital video.

Of course, this two-way flow of audio and video isn't a great idea to certain elements of the culture. If you haven't noticed, for example, there's a war underway between media companies and people who are tired of the gluttonous greed of a celebrity culture made possible by the money we pay for entertainment.

Harvard blogger, Dave Winer, is asking Democratic Presidential candidates to "make an impassioned plea to keep the Internet free of interference from the entertainment industry." SiliconValley.com's Dan Gillmor adds, "Keeping Hollywood's influence from wrecking the Net would, by extension, help solve the copyright disaster that's been building in America for decades."

These two, and others, are writing about this, because the status quo doesn't appreciate its fatted calf being whacked by a citizenry armed with weapons it can't control.

The media cartel, as Gillmor calls it, is winning a few battles here and there, but as long as the Internet remains free of their control, they will ultimately lose the war. The Recording Industry Association of America's lawsuits to stop the file-swapping theft of copyrighted songs and the Motion Picture Association of

America's victory with the FCC in the "broadcast flag" decision to stop the potential theft of copyrighted movies are desperate and defensive attempts by a Modernist institution to keep its place in a changing culture.

Meanwhile, and seemingly invisible to the status quo, a whole new order is being created and new rules of engagement written. It's no longer, "If we build it, they will come," for the builders aren't in charge anymore. To the Postmodern, it's the phrase I remember from first year Latin, "Veni. Vidi. Vici." We came. We saw. We conquered.

Reinventing Journalism

Citizen journalists. The Pajama Brigade. Call them what you will, but bloggers and their readers are quickly reinventing our trade from the bottom up. The essays in this section explore the history of journalism, the farce of "objectivity," and where I see our industry headed as the cultural change continues around and in our society.

The essay "News as a Sporting Event" is perhaps my best, and it describes where we've gone off the track in the world of professional journalism. What most professionals refuse to accept is their role in what's happening in our culture, so it's hard for them to understand why the people formerly known as the audience are looking to other sources. As Upton Sinclair once said, "It's hard to get a man to understand something when his salary depends on his not understanding it."

News Is a Process,
Not a Finished Product

November 9, 2007

L ike everybody my age, I remember where I was when President Kennedy was assassinated. I remember the crushing loss and how it impacted everybody I knew. My parents cried, and so did I. Young people today can read about it in the history books, but you had to be there to understand how it just ripped the collective heart out of America. We loved John Kennedy. There was a magic about life back then, an innocence and trust that vanished that day in Dallas.

I was in study hall in the cafeteria in high school. The school piped Walter Cronkite and CBS News coverage over the intercom, and everybody in the room wept quietly as we listened. It was my first experience with the process that is news, that compelling and magnetic sense of participating in history on-the-fly. There is nothing quite like live coverage of on-going news, and in the executive suites of newspaper moguls — with eyes glued on their television sets — a chill had to run down every spine.

The very definition of news was punctuated by this coverage. News is a process, not a finished product. It's always been that way, too. What changed back then was the ability of people to participate in the process as witnesses, and when Jack Ruby shot Lee Harvey Oswald on live TV two days later, we were never going back.

Live coverage evolved. There was the moon landing, the San Francisco earthquake, O. J. Simpson, and the twin towers going down. We were all there, together. I remember an old quote from Steve Friedman, then executive producer of The Today Show, that his innovation in the 70s of bringing live interviews to the program was based on viewers' innate desire to participate in history.

Cable news networks are the place where people can drop into the middle of the news process and experience that same sense of connection. But in an effort to maintain high levels of viewing after big events are over, the cable nets turn to hyperbole to create a sense of importance not justified by events. It doesn't work. Viewers, it turns out, are too smart for that.

But the reality that news is a process continues, and no communications invention in history makes that more evident than the Internet and the World Wide Web. The Web is neatly dismantling the concept of news-as-a-finished-product by appealing to the participatory spirit and offering pieces of stories as stories themselves. This is happening with frequency in times of major events, but it's also beginning to show up elsewhere. News-as-a-finished-product is bundled and presented in its entirety, whether it's the six o'clock news or the morning paper, but the Web allows people to unbundle specific items and "receive" them at will.

While media companies are aware of this, the idea of finished product news doesn't die easily. We're content to unbundle, for example, but that which is unbundled must also be finished. The story is the thing, we say to ourselves. But the reality is that the story is not the thing; the process is the thing, and the process doesn't require the finished product. This is the secret to news on the Web, the awakening to which has already begun and is best demonstrated in what has become the go-to news outlet for celebrity news and gossip, TMZ.com.

TMZ.com uses blogging software to produce a running account of news items, pictures-with-captions, snippets of ongoing stories, breaking news, and a clever, albeit snarky prose that doesn't take itself or its subject matter too seriously. TMZ's rapid success is due in large part to its approach to news. "Continual iteration" is their process, according to Bob Mohler, Executive in Charge, New Media, Telepictures Productions and one of the creators of TMZ.com. The format gives the writers and producers the freedom to publish partial stories.

> With the Anna Nicole Smith story. we were constantly updating on little tiny bits of information as the story progressed. One seemingly little item led to another, and we were constantly developing and updating the story. We owned that story, because we didn't have to hold onto stuff for some story that would happen later on.
>
> The ongoing blog is the finished product. Stories never finish. Anna Nicole stories are still coming out today. People may have needed it tied in a bow when they only had a half hour to publish their material. But news never ends. It's continuing to happen.
>
> Hollywood is a very controlled news town, where information is very agenda-driven. Publicity people call the shots and schedule things like red carpet events, sit down interviews, etc. Using blog software changed that for us, because we were able to go out and find our own news and sources and break our own news. (1)

Because their product is published in blog format, Mohler believes the cost of producing news is lower. There's no printing press or broadcast tower, and the cost of gathering the news is lower, too. No avids or betacams; it's all done with consumer or prosumer gear, including Mac laptops and Final Cut Pro editing software. Like others, Mohler finds it difficult to explain why traditional media outlets don't do the same thing.

Their name for the people who produce their material is "preditor," short for "producer/editor."

Everybody on the staff writes and edits. Everybody has access to the blogging software. "The blog platform is a great tool to try things quickly," he said. "If something doesn't work, you just set it aside and move on to the next thing." TMZ founder and show host, Harvey Levin, tells the staff that "done beats perfect," and this is their motto. Despite the race to be first, TMZ lives by traditional journalistic standards, such as fact-checking and sourcing. "We don't publish rumors," says Mohler. "Everything has to be sourced somehow."

Another big advantage to using blog software, according to Mohler, is how well it fits human nature. "Let's face it. People are lazy," he said, "and blog software lets people scroll down a page rather than commit to a link." The scrolling reality of TMZ flies in the face of what used to be conventional wisdom — that the print traditions of "above the fold" and "below the fold" apply to the Web. Mohler says that's not true, and this has opened new opportunities for advertisers as people are scrolling.

"The key to success in the future," he said, "is to continue to iterate and continue to try new things."

Meanwhile, TMZ's parent, America Online, is also adopting parts of the model for other news outlets. Milissa Tarquini, AOL's Director, User Interface Design and Information Architecture, says that the key is understanding that the idea of a "fold" is an illusion:

> During the early days of the AOL News reinvention, tracking data about the success of items below the fold of the TMZ site were uncovered that proved what the News team had been suspecting for a long time—that the fold is becoming less relevant in certain contexts and with certain content. We then felt completely confident that our new design, which incorporated a blog-like style and pretty long pages, would be successful and that the fold was one less thing we had to worry about. While we certainly didn't take any design cues from TMZ, the usage data from them, AOL News Daily Pulse and AOL Money & Finance supported the direction of longer pages and gave us actual numbers to use when challenged on the placement of certain items below the fold. (2)

Tarquini adds that TMZ.com's "tantalizing content" helps drive people down the page, but the real factor is the quality of what's being served. "Users will follow good content regardless of the fold line," she said.

TMZ's audience split is roughly 50–50 between men and women, which makes it somewhat of an enigma among entertainment outlets that normally skew far over to the female side. Its subject matter also appeals to a younger audience, and that means potential future news consumers are being exposed to the format of news-as-a-process.

Younger people are the key to the future of news, and most of them aren't even participating in "finished product news." No time. No interest. No relevance. Writing for Commonwealth Magazine, Dan Kennedy probed the reinvention of news with several observers and an eye towards capturing the attention of younger people. What he found suggests an open door for innovation.

- Tom Patterson of Harvard's Kennedy School of Government: "As they age, they'll probably consume a bit more news, but it's not going to get up there to the level of older people today."
- Judy Woodruff: "Much of the news young people see is not presented in a way that's relevant to them. ...We need to find out what they're interested in and address the news to them."
- David Kravitz of Blue Mass. Group: "Younger people are just more accustomed to interacting with the world through a medium like the Internet than through a medium like radio [or TV or newspapers], which is more like other people talking to you. To the extent that blogs are able to bring in a somewhat younger demographic than 'The CBS Evening News', maybe that's why, because it does become a conversation."(3)

News as a conversation is a key component of the contemporary process of news, because it's becoming increasingly clear that contributions by people who used to be just consumers of news are raising the bar for completeness of coverage and accelerating the news cycle that used to govern the process for the news-as-a-finished-product crowd. If you're the producer of the six o'clock news, your cycle is 24 hours. If you're the editor of TMZ.com, that cycle is immediate and on-going. Which is most compelling for young people?

This idea of a new news cycle was examined recently by Doc Searls, one of the authors of *The Cluetrain Manifesto*, and a thinker whose work is often cited in these essays:

> Here's the problem with most news: it isn't. It's olds. It happened hours ago, or last night, or yesterday, or last month, or before whenever the deadline was in the news organization's current "news cycle". It's not now.
>
> ...News is a river, not a lake. It is active, not static. It's what's happening, not what happened. Or not only what happened.
>
> But what happened — news as olds — is how we've understood news for as long as we've had newspapers. The happening kind of news came along with radio, and then television. Then we called it "live". Still, even on the nightly news, what's live is talking heads and reports from the field. The rest is finished stuff.
>
> There's a difference here, a distinction to be made: one as stark and important as the distinction between now and then, or life and death. It's a distinction between what's live and what's not.
>
> This distinction is what will have us soon talking about the life of newspapers, rather than the death of them.
>
> Because it's not enough to be "online" or to have a "presence" on the Web.
>
> To be truly alive, truly new, truly part of the life of its readers, a newspaper needs to be on the live Web and not just the static one. It needs to flow news, and not just post it.
>
> It needs to flow rivers of news, or newsrivers.
>
> A year from now every newspaper will have a newsriver — if not many of them. Most papers will copy other papers, of course. But one paper will start the trend, take the lead, and break the ice that's damned up their purpose in static sites and tombed archives.
>
> One of them will see that there's a Live Web as well as a static one. And that the Live Frontier is where the action is, and will be. (4)

Doc refers to the latest work by Dave Winer (the guy who basically invented blogging and podcasting), who is actually creating applications to turn RSS feeds into flowing "rivers of news," which are especially suited for mobile consumption.

News-as-a-process is more than just theory. It's being proven by blogs, sites like TMZ.com and others, including all of those run by AOL. This is the future for those who wish to be relevant, and there's no time like the present to get started. All it takes is willingness and a little (free) software. How exciting will it be to work where the only deadline is now?

This format could (perhaps should) be the home page of every mainstream news outlet, replacing the link farm that makes up traditional portal site home pages. We'd be judged by our work and not how many bells and whistles we used or page views we "drove."

The live Web is just waiting there for us to use it. What are we waiting for?

VOYEURISM: JOURNALISM'S
21ST-CENTURY CRISIS

February 26, 2007

In his book, *The Seven Habits of Highly Effective People*, Stephen Covey makes a remarkable observation about life: "You can't talk your way out of something you behaved your way into." (1)

This is the single most important problem facing journalism in the early part of this century, for we've behaved our way into quite a mess. What came first, our credibility problem or the personal media revolution? Or are they two sides of the same coin?

One of the biggest academic criticisms of Postmodernism is that its practices — especially deconstructionism — eventually lead to the chasing of one's tail. Modernism's roots attacked the faith of premodern times and the source code of western culture, the Bible—perhaps not the book itself but the belief in its absolute authority.

But Postmodernism isn't based on any historical or philosophical narrative, which is part of the reason critics say deconstructionism will always lead to nothing. However, this argument becomes irrelevant when the deconstruction process reveals existing assumptions to be the fruit of false assumptions, assumptions that seemed right at the time but that the clear lens of history has proven otherwise.

Nowhere has this been truer in my life than when deconstructing the roots of professional journalism. The trade became a profession when powerful people towards the end of the 19th century said it was. Examining their thinking tarnishes the nobility that professional journalists assume and helps explain the conundrum we've behaved our way into. This group — headed by Walter Lippmann and his friends from Woodrow Wilson's Creel Committee — used the ruse of objectivity in journalism to create a sterile environment for their newspapers that was more conducive to advertising.

In his powerful 1990 essay, "Journalism, Publicity, and the Lost Art of Argument," historian Chris Lasch noted what he viewed as an unhealthy relationship between the professional press and advertising.

> The rise of the advertising and public-relations industries, side by side, helps to explain why the press abdicated its most important function—enlarging the public forum—at the same time that it became more "responsible." A responsible press, as opposed to a partisan or opinionated one, attracted the kind of readers advertisers were eager to reach: well-heeled readers, most of whom probably thought of themselves as independent voters. These readers wanted to be assured that they were reading all the news that was fit to print, not an editor's idiosyncratic and no doubt biased view of things. Responsibility came to be equated with the avoidance of controversy because advertisers were willing to pay for it. Some advertisers were also willing to pay for sensationalism, though on the whole they preferred a respectable readership to sheer numbers. What they clearly did not prefer was "opinion"—not because they were impressed with Lippmann's philosophical arguments but because opinionated reporting did not guarantee the right audience. No doubt they also hoped that an aura of objectivity, the hallmark of responsible journalism, would rub off on the advertisements that surrounded increasingly slender columns of print. (2)

Lasch's deconstruction of Lippmann's child (he's known as the "father" of professional journalism) was bold and timely, because it came at a time when the tilt to a new definition of journalism was appearing — voyeurism. In very simple terms, voyeurism as news is the natural fruit of journalism that's designed to boost advertising. Gone are the days when advertisers only want to reach the elite. Mass marketing exists to reach, well, the masses, and reaching them *is* the core competency of contemporary media companies.

A quick check of Google:define reveals many definitions for the word "news."

- Information
- New information
- Unexpected information

"Aberration" is another definition. Dog bites man? Not news. Man bites dog? News.

Now we can add "voyeuristic information" to the list. This is not an academic definition; this one is based in behavior, the fruit of an industry that has redefined the mission of the business to the creation and maintenance of audience.

In the mass marketing paradigm, an environment that is conducive to real eyeballs and nothing else is the quest. So we can talk all we like about the lofty goals of journalism, but they crumble under the weight of the necessity to put eyeballs in front of our work.

Attention is solicited by news organizations through slick promotions, but people are wise to promos, so the solicitations come off as nothing more than hyperbole. Let's not fool ourselves by claiming that the marketing of news is the responsibility of only the marketing people. It is etched deeply now into the DNA of any newsroom in America, because the "business" of news demands it.

But hyperbole is not the case when events themselves occur that strike a resonate chord deep within people, one that seeks more, more, more. This is why Hurricane Katrina was such a blockbuster for the news industry. Hyperbole was blown aside by a storm, one that not only captured our attention but created that rare thirst for more information.

In this sense, the mission of "the news" is to satisfy that longing, and that's when everything clicks in the attention power curve.

But what about when there are no storms? What happens then?

This is when the real tragedy of contemporary "news" clicks in, for in order to fulfill the new definition of news, organizations must tap the base lusts of human nature, not the theoretical or the abstract. This is what gives us wall-to-wall coverage of the death of a person who gained notoriety via gossip and nothing else. This is why we must relentlessly pursue Britney Spears, always in hopes of (don't deny it) yet another tragic twist in her life.

This is not news, unless the definition of news is "voyeuristic information." Who does it satisfy? The reader, the viewer, the voyeur in each of us, our human nature. This is why researching news coverage is so difficult. People will tell you one thing, but their behavior belies reality. Scandal magazine sales have skyrocketed in the wake of Anna Nicole Smith's death, as have the ratings of the entertainment magazine shows. Why is this? Because people — regardless of what they say — want this kind of information.

We've all heard the old saw about driving down a street on which there is a lemonade stand on one side and an accident on the other. The attention of everybody in the car will be drawn to the accident, not the lemonade stand. This is why "if it bleeds, it leads," and so we have the sheep leading the sheep in shaping the whole of what is news.

Add to the mix the omnipresent and competitive pounding of 24-hour cable news channels, prime-time news magazines, and supermarket check-out stands with pictures of Britney's bald head, and it's hard to argue with the view that this is all we talk about.

And the astonishing and frustrating thing for news organizations about all of this is that it's led to a serious credibility crisis. The audiences that are drawn to these images and gossip are the same people that are telling us its our fault. This is the paradox of the "news as voyeuristic information" paradigm.

So who's to blame and what do we do?

The assigning of blame in all of this is counter-productive. It simply is what it is. Mass marketing demands a mass audience, and we will keep doing what we're doing.

Moreover, the reader might infer a suggestion that the audience is really to blame. After all, we're just giving them what they really want — as evidenced by their viewing. But this is just an excuse to validate and continue our behavior. Blaming the audience is also quite absurd, because our culture itself has no internal governor anymore. Without it, can we really say people are to blame for watching what we put in front of them? So if one wishes to assign blame, it must go to western culture as a whole, and who's capable of doing anything about that?

"I have seen the enemy," Pogo said, "and he is us."

If, however, voyeuristic information is a fruit of Lippmann's professional journalism, perhaps there is something we can do about that. The reality, however, is that the answer is being birthed outside our inner circle, which brings us back to the personal media revolution.

Lasch tracks the lack of participation in the political process in the U.S. with the rise of a professional press. He hammers home that what's lacking in contemporary journalism is argument, and that is what our culture so badly needs right now. Argument is what's protected by the First Amendment, not the bland "just the facts" vision of Lippmann, and yet it has been stripped from culture by a press that serves advertising and by that greatest of all argument-eliminators, political correctness. Only the status quo is served by the unbridled continuance of an argument-less press.

Within the personal media revolution, however, people are taking matters into their own hands, because journalism isn't really a profession in the same sense as, for example, medicine. It's not the sole purview of the elite, nor does it belong to any inner circle.

Anyone can "be" a journalist, and now that anyone can be a publisher, anyone can share their journalism with anyone else. Argument is evident again in the so-called "amateur" journalism of bloggers, and it has profound ramifications for our culture.

An important aspect to the personal media revolution is the social or "connected" nature of it. Bloggers and the technical community that serves them (made up, in part, of bloggers themselves) are creating marvelous tools to connect to each other, talk to each other, keep track of each other, and manage their place within the whole. This is counterintuitive to the traditional press, which has built its empire on remaining disconnected, except through hierarchical organizations that work to maintain the status quo.

As people are connected, they're increasingly turning to each other for all kinds of advice. This is evident in a GfK-NOP report last year from the U.K. that shows three-fourths of consumers prefer information from other people when making purchases. This is considerably higher than the media, advertising or even the Web. The numbers for word-of-mouth and the Web are trending upwards, while editorial and advertising are trending downward.

While these numbers come from the U.K., they reveal the nature of the business problem for traditional media, for in the end, it's really about money. If people are increasingly getting less information about purchases from editorial and advertising, where will the sellers of goods and services turn to reach an increasingly guarded customer?

In the U.S., there is a growing group of bloggers who are taking matters into their own hands beyond most. They are the group known as "mommy bloggers," (3) and they're connected, growing in numbers, and looking to themselves for answers because they feel institutions have failed them. This group represents a key demographic that Madison Avenue wants, and they know it.

In California, mommy blogger Mindy Roberts is involved in a new Web business called "Trusted Opinion." (4) The site allows networks of friends to post their thoughts about commerce. The opening target is a long-standing franchise of the traditional press, movie reviews, but Mindy says the plan is to turn Trusted Opinion into a universal rating platform for all manner of goods and services. It doesn't take a genius to see where this is headed, and the principal issue for the sellers of those goods and services will be the degree to which they're prepared to accept the customer's perspective on their wares.

You can't talk your way out of something you behaved your way into.

Are the writings of mommy bloggers journalism? Does it really matter? It's certainly not the voyeuristic information that currently defines the professional crowd, but woven between the anecdotes, the life slices, the live-blogging of events—including birthing—and the tragedies (all of which some would argue qualify as journalism) are found gems that would challenge anything the world of professional journalism could create in terms of quality, depth and the vetting of information. It is the blend, however, that pulls these people together, and that includes plenty of argument to support their views.

Is this an aberration or the leading edge of something significant? What will politicians do, for example, when confronted with this kind of organized force?

This essay should not be construed as a blanket approbation of the blogosphere, for there is plenty of mischief here in addition to some pretty darned good journalism. Then there is the matter of bloggers who secretly wish they were the mainstream and who sacrifice their passion for a place at the advertising feeding trough. These are the bloggers that get most of the attention from the mainstream, for they are its direct competitors. The perceived competition, therefore, isn't really over journalism; it's all about the money.

But there are, in fact, bloggers who are giving the world significant journalism, biased though it may be, and in so doing, returning argument to the public square or as Lasch calls it, "expanding the public forum."

The traditional press has no choice but to continue its quest for a mass audience and serve the harsh taskmaster that ad revenue has become. This will not change, nor should it. Business is business, and it's vital that traditional media companies stay alive and financially healthy. A sudden collapse of the Media 1.0 hegemony would destroy our economy, so the mainstream *must* live on.

This means that the changes necessary to evolve won't — in fact, can't — come from the legacy brand, for it has no choice but to play in the world of Anna Nicole Smith. If they don't, they run the significant risk of alienating what's left of their audience, for people have come to expect — whether they'll admit it or not — that one of the roles of contemporary media is to satisfy their voyeuristic information needs.

But this shouldn't stop traditional media companies from entering the Media 2.0 world and playing by its rules instead of their own. The opportunity exists to grow new brands, built on different guiding principles and unafraid of connecting with the people we're trying to serve. The experience can be humbling, but there is much the mainstream can do to actually advance the cause of expanding the public forum in the cyber world. By encouraging and supporting the effort, it won't matter how much its core efforts pander to voyeuristic information, because the higher calling of journalism—with argument—will be served elsewhere.

We might actually behave our way into something significant.

TRUSTING THE AUDIENCE
AND THE READERS

November 28, 2005

One of the fundamental beliefs of the Judeo-Christian experience is the inherently sinful nature of humankind. Since I
grew up in a Calvinist home, this was hammered into us around-
the-clock. Calvinism is an extreme form of legalistic Christianity,
where good behavior was the impossible goal of life, so we were
forced into good behavior (and a constant state of guilt). At the
same time, however, it justified all sorts of mischief, like when I
got caught stealing from the collection plate. After all, what do you
expect from a sinner?

Regardless of the extreme to which it is manifested, the belief that
humankind is essentially bad and needs redemption has been with
us for a very long time. It validates the need for war. It drives our
institutions and our Modernist culture too, because systematic and
rigid authority is in place to apprehend our runaway souls when
they get out of line. All authority in our culture, from God on down
to parents, exists to maintain civility in the face of our dreaded
sinful nature.

In politics, contemporary conservatism is built solidly on this belief, while tolerant liberalism seems to see other possibilities for people. And in media, the current debate about the mainstream media versus the blogosphere is rooted here too. After all, the argument goes, the self-centered and chaotic masses cannot be trusted to get things right on their own.

This was an essential theme of Walter Lippmann's in the early 20th century. He's the father of professional — read: objective — journalism, but his real passion was social engineering. A member of America's ruling class, Lippmann was so obsessed with the need for an elite (professional) class to run things that he routinely slandered the masses.

In his 1955 essay "Walter Lippmann and Democracy," Herbert Aptheker refers to Lippmann as an "offended and frightened snob" to say such things as these:

> "...there is no possibility that men can understand the whole process of social existence." Forgetting "the limitations of men" has been our central error. Men cannot plan their future for "they are unable to imagine it" and they cannot manage a civilization, for "they are unable to understand it." To think otherwise, to dare to believe that the people can and should govern themselves, that they can and should forge social systems and governments enhancing the pursuit of their happiness here on earth—this is "the gigantic heresy of an apostate generation..."
>
> ...Popular opinion is and must be opposite to the public interest—this miraculous public interest contrived by Mr. Lippmann, though never really defined. But then Mr. Lippmann being of the elite, knows the public interest when he sees it, and the one thing he is sure of is that his public interest is as public as the rich Englishmen's public school that is to say, it is private. Mr. Lippmann has extended the myth of the classless state of his earlier writings to the myth of a classless public interest which is knowable only to a private, minute elite. (1)

Remember, this is the man who fathered professional journalism. Is there any wonder the public is sick to death of it? The real threat to contemporary journalism from the blogosphere isn't amateur versus professional, ethics, reliability or any of that; it's the terrifying empowerment of the ignorant masses that is shaking our culture to the core. It's sinful humankind discovering that perhaps he isn't as bad — and therefore stupid — as he's been told.

If you believe, for example, that people will generally get things wrong, then your approach to informing them of "the news" is going to be hierarchical. Somebody "up there" has to determine what's important for those "down below." This argument is at the core of the gatekeeper concept of professional journalism.

If, however, you believe that people are capable of getting things right, then you'll include them in your journalism, because you believe they have something to add. Dan Gillmor, author of the landmark citizens media book, *We the Media*, made the observation long ago that "my audience knows more than I do." This is a shocking statement to mainstream media types, but it forms one of the foundational beliefs of the blogosphere. Gillmor even put chapters of his book online as he was writing it, because he wanted reader feedback before publishing.

Jeff Jarvis is one of the most outspoken evangelists for the idea of giving the masses a degree of trust, but he admits it's an ongoing learning experience. And it's that experience that is opening his eyes to a view of people that's considerably more tolerant than that of his mainstream critics. He recalls appearing on a CBS morning show in the 80s to talk about ratings, and the producer challenged him for defending the tastes of the viewing public. "That's no way for a big-media snob to act," she said. Jarvis responds, "But she was right: I was defending the taste of my fellow man."

> I have come to realize that if you don't have trust in the intelligence, taste, and good will of your fellow man then you can't believe in democracy; if the people are an idiot, why would you allow them to elect their leaders? If you're not a populist, then you can't believe in the wisdom of the marketplace; you can't be a capitalist. If you're not a populist, for that matter, then you should throw reform religion out the window, for why would you think that man could have a direct relationship with God?

But if you do trust — or better yet, enable the people — then wonderful things can happen. The Internet allows us to control not just the consumption but the creation of media and more. And once again, given half a chance, we the people can do amazing things…

…So both in terms of the good and the bad, the secret to success in world 2.0 is to hand control over to the people. If you mean that, if you really make that happen — providing raw material, connections, infrastructure, promotion, a marketplace, support, trust — then you can succeed. (2)

Another new media hero is Craig Newmark, founder of Craigslist, the consumer-generated online classifieds juggernaut. Craigslist has helped devastate classifieds revenue of the print media industry, but Newmark doesn't see himself as a business mogul, choosing instead the title of "customer service representative." He spends his time speaking with the users of Craigslist and working out problems on their behalf. "We have seen a genuine wisdom-of-crowds effect at work at times on our Website," he says.

His advice in the new media world is to get out of the way, which assumes a significant level of trust in people. When confronted with any problem, he simply says, "We'll figure it out." Where does this trust come from? "It's plain and simple," he says, "a great deal of actual, real-life experience."

People are very consistently very trustworthy, and very much okay. There are a few bad guys out there, a very tiny percentage, and people are generally aware of them. Give people the ability to deal with the bad stuff, and they deal with it. In our case, it's mostly our flagging for removal mechanism, though sometimes people email us in special circumstances.

Also, most of everything on our site is based on community feedback; we're dealing with that now regarding charging apartment brokers for rental listings in NY.

Normally, groups of people are smart about dealing with the bad guys, but some are very smart about inciting mob behavior, that's a problem, and we're still learning how to deal with that. We have that problem at craigslist, and the Wikipedia folks have a similar problem. We'll figure it out.

Newmark has announced his intentions to get involved in the journalism business, and it will be interesting to see what his belief system produces.

Google is another company that regularly invests its reputation and products in the people who use them. The company launches most new ventures in "beta" form and relies on the feedback of users to tweak them and make them better. As logical as this seems, it's a significant departure from the status quo in terms of new business development. Testing in our hierarchical culture is done behind closed doors, where mistakes can be hidden from the eyes of potential customers, but Google doesn't seem to care. The essential issue here is marketing. In a mass marketing culture, business needs to always put their best foot forward. In a culture of personal media, transparency is paramount, so Google says, "Here it is. What do you think?"

I work with a group that publishes an online magazine. We've been discussing the merits of blogging and blogging software, which has generated a bit of concern from the professional journalism defenders. One of my colleagues wrote that order (that hierarchical dream state) is evident in the magazine format and that it "adheres to the deepest ethics of journalism." He's afraid that without the editorial process "clear thought would disappear," because "thought requires care." The inference is that an orderly hierarchy is the only path to clear thought, and that assumes much.

Order is the god of the elites, because the thought of chaos is simply too much to bear. Despite the real life experiences of a growing number of intelligent people who are building an infrastructure through chaos, some of us cling to the fear that it will all crumble in an instant, and this view is only possible with a belief in the inherent sinful nature of humankind. It is a wall that separates in an age of disappearing walls.

One of the most common expressions heard in the blogosphere is that it is self-correcting. If you have experience with this phenomenon, you'll understand it, but it's undecipherable to mainstream media traditionalists. That's because the concept flows from a counterintuitive belief about humankind — our ability to fix some broken things without the assistance of a hierarchical order.

What most Modernist thinkers fail to realize in our increasingly Postmodern culture is that there is definitely something new under the sun today — silos of knowledge are being torn down and freely distributed to everybody, and this has profound consequences for the future. People such as Walter Lippmann looked down their noses at the concept of government of the people, by the people and for the people, because they viewed the masses as ignorant and incapable. Even if we give him the benefit of the doubt and grant that his belief may have been true a hundred years ago, it doesn't necessarily follow that it's true today. This is what's really changing in our world, and the old hierarchies of protected knowledge are being dismantled by what used to be the bottom.

Of course, this has not gone entirely unnoticed by the status quo, which has a great deal to lose in the new paradigm. Doc Searls paints a chilling picture of the future in a call to action essay entitled "Saving the Net: How to Keep the Carriers from Flushing the Net Down the Tubes."

> Are you ready to see the Net privatized from the bottom to the top? Are you ready to see the Net's free and open marketplace sucked into a pit of pipes built and fitted by the phone and cable companies and run according to rules lobbied by the carrier and content industries?
>
> Do you believe a free and open market should be "Your choice of walled garden" or "Your choice of silo"? That's what the big carrier and content companies believe. That's why they're getting ready to fence off the frontiers. (3)

We are facing a war for the very soul of our culture, and the side on which you fall depends, in large part, on your view of humankind. It is the most unreported story of our time. If you trust people to generally get it right, then you've no fear of handing over to them the power that comes with knowledge. If, however, you trust that people will generally get it wrong, then you'll see value in protecting such knowledge and continuing the path of hierarchical order. This is a considerable challenge for each of us.

Of all of the revelations I've had since I was a boy, none has contributed to my sense of well-being like the knowledge that I'm not, nor do I have to be, perfect. In taking such a position, I've discovered that nobody else is perfect either, and that includes those further up the hierarchical food chain. The greatest myth of the Modernist culture is that the elite are closer to perfection than the rest of us, and as more people discover that this isn't true, our democracy will only get stronger.

Get ready for a bumpy ride.

THE ASSUMPTION OF TRUST

May 27, 2004

Who's to blame that the news is often obsessed with pop culture at the expense of important (often foreign) matters?

A kerfuffle of sorts arose over this question recently at one of those gatherings of journalism elites in California. It began when David Remnick, editor of *The New Yorker*, blamed the public for failing to pay adequate attention to serious journalism by saying, "The public bears responsibility for what it watches, what it reads and what it ignores." Stanford Professor David M. Kennedy took him to task by comparing Remnick's quote with President Jimmy Carter's infamous "malaise" address, and added, "It's absolutely fatal to democratic theory to believe the public is incompetent. To whom else can we turn?" Kennedy said it was the media's job to make what's important more compelling.

This is a complex and important matter, for the real issue is not one of blame but one of trust. And on the mistaken assumption of trust rests all of contemporary journalism.

Let's begin with a question: Who or what gives anybody the authority to be a reporter?

Journalism schools only prepare people for our trade, and a degree isn't a license, so the authority doesn't come from education.

It certainly doesn't rest with the government, for then journalism would be mired in the political process. The First Amendment protects us from a Federal Bureau of Journalism Licensing. The authority doesn't rest with business or industry, because then only industry moguls would call the shots (a lot of people think that this is the case, but thankfully, it's not). The authority doesn't even rest with people who own printing presses or broadcast licenses or vast Internet holdings, although they may act as though it does. The truth is there is no conferrer of journalism licenses, because there is no authority to grant such — no person, no entity whatsoever to whom one can go to complain.

This is the crux of a very serious matter, because the true authority of any journalist in a democracy is a public trust, not the press card he or she might carry. This is badly misunderstood these days, and it's at the root of a whole lot of problems.

From the journalism side of this trust is an assumption that the press represents the public and, therefore, speaks on its behalf. When the press investigates, it does so as a representative of the people. Mess with the press, and you're messing with the people. That is journalism's assumption of the public trust.

From the public side of this trust is an assumption that the press has their best interests at core, and so consent and tolerance — rarely discussed forms of authority — are granted to those who investigate and report. As John Locke taught, however, one cannot tolerate unless one has the power not to tolerate, and this is what's happening today. The press has breached the trust as far as the public is concerned and now functions in its own best interests, and that has created two big problems. One, there's a void in the public information arena (more on this in a moment), and two, the press blindly assumes the trust is still in place, even though it functions as though its authority comes from someplace further up the hierarchy. This creates the illusion that the public trust is a given, that the press is actually doing the public a favor by shining a light on what it believes is truth — all in the name of journalism. That's why Mr. Remnick can blame his readers for their apparent illiteracy.

But journalism without the public trust isn't journalism at all; it's just a business.

When a reporter knocked at the door or called on the phone, it used to be that the weight behind their questions was that of a curious public, and it was considerable. Reporters want to believe that's still the case, but it just isn't. "Gotcha" has become a sad and self-serving game that the deluded press plays, but it's a power grab that the citizenry generally sees through. It's about marketing, personal and corporate. It's about manipulation for some form of gain. Who needs trust when you have clout?

On television, most people used to stay put when we told them to "stay tuned." The assumption was that there was something important ahead. Not anymore. We "tease" them, and well, guess what? They don't like being teased. And so they don't trust us anymore, but who needs trust when you think you have a captive audience or the marketing acumen to manipulate them hither and yon? Nowhere is the absence of the public trust in journalism more evident than in the hyperbole within television newscasts.

In TV news, we crossed the line between news and entertainment a long time ago, yet we wonder why the audience treats us like entertainers instead of journalists.

It used to be that we'd never consider showing a crime victim's body on the air, but now some version of the body shot is an integral part of every crime story. In truth, the only time you don't see this today is when there wasn't anybody there to videotape it. We also used to resist the exploitation of sobbing family members or friends, but that changed when the idea of touching viewers emotionally became more important than the story. Our audience used to trust that we wouldn't unnecessarily shock or distress them but no longer. After all, who needs trust when you've warned them?

We've convinced ourselves that such behavior is all right, because people "have a right to know," and we always run to press freedom whenever our business is challenged. The problem is that press freedom is inextricably tied to the public trust, and without it, such behavior is revealed as self-motivated and disingenuous. The biggest threat to freedom of the press is the press itself.

We're surprised when people object to Ted Koppel reading the names of war dead, so we write it off as politics. This stems from a belief that part of our role is to present things that people "need" to know, but again, this assumes that the public has entrusted us with the authority to do so.

They did once, but they don't anymore. We broke the promise upon which our relationship was based, and we deserve what we're getting. The question is — will we ever get it back? The answer is problematic, at best, because the real crisis revealed by the loss of public trust in the press is what it says about self-governance. Who wants to self-restrict when you can blame the audience, as Mr. Remnick has done?

In their recent book, *The Elements of Journalism*, Bill Kovach and Tom Rosenstiel argue that the purpose of journalism is to provide people with the information they need to be free and self-governing. By abdicating our responsibility to govern ourselves, we've also contributed to a self-governing crisis throughout the culture.

For all that we espouse the desire to run our own lives, the truth is we all need some form of government. Like Bob Dylan wrote, "You're gonna have to serve somebody." The choice we have in the U.S. is whether that governor is internal or external, and that poses perplexing and difficult questions in a culture that was built on the internal governor of religion but has evolved to the external governors of profit and the law.

When the United States was born over two centuries ago, its founders wrote a Declaration of Independence from British rule. It boldly stated that all men are created equal and that the rights of life, liberty and the pursuit of happiness were God-given and therefore could not be transferred to another or taken away. In making this statement, they rejected the hierarchy of the throne of England. The government they created was designed so that *the people* would run things through their representatives, and power was split between three branches of government.

That's because the authority of such a government was to come from the "consent of the governed," you and me. This is impossible unless those to be governed externally already have a modicum of an internal governor. In a culture based on oath, allegiance and promise, licentiousness is inevitable without such integrity. Promises based on nothing are meaningless. An oath sworn on one's own self has little meaning, since it can be broken with impunity. A real or perceived punishment must accompany the oath before it carries any weight. Locke knew this, which is why he had such difficulty with atheists in a democracy.

All government is about power — the granting or restricting thereof — and self-government is no different. What is different is that self-government flows from a bottom-up paradigm, one that begins with self-governing at the most micro of levels. That means each individual must find a way to govern him or herself before it's possible to participate in cultural self-governance. This is a primary missing ingredient in our culture today, without which we're like soup base without water.

Lying under oath in a court of law is a crime, but that's the be-all-and-end-all of it today. People who do so take a calculated risk and weigh the possibility of going to jail if found guilty of perjury. However, the oath taken in a court of law when our courts were founded carried a much stiffer penalty — that of hellfire and damnation. That was the essence of oaths. You didn't take them lightly, because eternity was at stake. This is one example governing from within, and it's what our way of life is built upon.

So this matter of public trust and the media is much more significant than it at first seems, for the self-governance of one demands the ability to test the self-governance of others. And isn't that actually what's happening when the press — with the public trust — knocks at any institution's door? Isn't that what our "checks and balances" accomplish — to assure that the self-governance of others is equal to our own?

Taking the public trust for granted while functioning as though our authority comes from a higher power has created a massive disconnect between the people and the press. And the people —

weary from decades of fighting this disconnect — have now taken matters into their own hands. With technology providing the means, a whole new genre of news reporting is springing up all around us to fill the information void.

Weblogs are increasingly representing the people, because they're written *by* the people. The journalism within the blogosphere is breathtakingly self-governing and self-correcting, and the energy flowing between the postings, links and comments is a gale of fresh air. The discussion is passionate, intelligent and involving. The public trust here isn't conferred on some detached, authoritative entity. It's in-your-face and open to challenge from any and all.

However, one must be a part of this phenomenon — as Bill Gates calls it — in order to fully understand it. Otherwise, the tendency is to view this historic transformation through institutional eyes and try to assimilate the movement into the status quo. It just won't happen, because contrary to what Mr. Remnick (and many others, including the father of professional journalism, Walter Lippmann) thinks, the public is a lot smarter than they're given credit for being.

This is the essence of the Postmodern movement, which is documented in this series of essays. It is the Age of Participation, in part, because Pomos view the Modern age of logic, reason and hierarchical authority — along with its need for citizen passivity — as having failed. Pomos don't trust experts, especially those who claim such a status based on some institutional authority. They trust those closest to them who've actually experienced the subject in question.

This is the power of the New Media known as blogging, and it has profound ramifications for the future of journalism's public trust.

ARGUMENT VERSUS OBJECTIVITY

December 5, 2003

TV News — and other forms of journalism of the future — will steadily drift away from the "professional" standard of objectivity and back to one that regularly incorporates argument into its soul. If you study Postmodernism, this conclusion is inevitable, and it will produce — I predict — a change in the culture as significant and lasting as the American Revolution. Moreover, this change will occur outside the institution of journalism and in spite of its ongoing self-examination.

To even begin understanding the dynamics of this change, one must first leave the safe pedestal of professionalism. This is why the institution will never "get it" and why the ultimate arrival of the new age will seem sudden, when it really has been bubbling and simmering for decades.

So set aside everything you've been taught and believe, and let's take a little trip back in time. If journalism is the first rough draft of history, then who were the first journalists?

Since the dawn of humanity, cultures have carried their myths and histories with them. These accounts reflected not only factual occurrences but also the cultural contexts within which they took place. As such, none would pass the muster of today's standards, because journalism goes beyond storytelling and includes, I believe, an element of investigation — an attempt to satisfy curiosity brought about by questions. This is the integral assumption upon which journalism is built and the missing element in much of today's junk.

Let's open the New Testament for a moment. The gospel accounts of the story of Jesus carry similar story lines, but Luke (who also wrote the book of Acts) adds elements that the others don't. Take a look at the way he begins his account:

> Most honorable Theophilus: Many people have written accounts about the events that took place among us. They used as their source material the reports circulating among us from the early disciples and other eyewitnesses of what God has done in fulfillment of his promises. Having carefully investigated all of these accounts from the beginning, I have decided to write a careful summary for you, to reassure you of the truth of all you were taught. (New Living Translation) (1)

Napoleon conquered Europe, yet he wrote, "Four hostile newspapers are more to be feared than a thousand bayonets." Revolutionary War era newspapers, many of which were shut down by the British for espousing their views, influenced the writing of the First Amendment, so that such opposition would never again be silenced in the new world. Facts don't need protection, but ideas certainly do.

The assassination of President Abraham Lincoln provides a useful look into the mind of mid-19th century journalism. A *New York Herald* dispatch from Washington during the execution of the four who conspired with John Wilkes Booth contained the following:

> The execution of his murderers to-day has proven us to be a law-abiding people; otherwise the miscreants who plotted and executed their great crime would have long since been torn to pieces by the people, who were as much convinced of their guilt before as after their trial. Everything has been done decently and in order, and the majesty of the law and of the nation has been vindicated, and the

guiltiest of the wretches have gone to answer for their crimes at
the great tribunal where no subterfuge will avail to hide their crim-
inality. (2)

Not much objectivity there. And of the four people hung, one was
a woman, whose death the reporter justified by painting a portrait
of a woman devoid of femininity.

> (Her) gray eyes were cold and lifeless and added to the mas-
> culinity of her appearance. They were seldom lit up by excitement
> or pleasure, though occasionally they gleamed with a furious or
> stealthy glare which indexed the bad passions of her soul...She
> appears to have been masculine not only in person and manners,
> but in mind. (3)

The point is that the roots of journalism don't include the pristine
notion that one should (or even could) stand afar off and report
facts without opinion or "argument" — to use historian Christopher Lasch's term. "The job of the press is to encourage debate,"
he wrote, "not to supply the public with information." He espoused
the idea that argument precedes understanding and is central to
democratic opinion formation. And democratic opinion was the
issue that split liberal thinkers in the years following World War
I, when the modern public relations era was born. One group, led
by Pragmatic philosopher John Dewey, believed that the public
could and should participate in democracy. Walter Lippmann, the
man who would later be called the "Dean of American Journalism," headed the other group and maintained that the public was
too ignorant to do any more than cast ballots once in a while.

The idea that the public might intrude into the affairs of "responsible men" was repugnant to the cynical Lippmann, who voiced his
social engineering vision in two important books, *Public Opinion*
(1922) and *The Phantom Public* (1925).

> A false ideal of democracy can only lead to disillusionment and
> to meddlesome tyranny. If democracy cannot direct affairs, then a
> philosophy which expects it to direct them will encourage the
> people to attempt the impossible; they will fail...The public must

be put in its place, so that it may exercise its own powers, but no less and perhaps even more, so that each of us may live free of the trampling and the roar of a bewildered herd." (4)

Walter Lippmann, *The Phantom Public*

He deplored what he saw as the uneducated manipulating the masses through the use of symbols and stereotypes and called for an educated elite to run things on behalf of everybody. Thus was born the "professional" journalist, one who was free of symbol and stereotype and would assist the other elite institutions in leading the country, something Lippmann had already done as an advisor to President Woodrow Wilson.

Dewey, on the other hand, was a firm believer that the open exchange of ideas permitted the people to govern themselves:

…the act of voting is in a democratic regime a culmination of a continued process of open and public communication in which prejudices have the opportunity to erase each other; that continued interchange of facts and ideas exposes what is unsound and discloses what may make for human well-being… Any fair-minded survey of suppressive acts in this country will demonstrate that their ultimate source is always a privileged minority (with the majority standing passively by and permitting it to occur). (5)

John Dewey, *John Dewey Responds* (1950)

The Postmodernist mind is eerily similar to Dewey's and immediately repelled by Lippmann's. Pomos look around and see ruin where the elites promised prosperity. The American dream lives on only for the privileged, and the resulting anti-institutional energy is fierce and unrelenting. Technology has leveled the knowledge playing field and has thrust the masses into unfamiliar territory, where the application of knowledge used to be reserved only for the few. The rational command and control of Modernism is under assault by people who find greater comfort in anarchy than what they view as the false promise of the shepherds. Postmodernism is the Age of Participation, and media executives who don't realize that will soon find themselves unemployed.

Walt Disney built his animation empire on the concept of "the plausible impossible." The term could easily be applied to the artificial journalistic hegemony known as objectivity — the silly notion that information without argument is what people want and need to live their lives. We stand on that self-hallowed ground, while the people rank us below used-car salesmen and trust of the news media is at an all-time low. Lasch noted the impossibility in an article he wrote in 1990.

> Our search for reliable information is itself guided by the questions that arise during arguments about a given course of action. It is only by subjecting our preferences and projects to the test of debate that we come to understand what we know and what we still need to learn. Until we have to defend our opinions in public, they remain opinions in Lippmann's pejorative sense — half-formed convictions based on random impressions and unexamined assumptions. It is the act of articulating and defending our views that lifts them out of the category of "opinions," gives them shape and definition, and makes it possible for others to recognize them as a description of their own experience as well. In short, we come to know our own minds only by explaining ourselves to others. (6)

This is why blogs are sweeping the Internet and have been embraced by a public hungry for argument. Bloggers are the journalists of tomorrow. They demonstrate a fundamental curiosity and the Internet affords them the ability to check facts. They offer arguments and links to reference material in support of their individual points-of-view, and as a whole, they make up a community of people who keep each other honest. In an article for Australia's Evatt Foundation, Tim Dunlop calls bloggers "the new public intellectuals" and gives an excellent example of bloggers setting the record straight.

> The *Guardian* published a report that said Paul Wolfowitz, the U.S. deputy secretary of defence, had claimed that the war in Iraq really was all about oil. Bloggers by the bucketload logged onto the United States Department of Defence Website, checked the transcript of the interview Wolfowitz gave, and reported in pretty quick time that *The Guardian* had got it wrong. They had used a German

translation of the interview that they'd then back-translated causing all the nuance to be lost in the process. Within half a day, many blogs had nailed the error and twenty-four hours later *The Guardian* had withdrawn the piece and apologised. (7)

Israeli Blogger Allison Kaplan Sommers recently gave an example of how the new media works:

1. Jeff Jarvis sees an item in the *Daily Telegraph* on the new BBC Middle East ombudsman and posts it on his blog, BuzzMachine.
2. Steven Weiss, one of the bloggers on Protocols, sees the item and posts it on his blog.
3. I see it on Protocols and post it on my blog.
4. Gil Shterzer sees it on my blog. He realizes that it hasn't hit the Israeli media yet — guess their London correspondents are asleep on the job. He e-mails Ynet, the Web site of Israel's largest newspaper, Yediot Aharonot, and gives them a heads-up. Ynet runs the item as one of their top stories.

So the story travelled from the British press to an American non-Jew's blog to an American Jew's blog, to an American-Israeli's blog, to an Israeli's blog, to the Hebrew press. (8)

The big problem in all of this for "professional" journalists is its randomness. It just doesn't fit into the command and control Lippmann/Modernist mindset. But that's exactly what gives it power in a Postmodern world, where chaos is the rule and disdain for anything elite provides fuel for the journalist fire.

Lincoln's "government of the people" was lifted from a statement made by Englishman John Wycliffe a few centuries earlier. Wycliffe is called by many the true father of the Protestant Reformation, because it was his English translation of the Bible that removed Christianity from the sole purview (and authority) of the Roman Church. When he finished it shortly before his death, Wycliffe said, "This book shall make possible government of the people, by the people and for the people." His argument was that only individuals who are self-governed internally are capable of governing themselves as a people. This idea lives on in Postmodernism and beautifully represents the concept of order in chaos.

No groups of elites calling the shots. No manufactured consent (to borrow Lippmann's phrase). Just people living together and governing themselves.

Idealistic? Perhaps. But the many voices of tomorrow's media (it's closer than you think) demand to be heard, and all great cultural changes of the past have been birthed in such cries. And if life teaches anything, it's to never underestimate the power of free communication.

The Changing Face(s)
of Local News

August 23, 2006

In the early days of television news, the people who worked in the industry came out of radio or newspapers. I cut my teeth in the business at WTMJ-TV in Milwaukee, a combination radio-TV operation owned by the *Milwaukee Journal*. That original newsroom was a cast of characters, many of whom definitely had faces for radio. The emphasis back then was on covering the news, not how it was presented.

There was no college degree to teach attractive young people how to be on TV. That came later as the emphasis shifted to presentation and promotion. One of the constant complaints about local TV news these days is that it's a mile wide and an inch deep, and the complainers point to this ;looking people, and so it goes.

But they're not watching them like they used to. Average local news viewing is down almost a third over the last ten years, and while most people point to the fragmenting marketplace, others are exploring the possibility that other factors are involved — the obvious being that people are turning away from local news, because there's something wrong with the product. Is there? That's a pretty big question for an industry that works its tail off day in and day out to serve the information needs of America's communities.

A visit to Dunedin, Florida, where Nielsen stores its paper diaries from markets, is an eye-opening experience and one that broadcast executives might find revealing as our audience universe continues to shrink. For in those diaries are handwritten comments from viewers — and more importantly, non-viewers — that offer insight. Based on my experience there, several themes occur when people explain why they don't watch:

- I get my news elsewhere (often the Internet).
- It's not relevant to my life.
- It's all the same.
- I can't stand the teases.

It would be presumptuous to declare that these concepts color the local news business "wrong," but let's keep an open mind for a moment. Perhaps people *are* turning away from the whole idea of commoditized news, with its predictable emphasis on breaking — usually crime related — stories, live reports, slick production and marketing that approaches "watch this or die" status. In many ways, local news seems to have become a caricature of itself, something to be mocked by Comedy Central and in films. Are we what they say we are? Perhaps more than we'd care to admit. Regardless, the popularity of The Daily Show with Jon Stewart suggests it might be more than just food for thought.

At WKRN-TV in Nashville, president and general manager Mike Sechrist and news director Steve Sabato think there's more here than meets the eye, and so they've embarked on a multi-faceted strategy to inject substance into local news through new media projects and a controversial concept called Video Journalists or VJs. The plan was implemented in 2005, and what they're learning has substantial ramifications for the whole industry. In many ways, they've gone back to the type of news that was done in the early days. While the station still cares deeply about presentation, the seesaw has definitely tilted towards the content. Steak over sizzle, as old timers would understand.

What's new is the VJ concept. Most people in the news department write, shoot, edit and host their own stories. This doubled the number of feet on the street and dramatically changed the way they go about gathering the news. There is no "talent/shooter" caste system; everybody's equal. Each has their own car and gear — and perhaps more importantly — their own beat to cover.

The newsroom comes closer to a meritocracy than the disciplined dictatorship that exists in many contemporary shops.

> The VJ concept has its detractors, usually photographers who feel two people will always produce better stories than one. The truth of this belief, however, isn't the issue in a world of increased expectations and declining resources, and the VJs bring so much else to the table that it's hard to argue with the formula. Good storytelling will always require work, and that's no different with one person than it is with two. The VJs like the idea of controlling their own pieces, and some of the best come from the ranks of the shooters.

When Sechrist and Sabato discovered that the system had virtually eliminated overtime — they begin each day with ten completed stories — they rolled that money into salaries and put everybody in the shop on the same pay scale.

But the biggest change that is occurring is with the types of people the station is bringing into the newsroom as a result of the VJ concept. With the newsroom looking for expertise first, the age of the glamorous "general assignment" reporter has come to an abrupt close.

"The VJ concept opens up all sorts of avenues in hiring," says Sechrist. "You're not bound by the traditional constraints of only looking at current reporters in other markets. Our Real Estate and Lifestyles VJ was once a photographer and real estate agent. We're looking for people with an expertise in certain areas. Smart, motivated self starters. We can teach them how to write, shoot and edit."

The station recently lifted the top investigative reporter in the state from The Nashville Tennessean, in part, because he wanted to be a VJ. He was the second top-line reporter the station has recruited from the newspaper in a matter of weeks, because the emphasis on substance outweighs the farm-system approach of contemporary television news. Sechrist explains:

> A majority of times you do not see the reporter in the story. This has an advantage of attracting people who are more interested in storytelling than seeing themselves on the air. To be sure it's advantageous if they have good "pipes," but it certainly takes the "appearance" prerequisite out of the equation. Local newspaper and radio reporters who have a wealth of local knowledge are now finding their way to the top of our candidates list.
>
> Our aforementioned real estate reporter has worked as a real estate agent. When she does stories she brings a wealth of knowledge that a GA reporter doesn't have. The morning meetings have changed from the typical four our five news managers in a room determining the day's coverage to a raucous free-for-all in the newsroom with all the VJs pitching their story ideas. To be sure, we still have desk people who keep track of breaking and developing stories, and some VJs are better with story generation than others, but it is a much better method which invites participation from everyone.
>
> We look for smart and motivated people in all sorts of disciplines. We are functioning more like a newspaper now with stories bubbling from the bottom up rather than the top down. (1)

The proof of the concept, of course, will come in the form of ratings, but there's more to the VJ concept than a new way to produce TV news. By placing the tools of the personal media revolution in the hands of professionals, the station is opening the door to uses of the material that go far beyond what's seen on-the-air. Many of the VJs also have blogs, and those will evolve to include their video. The idea is to turn each beat into an on-line franchise, and the options after that are pretty significant, especially as the audience/readers get involved.

Nashville has a remarkably cohesive and growing blogosphere, and Sechrist has announced plans to work towards a citizens-media-generated daily news program through them, and again, the flexibility offered by the VJ concept — and the eye-opening revelation that local amateur journalists can be very good and knowledgeable storytellers — make this a real possibility moving forward. What will this do for the people who don't watch local news anymore? Stay tuned.

The core competency of any newsroom is the news it creates, and WKRN-TV is pioneering a vision for tomorrow. "Pioneers always take a few arrows," Sechrist is quick to point out, and he's had many of his own — from the industry, his company and his own staff. Still, he says he'd never go back.

> I can't imagine not doing it this way. Our daily content has probably more than doubled what it was under the old system. There is an air of experimentation and innovation that was not possible under the old system where every crew had to produce one or two stories everyday no matter what. VJs can now pitch stories that may take two days or more to put together. Beat reporters are usually producing three stories per week giving them time to work their sources. It is a better way than the old. We are still learning as we go along but this newsroom is much better than it was a year ago. (2)

In Nashville, WKRN-TV is changing the face of local news, and while the ratings have just begun to strengthen, it's still too early to call it a ratings and revenue success. The newest hires — the top entertainment reporter from the newspaper (*Hint*: Nashville is an entertainment town) and the investigative reporter (*Hint*: Nashville is the seat of state government) — simply would not have happened had the station not deliberately placed a premium on local knowledge over style, and the VJ model is what brought that about. These people will need time to learn and produce, but the point is that the station has made considerable strides down a path that both Sechrist and Sabato see as inevitable for local news.

This has profound ramifications for people working in the industry and for journalism education as well. For if the farm system isn't as important as finding quality people with local knowledge, then young people who "want to be on TV" will have to take a different path. They may not need the skills they're being taught, because the tools of the trade are now easily acquired, and news "people" are growing up all around us — not just in the schools that form the front end of the farm system. Basic liberal arts may again become the foundation for people who report the news, and that may be just what the doctor ordered to stop the leak and bring people back to local news.

———————

Disclosure: WKRN-TV is my client.

THE CASE FOR MTV

August 11, 2003

P rior to launching Music Television (MTV) in 1981, then-Executive V.P. Robert Pittman did a little homework. "I love research," he said. "I don't say that too often, because it is something people look down on. But I use research to find out what people like and what they are doing." In his foundational MTV research, he learned the following:

What Teenagers Want:

- Irreverence
- Zaniness
- Instability
- Chaos
- A frenetic pace
- Lots of disjointed thoughts
- In-depth info about music

And so MTV was born, in part, to feed back to teenagers what they wanted. Can anyone my age look at that list and not recognize MTV? Its marketing success is the stuff of legend, but there's something else going on at Music Television these days that bears analysis as an information conduit for young people. The music of MTV shares the spotlight with a steady stream of useful information offered through the lives of everyday people.

MTV's version of "news" relates primarily to the music and entertainment worlds, and MTV is certainly not a "news channel" using recognized definitions of that term. But it is providing an information service to its audience that is robbing the TV News industry of viewers it used to take for granted.

And I think TV News leaders should pay attention.

MTV's programming lineup is filled with reality programs designed to meet the information needs of the MTV audience. What are those needs? Well, let's take a look at some of the programming.

- The Big Urban Myth Show looks at modern-day legends and helps viewers "decipher fact from fiction."
- Crib Crashers lets viewers watch as someone gets their "crib" made over in the same style as a celebrity's while teaching people "how we can use a modest budget to turn our domiciles into a full-fledged Crib-dom."
- Fraternity Life and Sorority Life teach viewers what this aspect of college life is all about through the sometimes bizarre stories of real fraternities and sororities.
- MADE is all about people who desperately want to change their lives and are willing to do just about anything to make it happen.
- Newlyweds follows a real life couple going through the ups and downs of just-married life.
- Real World and Road Rules have been around for a long time and are based on real people involved in a variety of situations — some natural, others contrived. As the promotional copy says, we "find out what happens when people stop being polite and start getting real."
- Taildaters is all about two people meeting for a date while friends and family tag along behind. It's a primer for dating.

- True Life is my favorite, a wonderful documentary show where the drama of everyday life is played out simply because it's drama. It's not about winners or losers. It's about tryers. This program offers the points of view of everybody involved in the theme and uniquely reflects "the state of youth culture at any given moment."

The point is if you are a young person in western culture, these programs meet your information needs about growing up and living life. No lectures. No lessons. No right way or wrong way. They simply express, through the life experiences of others, what life is or can be like for the target demographics of MTV. It's very postmodern and, frankly, it's brilliant. Reality works, because it can't be hyped and manipulated — things these people increasingly see through.

Now, if local news were to take each of these topics and do "special projects" on each, they would miss the mark MTV has hit in several ways.

1. There would have to be a point to each, a news "hook" upon which to hang the story. MTV viewers are saying, "Sometime there isn't a point. Sometimes it's just life."
2. There would have to be experts and resolution. After all, modernist news organizations believe in expert solutions to cultural issues. Not all viewers do, and this is even more the case with young viewers. Government is often included in news stories for this reason.
3. Along the same lines, authority would be presented in the form of an outside observer, often the news organization itself. This is a bunch of crap to postmodernists who believe anyone who lives the life is a greater expert than one who observes it or even studies it.
4. Artificial conflict in the form of "counterpoints" would be inserted to "move the story forward" and, of course, this is done in the name of fairness. Postmodernist young people view this as manipulative and another attempt to understand the un-understandable.

MTV's current "in search of" list looks like sweeps week fodder. Does Your Girl or Guy Flirt Too Much or Have a Body Image Dilemma? Have You Been Unfairly Fired, Suspended, Dumped…? Are You Gay, Lesbian, or Bi-sexual and Starting College? Do You Want to "Burn" Someone? About to Graduate and Looking for a Job? Do You Want to Make the Cheerleading Squad This Fall? Is Your High School Class Planning a 5-year Reunion? Were You Unfairly Branded a "Slut" — and Did Something About it? Are you Bicultural and Trying to Date while Stuck Between Two Worlds? Are you on ritalin, GHB, in an interracial relationship, an EMS worker…?

It's sweeps week all right, and it runs 24/7. Think about it. If this channel puts this kind of effort into providing this kind of information, why would its audience need to go anywhere else?

So what can a news director in Averagetown, USA learn from this?

- The world of information dissemination is evolving. Years ago, the MTV model would've been cost prohibitive. Tiny, hand-held cameras and laptop edit systems make following real life easier and more cost-effective. Maybe, too, it's time to redefine news. Aberration has become the norm, and people are turned off by it.

- Be honest and especially with yourselves. You aren't nearly as important as you think you are, and that arrogance is projected in your product. Your (potential) audience is a lot smarter than you think, and a great many of them have decided they just don't need you anymore.

- You don't have to sell so hard. Consider the concepts of attraction and leadership versus promotion and management. The harder you try to "manage" audience flow, the more you push people away. You have at your disposal airtime that advertisers pay thousands of dollars to obtain. Use it wisely. And please, please, please re-think the so-called "art of the tease."

- Stop assuming you know, and let your audience define their own information needs. Young people, for example, live for the weekend and yet the closest news organizations get to meeting that need is through a calendar of events on the morning show. After all, it's not important enough, right?

- You don't have to make sense out of everything. This is perhaps the most important lesson to learn, for it is this drive to understand (and especially to look like we do) that special interests have learned to skillfully manipulate. It's also what produces the air of elitism that accompanies much of TV news these days and separates you from people whose lives have taught them otherwise. The need to be authoritative is a death sentence when trying to communicate with people who reject authority.

I think MTV has earned the right to be taken seriously in the world of information television. Their storytelling methods are provocative and compelling, they understand their audience, they regularly meet the information needs of their viewers, and they do so with a non-judgmental respect that's refreshing. One does not have to like or accept the role they've played in our culture to appreciate the expertise with which they fulfill that role.

Mr. Pittman has long been gone from MTV, but his legacy is evident.

NEWS AS A SPORTING EVENT

April 27, 2004

There's an old psychology exercise that people use from time-to-time when they're trying to figure things out. It's called "why–because." A current conundrum is expressed, which is followed by the question, "Why?" The answer must begin with the word "because," and that answer must be followed by another "why?" The resulting tail chasing is designed to focus the patient on the uselessness of such thinking in addressing their feelings and their reaction to life.

Asking the question "why" is an important part of every reporter's job, but the extent to which it has grown to dominate the day-to-day operation of newsrooms has subtly turned the business into one that emphasizes blame over facts.

Every news consultant who says our viewers, listeners or readers want to "make sense" of the events of the day — and advises us to provide such perspective — is perpetuating the myth that we actually understand those events ourselves. This is an underlying assumption in Modernist newsrooms that must be challenged, for it leads to the self-destructive notion that all news can (and should) be covered as if it was a series of sporting events.

In the world of news as a sporting event, journalists posing as color commentators jump into the stream and give us context that helps us understand. We don't end up understanding, of course, because normalcy in such a culture is defined by winning. Right and wrong are classified with winning and losing, but who's defining right and wrong? For all the talk about campaign reporting being the equivalent of a horse race, it is amazing that observers don't see this equally reflected in crime, business, government and other reporting.

Since the days of Walter Lippmann and his "professional" cronies, we've tried hard to present ourselves to the public as an elite group of knowledgeable experts who can ferret out the truth about anything. Walter Cronkite's "That's the way it is" was more than a simple salutation. We've also tried to sell the idea that we do this, because we represent their best interests. Internally, we've fallen victim to our own hyperbole, and, in so doing, we've alienated our audiences, because people know it's just not true.

The Project for Excellence in Journalism released their inaugural and impressive "State of the News Media" earlier this year and noted that journalism "is in the midst of an epochal transformation, as momentous probably as the invention of the telegraph or television." From what to what is the essential question, and that understanding begins with the important changes taking place in our society.

We've entered a massive cultural shift in the west, from a time when the Modernist lordship of science and logic built the institutions that currently serve humankind (or do we serve them?) to a time when creations of the Modern era, especially technology, have empowered individuals in such a way that Modernism is no longer relevant. It's the Age of Participation, and the credo "I think, therefore I understand" has been replaced by "I experience, therefore I understand."

Of all the Modernist myths that currently dominate our culture, the most prevalent and, therefore, threatened is that everything in life is based on cause and effect. This is the pinnacle of logical thinking, and it's accepted as reality, sweeping aside in the process the unmanageable notions of time and chance. This myth is perpetuated daily by the news media, who've become accustomed to presenting stories as if they have endings similar to sporting events and can be analyzed as such.

- The Lakers lost, because Kobe didn't perform up to par.
- Howard Dean lost, because the Internet didn't perform the way he hoped it would.
- The people in the home died, because the smoke detector didn't go off.
- Police suspect the truck driver had been drinking before the crash.

The idea is that if we can just know the cause of everything, we can then prepare, so that it won't happen to us. This is the heaven promised by the gods of cause and effect and served by news-as-a-sporting-event. People don't want bad things to happen to them or their loved ones. We're content to travel down life's unpredictable road as long as we know when to duck. This is core human nature stuff, and it's the target of sporting event news.

Nowhere is this type of news more prevalent than in the coverage of our political world. An election is a natural sporting event, albeit one that lasts for months or even years. A Presidential election is like the NCAA basketball tournament on steroids. We have an elimination tournament in the form of primaries that culminates in the championship game in November. The sidebar political stories contribute to the overall story. For example, a *New York Times* piece on the recent 9/11 hearings carried this headline, "Evaluating the 9/11 Hearings' Winners and Losers."

Most that we classify as news begins with an event. I was taught long ago that the event was the first day lead and that reaction was the second. Attempts at understanding were reserved for later, but today, the "perspective" stories often shove aside the others as news organizations compete for "king of the know-it-all-mountain" status and the coveted marketing niche of "they help me make sense of the news." Who, what, why, where and when have become the servants of how and how come. Blame is now the first day lead. Technology and speed have enabled this occurrence, but it is our marketing that has provided the mandate to turn curiosity into conclusion in the name of cause and effect.

Our day-to-day behavior in obsessing over the "big story" concept has backed us into a terribly uncomfortable place, and as Stephen Covey wrote, "You can't talk your way out of something you've behaved your way into." We no more understand what's really going on than our audiences, so we either fake it or come off sounding like morons through content manipulation in the name of branding. Such efforts don't take place in a vacuum, however, and the audience is hip to what we're doing. Yet we express amazement that we have a credibility problem. We mistakenly believe we're providing meat for them to digest, when in fact, we're serving them Jell-O.

Consultants will argue that this is exactly what audiences and readers want. Life is complicated, the argument goes, and people want and appreciate help in making sense of what's going on around them. This again makes the false assumption that this is part of a news organization's mission and that we are capable of doing so. We have no special right to make this claim.

Howard Stern versus the FCC is a great example of a sports story in news clothing. Good versus evil. Big versus small. Winners, losers, good guys and bad. It's perfect. We're all clinging to our radios, TVs, newspapers and Websites to find out who's going to come out on top. This has special intrigue, for it's one of those cases where the winner can actually wind up being the loser and vice versa.

People are addicted to the sense of participating in history by watching on-going events unfold, and isn't that the same principal appeal of, say, the Super Bowl?

All of this, of course, creates wonderful diversions that the logical status quo uses. Non-important sidebars actually become the story, because of their ability to produce winners and losers. Meanwhile, the real issues of life go unreported. They don't have the same zing as sporting event news, and we're content with being a mile wide and an inch deep.

A case in point is the coverage of the biggest event of them all — war. Aside from the main event with its winner and loser, there are tons of side events with similar story lines. It makes for a marvelous and bottomless pit from which news organizations can pick and choose and put on their color commentary suits.

Lawyers have helped turn any kind of accident or mishap into a sporting event, because their lifeblood is cause and effect. Lawyers write the laws for our culture that they then use for their own benefit. This is one of those important and ongoing issues of life that is swept aside or overlooked by our lust for news as a sporting event. After all, why would we take on the group that provides us with the stories we really seek? So we end up serving the best interests of those who dine at the table of cause and effect.

The problem is that — at a very deep level — people know this is all bull. There is such a thing as chance. There is such a thing as the wrong place at the wrong time. Shit happens. Accidents happen. We can't live forever. Not everything is cause and effect. And it's so easy to root for any good guy until you've spent some time with somebody you thought was on the other side. Suddenly, you're left with sporting event confusion — rooting for both teams at the same time. What you thought was white is actually black and vice-versa.

Speaking of black and white, is there a more perfect bad guy in our world today than the Caucasian male? He's the cause of everything evil, right? The effects his villainous actions have perpetrated upon the world are nothing short of catastrophic. Yet, in an attempt to find victory in the middle of a losing effort, he actually admits he's the villain in the hope that people will ultimately forgive him and eventually like him. Penalty flag! This poor Dagwood is always on the losing team, but he sure wishes it could be otherwise.

We perpetuate other stereotypes and myths — the very things Lippmann sought to overcome through a professional press — in the name of cause and effect. Another black man in handcuffs. Another Asian math whiz. An athlete on drugs. Another corrupt politician. Another deadbeat dad. Another welfare cheat. Another victim who brought it on him or herself. Life is filled with pigeonholes that the media identifies and advances through the gods of cause and effect.

So along comes Postmodernism, which elevates experience and participation — because everything isn't black and white. Time and chance do play a role in life. There is order in chaos, and not everything is as it first seems. Deconstructing the misfortune of a friend can tell a story other than that which the culture deems true. The lure of cause and effect are, at best, demonic, because they produce a world that Pomos see as rigid, boring, predictable, confining and most importantly, unfulfilling.

The Internet plays a huge role in all of this, because its structure allows and encourages Postmodern inquiry. Pomos discover themselves in this environment and, more importantly, they find others of similar thought. They share their lives and experiences and uncover something profound — that the black and white, winners and losers, hierarchical world around them is self-centered and obnoxious. So they build their own worlds — their tribes.

Doing the news in such a world requires new definitions and a serious attempt to climb down from the pedestals we've created for ourselves. News is not a lecture; it's a conversation, and one that begins with a willingness to believe that the person with whom one is conversing might actually be more knowledgeable than ourselves. This is already taking place — and with great success — in a place known as the blogosphere.

For traditional media types, the biggest threat with bloggers is not the power grab, criticism or citizen reporting offered by those who work the blogosphere; it's this notion that the reader has a role in the discussion. This threat stems from a basic insecurity built on the assumption that the journalist has done the necessary homework and, therefore, ought not to be challenged. Moreover, he doesn't have time to be challenged, because he's off to the next event. These people live and work in a world seemingly beyond that in which their audiences live — untouchable professionals on a mission, the source of which no one can identify, because it wasn't commissioned by anyone.

People today are demanding to be heard, and the tools of the Internet are making that possible in growing numbers. Absent regulation or other obstruction, they'll ultimately win this sporting event story.

Why? Because.

THE NEW PUBLIC RELATIONS

March 24, 2004

A s the concept of professional journalism grew in the 20th century, it did so alongside its twin sister, public relations. Historians like Christopher Lasch have noted that the rise in the
professionalization of the media tracks perfectly with the decline
in citizen participation in the political process. This is no accident,
as we'll see in a minute.

There would be no professional news without professional public
relations, and there would be no professional public relations
without professional news. They are two sides of the same coin.
In fact, when most television news people consider careers beyond
TV, the most common first choice is PR. Why does that make so
much sense? Because the industries are so intertwined as to be one
and the same. PR serves a valuable function in the news gathering
and disseminating process, providing important insight in the quest
for truth.

The discomfort expressed by professional journalists recently in
the wake of the discovery that a politically-driven Bush administration video news release (VNR) was carried by over 70 TV stations unawares is simply evidence of the self-deceit perpetuated
by the myth of objectivity. The irony of their reaction to this gaffe

(CNN's news feed failed to identify it as having been prepared by the Bush administration) is that it supposes their "objective" news was tainted by a point of view — as though there's no POV the rest of the time.

In many ways, all conventional news is public relations. What's really at issue here is who gets to decide what's news and what isn't. Power is the central issue. The myth of objectivity gives journalists a (non-existent) duty to maintain an arm's length from positions within issues. A VNR is designed to provide one of those positions. Since a journalist believes that the point-of-view expressed therein is only a part of "the news," they must maintain a wall between themselves and such things as press releases and VNRs. But this is illusionary, because there is no such thing as objectivity. Hence, the wall is artificial; the distance is self-serving; and the issue of power is laid bare. Contemporary journalists view themselves as "above" the various positions within issues. This is at the heart of everything that's wrong with contemporary journalism.

Most that qualifies as news these days begins with an event. Events are just that, but reaction is always the second lead, and therein begins the process of identifying cause and effect, the twin gods of Modernist thinking. The professional journalist steps to the plate armed with sources and an unwritten mandate to investigate. The public relations industry isn't far behind, spinning and whirling events to sell their message, be it social, political, business, academic or otherwise. It may be the PR person's message that makes it to center stage, or it may be somebody else's. In many cases today it's often the journalist's own message, though he or she usually doesn't think so.

The cultural shift to Postmodernism is eating away at the foundation of all institutions, including the media. Pomos reject the hierarchy inherent in Modernism, and technology is enabling them to do something about it. The very definition of news is changing, as everyday people discover that with an Internet connection and some simple software, they, too, can be journalists. The concept of news as a conversation flows from a bottomless pit of frustration created by decades of being ignored in the public square and elsewhere.

Much has been written in this space about the father of modern journalism, Walter Lippmann, and his social engineering views of the early 20th century. In Lippmann's mind, people were incapable of governing themselves, a job he felt was better suited to an educated elite class, among which he included journalists. Lippmann was a high-profile member of the Committee for Public Information (CPI), also known as the Creel Committee. Every serious student of journalism should study this era and especially the people on the committee, for it was a major turning point in the world of public information.

Here's the context: Woodrow Wilson was re-elected in 1916 on a platform of "He kept us out of the war" but subsequently found himself in the position of having to do just the opposite. Since public opinion was dramatically against entering the war, Wilson created the Creel Committee to turn that opinion. They did, and in so doing birthed not only the professional journalist, but also the professional PR person.

One of Lippmann's Creel Committee brothers was Edward Bernays, a nephew of Sigmund Freud. Another was Ivy Lee. Some historians regard Lee as the first real practitioner of public relations (he invented the press release), but Bernays is generally regarded today as the profession's founder. He was the first PR theorist, drawing his ideas from his uncle's theories about the irrational, unconscious motives that shape human behavior.

He saw public relations as an "applied social science" that uses insights from psychology, sociology, and other disciplines to scientifically manage and manipulate the thinking and behavior of an irrational and "herdlike" public. In his book, *The Engineering of Consent*, he wrote, "If we understand the mechanism and motives of the group mind, it is now possible to control and regiment the masses according to our will without their knowing it." (1)

In another book, *Propaganda*, Bernays wrote an even more chilling message, "The conscious and intelligent manipulation of the organized habits and opinions of the masses is an important element in democratic society. Those who manipulate this unseen mechanism of society constitute an invisible government which is the true ruling power of our country." (2)

Josef Goebbels used Bernays' books, among others, as a basis for his destructive campaign against the Jews of Germany. Until that happened, "propaganda" wasn't considered a pejorative term.

Lippmann and Bernays were similar thinkers, each believing that to get anything done, the masses would have to be somehow herded. This was social engineering in its purest form, and around it have sprung the institutions of the professional press and public relations. No wonder there's an epidemic of voter apathy in this country. No wonder the public is revolting in the new century. Who wants to be herded and controlled?

I ran the Assignment Desk for a large market station during the 1973 energy crisis. Years later, in reflecting on my career, I came back to this event as my first experience with being used. Smart environmentalists exploited the long lines at gas stations to tell the world that we were running out of oil and that this was a contributing factor. We did stories with these people, because we were trying to understand what was happening and pass that understanding along to our viewers. All we did was cloud an economic, business and political issue.

In 1990, I read an article in The Animals' Agenda, a mouthpiece for the animal rights movement, that was enlightening, so I kept it. The article, called "Dealing With The Media," was a guidebook for manipulating the press.

> You are the one who can control the way the story will be covered. Begin with the local angle on your issue. To insure a serious and sympathetic article, describe one or two specific acts of cruelty that everyone can recognize as abusive. Then talk about your personal experience — what moved you to become involved in animal protection. Show the reporter you are motivated on a personal level by compassion. Finally, you must combine the personal

with the philosophical. Few reporters have read Singer or Regan, and they rarely do background research. By explaining the underlying philosophy of the humane movement, you eliminate the possibility you'll be portrayed as a bored cat lover looking to keep busy.

Be vulnerable. Reporters love people who open up emotionally. If you have a poignant story about seeing a dog die, tell it, even if it makes you cry. Especially if it makes you cry. (3)

This is the "control" of which Bernays and his contemporaries spoke. Thankfully, there is a new form and format growing rapidly today, one with roots from a much more people-friendly perspective. In *The Cluetrain Manifesto*, Doc Searls and David Weinberger wrote of PR people:

Ironically, public relations has a huge PR problem: people use it as a synonym for BS. "PR types." We all know what that means: they're the used car salesmen of the corporate world.

But, of course, the best of the people in PR are not PR Types at all. They understand that they aren't censors, they're the company's best conversationalists. Their job — their craft — is to discern stories the market actually wants to hear, to help journalists write stories that tell the truth, to bring people into conversation rather than protect them from it.

In the age of the Web where hype blows up in your face and spin gets taken as an insult, the real work of PR will be more important than ever. (4)

If markets really are conversations, as *Cluetrain* asserts, then the work of Robert Scoble is writing the rules of a whole new form of PR. From his office at Microsoft in Redmond, Washington, Scoble talks with consumers, writers, critics, suppliers, customers and competitors in a way that is decidedly Postmodern. His blog, Scobleizer, is a unique blend of the person and the company. Scoble works for Microsoft and writes about Microsoft, but he does so as part of a conversation, not as from the mountaintop. He doesn't work for the PR department, although he's quoted more than anybody with a PR badge.

"People don't trust corporations," he says. "They trust individuals." And they trust Scoble, because he has a three year history as a blogger, even as one who used to attack Microsoft. That gives him what he calls "street creds" that traditional PR people would never have. That he is still free to take his employer to task (and he has) is a central factor in maintaining that trust.

"I don't speak for Microsoft officially," he says. "I try to give the insiders opinion of what's going on, which is often useful, but I let the executives do the product announcements, etc. I'll watch what's being said and comment about them later on."

Affable and friendly, Scoble is more like a neighbor than a corporate flack, and that's why he's been so effective at inserting Microsoft into a host of technical community conversations. "Have you noticed that the shrillness is gone from the community?" he asks concerning the views of former Microsoft critics. "They were like this, because they didn't think they were being listened to." Scoble listens and writes and links, and he has opened a welcomed doorway to a formerly impenetrable fortress.

His "Corporate Weblog Manifesto" is must reading for anybody in the public relations industry.

> Tell the truth. Post fast on good news or bad. Use a human voice. Talk to the grassroots first. If you screw up, acknowledge it. Never lie. Never hide information. Be the authority on your product/company. (5)

These, and more, are the lifeblood of the new public relations.

Scoble says posting fast is one of the most critical things in today's environment. By the time most corporate PR departments have prepared the "official response" to an event, most news organizations have long since made up their minds and are only looking for a quote. News moves at Internet speed these days, even (and often especially) overnight. If he can post comments early in this process, the chances are much better that they will be considered as the story develops, rather than the story taking off based on the reporter's own knowledge or bias.

One of the refreshing things about Scoble and his manifesto is the lack of rules, guidelines or orders under which he must work. "There are no official restrictions," he says, but he is quick to point out that he knows what he can and can't do, much of which is basic common sense. His gut is his governor, not some codified set of instructions from on high. This, of course, terrifies traditional PR types, who live and work in a tightly controlled environment.

But control is exactly what's under assault in today's Postmodern world. The Lippmann/Bernays issue of who gets to decide what is and isn't news was never supposed to include the readers and listeners and viewers. That's the paradigm shift. People have increasing control over their own lives, including the information that influences their beliefs and opinions.

We have to adapt to them, for a change, and that's great.

NEWS IS A CONVERSATION

January 13, 2004

I was a news director in six markets and a manager in several others. As an incoming news director, my first order of business was always to survey the staff. My experience in the business taught me that the people in the trenches had the answers to most of the competitive questions about the market, and my job was simply to organize their thoughts. Not only did the troops feel good about being asked, but the task accelerated my understanding of the market as well. The lesson for all managers is simple: the people closest to the product — and therefore the conflicts that accompany its creation — generally have the collective business answers you seek.

I find this is also often true about life, which is why the matter of an elite class running things from arm's length is an issue with me. The institutions of the world would do well to listen to the people on the street, for their view is quite different than the opinion of those atop their pedestals. Of course, they have no incentive to do so, so the smokescreen of polling is offered as an attempt to hear the voice of the people. This is not only true in the business world, but it's the mainstream media's sad excuse for interactivity. Whether it's polling the audience to see what they like and don't like, or sponsoring issue and political polls, they're inherently biased by the questions asked, and the press is able to interpret and control what results are reported.

There's a new movement underway today that says relevant journalism could be — and perhaps should be — a conversation, not a lecture or the squawk and noise that comes when journalists talk to each other, and today's media, with a little modification and a new point of view, could provide a forum for such conversations.

The essential conflict between the old and the new in journalism is the belief by those of the new breed that ongoing feedback — and interaction with that feedback — advances a story. It does so by moving the assumptions of the original piece in directions unknown, and this frightens the mainstream press, who insist that journalism isn't journalism without the editorial process and, by default, editorial control.

So let us examine that postulate. Editorial control means that all copy and pictures associated with communicating a work by a professional newsgathering agency are screened by someone other than the reporter to assure the story complies with the standards and policies of the agency. Implied in this is the understanding that the news organization also is charged with the duty to pursue what it considers news and how it is reported, although one is free to ask from whence cometh such an assignment. This is the editorial process. It is assumed that such decisions and screening are necessary, because the process protects the professional organization from such nastiness as lawsuits for libel and slander while passing along its fruit to the public. But buried in this assumption are two core beliefs: that only one with proper intelligence, training and experience can function in such a capacity, and that the public requires such a screen. The latter isn't talked about and perhaps not even acknowledged, but it's definitely there. "This is important." "That isn't important." These are judgments made by editors daily, even in the process of copyediting.

Media high priest, Tom Brokaw, acknowledges that people today get their information from a variety of sources and, "By the time people get to us, they know what's happened that day." But he goes on to explain his role, the role of NBC Nightly News. "What we have to do is put this in a coherent form for them at the end of the day." In other words, let their editorial process and control work to digest and summarize the news, so that we can make sense of all those incoherent (for us) bits and pieces. What would we do without news in a coherent form?

In truth, the editorial process works on many levels to assure that, in terms of both style and message, the news agency is set apart from everyday people. To be sure, this is a pedestal, and it engenders an air of arrogance that news people themselves can't seem to see. For upon what does such control base its pronouncements and judgments, if not the personal, albeit educated viewpoints of the controller? To continue reporting the news like this, the organization itself must view its members as a special class whose training gives them the ability not just to package the news coherently, but also to give coherence and meaning to the news events by their analysis, presentation, and dissemination of the facts.

So editorial control is really about power and authority, and not just over words. It's Walter Lippmann's social engineering dream, the masses following an elite, educated class, and it's the core reason mainstream journalists look aghast when somebody suggests letting everybody play the news game. Who wants to give up power and influence? In fairness, journalistic power was in place long before Lippmann. There's the wonderful Mark Twain quote, "Never pick a fight with a person who buys ink by the barrel," but during that time, the press was passionately opinionated and openly represented points of view. Lippmann is the one to brought forth the idea of an objective, "professional-class" journalist, who would stand in the gap between the masses and those alleged to be in power.

It is this power and influence that drives mainstream journalists to look at new media types, especially bloggers, and describe them pejoratively as the "vanity press," "self-important," or worse. The question, of course, is if bloggers derive their sense of importance from themselves, then from whom does the mainstream press derive theirs? You see, there exists within journalism today a belief that this power and influence of theirs is a right, a guarantee given to them by some higher authority, and therein lies the rub.

This belief is further enhanced now that certain, very well paid journalists find themselves on the same societal and cultural levels as those about whom they report. This is treasonous, for the roots of journalism are fed by the blood of those who gave their lives for the free flow of information. As a profession, journalism was never intended to be a get rich occupation. Lippmann and his cronies gave us that.

At the height of the Internet bubble, four people with deep roots in the Web wrote an important and prophetic little book called *The Cluetrain Manifesto*. Three of the authors, Doc Searls, Chris Locke and David Weinberger helped pioneer Weblogs and are regular bloggers. The book's "95 Theses" are well known among those who understand the core value of the Internet, including Howard Dean campaign manager, Joe Trippi. Dean has been referred to as "The *Cluetrain* Candidate," and Weinberger is a Dean consultant. Here are the first ten of the "95 Theses":

1. Markets are conversations.
2. Markets consist of human beings, not demographic sectors.
3. Conversations among human beings sound human. They are conducted in a human voice.
4. Whether delivering information, opinions, perspectives, dissenting arguments or humorous asides, the human voice is typically open, natural, uncontrived.
5. People recognize each other as such from the sound of this voice.
6. The Internet is enabling conversations among human beings that were simply not possible in the era of mass media.
7. Hyperlinks subvert hierarchy.
8. In both Internetworked markets and among intranetworked employees, people are speaking to each other in a powerful new way.

9. These networked conversations are enabling powerful new forms of social organization and knowledge exchange to emerge.

10. As a result, markets are getting smarter, more informed, more organized. Participation in a networked market changes people fundamentally. (1)

Regrettably, the vast majority of television and news executives didn't get onboard the *Cluetrain* when it passed by their offices years ago. If they had, they might understand the current reality; that, like markets, news is a conversation.

Blogger Jeff Jarvis has been using "news is a conversation" to describe the evolving arena often referred to as "the blogosphere," and he cites the *Cluetrain* as a major influence. "Getting to the true news," he says, "is an additive process, back and forth. News has always wanted to be a conversation, but we've always worked in a one-way medium. Whereas it used to be gatekeeper, source, gatekeeper, source, it's now gatekeeper, source, audience, gatekeeper, source, etc."

"This is the first time we've truly had a two-way medium," he adds, "and we're still trying to figure it all out."

One thing we do know is that the audience itself can and does function as editor in the blogging process. Dan Gillmor, columnist for the San Jose Mercury News and himself a blogger, puts it this way, "I like the idea that people are watching what I say and correcting me if I get things wrong — or challenging my conclusions, based on the same facts (or facts I hadn't known about when I wrote the piece.) This is a piece of tomorrow's journalism, and we in the business should welcome the feedback and assistance that, if we do it right, becomes part of a larger conversation." (2)

As Jarvis, Gillmor, the authors of *The Cluetrain Manifesto*, and many others have discovered, the significance of this new medium isn't power. It's about niche, yet when the mainstream press looks at it, importance is automatically assigned to those with the largest or most influential audiences. This is their hierarchical, Modernist worldview, and it blinds them to the truth about the Internet in general and blogging in particular.

The good news is that the press is beginning to pay attention, and the *Cluetrain* is still out there for them to climb aboard.

The editorial process certainly has its place in world of journalism, and as a recent commenter on my own blog pointed out, bloggers feed off the work of mainstream journalists. There is a symbiotic relationship between the two, and I'm certainly not suggesting one will replace the other. There is, however, a reformation underway, and while nobody knows exactly how it's going to play out, I think it'll be good for everybody in the end. Bloggers, who don't necessarily care, will find validation in the journalism world, and mainstream news people will be forced to stop giving only lip service to interacting with their audiences.

And instead of turning to elite experts to guide us and solve all our problems, we might actually find that the answers we seek are with the people out here pounding the pavement and living the life that those experts only touch from a distance.

Wouldn't that be something?

THE RISE OF THE
INDEPENDENT VIDEO JOURNALIST

September 1, 2003

There's an old story about a father disciplining his son. "Sit down," the man says, and the boy refuses. "I said sit down," the father demands, but the boy continues to stand. The father grabs the boy's shoulders and forcibly puts him into the chair, whereupon the lad says, "I'm sitting down on the outside but I'm standing up on the inside."

As the cultural shift of Postmodernism continues to envelop authoritative logic in the West, new ideas and new concepts are emerging to fill the Modernist void. This is happening without the approval of those in charge, mostly because they're driven by an opposing worldview and can't see it. There's no secret organization meeting in some mountaintop hideout and pulling the strings of this movement. No marching on Washington or waving of banners. Driven by technology, the Postmodernist movement is occurring at a level beyond the reach of manipulation, where human nature itself calls the shots. It is a time in history when one must step back and take stock, because the status quo is crumbling under its own recalcitrant weight. It's sitting down on the outside but standing up on the inside.

Nowhere is this truer than in the world of television news. This elitist, Modernist institution stubbornly clings to 20th century concepts with the feigned confidence of a professional wrestler engaging a 40-foot python and being slowly strangled to death. Technology is evolving television news to Video news, which inevitably will evolve to Video News on Demand (VNOD).

The Video Journalist movement is sweeping Europe, thanks to Michael Rosenblum and his vision of television newsrooms that resemble newspaper operations. I've seen the results and heard from these VJs who're on the cutting edge of a genuine revolution in television newsgathering, and the results are provocative and encouraging. Here in the U.S., Dirck Halstead's Platypus movement is bringing a similar revolution to print journalists who've discovered they're no longer bound by the rules of text and still photos. Multi-media is the name of the game in today's environment.

In a nutshell, Rosenblum's idea is to eliminate nearly all of the 2-person news crews in a newsroom, remove the edit bays, get rid of most of the ENG gear, and then equip everybody with small digital video cameras and laptop edit systems. The result is a reporter-driven newsroom that functions like a newspaper. Producers have much more material from which to choose for their programs. Field people aren't stressed by turning a package and a v/sot in half a day, and the reporter dynamic in the field changes, because a television crew with all their gear doesn't become a part of the show. The little cameras don't dominate the scene, and people are much less intimidated, which makes for better interviews, etc. Prima Donna reporters can no longer lean on gifted shooters, and the gifted shooters become the star reporters. Since everybody edits their own pieces on their own systems, everybody "thinks" television, and the quality of the work goes up.

And it costs only about $10,000 to fully equip a VJ.

TV news photographers despise the concept and go out of their way to vilify Rosenblum at every turn. This is lunacy, because the whole idea is built upon the recognition that video is the foundation of TV reporting — something news photographers have been preaching forever. What the VJ concept offers to photographers is job security and the chance for vindication in an industry that has increasingly rewarded pretty faces over quality work. Moreover, there are still live shots and places where 2-person crews are necessary. (Although Sony makes a wonderful and inexpensive little camera with face recognition software that'll follow a reporter's face in a crowd, perfect for those walking, talking stand-ups without a separate shooter.)

The VJ idea hasn't fully taken root in the US yet, although embedded reporters used it during the Iraq war with stunning success. It is only a matter of time. The economics of the move make it highly attractive to increasingly cost-conscious station owners. While cost savings may be the impetus that drives the American foray into this realm, it will be the new newsroom dynamic and product that keeps it around.

However, in a Postmodern world, the VJ concept takes on significance far beyond the newsroom, because it opens the video news door to anybody. Postmoderns (Pomos) reject elitist authority and the "thus saith the anchor" implication of typical 20th century newscasts. Pomos gravitate to the idea of tribes and a multicultural mosaic that doesn't have to make sense. All points of view are relevant and therefore worth consideration. Pomos don't want information predigested, like the mama bird of contemporary journalism provides. They feel they can do that themselves, thank you very much. Moreover, Pomos view as dishonest the idea of professional objectivity and choose instead to have their information needs met in other ways.

As such, the idea of Independent VJs who represent various points of view is very Postmodern and, therefore, inevitable as the evolution of video news continues. As with everything else Postmodern, technology drives the train for video news. For the Rise of the Independent Video Journalist to happen, four things need to be in place, all of which are already there or very close.

1. Playerless video streaming technology and bandwidth provide steady, high quality Internet pictures that users of all ilk and hue will accept. Video doesn't drive the Internet yet, but

by 2010 it will share the stage with the other efficiencies of a wired world. It's unlikely consumers will fully embrace the idea of combining their TV set with their computer until the same box runs both and the video quality of both is interchangeable.

2. Video-on-demand (VOD) takes the place of broadcast schedules as the principal method by which people watch television. The TiVo personal video recorder (PVR) model is changing the way consumers relate to entertainment and information programming by empowering them to watch what they want to watch when they want to watch it. VOD makes sense in a Postmodern news world too, because it puts decision-making in the hands of the user instead of an Executive Producer somewhere else. Pomos want to participate in their world, and PVRs make that possible.

3. Point-of-view journalism becomes an accepted part of information programming. Special interest groups representing specific points of view will get into the VJ business, because it makes economic and political sense for them to do so. Pomos think information should be free, so who's going to pay for video news in the 21st century? Advertising? Perhaps, but not in the form we know today. The first thing every PVR owner does is remove the commercials from their viewing. One day, an Independent VJ in, say, New York will be paid by the Sierra Club or PETA or Ford to ensure their perspective is presented in daily stories about virtually anything. This is not to suggest the VJ will do only stories about Sierra Club or PETA or automotive issues; rather, that their perspective won't be omitted in the pieces he or she does do. Remember that Pomos embrace the idea of different perspectives as they continuously scan their surroundings in search of comfortable tribes. There is a subliminal honesty to point-of-view journalism that also fits the Postmodernist ideal, along with a realism and practicality that Postmoderns appreciate.

4. Internet video news portals take the place of or supplement news organizations in offering Video News On Demand (VNOD) to users. Since the Independent VJs don't work

"for" these portals and, in fact, may never visit the building that houses such, the Internet becomes the most efficient method of getting their stories to end users. Each Independent VJ could have their own Web-based Video blog or archive from which these portals would cherry pick the VJs latest offerings. Google News has pioneered software that presents text-based news in a similar manner, and these video news portals could function in the same way. On Google, for example, the same story is presented from multiple perspectives based on the news organization providing the story. This gives readers a well-rounded view of a particular issue, especially when various international spins are presented. In the same way, video news portals would provide viewers with multiple points-of-views on stories based on the published biases of the various Independent Video Journalists selected by the portal.

Word-of-mouth, jungle drums and smoke signals aside, the news/information spectrum we have today began with a single tool, the printing press. Then came radio, followed by television, and now the Internet. Each has its own unique niche, something it can do better than any of the others, and that niche guarantees each a future. Printed news — whether newspaper or magazine — provides depth, which can be picked up and put down. Radio occupies only the sense of hearing, which means listeners can do something else while participating. It can provide information immediately too, but so can television. TV's niche, however, is that it occupies two senses and can "take people there" better than radio. The Internet bests its competitors, because it can provide all three forms of communication in addition to being a 2-way medium.

The extent to which television news is clinging to its niche while ignoring the natural transition to Video News On Demand (VNOD) via the Internet is both self-destructive and sad. Today, events drive television news, because covering events — especially compelling breaking news — is what TV does best. But where there is no event, TV operations attempt to create them through manipulative marketing gimmicks and hyperbole. Meanwhile, people, especially Postmoderns, are turning away in droves.

Local television stations are the natural choice to move VNOD forward and reap the financial benefits thereof. However, the price of admission to this dynamic new world is so reasonable that outside investors could easily steal the niche right out from under stations. This is a business threat that station owners should take seriously. Already the Platypus movement is training print journalists in the art of video journalism, and some newspapers are drifting into the video news business.

Marketing guru Craig Marshall gave six rules for managing change, and they are especially appropriate for television news leaders today.

1. Challenge the status quo.
2. Utilize consumer research.
3. Analyze your current strategy.
4. Recognize paradigm shifts.
5. Constantly monitor change.
6. *Make* the change.

Make the change, TV News. Stop standing up in the face of a vastly more powerful entity that is insisting you sit down.

NEWS ANCHORS:
AN ENDANGERED SPECIES

October 30, 2003

L eslie Wilcox anchored the news for us when I was the news director at KGMB-TV in Honolulu in the late 80s. Leslie grew up in Hawaii and could pronounce names with multiple vowels like nobody I'd ever met. This, of course, made her perfect to sit in front of a TV camera and read the news in Hawaii. However, international news in those days was dominated by stories from eastern Europe, where multiple consonants made names torturously difficult for her to pronounce. One night she came up with a brilliant idea just before airtime, while proofing a story with one of those names. "I'll look in the phone book and see if anybody here has that name, call them and get them to pronounce it for me." Sure enough, there was one person listed. She hastily punched the number, now breathing rapidly with excitement.

"Hello," came the voice at the other end.

"Hi," she said quickly, "This is Leslie Wilcox with channel 9. I have a story to read in a few minutes about somebody with your last name, and I can't pronounce it. I'm wondering if you could say it real slow, so that I could write it down phonetically."

There was a pause, then the man said, "Sssmmmmiiiittthhhh." She had dialed the wrong number.

So it is that the most memorable stories of my career generally involved anchors, that peculiar breed of egomaniacs with inferiority complexes that give the news to us night after night — human beings who'll risk unspeakable embarrassment for the strokes that come with being on TV. And "being on TV" is what it's all about these days. The first question I always used to ask young people looking for a job was, "Why did you pick this business?" The answer evolved over my 28 years — from "It's an opportunity to make a difference" to "Ever since the local anchor visited my school in 9th grade, I knew it was what I wanted to do."

And so the communications schools of our country have pumped out anchors and wannabe anchors for the past couple of decades, and the industry is awash in those "cosmetically suited" to being on TV — regardless of their journalistic abilities.

But all that's about to change.

The industry's obsession with celebrity and the easy marketing thereof is meaningless in a Postmodern world that has demystified the industry and its hype, rejects elitism and doesn't need its information spoon fed by good-looking faces anyway. As the world of video news shifts to a broadband environment, where users can pick and choose what they want to watch and when they want to watch it, there are powerful forces at work that will make news anchors unnecessary.

Firstly, time is precious to the Postmodern (Pomo). It "belongs" to me, and I can read a story faster than anybody can read it to me. I'll read my own stories and make my own decisions about those I choose to explore further. I don't need you to do that for me.

Secondly, in selecting the video stories that I want to watch, I'd rather have the reporter who was there give me his or her take on it than somebody sitting in a studio. This is essential Postmodernism — that if I can't experience something for myself, I want only someone who's been up close and personal with the thing to share their experience.

Thirdly, the only "personalities" I care about are those who share my beliefs and provide the arguments that I need to communicate those beliefs with other members of my "tribe." I don't care what these people look like or sound like. What they say is paramount.

Finally, I'm out here slugging it out with everybody else, and I have little time or respect for people on pedestals, especially those who don't have a clue as to what I'm going through. The pejorative term "media elite" is generally used by conservatives to slam those with a liberal bias, but, for Postmoderns, it goes way beyond that.

Media critic, Howard Kurtz, says it beautifully, "Reporters may once have been champions of the little guy; now they are part of a smug insider culture that many Americans have come to resent." Referring to former ABC reporter, Sam Donaldson, Kurtz wrote, "By his tone, stance, manner, hair, he…maintains: I impart the message (indeed, I am the message)."

In a Postmodern world, where the power is with the information consumer, this elitist gap is a huge liability.

The Pomo's disdain for elites has little to do with counterculture energy, as some believe. Modernists cling to logic and reason and math and science — that which is proven and, therefore, reliable — all of which elevate education and those privileged to have such an education. And what is education if not the acquiring of knowledge? What a lot of people don't see is that the technological advances of our Modernist culture have put that knowledge at the fingertips of anybody, and the need to learn has been replaced by the need to apply. To the Postmodern, that means the playing field is level. All he needs to learn is how to work the gadget.

In other ways, the TV industry itself is guilty of erecting the pedestal that separates news people from viewers. For example, the TV news consulting firm, Audience Research and Development (AR&D), coined a phrase that has been used for years in positioning anchors with the audience — the Command Anchor. The talent side of what used to be AR&D is now called "Talent Dynamics." Here's what their marketing material says about the concept:

> I will guide you through this newscast. You've been busy with your life all day, but you want to know what else is going on in your world. I've been here watching and investigating for you. Sit back, relax, watch and listen; I'll see to it that you are brought up to date.

The ideal command anchor

> Viewers form a relationship with their news anchors. The greater the perception of an anchor in "command" of the newscast content, the stronger the relationship and, therefore, the bond. Longevity in a market is a sure path to Command Anchor status, but we can speed up the process.

In a passive audience environment, this is terribly smart. We build newscasts in such a way that the audience believes the anchor is in charge. Story intros and outros are crafted, so that the most important facts of the story are given to the anchors, not the field reporters. When there's "team coverage," guess who leads the team? Anchors recap or summarize big stories to further the notion that they are in command. They thank and congratulate people in the field, which leaves the impression that the work was done for them. People follow people, the old saying goes, and that's a critical factor in the marketing of television news. Local television anchors are often *the* celebrities of the communities they serve. The more popular they are, the greater the likelihood the community will watch their newscasts. So what's wrong with positioning them as such?

The problem is the world is changing, and these strategies are actually driving people away. The audience is no longer passive, and the very attributes that help boost an anchor to Command status are those that create the air of elitism that Postmoderns find so repugnant.

The Pomo says, "I don't want to sit back, relax, watch and listen anymore, and if I do, it's certainly not going to be to hear from your world. In mine, there's not a violent crime on every block, cynicism isn't the rule, and I really don't care if the President is bedding the interns. There's suffering out here, but it's not in the forms you see, and we're getting along in spite of it all anyway. Besides, we know more about "doing TV" than you think, and we're not fooled by your hype. Thanks, but no thanks."

Howard Kurtz summarizes it this way:

> This is, finally, how an elite loses its position. The members of the elite just start to seem like dinosaurs. Life happens in exciting, interesting, novel ways, but they aren't part of it. They live some past life, or live in memories of some past life. The American people, riding economic and social forces, go one way — demonstrating an uncanny ability to get hip in an instant — while the upholders of conventional thinking are, necessarily, left behind.

The television news anchor is an endangered species. Even now, staff cutbacks generated by economic pressures are gutting a local station's ability to gather the news, which places even more emphasis on the personalities delivering it. The more that happens, the more an increasingly Postmodern audience departs, and the cycle just continues. Meanwhile, people are turning to other sources to have their information needs met, and technology is responding to the demand. Eventually, anchors will be reading to smaller and smaller audiences, until they're swallowed up by an entirely different landscape.

Don't get me wrong. I think there will always be a need for anchors during live, breaking stories involving multiple crews in multiple locations. This necessitates somebody to play the role of "hub," tying all of the elements together. TV execs know this, and one of the problems with contemporary television news is that it "manufactures" big, breaking stories to reproduce this effect day after day. It wears thin on a generation hip to marketing, and in most cases, there just aren't enough such stories to justify the celebrity anchor salaries.

The video news people of tomorrow will be very different from those of today. You'll write, shoot and edit your own material. The ability to write will be paramount, for — in an on-demand world — people will read your words before they watch your video. Your compensation will be based on your work, not your appearance or your Q score. You'll make a living, but it won't be extravagant. There'll be a premium on what you say, so your point of view is what'll separate you from the rest and determine your following. You'll likely have a blog and your own Web address.

These are exciting, pioneering times for television news and for the people who work in it. What may appear on the surface to be a tragedy is actually a doorway to incredible opportunities, both for those who do the news and those who consume it. Marginalized voices will have their day, and we'll able to choose for ourselves from an amazing array of new perspectives. And as the consumer guides himself through the news of the day, reporters will have their stories all to themselves, which, I believe, will mean better told, multimedia-displayed stories.

And that's something even Mr. Smith in Hawaii will appreciate.

PARTICIPATORY JOURNALISM

October 10, 2003

In my favorite Peanuts comic strip, Lucy notices something on the ground and declares, "Well, look here! A big yellow butterfly." She adds that it's rare to find one this time of year and states that it probably flew up from Brazil. Linus looks closely and announces, "This is no butterfly...this is a potato chip!" Lucy gets on her hands and knees and says, "Well, I'll be! So it is! I wonder how a potato chip got all the way up here from Brazil?"

So it seems with TV executives who deny their world is collapsing around them and insist that any glitches in the system are only temporary. When the validity of the collapse finally hits home, they continue in the belief that it's either temporary, or that somehow we'll figure it all out. A shrinking local news audience is the butterfly-turned-potato chip of local television. According to a recent survey by the Pew Research Center, 77 percent of Americans watched local news ten years ago. By 2002, that number had decreased to 57 percent. The response has been to cut staff and expenses while adding more shows in an effort to maintain market share. That's the Brazil effect, because there are other options.

Meanwhile, others, including news people caught in the middle, are at least asking what to do, but in order to answer that fully, one needs to first understand how we got where we are. Why don't people watch the news anymore? "Bringing people back" isn't the issue, because the problem is what we're trying to bring them back to! The world we used to know doesn't exist anymore, but we operate as though it does.

Technology is creating a new culture, Postmodernism, and Pomos, as they're known, seek something different. It's the Age of Participation. But audience participation means rubbing elbows with real people, something we don't seem to do very well from our arms-length position as professional authorities.

A little history: In the 1920s, newspaper mogul Walter Lippmann wrote a series of books that provided a founding chapter for modern journalism. He built a rationale for a journalism guided by a new idea: professional objectivity. As historian Christopher Lasch wrote, "In Lippmann's view, democracy did not require that people literally govern themselves. Questions of substance should be decided by knowledgeable administrators whose access to reliable information immunized them against the emotional 'symbols' and 'stereotypes' that dominated public debate. The public, according to Lippmann, was incompetent to govern itself and did not even care to do so." And so was born the fetish of objectivity that has served the industry well — until the Internet came along and spoiled all the fun. Modernism, with its core beliefs in science and reason, has been replaced by the new culture where experience is revered. "I don't need your experts!" cries the Pomo.

Lasch also makes a compelling argument that Lippmann and his contemporaries were more interested in creating a sterile environment in which to sell advertising than establishing professional high ground. It worked. Media moguls became wealthy media moguls and then reporters began to demand a cut. The Lippmann legacy of elitism was bad enough, but when coupled with the late 20th century cult of celebrity — spawned by all that wealth — the separation from real people was complete. News people, feeling themselves on the same level as the authorities they covered (or perhaps even a cut above), took the concept of the media elite to a whole new level. Caught in a Web of self-importance, the Fourth Estate has drifted far from its original calling. And we wonder why people don't watch anymore.

There have been spotty attempts here and there to reach out and touch real people, but as a whole, the industry is still high on its pedestal. Community news had its moments in the 90s, when smart editors and news directors "got involved" by taking advocacy positions on issues important to everyday people. While some outstanding work was done, the efforts went the way of the hula hoop, victims of cost-cutting and consultants, who emphasized presentation over content.

But there's a new light on the horizon that illuminates the core of the problem, because it includes a fundamental change in the definition of a journalist. It's called Participatory Journalism, and its mission is to get everybody involved in the process of gathering and reporting the news — including those everyday people.

Online Journalism Review makes the statement that "Participatory journalism is a slippery creature," and then asks the question, "Everyone knows what audience participation means, but when does that translate into journalism?"

I love what NPR's Daniel Schorr said: "Freedom of the press used to be freedom for those who had a press. Now, with Internet publishing, everyone has a press, and this democratization could help mark this shift between Modernist elitism and Postmodern democracy."

Weblogs are gaining in popularity and credibility daily, and even mainstream Modernist news institutions like the *New York Times* are exploring adding them to their mix. Bloggers are an interesting lot with some wonderful insight into life in these United States. Ah, but the elite objects to its fatted calf being whacked in such a manner! We're actually coming up with terms to separate us from the bloggers, such as columnist Maggie Gallagher's "Journalistic Journalism." What the heck is that?

Three years ago in South Korea, a group of smart and enlightened folks came up with OhMyNews!, a New Media concept for journalism. By anybody's measurement, it has been successful. In just three years, the Website of "citizen journalism," as they call it, has seen its full-time staff grow to 53 — including 35 full-time reporters and editors — and the number of "citizen reporters" writing for the site grow from 700 to about 26,700. Citizen reporters submit 200 articles every day, and a million readers visit OhMyNews! each day. The site mixes straight news reporting and commentary. Its influence at the grassroots level has been widely credited with helping President Roh Moo-hyun win the popular vote last December. The OhMyNews! slogan is "Every citizen is a reporter." No pedestal here!

Dan Gillmor, SiliconValley.com blogger and tech columnist for the *San Jose Mercury News*, writes, "OhMyNews! is transforming the 20th century's journalism-as-lecture model — where organizations tell the audience what the news is and the audience either buys it or doesn't — into something vastly more bottom-up, interactive and democratic." Walter Lippmann must be rolling over in his grave.

OhMyNews! may not be *the* model for news in the 21st century, but it bears consideration for an industry that's going nowhere fast. It's a simple and relatively inexpensive concept for TV stations to try. Somebody's going to do it, so why not you? Here are five suggestions to jump start the idea.

1. Create a reality show wherein viewers "compete" to be citizen reporters. Make a big deal of it. Winnow the field down to, say, twelve finalists, and build the show around them. Let each go out and do a story and have your audience "vote" on the five or six that will become your citizen journalists.

2. Equip them with consumer level digital video recorders and laptop editors (Approx $10k each). Give them the training they need and turn them loose. You'll obviously want to maintain editorial control, but give them as much room as you can to report stories their own way. Pay them a stipend for each piece they generate.

3. Mix their stories into your news with or without fanfare. You could flag each story for what it is, or let it stand on its own.

If the OhMyNews! experience teaches anything, it's that the professionals will be surprised by what these people turn up.

4. Make one newscast a "citizen" newscast. It doesn't have to be in some highly visible daypart. People will find it. Stream this program and make it available on your Website.

5. Get them together as a panel to comment on news regularly. Let these people represent the folks on the other side of the glass. Put them in a studio setting and roll tape. It would make a great Sunday feature.

A recent Gallup Poll shows six of ten Americans feel the media is biased. Most of those think the tilt is to the political left, while others think it leans to the right. This is evidence that the artificial journalistic hegemony of objectivity isn't working with the people it's supposed to serve. It doesn't work, because it can't work. The best a professional journalist can be is fair, and there will always be a place for that. And, to a certain extent, people will always need the editorial function provided by a professional press. There are some things people just need to know as opposed to what they want to know, Postmodern or not.

This is the most amazing time in the history of journalism. Technology has opened doors we couldn't imagine even 20 years ago. Rather than shrinking back under the cold blanket of the Brazil effect, let us open the floodgates of creativity and let the sun shine in. The answers are right in front of us. Participatory journalism, in one form or another, is surely one of them.

SECTION III

The Postmodern Culture

Our culture is in the midst of an epochal shift. Absolutely nothing is being left untouched, from religion to education to entertainment to politics. The Age of Participation demands of local media companies that we engage those we wish to once again count among our "audience." The essays in this section explore the definition, history, impact, influence, and future of Postmodernism in our culture, offering insight into how we got here and where we are now going as the shift continues.

"The Power of Attraction" remains the key in understanding how business and industry need to approach consumers online. Carpet bombing people with ads is one of the main reasons they're leaving tradition information sources, and media companies (and advertisers) need to learn a whole new skill set, all of which revolve around attraction, not promotion.

A POSTMODERN WAKE-UP CALL

December 14, 2002

I heard a report the other day about math and science scores in American public schools as compared to the rest of the world. We don't do very well, folks, and that has all the usual suspects pointing fingers of blame. Politicians on both sides of the aisle use statistical stories such as these to argue their own agendas, but everybody seems to miss the reality that we, as Americans, live in a culture that views such teaching as increasingly irrelevant. Whether that's good or bad is not the point of this essay. I merely wish to point out that my daughter's calculator makes her legitimately ask why she needs to memorize math tables.

Math and science themselves have created the tools that allow the users to move past learning fundamentals and into application, the experiencing of the knowledge as opposed to the learning thereof. This is basic Postmodernism, a fun little cultural change that has happened in my lifetime, and one to which few local media people have paid much attention. Too bad, for without this understanding, none of what's happening in the business of TV news makes much sense, nor does there seem to be any way to plug the holes of this sinking ship. The truth is that a sinking ship eventually sinks! I say, "Let it go and build one that can stay afloat in the 21st century." But that requires a fresh perspective on life in these United States.

What is Postmodernism?

I don't believe there is a single, universally accepted definition of this term. As a movement, it essentially points to the end of modernism, a cultural era that touted science, logic, and the mind of man over traditions, especially religious ones. I also doubt that there is such a thing as a pure postmodernist, for that would mean somebody completely anti-intellectual and entirely relativistic. In fact, it's very difficult for a logical modernist to accept or even understand concepts so contrary to his or her own core perspective. Therefore, rather than taking a standard definition from a philosophy text, it will be more useful for this discussion to compare Postmodernism with modernism on a few important levels:

> Modernists share a universal faith in logic and science. Postmodernists (Pomos) see the realism of limitations.

Words like purpose, design and hierarchy are modernist, while postmodernists would rather use play, chance and anarchy. Pomos don't completely reject logic, but their own experiences tell them that order isn't over all, and they passionately despise what they see as the inherent elitism of hierarchy.

Modernists view much of life of life at arm's length. Postmodernists experience it as participatory. Life is not "out there" to Pomos; rather, it is all around us — something that we can have as little or as much of as we choose.

One of the most defining differences is with God, where the modernist would first see God, the Father. The postmodernist would see God, the Holy Spirit. God, the Father, represents distant authority, which Pomos reject, while God, the Holy Spirit, is among us, something we can experience for ourselves.

For the modernist, the parts logically make up the whole, but the Pomo views the whole as greater than the parts.

> *Premodernism*: "I believe, therefore I understand."
> *Modernism*: "I think and reason, therefore I understand."
> *Postmodernism*: "I experience, therefore I understand."

Most people I know today are a combination of modern and post-modern thinkers, but the shift from one to the other is unmistakable, if you allow yourself to see it. What's interesting is exploring the various writings about Postmodernism, because everyday events begin to make sense. My generation has helped create a world wherein this postmodern thinking can flourish. My daughter's calculator, for example, permits her to use math, something that I couldn't do without memorization and discipline. Likewise, the Internet enables her to use science, because knowledge is there at the click of a mouse. "Use it" is very postmodernist, while "study it" is very modernist.

Armed with knowledge and information promised by the Internet, postmodernists are a serious threat to every institution in America whose power is derived from protected knowledge. Why do you think the American Medical Association was quick to create a lobbying arm that would keep informational medical Websites under its purview? The AMA is an entity governing a modernist institution whose members are licensed based on knowledge. Pomos don't believe anybody should have to pay for knowledge, and they reject the idea of governing bodies, because they view them as self-serving. Modernists would argue this is really about protecting consumers from the unscrupulous, but postmodernists would say it's about the AMA protecting its own interests first.

I believe this cultural shift has significant ramifications for the news business. Postmodernism wants to play and experience, and it will not sit still for lecturing and passive participation — both of which are fundamental essentials of TV News. The anchor is a traditional authority figure. Postmodernists abhor authority, especially what they view as elitist, and the more we try to promote that, the more the postmodern world moves away. The more we try to educate, the farther away moves the audience. They don't wish to be taught; they wish to learn by participating. Postmodernism sees through our bells and whistles, our live shots, our promotional copy, and our trickery. The more we attempt to explain what we view as out-of-control, the more we lose postmodernists, who view anarchy and chaos as acceptable realities and reject the modernist idea of a logical way things "ought to be."

The "broad" in broadcasting is gone forever. The very ideas of community and group identity have changed. "Tribes" is a word often heard in postmodernist discussion; diversity is a righteous concept among Pomos. Tribes transcend communities. A mosaic that spreads beyond anybody's melting pot has replaced yesterday's logical, American mindset. This also runs counter to modernist news organizations, which still operate with a logical belief that the whole (community) is the sum of its parts and that we're all in this together.

10 ideas for consideration

So how does one "do news" for postmodernists? In my opinion, the following ideas are open for discussion:

1. Firstly, there *is* no news except television (better: "video") news. Pomos want to see and hear for themselves, not read about it from a distance.

2. News must be available 24/7. Gone are the days when people will tune in at a specific time to be "given" the news.

3. There's no such thing as a newscast in a postmodernist world. Stories must be available simultaneously, with the viewer able to select at random. Pomos don't believe they should have to wait for anything.

4. News must not be afraid to present the absurdities and contradictions of life as parts of the reality of a multi-cultural, diverse world.

5. News must include everybody's perspective, identify the organization's own perspective, or give none at all. The artificial journalistic hegemony known as objectivity is dead. It never was real and Pomos see through it.

6. News must give up its obsession with stardom and celebrity. Postmodernists reject authority and elitism (news-

casters and reporters) in favor of participation and the knowledge acquired therein.

7. Reporters could and perhaps should represent the various tribes. This would provide sort of a global view from which viewers could pick and choose. "Now what?" is an important question for postmodernists, but only insofar as they can make up their own minds.

8. "Live" is hypercritical, for the Pomo wants to participate more than anything else.

9. News must be interactive, but the goal is participation, not driving viewers to goals or solutions.

10. I believe it's time for TV stations to spin their news departments out as wholly owned subsidiary companies and permit them to seek their own distribution outlets. Create a licensing arrangement with the parent company for broadcast rights, and let the laws of the market determine who continues and who doesn't. Despite their similarities, broadcasters are not Web people, because their interests conflict. Consequently, TV stations only play with the Internet, and in so doing, they miss the point of the technology. They also deny and ignore the primary conduit to the whole postmodernist movement. It will stay that way unless the news becomes its own master, complete with the option to decide how best to distribute its product.

Chasing the young demos

Young people are vastly more postmodern than their parents, and the gap between generations today is far more than simply one of age. This is critical for television people to understand, for it offers an identifiable clue as to why TV News audiences are getting older and older. If you want to catch trout, you must use trout bait. The currently accepted philosophies of television news will never be attractive to postmodernist-leaning young people.

The digital era, created by the logic of a modernist world, has done far more than simply empower young people with knowledge. It is the force accelerating an enormous cultural shift and leaving broadcast news organizations in a very fragile position. Like Dorothy, Pomos have cast aside the curtain and revealed the Wizard for what he really is — a profit-motivated entity that they believe has fooled people for decades.

To paraphrase Murrow: "We can deny and ignore this shift if we choose, but we cannot escape responsibility for the consequences."

THE JEWEL OF THE ELITES

October 3, 2005

One of the great heroes of history was John Wycliffe, the 14th-century English philosopher and politician responsible for the first common English language translation of the Bible. "This book shall make possible," he said, "government of the people, by the people and for the people." (1) He was one of the most important founders of the Protestant Reformation, and there are fascinating parallels between his life and times and our own.

Wycliffe fought the authority of the Pope and the institution of "The Church" by challenging Rome's assumed right to tribute from foreign lands. He railed against what he viewed as dictatorial oppression of commoners by church elitists, and he likened the Pope to the antichrist of the Bible. So heretical was his attack on the hierarchy that decades after his death, church leaders had his body exhumed and burned simply to make a statement.

By placing the Bible in the hands of commoners, Wycliffe destroyed the secret weapon of the church hierarchy: protected knowledge. His opponents responded with the statement, "The jewel of the clergy has become the toy of the laity." (2)

So it is today as the personal media revolution undercuts the institution of the press, but the energy behind it all is actually much larger. Knowledge is empowering the commoners once again, and the jewel of the elites has become the toy of the masses. It is and will change our culture beyond even that of the Protestant Reformation, because it reaches into every aspect of life.

What happens when the jewel that presents itself as expertise is shared by all? The *knowledge = expertise* equation is coming apart under the postmodern weight of experience and participation. "Who are the real experts?" we're beginning to ask, and increasingly, we're finding that "they" are us.

Jay Rosen, journalism professor, author of PressThink and a brilliant observer of life, noted at a recent gathering of Big Media executives and bloggers in New York that the nature of authority is changing in our culture. He used the example of a person who goes to the doctor and gets a prescription for an ailment. The doctor explains how the medication will work, and the patient nods and proceeds to the drugstore to get the medicine, along with (perhaps) an explanation from the pharmacist about how the medicine will work. What's new in our world is that the patient then goes home and gets on the Internet to research the thoughts of others who've used the medicine in order to discover what *they* think about how it works. This impacts the doctor's authority. The doctor is still the doctor, but gone is the automatic acceptance of his or her words as gospel. This is due, in part, to a breakdown in the modernist, *knowledge = expertise* equation.

Corante President and COO Stowe Boyd says people increasingly view the institutions that are supposed to serve them as suspect, so they're turning to each other for authoritative perspective.

> We look to ourselves, through the Internet, our third space, to find the answers to our questions. Individuals, through first person perspective, command authority in such a context, not large organizations. It is the organizations, and their chronic failures of trust, that have led people to look elsewhere. As a result, the trappings of old style authority — association with a national newspaper or media network, government agency, or other professional associations — does not confer trust or credibility as it once did: on the

contrary, it may arouse distrust and even contempt. In the post-modern era, it is the individual, true voice that is trusted, and that trust is the result of hard won respect arising from a long period of open public discourse. (3)

Modern institutions were all created to serve the common good. That calling has been replaced, however, by self-preservation, something that's becoming increasingly obvious to everyone except the institutions. Each now seeks to create an artificial sense of dependence through the lure of success and happiness.

Government: "You are unable to take care of yourselves, much less govern yourselves. You can find success and happiness only if we make it happen. You need us to make legal that which will make you happy and successful."

The Law: "There are bogeymen out there to rob you of your success and happiness, and you need our protection. Besides, it's a complex society in which we live, and you need our help to simplify it for you."

Business: "We provide the means for success and happiness. You need us to make the 'things' and services that will make you happy."

Religion: "Only God 'out there' can provide success and happiness, and you need us to bring Him to you."

Education: "Only an educated mind can bring success and happiness, and you need us to give you that."

Media: "Only we can make you aware of what will make you happy and successful. You need us to entertain, inform and enlighten."

Medicine: "You cannot be successful and happy without a sound mind and body, and you need us to give it to you."

Finance: "You can buy whatever you need to be happy and successful, and you need us to show you how to get it."

The response has been the creation of a participatory culture, one wherein we share knowledge and experiences with each other in the hope that we will better our lives. Since the institutions have an ulterior motive (self-preservation), we're increasingly trusting ourselves. Technology is providing the means, and the economy, in many ways, is providing the demand. If I don't have health insurance, for example, I'm more likely to run my symptoms up the flagpole of my network than to march willy-nilly to the doctor's office, and that's because the cost comes out of my pocket, not some third-party insurance provider.

This is a profound threat to the modernist world view and especially the *knowledge = expertise* equation.

A friend of mine is the head of counseling at a large drug and alcohol rehab facility in the South. As insurance companies began to put the squeeze on paying for the treatment of alcohol and drug abuse in the 90s, these institutions had to comply with increasingly restrictive accreditation requirements. Threatened with losing all those patients, my friend's facility became more interested in pleasing the insurance companies than in treating the problems of alcohol and drug abuse.

This was demonstrated when the place was forced to terminate a man who had led family sessions there for over 15 years, because he didn't have a Master's degree in psychology or therapy. According to my friend, this fellow was the best in his field. He had a gift for reconciliation and was able to restore the families of thousands of suffering individuals. Insurance company rules, however, said that such a person had to meet certain academic requirements, and if the rehab facility wanted to be eligible for insurance company patients, they had to replace him with somebody more "qualified."

This is an outrage, and yet these kinds of stories are everywhere. When self-preservation becomes the dominant behavior, institutions are revealed for what they are, not what they say they are. And as Stephen Covey wrote, "You can't talk your way out of something you behaved your way into."

The status quo would argue that the restrictions provided by accreditation are necessary to prevent genuinely unqualified people from getting into such positions, but this belief assumes much and most often comes from the guardians of the hierarchy — the American legal system. Testifying in court, for example, on any matter that can seemingly be quantified always brings about the question, "What qualifies you...?" Any system that follows a set of rules — whether they are good rules or bad — demands accountability in the form of expertise. This seems wise, but it often produces an assault on common sense, because no set of rules can take that which isn't quantifiable into consideration. Live by the rules, die by the rules.

In a participatory culture, however, experience takes its rightful place alongside knowledge, because the validation of expertise comes from the bottom, not the top. If my doctor prescribes a medication that I learn is highly suspect among people who use it, I'm going to question the prescription, regardless of what any "expert" says.

The modernist mind argues that all of this is absurd — that truth exists in absolute realities that can be dissected and studied. Everything is cause and effect, they say. There's no room for randomness or, God forbid, chaos. But this view is directly challenged by the participatory culture.

Television stations spend a fortune on equipment for the weather department, because weather is often the most important news franchise in any market. The meteorological "experts" then spend hour after hour teaching the community about weather, including what to look for on a radar image and how to track a storm. I've long been an advocate of creating hands-on access to this type of equipment for Internet users, because it fits with the participatory culture concept. This view was challenged during a roundtable discussion at Ball State University by a man from Florida who said that when the chips are down — and a hurricane is approaching — he'd rather hear from the institutional expert.

I would too, but I'd also want to see for myself. If Katrina taught us nothing else, it's that our hierarchical systems can and do fail.

Participatory culture will take down the economy unless current institutions wrap themselves in it. What's needed is a vast economic overhaul in order to save capitalism — if it needs to be saved at all.

What happens when participatory law releases the grip of lawyers on the law — when a plaintiff or defendant can stand in a courtroom armed with a legal "brain" capable of analyzing facts and providing legal expertise? Or when this brain can respond tit-for-tat to the volumes of paperwork with which law firms attempt to drown the little guy in protecting the status quo? Will we one day have a "lawyer-in-a-box" computer?

What happens when participatory medicine — funded by the insurance industry — releases the grip that doctors have on medicine? Will we one day have a "doc-in-a-box" computer? (Not if the AMA has anything to say about it.)

What happens when all aspects our culture become genuinely participatory? Who makes the money? Where does it go in the economy? These are difficult and troubling questions, because our modernist minds cannot grasp such a world.

And for the news media, these questions are enormous. Rosen writes:

> …journalism is trying to protect itself while the public is saying "we don't need you anymore." So while the revolution invites them to participate, the reality is it doesn't need them to participate. The institution doesn't control the societal role it used to control, and this is a significant change in culture. If you think today's cultural wars are nasty, wait until we get further downstream with all of this. The

people may, in fact, build their own institutions, but they won't be the same as the ones that exist today. The biggest problem with journalism — and any institution today — is that it has lost its authority. (4)

Author, philosopher, educator and blogger Dr. David Weinberger is actively exploring the roots of knowledge. He writes that "knowledge is literally a matter of conversation. It's disagreement with people who stretch you. Knowledge is the continuing conversation, not the result of it." In this view, knowledge is ever-evolving and changing as humankind searches for truth.

> In these billions of conversations, we attempt to work out what's true. But, especially as the conversation goes global and involves people with deep differences, we (= I) have no hope of ever resolving issues and creating anything like an eternal tree of knowledge. That dream of Reason is gone. (Appropriate exceptions admitted.) Instead, for the rest of our time on the planet, we will be iterating differences, hopefully on an increasing ground of commonality. But we're never going to all agree and fall silent. That's not even a desirable outcome.

This is radical thinking and another profound threat to modernism, because it takes into account the role of experience in the production of similarities and differences. It also forecasts commonality rather than lock-step agreement.

The longer people are exposed to computers that assist in their thinking, the greater the likelihood that they will resist blind faith in the institutions of humankind. The Internet accelerates this and the architecture of the Web itself — with its deconstructive links and references — produces a thirst for knowledge through experience. So in the application of the jewel of knowledge, the new equation is *knowledge/experience = expertise*, and it's very much a bottom-up phenomenon.

But the status quo will not easily let go of its jewel. Just as Rome did during Wycliffe's day, we can expect — as Jay Rosen predicts — escalating and nasty conflicts. And while it may take generations, we can also expect that the reformation will win out in the end, because people united against tyranny — regardless of how it's dressed — will always come out on top.

After all, the jewel, as Wycliffe taught us, belongs to everybody.

REINVENTING NEWS
FOR THE 21ST CENTURY

September 24, 2003

A friend and I were watching one of those Microsoft Server2003 commercials the other day. You know the ones. The geek IT guy is trying to explain to blank-faced executives how switching to the new servers has improved efficiencies. He gives up and says, "It'll save us 2 million dollars," and everybody gets it. My friend looked at me and said, "That's me. I don't understand any of that stuff."

So it is in trying to explain Postmodern trends to Modernists, who think in terms of order, logic and reason. Postmodernists elevate experience over reason and are perfectly comfortable with chaos. The language of metanarratives and perspectivism can choke even the best of us, and rather than try to understand, many people choose instead to live in a state of denial. In business, this can be fatal, for contempt prior to investigation, and especially in the form of denial, has always been a barrier to growth and progress. Of course, one of the problems in attempting to understand Post-modernism is that it can't be understood through Modernist logic and order. It's the IT geek talking to the sales guy — a different language. To be successful in the business of TV news (or any business) in the 21st century, we're all going to have to learn a different language.

Postmodernists (Pomos) aren't a subculture. They don't exist as an organized group with a set of guidelines for membership. They can't be studied, tracked or monitored. "They," in fact, are really "us." We're all Pomos in the sense that technology has given birth to the Age of Participation. We don't need to study things we can experience for ourselves now. And when it's something a Pomo can't experience, he will only pay attention to someone who's been there and done that *recently*. In the trenches. Not the school superintendent who works in the office downtown — the teacher in the classroom. Not the hospital spokesman who works in the office on the first floor — the ER nurse.

Screw the official company line. If it affects my community, I want to hear from the guy doing the bleeding or mopping up the blood, not the spin doctor.

Young people are vastly more Postmodern than their elders, but age alone doesn't make one Postmodern. It's more a matter of how deeply one wishes to live the life made possible by technology. The older a person, the more likely they are to be intimidated by technological advances of the digital revolution and, as such, cling to the tenets of Modernism.

There's an old saying that God won't do for you what you can do for yourself, and technology is permitting us to do a whole lot more for ourselves these days. God-like Modernist institutions of every hue are under attack, or so it seems. Does a recording artist need a record company to sell music to consumers? Does an airline need travel agents to sell tickets? Do consumers always need a doctor's appointment to analyze their symptoms? Do we need to wait until the evening news comes on or the paper is delivered to have our information needs met? There are countless other examples, and yet on many levels, there remains a rather obstinate disregard for this as anything more than a phantom blip on the radar.

At a recent presentation, I was asked if I thought this was just a passing phase. "If you're not a liberal by the time you're 20, you have no heart; if you're not a conservative by the time you're 30, you have no brain." That kind of thinking. It's an interesting question, but the problem is it comes from a Modernist understanding of life. After all, haven't young people always been rebellious? Isn't youth always seeking its own identity? Don't people always grow out of these things when they cease to have so much free time? Haven't we been through this kind of thing before?

No, we haven't, because this youthful revolution is driven by technology, and it will only accelerate as time goes by.

Slate columnist, Bob Walker, recently wrote of the battle over downloading music for the *New York Times*. Bob's a smart guy, but he dismisses the entire matter by asserting that the forces behind it are nothing new. He states that youth is the time of experimentation and adds, "Younger people with fewer responsibilities have much more time to devote to pleasure seeking of all sorts than they have disposable income to pay for it. And at college especially, they are part of a tight-budgeted community, and the culture of sharing is stronger at this age in their lives than it will ever be again." (1) Nice and logical. The only exception this time, he writes, is that young people have a greater "facility with technology" than grown-ups. He doesn't speculate what will happen when these young people take their facility into adulthood.

Postmodernism is not a trend. It's not a passing phase or fad. It's a bona fide cultural shift that must be acknowledged before the language of change begins to make any sense.

This is absolutely critical for local television and especially TV news, as broadcasting faces challenges that were unthinkable just a few years ago. Cultural historian, Leonard Sweet, writes, "Postmodernism is a change-or-be-changed world. The word is out: Reinvent yourself for the 21st century or die! Some would rather die than change." The way many make that choice is to deny the evidence. TV News executives who continue to force 20th century philosophies and methods on their viewers will soon find themselves out of work. If you're in the TV news business, it's not too late to reinvent yourself. Here are 10 things you can do today.

1. Get off your pedestal, please! The anchor-in-charge-of-everything image is offensive to Pomos, who shun authority as nothing special. Elitism is fingernails-on-the-chalkboard to Pomos. We're just not as important as we think we are, and climbing off the pedestal helps us view our audience with the respect they now demand.

2. Get out of your box, and, managers, *let* people get out of the box. "I can't go over 1:20 on a package." "The research shows people want it this way." "The meters don't lie." Meanwhile, you're losing viewers with every book.

3. Get relevant! And start by defining relevance. There are a lot of reasons young people don't watch the news, but the biggest one is there's nothing on that's relevant to them. Pomos have information needs. What are they? How do you meet them?

4. Get involved in your community. Why are we so afraid to take a position on an issue and go after it? Pomos see through the artificial journalistic hegemony called objectivity, so why can't we? Pomos like a little argument with their information, as evidenced by the variety of information portals Internet users seek to develop their own opinions. Local news Websites aren't among them.

5. Get local! Forget about what "worked" in Pittsburgh or Miami or Dallas. The homogeneity generated by news consultants has taken the local out of local news and replaced it with franchised fear. Watching the news in Anytown, USA is like a drive through the suburbs. It all looks the same.

6. Empower your viewers to participate. OhMyNews! in South Korea has hundreds of users reporting the news and is turning the whole concept of journalism on its ear. You don't have to go this far, but get your audience involved in what you do day in and day out. Remember, Postmodernism is the Age of Participation.

7. Rethink and reinvent the art of the tease. You can't force people to move from one daypart to another anymore. It's insulting to Pomos, who want what they want when they want it, and you're pushing people away while trying to attract them.

8. Seize control of your Website. I've written extensively about this, but it bears mentioning again here. You are missing your best chance to recruit Pomo viewers by giving content control of your Website over to somebody who doesn't necessarily have your best interests at heart. The technology exists for you to do quality Video News on Demand online. Seize it.

9. Think multi-media at all levels in the news gathering process. TV News and Newspaper news are converging online. Your greatest future threat is not your television competitors, but your local paper, assuming they're actively pursuing an online business model. There are only failures of creativity when it comes to digital communications, because if you can think of it, you can do it. Text, slide shows, video, graphics. These are all tools at the disposal of a news reporter in a digital world.

10. Embrace the VJ and Platypus movements. Michael Rosenblum and Dirck Halstead are rewriting the rules for electronic news gathering by putting small cameras and laptop edit systems in the hands of journalists. Stations that embrace the technology will find new opportunities and a staff more inclined to reporting than entertaining.

There's no magic formula for TV News success in a Postmodern world, because everything's disposable and there are no guarantees in an environment that rejects the rules of order. It's not that Pomos are inherently cynical, even though they distrust authority. They just want to experience before accepting. "Show me," doesn't work anymore. It's more, "Let me do it myself." For example, in the case of the recording industry, a Forrester study showed that those most inclined to download music (the bad guys) were actually the most inclined to buy CDs, too (the good guys)! That kind of chaotic thinking makes no sense to Modernist recording company executives, who're beating their heads against the wall trying to figure out how to stop what they view as an evil. TV stations do the same thing when they emphasize stealing viewers from competitors instead of exploring multi-media, digital options to recruit new ones.

Reinvent yourself for the 21st century. It's not too late.

THE DEMOGRAPHIC CANDLE

February 17, 2004

In Barbara Ehrenreich's fascinating book on working class life, *Nickel and Dimed, On (Not) Getting By in America*, she takes a potshot at her own class. "We always have a plan or at least a to-do list; we like to know that everything has been anticipated, that our lives are, in a sense, pre-lived." (1) How true this is for those who have it made. The paradox of prosperity is that discontent increases with opportunities for acting on it. You don't worry about losing something if you don't have anything to lose.

Ms. Ehrenreich's statement is also a mantra, of sorts, for the business world. The "pre-lived" business life is built on an everything-is-anticipated, command-and-control paradigm. It creates spending budgets based on revenue projections required, not to run the company, but to keep shareholders happy. This strains everybody below, because the job really isn't about the job; it's about serving the owners who, it turns out, really aren't the managers, executive staff or the Board of Directors. This model has served free enterprise well, but it guts industries that draw lifeblood from the wellspring of creativity.

Creativity lives in today, and that's hard to do when you're consumed with tomorrow.

The entertainment industry is a good example. Risk-taking is long gone, replaced by "what works" in terms of repeatable cash flow. And so every CD sounds the same, every movie seems the same, and only predetermined bestsellers are published. The arts no longer reflect the culture; rather, the arts reflect the artists' needs to make money for their owners. Yes, owners. Rationality has taken creativity's place, and the result is a homogenous mass of sights and sounds.

Television has not escaped the steamroller. "What works" is repeated at all levels of programming, and every newscast looks the same. Television has placed its ability to innovate on the altar of the pre-lived life. The business isn't even at a crossroads anymore. We passed that a long time ago. We're already far down the road on the wrong path.

An essential part of living the pre-lived business life is that you dare not get into a conversation with your customers. The rationale is that you just don't have time. After all, if your nose isn't against the grindstone, somebody else will get the grain made before you do. And somehow, that translates into a fate worse than death; so all energy is devoted to the task at hand.

For television, the decision not to listen to viewers and potential viewers has been a disaster. Broadcast companies spend a fortune regularly on research and come away with a sense that they have, indeed, been conversing with viewers. This is a false assumption for several reasons. One, we talk to them, but we don't listen. Two, television research is generally limited to people watching TV or, more often, a certain group of people watching TV. News research, for example, talks to news consumers. It's an echo chamber that is a net liability in a shrinking universe. Finally, significant, albeit critical things people say are dismissed with logic such as:

- "That's not our target demo."
- "We can't do anything about that anyway."
- "Don't worry, that's an extremely small group."

- "They're just a bunch of weirdos."
- "That can't possibly reflect the majority."

So here we are down the wrong path, and we're looking around and wondering what happened? The fault, dear Brutus, is in ourselves. Having dismissed important messages that our viewers were clearly sending, the ground beneath our feet is shaking and beginning to crumble.

These messages have come from opposite ends of the demographics spectrum. The result is an industry that resembles a candle burning from both ends. Both sides will meet soon, and all we'll be left with is a smoldering wick. Here's why.

The pre-lived business life requires maximum revenue to produce maximum dividends all of the time. It's the only way to hedge against tomorrow. The communications industry has determined that, for television, this means ad revenue from sponsors targeting a youthful audience. Hence, programming — and to a large extent the news — has slowly and deftly evolved to appeal to a younger crowd. The number of the young demos attracted determined "what worked." And when something did "work," it was duplicated ad nauseum.

The result is that older people — those people who grew up with the industry and were loyal through and through — have given up on television. They've been telling us all along that they didn't like the youthful tilt in programming. Too much sex. Too much violence. Too many low-life reality programs. Too many insults to intelligence. Bring back the good dramas and comedies. Over and over, we've heard this. And now these people find contentment with HGTV, The Food Network, and other specialty cable channels.

So the plus-fifty crowd is one end of the burning candle.

At the opposite end is the very group that TV is trying to reach for their advertisers, the 18-49 year olds. And what's happening there? Disruptive innovations are moving them to other technologies in droves. For them, watching TV includes playing video games and watching DVDs. Digital recorders allow them to be their own programmers *and* skip the commercials. Then there's this little thing called the Internet.

In their groundbreaking and ongoing study on the Web's impact on culture, the UCLA Center for Communications Policy found that the time Internet users spend online (11.8 hours a week on average) comes from their television viewing time, that this is more pronounced with young people and experienced users, and that the fastest growing segment of the Web — broadband — accelerates the switch. This move away from television and to the Internet will only accelerate as Web users become more experienced.

For Postmodern young people, ownership of time is a serious matter. Young people work a lot of hours to afford the things they want and feel they deserve, so the value of the digital video recorder (TiVo) technology is not so much one of coolness as it is practicality. If you can skip commercials, that's a full hour of prime time gained.

Another factor that many broadcast executives miss is that this 18–49 age group is remarkably media savvy. They've been bombarded with messages since they were toddlers, and they're not ignorant of what's really going on. They recognize how things work and view programming decisions and advertising that targets them as insincere and manipulative. When combined with technologies that offer entertainment alternatives, their choice is obvious.

So the candle burns at both ends.

One of the people watching all of this is Tim Hanlon, Senior Vice President and Director of Emerging Contacts for Starcom Worldwide. His voice represents the people who pay the bills for TV, the advertisers. Despite the challenges facing television, Hanlon is bullish on the future and an evangelist for change. He's become somewhat of a lightning rod on behalf of the advertising industry, a voice unafraid to call a spade a spade. "The sampling methodology of TV is not keeping up with developments," he told a conference in Florida recently. "A more data-centric view is required.

TV today is less about watching TV than it is about consuming video in many different environments."

These are important words for broadcasters to understand. The cable industry is developing their own audience measurement tools, because, as Hanlon says, "They know there's gold in them thar set-top boxes." Advertisers are shifting millions of dollars to the Internet, because they're beginning to understand the medium and its ability to deliver targeted audiences.

Television long ago gave up ruling the roost, and the industry needs to accept that it is now just a part of a much bigger multi-media reality. When it does, television will discover that it has options far beyond what it believes. To fully utilize the creativity at its disposal, however, television has to give up — at least for a season — its addiction to the pre-lived life. Innovation is the key-word for the next few years, and fresh air demands freedom.

And nowhere is this truer than with television news. The candle is burning at both ends on the local level too, and local news needs innovation badly. And the sad part here is that there are so many wonderful options available to bring video news to local con-sumers via New Media outlets, yet the industry sits defiantly in a 20th century rut. In order for local news to participate in the rev-olution underway, it has to stop seeing itself behind a podium in front of thousands of attentive and adoring fans. Every tool that technology has to offer — from broadband video to RSS readers to mobile phones — can be used to communicate local news to local people, and it's high time stations got into it with vigor. Moreover, there has never been a time like this where it was pos-sible to actually include everyday people in the news mix, and that ought to stir creative juices instead of stifling them.

The barrier to stepping into the new world is only fear, one that's based in the illusion of control offered by the pre-lived life. There are no guarantees in life, not even those we used to mistakenly take for granted in the days of double-digit growth.

This is the most amazing time in communications history. Television has the means and the creative people to be competitive in a multimedia environment, but first it has to get into the game. I'm waiting to hear of the broadcasting CEO who stands before shareholders and says, "No more running! It's time to invest instead of retreat!"

THE UNOBVIOUS RESULT OF THE WEB

February 3, 2004

Television news is awash in a sea of change brought about by disruptive innovations in technology. We're hearing smart people talking about a post-broadcasting, post-mass market world. The head of the FCC suggests that a tower and transmitter are no longer necessary to be a TV station, that one can "ride the infrastructure" of the Internet to business success. Sweeps are coming to an end, and so is the viability of the 30-second commercial. Taken together, these suggest a very gloomy future for broadcasting.

But does it have to be that way?

In order to see the real future, one must step away from the forest and get away from all the noise, because these changes are really all about people, and not merely the technology. Our culture is changing, and unless and until you can see that, any attempt to "correct" for change will ultimately prove to be shortsighted at best. But if you can see it, that knowledge will alter your plans — even those for tomorrow — because there is certainly a place for television and television news in a Postmodern world.

Premodern: I believe, therefore I understand.
Modern: I reason, therefore I understand.
Postmodern: I experience, therefore I understand.

There's some of each in all of us, and one doesn't fully replace the other. And it's not like you can look across the room and say, "Look! There's a Postmodernist!" We're talking about a cultural shift, not necessarily a person.

Postmodernism is the Age of Participation. Postmoderns (Pomos) distrust institutional authority figures and intuitively trust those who've actually experienced the things that Modernists only study. It is through these experiences — and to a great extent, shared experiences — that people are forming their tribes.

So significant is the impact of Postmodernism on the media and the future that it simply *must* be understood and discussed. It's critical knowledge for the industry, because news people who make no attempt to understand the culture within which they now live and work are doomed to helplessly inept and shallow reporting. This used to be a business that required thinking, and it has for too long been driven towards the cliffs of irrelevancy by self-centered foolishness like greed, avarice and a lust for power. If one wishes to "do TV news" in the future, one must first accept the realities of the force behind the many changes in the media landscape. It's the Internet, but the Web is really just a tool. It's technology, but appliances simply do what people tell them to do. The energy behind it all is people, angry, frustrated people who've been left out for too long. Pomos look around and see failure where the "professional classes" — who were supposed to make everything work through logic and reason — have screwed it all up.

I capitalize Postmodernism for a reason. This cultural change is of epochal proportions, and depending on the level of one's understanding, the events unfolding before our eyes daily either make sense or they don't.

Take, for example, the case of Howard Dean and Joe Trippi.

Dean fired Trippi in the wake of his loss in New Hampshire. Trippi was the campaign manager, and the campaign wasn't working, so the move was understandable. Dean then hired Washington insider and lobbyist, Roy Neel, to run his campaign. The Postmodern campaign, which got all the attention for the new ground it broke, has been jerked back to one of Modernist logic and reason. And of course, this has brought about the inevitable arguments from various circles attempting to explain how the Internet candidate created by Trippi and others bombed so badly in the real world. Everybody, it seems, has an opinion.

One is particularly noteworthy for this discussion. It's from Richard Barrett, a conservative California computer geek (said with a smile), political activist and blogger.

> Dean's problem is the Deaniacs. The Internet-driven campaign has enabled him to amass a large following, but they're primarily unbalanced people, fanatical followers, extremists, and wackos. In my experience with Internet-enabled activism, these are the kind of people most attracted to online chat and email wars, so an organization that's going to use these tools to recruit has to prune the weirdos before they run off the mainstream people you need to reach out to the undecided mainstream people whose support you really need in the voting booth. Others have written that the orange-hatted, tattooed, and body-pierced volunteers who flew into Iowa alienated the actual voters, and that's real.
>
> When your core group of volunteers is weirdo, you pretty well guarantee that only weirdos will join the campaign later on, because normal people don't want to hang out with a bunch of lost pups looking for a father figure or a messianic jihad. And when your volunteers are as large in numbers as they are loose in marbles, the constant contact the candidate has with them can't help but rub off in the kind of mania Dean displayed in the "I have a scream" speech. And volunteers are the life-blood of the campaign, doing all the indispensable phone calling, door knocking, and talking to voters one by one. Without a core group of people both dedicated and sane, a campaign can't go anywhere. (1)

A simple explanation of this rant would be that Dean's was a bottom-up, decentralized Postmodern campaign, empowering people (all types) at the edge of the political process, and that Barrett is a top-down Modernist thinker (sane, logical, rational) all the way. There's truth to that, but it doesn't go deep enough.

In the middle of World War II, a major cultural event took place that didn't get a lot of ink. The man who would later be called "Hitler's Pope" issued a decree that injected life into the roots of what is now called Postmodernism. The date was September 30, 1943. In his encyclical *Divino Afflante Spiritu*, Pope Pius XII encouraged scholars to pursue knowledge about the writers of the Bible, for they were "the living and reasonable instrument of the Holy Spirit...." He wrote:

> Let the interpreter then, with all care and without neglecting any light derived from recent research, endeavor to determine the peculiar character and circumstances of the sacred writer, the age in which he lived, the sources written or oral to which he had recourse and the forms of expression he employed. (2)

This was a stunning decree, because, according to Catholic tradition, the Vulgate (Latin) Bible of Saint Jerome was the absolute depository of divine truth, the source, sole and authentic, of God's word. While the encyclical was hailed by scholars as a way to produce a more meaningful Bible, it produced the unintended consequence of a license to challenge authority.

The modern term for what the Pope suggested is deconstructionism, an intellectual challenge to the attempt to establish any ultimate or secure meaning in a text. Using language analysis and examining the author and the author's sources, it tries to "deconstruct" the gender, racial, economic, political, and cultural biases that "infect" histories and statements of "truth." It's been around academic circles for 30 years, and it is closely associated with academic Postmodernism, because it views concrete experience as more valid than abstract ideas and, therefore, refutes any attempts to produce a history, or a truth.

But how does that play out in real life, and what does it have to do with Howard Dean?

In an important essay, "Why the Web Will Win the Culture Wars for the Left: Deconstructing Hyperlinks," Chicago attorney and critical theorist Peter Lurie convincingly argues that a cultural swing to the left is inevitable, given the nature and structure of the

Web itself, not the content it contains. He writes that the process by which users search for and use content on the Internet forces people into a Postmodernist mindset — whether they realize it or not.

> The content available online is much less important than the manner in which it is delivered; indeed, the way the Web is structured. Its influence is structural rather than informational, and its structure is agnostic. For that reason, parental controls of the sort that AOL can offer give no comfort to conservatives. It's not that Johnny will Google "hardcore" or "T&A" rather than "family values;" rather, it's that Johnny will come to think, consciously or not, of everything he reads as linked, associative and contingent. He will be disinclined to accept the authority of any text, whether religious, political or artistic, since he has learned that there is no such thing as the last word, or indeed even a series of words that do not link, in some way, to some other text or game. For those who grow up reading online, reading will come to seem a game, one that endlessly plays out in unlimited directions. The Web, in providing link after associative link, commentary upon every picture and paragraph, allows, indeed requires, users to engage in a postmodernist inquiry. (3)

In this sense, blogging itself is an exercise in Postmodernism, regardless of the content or cultural leaning of the blog, and Mr. Barrett and all others are furthering the advent of a Postmodern world, whether they intend to do so or not.

> Surfing mimics a postmodern, deconstructionist perspective by undermining the authority of texts. Anyone who has spent a lot of time online, particularly the very young, will find themselves thinking about content — articles, texts, pictures — in ways that would be familiar to any deconstructionist critic.
>
> HTML, hyperlinks, frames, and meta-tags are the essential building blocks of the Web. They combine to create a highly associative, endlessly referential and contingent environment that provides an expanse of information at the same time that it subverts any claim to authority, since another view is just a click away. (4)

And so in the case of Howard Dean, one could easily argue that while losing the battle, he and Trippi and the others who created his original work have already won the war. The leftward tilt will be increasingly resisted by the right, who'll continue to use the Internet tools available to them and, in so doing, continue the shift unawares. Fascinating.

The bursting bubbles of the Internet — whether the tech stock collapse or Howard Dean — are insignificant compared to the next one that will come along, and sooner or later everybody will figure out that the Postmodern ideas of rejecting authority and decentralized power are the norm, not the weird. Then where will we be?

Some argue that Lurie's conclusions are quite a leap, that the places where conservatives hang out on the Web will do just fine. But the scenario Lurie paints is valid, because he speaks directly to the influence of the Web on young people, those who have yet to form social, much less political beliefs. "The Web is a postmodernist tool," he writes, "that inevitably produces a postmodernist perspective. It is an unobvious result."

And in the middle of this, the (new) media will play an extremely significant role, for the inherent, hidden danger of such a culture is the echo chamber phenomenon, wherein Postmodernist tribes listen only to each other and free speech loses its value. Those who view the Weblog concept as the future news architecture dismiss this as specious, because bloggers regularly "touch base" with mainstream media sources before sharing their findings and arguments with readers. While this is currently true, it doesn't necessarily follow that such will be the case downstream. What will be the "mainstream" of the future? These are the same people who argue that we are witnessing the end of the mass market — a vision I happen to share — yet they fail to follow the argument to its end.

Ultimately, news reading and viewing decisions in a Postmodern world will be up to those at the receiving end, not a hierarchical, "professional" press dispensing filtered happenings from the mountaintop. Pomos reject authority, especially anything smacking of elitism, and that would include anything under the banner of today's mainstream press. Mr. Barrett's notions of weirdos, wackos and sanity come from an institutional, Modernist value perspective. After all, who's deciding the difference between weird and sane, if not some real or imagined authority? In the Postmodern view, one man's wack is another man's sane, and so it goes.

Attempts to be all things to all tribes in a Postmodern world is problematic at best, but it's the most likely road "professional" news people will follow in the short term. We'll also likely see early competition for the biggest tribes, because the broadcasting mindset doesn't leave easily. If it's the end of mass marketing, then niche marketing (known as "contextual marketing" in Webspeak) is where we're heading. If it's the end of broadcasting, then let's look at the benefits of narrowcasting.

To survive in the years ahead, local television stations are going to have to become multimedia production and distribution companies. This is the inevitable conclusion offered by an increasingly Postmodern culture, and it's where, I think, broadcasting companies need to invest their futures.

THE POWER OF ATTRACTION

August 2, 2004

I was hopelessly naïve when I was young, as I think most kids were who grew up in the 50s. My father's growing-up speech ("Terry, you're at that age where hair is going to start growing in strange places.") didn't equip me to handle the girls with whom I so easily fell in love. I also wasn't equipped to handle the girl in the pink halter top who tried to seduce me at one of our concerts. "I just *love* banjo players." Yikes! I ran.

Seduction, I have since learned, is a power game. It's remarkably simple, yet complex in its rules, and, of course, some are better at it than others. Here's the essence of the game:

I want you to want me more than I want you.

Most people attribute the word to the dating scene, but seduction takes place in every walk of human life. It's an important word in discussing anything associated with the media, because mass marketers are doing their best to seduce all of us with a relentless stream of winks and smiles. The truth is they want us more than we want them, and the trick for them is to turn that around. An enormous industry is based entirely on this concept.

Attraction is certainly a part of seduction, but there's an important difference that often goes unnoticed or certainly unacknowledged. One can only make himself or herself attractive up to a point. Ultimately, the attraction decision (consciously or unconsciously) is made by the one being courted. This decision is the target of seduction, and it's where the media status quo is most threatened by the empowerment of the individual in our increasingly Postmodern world. Technology is only the catalyst in the cultural shift underway. People are what's really driving it all, and that's why the power of attraction is so crucial to future media success. Mass marketing exists in a one-to-many world, whereas attraction works on a level of many-to-one. This may seem like splitting semantic hairs, but the difference is really quite profound.

In the Postmodern worldview, people are united through the concept of tribes, where attraction takes center stage. This is difficult to grasp from a Modernist perspective — which, it is fair to say, includes just about all of us — because we're blocked by logic and history. The word conjures up images of human beings living in groups on river banks before Caucasians arrived in North America, villages with a chief in charge.

The problem with any purely Modernist understanding is that it can limit what's possible, and, therefore, this cultural shift is taking place largely beyond our comprehension. If we don't see it, it must not be there. We either ignore the reality entirely, then, or we attempt to assign logical interpretations that make us feel comfortable in our ignorance.

A case in point is the discussion currently underway regarding the influence of bloggers and the blogosphere — a remarkable Postmodern development. Attempts to assign rankings to various blogs to determine their influence are based on the hierarchical (and therefore Modernist), mass-marketing concepts of reach and frequency. Traditional journalists fear bloggers are whacking their fatted calf, and many bloggers are actually joining in this misdirected fear-cum-anger. The ensuing debates over credentialed versus uncredentialed, opinion versus objectivity, checks and balances, echo chambers, and — most importantly — who has the greater ability to influence the masses, all lock the debaters into purely Modernist arguments. In so doing, the point is missed entirely, and that is that influence in a Postmodern world is entirely the opposite of convention. Individuals now determine their own influences. Think about that for a minute. Do you ever wonder why nothing you try seems to be working anymore? There's your answer.

The Democratic National Convention introduced bloggers to the world of political conventions for the first time. In fact, it was one of the big stories of the convention. Stories about this band of renegades descending on Boston were everywhere, and now we're in the process of deciding what value, if any, the blogosphere brought to political journalism.

A few of my favorite bloggers were there, including Jay Rosen and David Weinberger. I'm so familiar with each that it was like having trusted friends present, people through whom I could let my guard down enough to actually look inside the Fleet Center. Both did an excellent job, but I wrote a note of thanks to Weinberger.

> This new journalism we practice is very much like surrogate eyes and ears offering vicarious experiences for those of us who can't be everywhere, and it works because — in the Postmodern model of tribes — I feel comfortable allowing myself inside your thoughts and emotions. You generally think the things I would and feel the things I feel, so you ask the questions I would, see the things I want to see, and float the ideas and reactions that are so much a part of me. The result is a very satisfying and knowledgeable conversation that takes place in my mind, and it goes way beyond the simple and detached who, what, why, where, etc. Shared experiences is the most powerful dynamic of the whole tribes concept, and I think it's the real value of blogs and blogging. It's neither vertical nor horizontal. In a mystical sense, it's more like an internal connection that transcends the logic of the senses. It's quite intimate, I think, and you've got to be a part of it in order to understand.

Jay Rosen and David Weinberger are members of my tribe — *my* tribe. They don't know this, of course, and that's fine, for the first rule of Postmodern tribalism is that each individual gets to choose his or her own tribe members. In that sense, each person is their own tribal leader and that role is absolute, because one isn't subject to group-think, being out-voted, or submission to any form of hierarchy. Tribe members don't have to acknowledge membership or even be aware of it. The make-up of the tribe is ever-evolving and amoebic.

Bloggers, therefore, function in tribal membership roles, not leadership. This is contrary to Modernist notions of influence, because the power of influence lies in the hands of those being influenced. Hence, conventional rules and roles don't apply, and that leads to the second rule of Postmodern tribalism: attraction is the defining dynamic of influence.

Weinberger gets this where many don't. "Weblogs filter readers," he writes, "the way people filter friends. That is, to the extent to which a Weblog is a personal expression — leaving out some of the more "professional" blogs — the Weblog attracts readers for the same sorts of reasons that people make friends. Mass media write for mass audiences. Bloggers write for people who know them."

I'm regularly jolted by the things complete strangers say to me as a result of my own Weblog. Clearly, I am a part of many tribes, few of which I have any knowledge of whatsoever. However, I am keenly aware that there is something about the content of my blog that brings certain people to it. I know this, because I've done little to "market" myself in the tradition sense. I have a mailing list made up entirely of people who've asked to be a part of it, but that's about it. The blogosphere has its own way of promoting, and I'm content to just let that happen. The best and smartest thing I can do is get out of the way. This is the concept of attraction that is so difficult for hierarchical Modernists to understand. It's just too, well, random.

It's also at the heart of attempts by some to "rank" bloggers based on influence, as defined in terms of reach and frequency. Bloggers each reach certain people, the argument goes, who then reach others, and so on down the pyramid (the masses, it seems, always live at the bottom of some pyramid). Companies who offer ads to bloggers, like Blogads, are betting on this paradigm, and many bloggers are hoping it will form the essence of a business model for them. It may or it may not, but this is an example of applying top-down (Modernist) thinking to an innovation that is clearly bottom-up, and blogs and bloggers who function this way are nothing more than another form of hierarchical media. If they continue, they will ultimately be replaced by others who aren't so inclined, for in adopting this perspective, bloggers are trading the concept of conversations for just another bully pulpit. What is the message, after all, from those who provide site statistics to their readers if not to point out their position on the pyramid?

In life, there is intended influence and unintended influence. The former is the work of, among others, journalists, entertainers, PR flacks, advertisers, politicians and all sorts of bullies. The latter is that which resonates within, a picture that inspires, the voice of a friend, human touch, a laugh, a right word spoken in time of need. The line between them cannot be deliberately bridged, for the right to be unintentionally influenced belongs to the individual, and that is powerfully enabled by the Internet.

One of the lessons that the Net is teaching marketers is that this law of attraction can be successfully used to market products and services in unconventional ways. The best example is the growing understanding and use of viral marketing. This is a new industry built on what appears to be a chaotic foundation — that people will carry your message for you if given a compelling vehicle. You don't "buy" rating points, page views or any other scientific measurement with a viral campaign. You simply put it out there and let it happen. You can test it until the cows come home, but the overriding issue in any viral campaign is faith.

People are seduced by viral campaigns, not hit over the head. It is the power of attraction at work, and it offers an important reminder for those of the blogosphere who are trying to figure out (read: control) where this is all going. The pyramid has been inverted, and the people are now in charge.

Disruptive technologies are empowering individuals far beyond anything we've ever known before. This is either true or it isn't (it is). If it is true, then the relationship between buyer and seller can only produce a buyer's market. This is true whether you're a blogger, the *New York Times*, Proctor & Gamble, or a local television station. Our energies need to stay focused on making ourselves more attractive on every level instead of wasting our time and resources on clever ways to promote ourselves.

We may just find that, in the game of seduction, the best strategy is often to stop wanting the other so much. That can be very attractive.

RIGHT BRAIN RENAISSANCE

November 9, 2006

What will history call the postmodern age, and what events will it judge as watershed on the road we now travel? The counterculture movement of the 60s? The fall of the Berlin Wall?

The modern age essentially began with the "Enlightenment" (including the Age of Reason and the Renaissance), when the marvel that is the human mind was exalted against the authority of "The Church." Religious leaders of the time — along with those who benefited from their largess — fought it tooth and nail, but the new age dawned anyway.

And it was inevitable, wasn't it? It really began with the Bible being put into the hands of everyday people, which led folks to the belief that those high priests weren't so high after all.

Postmodernism finds itself in similar territory, and while its fruit is all around us, we're a little bit too close to it to start defining events. There is one, however, that I believe history will judge kindly as a catalyst of change — a renaissance of the right brain in our culture. I call it a renaissance, because I believe there was a time long ago when creativity and the arts were given their cultural due. This contemporary right brain revolution is evidenced

173

by things great and small and has profound implications for the future.

We make plans and set goals, for example, based on left-brain formulas. In the media world, that means we find where we want to go and craft logical plans to get there, and this has — and will continue — to serve us well. But we've entered an upside-down world in media today that demands right brain goal-setting and planning.

I cannot tell you how many people I encounter in the media boardrooms of the U.S. who are waiting for the left brain plan before moving into the Media 2.0 world. Yet the conventional wisdom among those companies (and their supporters) who are already into the Media 2.0 space is to just build it and create the business later.

Let me state up front my bias to this end, because I am right brain dominant, although I'm able to perform logic and reasoning functions — according to experts who've probed me — through intelligence. My default setting, however, is on the creative side.

There are two kinds of creativity — that which flows from known parameters and that which begins from beyond. The person who wrote the song is different from the one who remixes it, but both are demonstrations of the right brain. While they share a common ground, they are separate gifts. One who begins with a blank slate sees things beyond one who begins with pieces already in place or within already known parameters.

Creative engineers work within that which is known, and this I find to be an extension of the modernist culture. This kind of creativity drives the modern culture forward, but that which is known has creative limits, and that's one of the reasons it cannot continue to dominate the world.

But the artist has no boundaries except those she creates for herself, for the right brain is wired differently than the left.

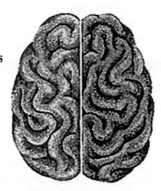

Left Brain Functions
Language
Science and Math
Logic
Analytic Thought

Right Brain Functions
Art and Music
Intuition
Creativity
Holistic Thought

The evidence of a right brain renaissance is everywhere. The value of YouTube, for example, isn't in the eyeballs viewing illegally uploaded materials; it's in the millions of creative works being posted by everyday people. Even Hollywood has recognized that its system doesn't have a lock on creativity, as talent agencies are now looking to the Web for new prospects. Welcome to the cutting edge.

Have you ever really spent any time on Flickr? It's bursting at the seams with marvelous photography by amateurs who've found an online studio for their work. Institutional photography may not recognize the work on Flickr as "legitimate," but tell that to the people who are using the site to share their work with others.

And the communities that just these two sites are spawning are filled with creative people seeking outlets for their work.

New art forms are exploding. Whoever heard of photoshopping or other forms of digital art just a few years ago? We're inventing whole new virtual worlds such as Second Life, and video games have taken on a life of their own. Nobody knows where it's going. Nobody.

Who would argue that Chris Anderson's brilliant discovery of The Long Tail and his exploration of new media economics isn't inspired? The Web empowers the long tail, so not only are we innovating new worlds but also new economies.

Institutional modernist leaders look at all of this and scratch their heads, because it's taking place without their permission. Traditional rules and systems are being by-passed and with alarming speed, and the loss of (their) order is frightening and dangerous. It's foolish, however, to think there is no order as the rules of the right brain world are being written.

Everything about the modernist culture is driven by the left side. How often do we complain that the world is run by the bean counters? That's the left brain at work, the author of the bottom line. Our government is more a government of rules than of the people, and so, where that which is new rears its (ugly) head, we create a new set of rules to bring it into control. While this is a necessary function in a civilized culture, there is ample evidence that, well, it's just gone too far.

Lawyers and the legal system count on left brain rule, and while you can call "creative" some of the manipulation of the law, it is still based on the godlike assumption that the law is the law is the law. Judicial activism, where law is made from the bench, is just another form of logic and reason applied to other left brain work. The law is all about justice these days, but what about mercy? And if mercy is not relevant to culture, then why do we have judges?

Our culture's system of education is based almost entirely on left brain thinking and systems. Hence, I found myself bored by school and excited by that which was beyond the senses and the ability to measure. I was accused of being "too sensitive" by adults, and I wonder if they really knew what they were saying. "Stop being so sensitive, Terry Lee!" was something I often heard. How exactly does one stop being who or what they are?

Consequently, I always felt a bit out-of-step with my surroundings, and I still do in many ways. This is why I don't play well with rules and why I'm able to develop theories from assumptions that others find, well, different.

One of those assumptions is that the page is turning in our culture from modernism to Postmodernism, something I accept without a great deal of internal argument, for to me, the things I see taking place in our world make "sense" only when viewed as part of a postmodern shift. They make no sense otherwise. Much of Media 2.0, for example, is counterintuitive to the logic and reason of modernism, whereas Media 1.0 is modernism's crown.

This series of essays is called "TV News in a Postmodern World," because without that framework, it's much harder to view the changes around us as anything other than technology or new distribution systems. TV News doesn't need TV anymore, and the definition of news is now in the hands of consumers, not an elite group of journalistic royalty. Some of it these days is actually being created by amateurs, and that's only going to increase. Why?

Because Postmodernism views much of the fruit of modernism as failed and challenges its basic assumptions (grand narratives) of ordered hierarchy, elitism, and the lordship of science.

The Internet and especially the World Wide Web, while authored by science, are the tools of curiosity and imagination, and structurally put people in a countercultural driver's seat, because they can — through exploring links — deconstruct any assumption presented to them by the culture's elite, and that includes all institutions of power. This is power in the hands of the masses never dreamed of before, and where it's going is scary as hell to a society of order.

But I don't share this fear for several reasons. One, I take John Dewey's position over that of Walter Lippmann's, that the open discussion of ideas — even heated and stridently partisan — is necessary for human well-being.

> ...the act of voting is in a democratic regime a culmination of a continued process of open and public communication in which prejudices have the opportunity to erase each other; that continued interchange of facts and ideas exposes what is unsound and discloses what may make for human well-being...Any fair-minded survey of suppressive acts in this country will demonstrate that their ultimate source is always a privileged minority (with the majority standing passively by and permitting it to occur).
>
> — John Dewey, *John Dewey Responds* (1950) (1)

Lippmann (the Father of professional journalism) took a completely opposite position, and his view has been the dominant thinking of our modernist culture:

> A false ideal of democracy can only lead to disillusionment and to meddlesome tyranny. If democracy cannot direct affairs, then a philosophy which expects it to direct them will encourage the people to attempt the impossible; they will fail...The public must be put in its place, so that it may exercise its own powers, but no less and perhaps even more, so that each of us may live free of the trampling and the roar of a bewildered herd.
> — Walter Lippmann, *The Phantom Public* (2)

Two, I think our culture is sliding into the muck in a hurry, but this downward spiral is nothing new. The ideas from the elite are old ideas, because, well, they need old ideas to sustain what they have, but that does nothing to solve the downward spiral. The left throws money at poverty, and the right gives the money to business in hopes it will "trickle down." Neither does anything to fix the problem, but both are politically expedient.

There is no institutional cure for a disease that is incubated institutionally. Hence, I'm more than willing to let the masses try and figure it out. We certainly can't do any worse than the elites.

Three, technology is the servant of humankind, not the other way around. Our institutions are built upon protected knowledge and the extent to which that protection breaks down is the extent to which we'll be able to one day manage ourselves. I don't claim to have answers that will satisfy how this will come about, but I have faith that — as long as the flow of information is free — we'll be able to figure out ways to use technology for the general betterment of the people.

Already people are helping themselves in the world of healthcare. Who hasn't researched their own symptoms before or after seeing the doctor? And self-help chatrooms and discussion boards are a mainstay of many who suffer from mental and other illnesses. Are they talking with a doctor? No, they're talking to and helping each other.

I view Postmodernism as the Age of Participation. Just as the dark ages were brought to a thankful end through an enlightening, the fruit of a closed culture of elites is coming to an end through the increasing ability of every day people to share in the knowledge upon which the culture was built and is sustained.

And just as "the church" didn't disappear after the Enlightenment, elitism won't entirely disappear either as the culture drifts deeper into Postmodernism. But those who choose to ignore the people won't be among the favored in the years to come, because the power to decide who's on top is increasingly theirs.

The 21st century could get very ugly as all of this plays out, which is why we so desperately need original thinking right now and why we're witnessing a renaissance of the right brain. To quote a very old book, "He who has ears to hear, let him hear."

POSTMODERNISM'S MOST
IMPORTANT GIFT

October 30, 2007

While the academic and religious worlds continue to shake self-serving fingers at what they view as the absurdities of Postmodernism (it is absurd to the linear, rational mind), the cultural shift just chugs along. Like an old steam engine with its cowcatcher pushing aside obstacles that might block its path, our culture is becoming more participatory and networked, with a subtle decentralization of power left glistening on the tracks as the locomotive rolls by.

The nature of authority is changing, because people don't have to blindly accept what others say anymore. We can increasingly find out for ourselves. Whoosh, the train pushes institutionalism aside. Reason, it's becoming increasingly obvious, isn't living up to its potential to solve problems — except for the established haves — so people are turning to each other. These problems are widespread and growing.

There is no unified definition of Postmodernism, because by nature, it must resist codification. This is maddening to logic and reason, who then dismiss it as folly, or worse, try to explain it in logical terms. This is a shame, for there is at least one enormous intellectual upside to postmodern acceptance.

The first assumption about Postmodernism is that it demands the challenge of assumptions, which is enough to strangle the ganglia of any left-brained, linear thinker. Postmodernism doesn't say there are no absolutes, because, well, that would be an absolute statement, wouldn't it? This is what comes from the silliness of trying to wrestle with logic something that exists in the slippery and greasy pit of chaos. While there may well be absolutes, the source of that determination is fair game in the questioning of assumptions. This is why religion views postmodern thinking as anathema. Faith is the determining factor, but faith in what? And so it goes.

Postmodernism's great gift to humankind is this challenging of assumptions, and this is an important matter for our new century. Why? Because in every walk of life, our failed institutions are rooted in assumptions that need challenging, if we are to progress as a culture.

If you honestly believe things "work" in our modernist world, consider a recent Ben Stein column in the *New York Times* where he addresses the banking crisis brought on by foolish (or clever) executives who used the system to get rich with very risky loans.

> I could easily be wrong, but I suspect that at the end of the day, you and I will be bailing out the hundred-million-a-year finance titans who messed this up in the first place. This is what happened with the savings-and-loan disaster. The S&L chieftains…became multi-millionaires and billionaires by wheeling and dealing with government-insured money. When the loans went bad, you and I picked up the bill while the bankers went shopping for their Bentleys. (1)

What is it about our world that enables people to get away with such? Why do we create rules that only benefit the haves, to the detriment of everybody else? The answers lie in the basic assumptions of how modernism can only serve the elite, for where the mind is god, those with institutional intelligence have the upper hand.

So Postmodernism comes along and says, "The cultural narrative that allows this is flawed." This isn't demonstrated in some organized "program" or rebellion; it's played out every day in little ways that evidence the disenchantment of the masses. Web technology is aiding the mission, because every link that leads to discovery opens the mind to possibility — another link — and that includes the hows and whys of the ways things work in our culture.

The Electronic Freedom Federation, among other things, fights the ridiculous end of modernism's spectrum by refusing to accept the actions of certain lawyers. The EFF recently took on the complaint of Stephanie Lenz, the mother of 18-month-old Holden Lenz, about whom she had posted a 29-second home video on YouTube. The video had been seen by 28 people when she received notice from YouTube that they had removed the video for copyright infringement. Prince's tune "Let's Go Crazy" was playing in the background, and his lawyers filed a complaint with YouTube, which the Website was obligated to honor.

When this kind of thing happens, people just scratch their heads in amazement, and what most people don't understand is the degree to which the cumulative rage over hundreds of such little things is blowing back into the faces of a culture that permits them in the first place. These kinds of things aren't necessarily happening more these days, but we are increasingly aware of them, thanks to the information explosion enabled by the Web.

Twentieth-century philosopher Alan Watts studied eastern cultures, not because he wanted to convince the West that the East was better, but because it helped him understand the assumptions of the West. "You don't understand the basic assumptions of your own culture," he told IBM executives in the early 1970s, "if your own culture is the only culture you know. Everybody operates on certain basic assumptions, but very few people know what they are."

> The assumption of Judeo–Christian culture is that man in his nature is sinful and therefore can't be trusted. The assumption of at least ancient Chinese culture is that man in his essential nature is good and therefore has to be trusted. They say to us, "If you can't trust your own basic nature, you can't really rely on the idea that you're untrustworthy. Therefore, you're hopelessly fouled up." (2)

When I first began writing these essays, I noted early on that I write because it is the most efficient way I know to challenge my own assumptions. Challenging your assumptions is a heady but necessary task, if one is to be relevant in a changing world. And the longer I've been writing, the more convinced I am of Watts' conclusion that very few people know the underlying assumptions of their own lives.

I have found this assumption business to be especially useful in studying matters of media in the throes of change. In working with traditional media companies, for example, all questions about the Media 2.0 world flow from certain assumptions that would best be set aside in the reinventing of business models for the future. I was in a meeting once with a major media executive who'd just seen my "unbundled" presentation and asked, "So how do you find mass quickly in this paradigm?" Mass marketing and all its concepts are this fellow's life, so it was a natural question to ask. He was looking at a different culture though the eyes of his own, and his view came from assumptions that aren't necessarily true.

Here are ten assumptions about media and marketing that need challenging:

1. The best way to communicate with people is in a mass. It is, perhaps, the easiest and most efficient way to communicate *to* people, but it is the least meaningful and efficient for communicating *with* people. This means that the entire mass marketing paradigm is built on one-to-many applications, which will result in serious tail chasing in the two-way world of the Web.

2. Getting to mass quickly is needed only in an emergency that threatens the mass. This assumption affords us the time to shape and mold messages in a way that serves the best interests of the one. This is also the birthplace of "the tease," time-based news distribution ("film at eleven"), and the absurd notion that we can get away with routing people through the hoops and passageways of our Web "portals" before getting what they want.

3. The mass wants or, more often, needs to be approached. This is the great illusion that feeds all of mass marketing, an assumption that people are just sitting there — eyes propped open with toothpicks — waiting to be tapped on the shoulder or screamed in the face. It is this more than anything else that fuels the technology-enabled revolt of the people formerly known as the audience.

4. Mass is the only means to achieving the desired communications end. This assumption, perhaps more than any other, needs challenging, because it's at the core of the advertising disruption of Media 2.0 and, subsequently, the paradigm that supports contemporary media. The reality is that mass may indeed be the best means for *some* communications, but certainly not all.

5. Brand building is the most important element of selling. Fostered by the likes of Ries and Trout — who identified "immutable laws" of marketing — the concepts and practices of branding are so overused as to be ineffective. This contributes to marketing-over-product as the accepted means to profit in contemporary capitalism.

6. Reach (the size of the mass) and frequency (the number of times you reach the mass) are the metrics that matter most in the buying and selling of goods and services, and that any behavior with the mass in its entirety is acceptable in the furtherance of commerce. This blindness to anything else stops innovation in its tracks and contributes to the difficulties that all media companies are having with regards to revenue.

7. Listening to the mass is necessary only insofar as to further the goal of assumption number one. Research, therefore, which alleges to begin with no assumptions, may exclude data relevant to the interviewees but irrelevant to the task of reach and frequency.

8. Money spent on marketing to the mass is as or more important than money spent on the product or service created to serve the mass in the first place. This is the fool's folly of the new millennium, because it assumes that brand loyalty

can be purchased, regardless of the quality of the brand itself. The natural fruit of this assumption is hyperbole.

9. People don't really mind being considered targets to be hit, an enemy to be battled, prey to be pursued, uninformed to be educated, misled to be guided, pedestrians to be driven, and valued only to the extent that they "consume." These, of course, are unspoken assumptions, but the exist nonetheless in the mind of mass communications world.

10. People who are aware of our assumptions will function as though they are not. The great illusion of the world of mass marketing is that the people we fooled once can be fooled again and again, and that we begin each task with the assumption of a clean slate upon which to draw. Like *The Emperor's New Clothes*, marketers simply refuse to believe that they are marching the streets naked, their garments too transparent to be effective. And yet they march on.

The above list doesn't even consider the assumption that this is the way it has always been done and that therefore it will always be so. This is the kind of stuff upon which all of contemporary media and marketing is based, and it's about time we talked about it honestly. Postmodernism offers no answers, but asks questions that might lead to answers, if we're willing to ask them.

The greatest mistaken assumption about Postmodernism itself is that it attempts to replace, is replacing or will replace modernism entirely. This all-or-nothing view is absurd, because logic and reason (and their offspring, math and science) are critical to the well being of our culture (any culture) in a hundred different ways.

But should logic and reason dominate the culture? Should the left brain rule the right? These are different matters entirely.

How
the Web
Works

Fundamental to the reality of the New Media world is understanding that the Web is not TV. Interaction, not passivity, rules online. The Web cannot be manipulated into mass audience. Our usual rules don't apply. The essays in this section explore how the Web truly works, enabling readers to expand their understanding and opening new vistas for their own ideas.

Perhaps the biggest problem for local media companies regarding the Web is that its structure, behavior and activities are mostly the opposite of what drives companies built on a mass marketing model. I see this up-close and personal in my work, so many of my essays have involved trying to teach people about how the Web works. Most of my favorite essays are here, especially "Links, the Currency of the Machine" and "The Local Web."

2008: EMBRACING THE (REAL) WEB

December 28, 2007

We got our first television set in 1952 when I was six years old. I had a kidney disease and was bedridden, so the new invention became my friend. Radio held me in its grip with super heroes and Western dramas, but TV made me smile.

My favorite show was "Andy's Gang," featuring Andy Devine, Froggy the Gremlin, Midnight the Cat and Squeaky the Mouse. "Plunk your magic twanger, Froggy," Andy would shout in his raspy voice. There would be a flash of smoke and a *boing*, and then Froggy would appear with his greeting, "Hiya, kids. Hiya. Hiya."

Television back then was unbelievably boring compared to today. It's easy to understand, when you consider that much of what passed for programming in the early 50s was actually radio with a camera. Television programming was created by the radio executives who owned the television networks. Froggy, for example, got his start on Smilin' Ed McConnell's "Buster Brown gang" radio show in 1944, along with Midnight and Squeaky.

Comedy programs such as The Jack Benny Show, dramatic anthologies such as Kraft Television Theater, quiz shows such as Name That Tune, and variety programs such as Arthur Godfrey and His Friends borrowed heavily from popular radio formats. Other early programming was theatrical — cameras on a stage.

It is in this vein that television programmers have tried to adopt everything about TV to their little corners of the Web, and it is here where mistakes have been and continue to be made, for the Web is not broadcasting — not even close. The Web is also not a newspaper — not even close there either, and yet newspaper companies view it with the same eyes as their broadcast counterparts — extensions of their legacy businesses.

Newspapers and television stations are mass marketing vehicles. By nature and structure, the Web dismantles mass, and this is the essential problem. It's not the Web's fault; it's the fault of those who only see it as a vehicle for redistribution of content and the business paradigms associated with that content.

Every Website is equal in the structure of the Web. They're each just a pixel on the page that makes up the whole. This Website is a pixel. Your Website is a pixel. Google is a pixel. And so forth.

Consequently, we have traditional media who have played with the Web instead of embracing it, and a change in this kind of thinking will dominate new developments for local media companies in 2008. We have no choice. 2009, with a new President, no election or Olympics, economic uncertainty, and digital television on top of already decreasing revenues, looms like a tidal wave just a few miles off shore. As AR&D president and CEO Jerry Gumbert puts it, "2008 will be all about getting ready for 2009."

He's right, and this will mean acceptance on a level we've yet to witness in the executive suites and in the newsrooms of media companies and a willingness — even an eagerness — to move forward to become local portfolio companies, with traditional media, perhaps, moving from center stage. Along with this move will come a resource shift away from the portal Websites that host our traditional media brands to business opportunities that will fund, in part, the future mission of the journalism we all hold so dear.

The result will be genuine efforts on the part of companies to return the handshake that the Web offers to them, to become more than merely destination Websites or application platforms. Media companies will meet the (Real) Web in so doing, and learn to play by different rules, those already well-known in both the abstract and in practice throughout Silicon Valley and in the work spaces of thousands of companies who learned years ago that the Web will never be dominated or manipulated, and that if you want to do business here, you have to be prepared to play by its rules.

Attraction, not hyperbole, is what works here, for the supply and demand equation has been turned upside down.

Nokia issued a report last month expressing their belief that 25 percent of media consumption in 2012 will be peer-to-peer, people entertaining themselves, their families, their friends and their tribes. Even if this prediction is optimistic, the truth is entertainment is moving in this direction, and the smart local media company will seize the opportunity it provides. (1)

And the opportunity is significant, because the people formerly known as the audience want to know what we know and do what we do, and any model that enables this will be successful.

Unless you've actually looked, for example, you cannot comprehend the volume of video being produced in schools across the U.S. Who's teaching them to do it right? Should we have a role in that? Where is this video displayed? What will these students do with their video skills as they get older? Are these not the future employees of television stations? What will a television station look like downstream?

A prototype of sorts is Maui Today, an online video platform — a new term to describe what used to be a "television station" — serving the entertainment and information needs of the people of Maui. Maui Today is lightweight, original, and loaded with content — some professionally produced, the rest created by the (lucky) people who call Maui home. Like other hyperlocal models, this one "works," because the community supports it, not because some bigger media company is trying to make it part of their portal.

2008 will also be a year in which at least some local media executives grasp the reality that their monopoly on news and information has disappeared and that the only future they have is enabling the rise of personal media (including advertising) in their communities. This is difficult to accept, because it runs right into the most basic beliefs about the news business and its traditional sources of revenue.

A recent discussion thread via Poynter's Online-News email list raised the issue that we've got to "figure out ways to monetize our content." This is the dream of traditional media, but it is one from which we must be willing to awaken. *L.A. Times* columnist David Lazarus spoke for many when he lamented the following:

> Newspapers, including this one, give away the store online, all the while wringing their hands about declining revenue and circulation. Everyone says the Net represents the future of journalism, and that's probably true. But at this point, no one knows how to make much money at it.
>
> I'm scratching my head trying to come up with another financially challenged industry that found salvation by charging people nothing for its output. (2)

Like other observers, Lazarus went on to predict serious difficulties for our culture as a result.

> Here's the thing: As long as the big papers give it away free, the little papers will have no choice but to do the same. Before you know it, no more little papers.
>
> Meanwhile, blogs will continue sprouting like crab grass throughout the electronic ether. Soon, the line separating quality journalism from utter hokum will be too blurry to discern. (3)

This is overstated, and the problem with this kind of thinking is that it insists that there are only two ways to make money as a media company, both tied to the output of the newsroom: use the scarcity of the special nature of our content by charging for access to it or charge advertisers for adjacent positioning. This is textbook Media 1.0, and the Web is so much more.

Content scarcity is history. It will simply never support significant revenue growth for two reasons. One, content is plentiful on the Web. Everybody makes it, and as Lazarus points out, it's free. Two, we don't have the resources to make enough of it to satisfy reach/frequency advertising models. "More, more, more," we cry, but it's driven by an impossible strategic concept.

"Free is not a business model," says Web economics guru Umair Haque, "It's a strategy." The business model is what needs reinvention, and that's what we'll see happening as more companies embrace the (Real) Web in the year ahead.

For what this really means is that the end of the ad-supported content model as the sole revenue source for all media is growing closer. Advertisers have needed mass media, because it was the only way to reach potential customers. Classifieds have been the business model of newspapers for a very long time, because the community paper was the logical path for enabling commerce. That role for papers is gone now, and efforts to resurrect it will never be completely successful. The model is in full-blown decay, and other forms of ad-supported content are headed down the same path.

So do we just give up? Of course not! We're in a transition period, and there is still plenty of money to be made the old-fashioned way, but in our minds, we must surrender to the inevitable, for it's the only way we'll move forward in the new world. When the ship you're on is sinking, you make every effort to keep it afloat. But when its doom is certain, your only choice is to find something else that floats, and this is what will produce a real shift in local media during 2008.

We have to, for 2009 looms as a cloud of locusts on a meadow rich with life.

We'll see more companies putting less emphasis on their branded Websites and transitioning to pure Web-based entrepreneurial activities. This will mean local control of the technology and the ad-serving necessary to grow and a rethinking of the essential mission and methods of local media. Those who succeed will be those who can work without static plans, for everything is simply moving too fast for "one potato, two potato, three potato, four" thinking. The goal is what matters, and we must be willing to stay goal-driven.

By this time next year, many local media branded Web efforts will involve some form of continuous stream of news and an awakening to the reality of news as a process, not a finished product. It's the logical format to serve an audience largely at work, and the RSS feeds from such an effort can be used in any form of unbundled media play.

2008 will also bring new challenges to and pressures on the concept of net neutrality, mostly built around the real or perceived need to expand the pipes of the Web to handle the increasing bandwidth demand of broadband and other video applications. It's a fairly safe bet that we'll have a tiered Web within the next 24 months, that the flat rates we've known since its inception will move to flexible rates based on bandwidth usage.

And as more local media companies come in touch with the (Real) Web, we'll see more Web-only sales people and a reduction in convergence sales. This is inevitable (and necessary) for companies to grow pure Web revenue.

Above all, 2008 must be a year of action for everybody. We cannot afford to be lulled to complacency with political or Olympics ad revenues. Everything is *not* okay, and this includes our dependence on our portal Websites.

The life of the Static Web (4) — during which we duplicated local media online, like the early television programmers did with radio programs — is evolving into the vastly more flexible Semantic Web (5), and future relevancy depends on our ability to function beyond simple content creators.

Embrace the (Real) Web in 2008. It's the only way to create sustainable growth for the years that will follow. Venture capital money is flowing into pureplay media start-ups, because investors see opportunities in the inaction of media companies already in place.

We cannot sit back and let this happen unchallenged any longer.

CREATING SPECTRUM WITHIN SPECTRUM

September 20, 2007

Mine was the last generation to have known the awe and wonder of downtown, that centralized beehive of retail and business activity in the community. There was no Wal-Mart when I grew up in the 1950s in Grand Rapids, Michigan. There were no malls, at least none that I can recall. If you wanted to do serious shopping, you had to go downtown, and I feel fortunate to have grown up when downtown was the place to be.

In Grand Rapids, we had department stores with odd names like Herpolsheimers (HER-pole-shy-mers), Wurzburg's, and Steketees (like Chickadees). Wurzburg's was my favorite, because they sponsored the annual Christmas parade, so the real Santa was there. During the holidays, these stores all competed to see who could create the best window displays, and it was magical, especially when it snowed.

Herpolsheimers, Wurzburg's, and Steketees also competed for customers in that closed space called downtown, and what happened to them is what's happening today in the world that these essays probe: television — and especially television news — in our increasingly postmodern world.

One of the central questions for local media companies these days is "How do I expose my work online to a wider audience?" Nearly everyone in any community is online these days, but local media company Web efforts are limited to those they already reach on the air or in print, and that doesn't translate to a lot of new revenue. This is at the heart of the Yahoo! newspaper consortium deal, because Yahoo! claims it cumulatively reaches 70% of the users in any market, while the newspapers only reach around 40%.

For television, this is an equally perplexing matter. While people are watching more television, that viewing is so fragmented that the ratings for individual programs are shrinking at alarming rates. Hence, the universe in which a local station operates is getting smaller, so we're shifting our focus to where the money is going. While the new world is exploding with growth and is exciting beyond anything in recent memory, it's a damned frustrating place in which to work, for the "audience" is fluid, nimble and mobile. If only they'd just sit still!

They won't sit still, and worse yet, they want to watch certain things while bouncing from here to there. Hence, the titanic battle between the entertainment industry and iTunes and YouTube over who will be the ultimate host of copyrighted videos online. It's the most significant Web issue these days, because there's an incredible amount of money at stake. And even more than that, it's a business war to see who will be the control panel when the marriage of the Web and our television sets is complete.

For the copyright holders, it means a bright future, if they can maintain control of videos they see (and the law sees) as theirs. For people who the industry once considered customers, the winner will get their allegiance, assuming they have a say in the videos that they see as theirs. The more the industry behaves as if people are merely "consumers" of their "products," the less likely it is they will come out on top, because the choice — at least for now — belongs with the audience for these videos.

Let's step back for a moment and view this matter from another direction. The creators or licensees of anything copyrighted have historically been able to ply their wares in authorized spaces and places, what I'm going to identify here as various forms of "spectrum," to borrow a term from broadcasting.

Movie studios used to work only within the distribution chain of movie theaters, a form of spectrum that permitted them — and only them — to compete with each other for the eyeballs of moviegoers. This was and is a tightly-controlled, closed network of spectrum. The era of video tapes brought a completely new revenue stream to the studios and spawned a new distribution network — the video store. It wasn't until digital video came along that studios began to realize the loss of control over their spectrum.

The music industry worked within the spectrum of radio, which drove people to buy records at record stores. In my youth, we bought and swapped records with our friends, and nobody argued with the fundamental fact that those records were ours to do with as we pleased. Radio stations also worked within this spectrum to profit from advertisers who wanted their products adjacent to "Wake Up, Little Susie." It was a beautiful thing. 8-track and then cassettes followed, and soon we were walking around with "our" music thanks to Sony and the Walkman. This was all new money for the music industry, and everything was fine until digital audio signaled trouble for the closed network.

The television industry (joined at the hip with the studios) functioned within the closed network of broadcast spectrum, a license for which remains an enormously profitable proposition. When the cable and satellite industries swooped in, this closed network was expanded from without, but there was enough room for everybody to be happy. While digital TV has broadened the network more, it is still very much closed, but this business with the Web threatens to blow that apart.

Telephone companies used to function within the highly closed network of lines that crisscrossed our towns and connected us with each other. The age of "Ma Bell" and its lack of competition meant monopolistic control of the spectrum and everything related to pricing. Cellular phones work within yet another layer of spectrum, the closed nature of which brings profit to the pockets of those who control it.

In each of these cases, the institutional player has been able to increase profits by bundling crap with quality, and that's the real problem from the end-user's perspective. Sandwich a loser between two winners and suddenly the loser becomes a winner. Put two great tunes on an album with ten throwaways, and you can charge extra for those hits. Force people to subscribe to lousy channels in addition to the good ones. Add fee after fee to enable people to get what they want, because you own the lines. Crank out a steady stream of mediocrity in the hopes that one will reach blockbuster status.

These are the worlds in which incumbent communications businesses work. Each is being disrupted by the Web, and each is throwing everything they've got at "the problem" of maintaining the closed nature of their former spectrum.

What makes the Web so different is that it is an entirely open network, although the deep pockets of the status quo are lobbying everyone with breath to change that by creating tiers of service. The argument in Congress is that we're running out of bandwidth, which means a *ton* of money to beef up the Internet, and the people spending that money should be entitled to profit from the build-out. While that's certainly true, the reality is that this disguises what is essentially an attempt by the incumbents to restore some form of command and control mechanism (tiered pricing) to the open network. This means that those with money will be the only ones able to advance the spectrum, and this is exactly the old profit model wearing new clothes. But I digress.

On the Web, all of these individual companies are merely pixels on the overall page, blips in a spectrum of equal blips. There's no doubt that mass marketing muscle in the worlds within which the incumbents currently play gives them an advantage over the other blips, but it doesn't influence the essential infrastructure. This is why innovations from other blips can explode across the entire Web and why we're seeing new models being developed everywhere.

So now let's look at this thing between the networks, the studios, YouTube, and iTunes and examine what's really taking place — an attempt to create a new "spectrum" within which the creators of content can apply old rules. Each wishes to be the aggregator that people use to access "their" videos online and eventually through their TV sets. The problem is that neither aggregates all, and that defeats the intended purpose. The only way this will ever happen is if everybody works together, and that's contrary to traditional rules of engagement.

YouTube has created a spectrum for the prosumer movement. It's exploding, because anybody can be a studio, a newspaper, or a TV station today. You can create your own music and get recognized. The networks and the studios are terrified by this, and rather than find a way to play within this spectrum, each has chosen to try and create their own.

iTunes has created a spectrum for distribution of music and videos to Apple's assortment of devices. The networks and studios don't want to play here, because Apple controls pricing, and the arrangement destroys their ability to bundle crap with quality.

So what do the incumbents do, besides lobby the government for protection? They try multiple distribution outlets, which — from a brand extension perspective — is no doubt smart. In the case of Hulu.com, NBCU and News Corp are trying to create their own new form of spectrum, which would actually make a lot of sense if everybody decided to pool their resources. And I think this is what they originally envisioned, but the other players were a little too proud to get in on something that their competitors created. Of course, if the original vision included NBCU running things, then it was ill-conceived from the get-go.

These are difficult times for incumbents, to say the least, but extending their business models to the Web will only have limited success, because the basic structure of the beast is contrary to theirs. Even people within those businesses who "get" this, don't know what to do or are thwarted by inertia and structural barriers that block getting anything done.

I'm waiting (but not holding my breath) for an arrangement between all incumbents that allows them to move their competition between each other to a single platform on the Web, to operate as they wish within this specialized platform. Think of it as moving their existing spectrum to cyberspace and operating therein. If you want network television, for example, you go to the network television platform. If you want movies, you go to the movie section, and so forth. This could actually be done — and it would be useful for "consumers" — but it would require individual companies within these industries to work together, and that is very unlikely to happen.

For local media, the same thing could be done. If users wanted access to local news video, they would go to one place, where all local news video was available. This would create a form of spectrum within the whole, where individual players could duke it out just like they do in their own universe today. The problem, again, is that it would require separate companies to work together, and that's highly problematic. The number one station would tell the others to go to hell, because they think they can a) do just fine on their own and b) it would "cheapen" them by putting their work on the same stage as their competitors.

Would this station prefer their work to stand alone as a blip in the overall spectrum of the Web or be a part of a bigger blip, a piece of spectrum designed specifically to better enable users to find their work? And this same number one station is scratching its head, trying to figure out how it can attract a larger audience.

For the answer to this dilemma, let's go back downtown, to that piece of closed retail spectrum. As people moved to the suburbs, the retail world understood that it had to be where the people were. It could not expect the people to come to them.

And so the suburban shopping mall was created, and what is a mall but a group of competitors banded together for the convenience of shoppers? Would the number one department store refuse to anchor the mall, because its chief competitor was on the other end? Of course not!

But here's the rub: shopping malls weren't created by the department stores themselves. They were content to work from downtown locations as the suburban drift disrupted their world. Malls were built by outside developers, who could see what was really taking place. The same could be said for the communications world as regards the disruption of the Web.

Herpolsheimers, Wurzburg's, and Steketees are all out of business today. Had they taken a more proactive role — one that actually would have been viewed as cannibalizing their own business models — they would not only be in business, but they'd likely own the malls in which department stores are now only tenants.

This idea of competing against yourself is central to overcoming disruptive innovations. The history books are filled with stories of those who chose only to defend themselves against such forces, and when television broadcasters — the creators of the video communications niche — decide that they'd rather go down fighting than live to fight another day, their fate is already sealed.

The ghosts of my youth testify it is so.

LINKS, THE CURRENCY
OF THE MACHINE

March 19, 2007

L ong ago on some distant shore, our ancestors looked up at the night sky and felt two contrasting emotions. The awe and majesty of the heavens awakened a sense of insignificance and aloneness, the kind that comes when confronted with the magnitude of life itself. As these same eyes were opened to a powerful sense of oneness with all that majesty, the human quest for meaning was birthed.

Yet countless eons of mythology, religion and science have brought us no closer to unlocking the mystery, and the best we can do as the human race is to say, "To each his own."

It is with a degree of similar awe that we stand today considering the Machine that Kevin Kelly described in his seminal 2005 essay, "We Are The Web," a futuristic glimpse into what it is we're all building together with this thing called the World Wide Web. Dwarfing all efforts to create the ultimate science fiction "supercomputer," the Web is a living and growing mass of artificial intelligence, and we are amazed and just a little bit scared.

> In 10 years, the system will contain hundreds of millions of miles of fiber-optic neurons linking the billions of ant-smart chips embedded into manufactured products, buried in environmental sensors, staring out from satellite cameras, guiding cars, and saturating our world with enough complexity to begin to learn. We will live inside this thing. (1)

Kelly went on to give the Machine a kind of Tower of Babel twist, because we're all building this thing together. We are the Machine. We are the Web.

> When we post and then tag pictures on the community photo album Flickr, we are teaching the Machine to give names to images. The thickening links between caption and picture form a neural net that can learn. Think of the 100 billion times per day humans click on a Web page as a way of teaching the Machine what we think is important. Each time we forge a link between words, we teach it an idea. (2)

The word "link" is at the heart of all that is the Web, and it is vastly more important than any of us realizes.

The idea of links and linking is Web 101, and it's overlooked in its significance by traditional media companies, whose best and brightest generally think of links as only a way to move people around our sites or connect our content to interested parties. But links and linking are the real currency of the Web — with a value greater than cash — and one that might some day actually become a form of cash in a Web-based economy.

There already is a dollar value placed on links, and it's found in the seedy underbelly of the Search Engine Optimization world.

While the majority of industry practices are aboveboard, many companies clog the comment sections of blogs with false entries that create links for clients. Since search engine algorithms view links as a validation of influence, this actually raises the unscrupulous companies' clients in search engine rankings.

These same companies create sites known as "link farms" and build phony blogs known as "splogs" in order to drive client rankings up the search engine chain through links. While the search engines are aware of this and take measures to block these kinds of tactics, it is still a thriving business. That's real dollars attached to links.

Digg, the popular social-bookmarking site, is built entirely on links to stories that the users vote on to determine ranking in the community. Here not only do the links have value, they function as the content of the site and are manipulated by core users in an endless popularity contest to see who can control the home page. Links have tremendous value here, because a single home-page link can mean thousands of unique visitors in a very short time.

Another popular social-bookmarking site, Del.icio.us is a place where people store — you guessed it — links.

Links have value. They are the currency of the Web, and as the Machine gets smarter and is able to qualify and validate links, their value will increase. Like any other currency, they will be traded for goods and services. If you link to me, I should pay you for that, because it has real value to me. As media companies, we should think carefully about this.

Λ permanent link — or as least as permanent as the Web permits — has the highest value, for it keeps on giving.

Technorati, the blog search engine, uses permanent links, in part, to measure authority — a Website's ranking against others. Remember that links are considered a measure of influence, and this is an important metric in the Media 2.0 space.

For example, my blog (The Pomo Blog) is ranked at 14,498 of 71.6 million blogs that the company tracks. This isn't because I'm able to manipulate my way up the ladder; it's based on the links to my posts. As you can see at this writing, there are 463 links from 247 different blogs. The blogosphere itself determines the rankings based on its "acceptance" of the things I write about.

The only way to move up in ranking (if that's what's desired) is to write more posts, comment on other blogs, and generally behave like a grown-up. The Golden Rule is at work here, too, because the best way to get links is to give them. And all the while we're doing this, we're teaching Kevin Kelly's "Machine" to think.

Links from blogs are probably the most important reason for mainstream media companies to stay clear of pay walls in making their work available to the rest of the world. The *Wall Street Journal*, for example, is happy with the money from its corporate-paid subscription model, but the truth is the paper's stock as an influential voice in the culture can only go down. The Journal recognizes this and selects certain items that it offers to bloggers free daily in hopes of their links, but this is viewed by many as condescending and manipulative.

Technorati founder Dave Sifry regularly publishes data showing the most linked-to Websites. The following image (page 206) shows the *New York Times* is the top recipient of links and therefore the most influential information Website in the world. The gray lines represent media companies (including Google and Yahoo); the black lines represent blogs.

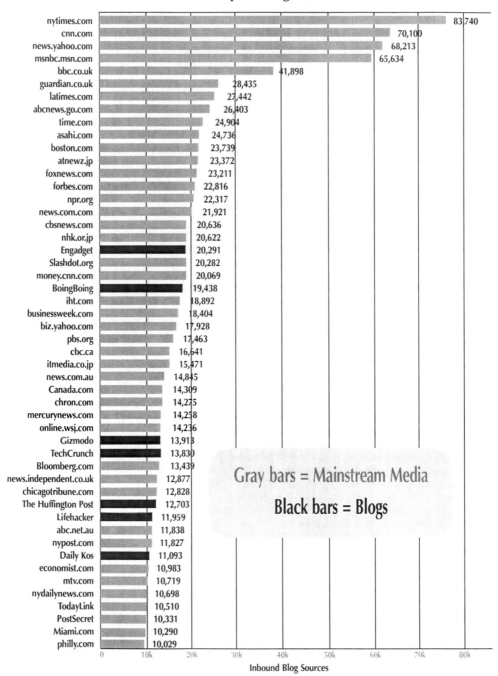

Q4 2006
Top 50 Blogs and MSM

Gray bars = Mainstream Media

Black bars = Blogs

Inbound Blog Sources

This will all be monetized one day. The Machine will make it easy.

Two years ago, when Sifry first published this graph, the *Times* was on top with 33,000 inbound sources. In just 18 months, that had expanded to what's shown (*opposite*): 83,740. This is an indication of not only growth in the online information space but also of the value of those links to the *Times* and its advertisers. That the paper puts its archives behind a pay wall kills many of those links, however, and sooner or later, they'll have to address the issue. The Machine has a long memory.

Another thing that's changed dramatically about this graph in two years is that the top 50 is almost entirely mainstream sources, whereas blogs made up about half in 2005. This is likely evidence of the awakening by these news organizations that's taken place since then, along with advances in the application of RSS and the distributed media culture.

The professional news industry is, of course, quite content to sit back and let others link to it. It's a traffic strategy. This despite the fact that many in the business criticize the linkers as parasites who build reputations and audience by linking to their work. This is an absurd and dangerous perspective, because there are millions more red lines in the long tail of the above chart than the blue lines that sit at the top.

The mainstream press views outbound linking as irrelevant — or worse, suicidal. The idea is to assemble crowds in one place rather than disperse them to the winds. Besides, the mere thought of actually linking to another person or organization is anathema to the concept of original reporting or scarcity of content, and the whole traditional press suffers as a result.

It suffers, because the news is bigger than that which any limited, single organization can get its arms around. It suffers, because its unwillingness to participate in the conversation that is news leaves it isolated, naïve and mere pawns of the status quo. It suffers, because without participation, the press will never discover the wonder or the tools of the Personal Media Revolution. And it suffers, because in the end, the Machine will calculate its value downward in the overall scheme of importance.

And given how search algorithms work, an outbound link from *The New York Times* would carry more weight than, say, *The Seattle Times* and thus be worth more Web currency.

Things are very different in the blogosphere, however, where bloggers lift each other by participating in each other's conversations and *the* conversation that is "news" via the Machine. If the traditional press could bring itself to function as the life of the party — the guy who brings the best stories, shares them with partygoers, and takes the time to listen to everybody else's stories — it could function in a valid role as "conversation starter" with all the benefits of the above.

That's because all of the tools that the blogosphere uses to form a gigantic handshake for the flow of information are there to serve the conversation, not the one-directional necessity of the mass-marketing business model. It's easy for us to see why we want everybody linking to us — and we should do whatever we can to make that as easy as possible — but the conversation will be served, because, as Kevin Kelly so brilliantly put it, "we" are the Machine.

The World Wide Web is a postmodern marvel of collaborative participation, and humankind stands once again at the shore of its own existence, a link away from everything.

> From this embryonic neural net was born a collaborative interface for our civilization, a sensing, cognitive device with power that exceeded any previous invention. The Machine provided a new way of thinking (perfect search, total recall) and a new mind for an old species. It was the Beginning. (3)

Links are the new currency. We should buy and sell wisely.

THE LOCAL WEB

January 22, 2007

In the early days of television, the networks needed affiliates in
local communities in order to establish scale for their programs
and their advertisers. Back then, the networks paid handsomely
for this, so the owners of local stations got a huge chunk of their
revenue from outside the market. This revenue has slowly disappeared, so the evolution of local television has been, in a very real
sense, the evolution of local advertising.

One of my fondest memories is of the day when the production staff
at WTMJ-TV in Milwaukee played a prank on legendary weath-
erman Bill Carlson for one of his live coffee commercials in the
early 1970s. They glued the cup to the saucer, so that Bill had to
lift the whole thing to take his customary live "sip." It was hilarious, but Bill covered it like the pro that he was. These types of
ads "evolved" out of local television as the business matured. Oh,
for the days of being a kid.

In today's world, the network model of television's infancy is broken in many ways. What message does the lack of network compensation send if not that the "networks" really don't need the
affiliates anymore? Wired solutions have rendered over-the-air signals almost irrelevant. Satellite and cable companies would love
programming feeds directly from the networks, and direct-to-consumer programming options via the Internet make the future even
murkier for local television.

But if local TV is about local advertising, to where will local advertisers turn in a world of diminishing relevance for broadcasting? This is a question of profound implications, but it's one that ought to give all local media companies hope for the future, for the real growth in Internet advertising over the next decade will be at the local level. And the evolution of local media on the Web will, once again, be about the evolution of local advertising.

Key to the development of a local online ad market is the identification of the local Web, and this offers a remarkable opportunity for those willing to explore this territory today. In the not-too-distant future, everyone will have access to the local Web, but this access is unavailable today, because the database hasn't been created. It exists in bits and pieces, but no technology can replace the human research necessary to build the initial database. This is a task that will pay huge dividends to the one who creates it, market-by-market, and there's no reason this can't be done by a local media company.

As the Internet matures, many of the applications and tools that helped make our world seem smaller will increasingly make our local communities seem bigger. This will occur in stages and over time, but it will happen, because the URL and IRL worlds can only meet where people live, and that means at the local level.

The enormity of the Web has been at the core of nearly every advertiser-supported business plan since the beginning, but, thanks to social networking sites like mySpace and Facebook, the younger generation of Internet users is building their experience from the community that exists around them in real life. You can say what you want about how the Web connects people from far and wide, but to today's youth, it's an efficient and fun way to stay in touch with their real life friends.

This is a new phenomenon, and one that we would do well to watch. Like cell phones, social networking sites allow people to share news and information about each other with each other, and it's not all about friendships that are Web-only. This means the Web is increasingly becoming a local animal, and this bodes well for local retailers and others who are interested doing commerce with their neighbors.

The Internet pure plays all recognize this, and there is a race underway to see who can seize local territory first.

It's no secret that local ad dollars was the prize that drove Google as it leveled the playing field by giving small advertisers access to search results just like everybody else.

The quest for local dollars was at the core of Yahoo!'s thinking when it announced an alliance with newspaper groups to merge online jobs classifieds and build content partnerships. In a *Newspapers & Technology* sidebar story about the arrangement, are these key statements:

> "Industry analysts agree with us that the local advertising opportunity is tremendous," said Hilary Schneider, senior vice president of Yahoo Marketplace, about the site's alliance with eight major newspaper publishers.
>
> The new partnership will make a big difference in the way companies advertise and the way they interact with consumers, she added.
>
> "We believe the local segment is largely untapped and provides significant opportunities to expand audience engagement and grow local advertising." (1)

Already, the world of Internet advertising is showing signs of a shift to this "untapped" segment, and this is both good news and bad news for local media sites. It's good, because money is finally beginning to open up to support local Websites. Agencies and advertisers at the local level are experiencing the awakening that took place at the national level during the past decade, and this is promising for local media companies and other entrepreneurs. It's bad news, because, as the education process for local advertisers shines a spotlight on Web analytics, a dirty little secret about advertising on local sites is being illuminated: much of the traffic on local media sites comes from outside the market.

212

This the natural fruit of networked media sites driven by third-party providers, whose business model is the creation of scale to deliver ad impressions to national advertisers and special section sponsors who don't care where the eyeballs come from. Deals these companies have made with the major portals brought the news from local communities to the rest of the world, and that meant significant traffic for local sites. A big story in, for example, St. Louis will flood the local media sites with eyeballs from outside the market. In Denver, 70% of one station's traffic came from outside the market during a month when a big story originated in the market.

This is not what local advertisers are seeking.

Local advertisers want to reach local consumers, and historically, this hasn't been easy online. The Web offers so many options and so much flexibility that the numbers of users at the local market level just haven't been there to make an advertiser-driven business work. Technology is changing this, however, because the Web — and especially in the Media 2.0 world — is much more about direct marketing than it is mass marketing. If advertisers know where local users have been, they can reach them anywhere they might go.

Smart local media companies will invest resources in this area, because this is where the real growth will be downstream.

In order to achieve scale, Internet start-ups have historically had to take a global view of the Web. Investors have always wanted to make money off their investments, and in the early days of the Web, that required a big, big picture. Whether the revenue model was advertising or B2C, the ability to put lots of eyeballs in one place — or in many joined places — was a necessary component of success, and that meant an application that served with broadest possible reach.

As a result, we've come to know Amazon.com as a global bookstore, Google as a global search and advertising engine, mySpace as a global community and Yahoo! as a global portal to everything. In many ways, we've been able to overcome the prisons of time and space to interact and do commerce, but this is an artificial reality — a romantic, wormhole-esque illusion that feeds human nature yet sucks the life out of it at the same time. Don't get me wrong. The global village aspect of the Web is certainly one of its charms and one that will have permanent influences on global politics and economics, and it's been pretty cool to order something from Japan or interact with my family in the Middle East.

But most of my shopping still takes place at the mall or the supermarket, and the need to hug my loved ones doesn't change just because I can see them via a Web camera.

Ask anyone in Atlanta who's had an online "relationship" with someone in Los Angeles, and you'll get the same story: it was good for awhile, but he wouldn't move — or she wouldn't move — and eventually distance killed it. Or worse yet, somebody did relocate only to discover that Dr. Jekyll was really Mr. Hyde.

Ask anyone who's had a bad experience with a product that didn't arrive on time, never arrived, arrived damaged or wasn't at all what it looked like on the site, and you'll hear complaints reminiscent of the old Sears Roebuck catalogue days. There's a reason why local grocery-shopping sites didn't work back in the bubble days.

But this illusion of oneness has sustained early efforts to do business, and there are a lot of success stories to that end. Nevertheless, as the Web matures, the emphasis must shift to local, because that's where the people live.

More and more people are shopping online and feeling comfortable in so doing. According to comScore Media Metrics, "overall non-travel (retail) e-commerce spending increased 26 percent this holiday season versus 2005 to a record-setting $24.6 billion." But doing commerce on the Web — at least in its current iteration — will always be just a small drop in the gargantuan bucket of overall commerce, and that's why local advertising is so important.

The opportunity for online local advertising is there, but before it can find its rightful place in the local community, the local Web community must be defined, identified and nurtured.

Local agencies and advertisers also need to go to school on Web advertising, because their ignorance stands as a structural barrier to growth of the local online ad market. In Nashville, the WKRN-TV sales department didn't wait for that to happen. They took it upon themselves to become *the* knowledgeable source in the community, and that has paid significant dividends. The advertising community there recognizes their expertise, and that has meant the lion's share (in some cases *all*) of local buys. This, too, is an opportunity for local media companies everywhere.

Some will argue that the illusion of anonymity is one of the real attractions of the Web, and that this illusion is harder to maintain at the local level. But this reveals a mistaken assumption about the local Web, one that is only revealed by spending time on sites frequented by local people as groups. The MySpace generation is very much about gathering online with their identities intact (although in most cases — two-thirds, according to Pew — private to outsiders), and this is something that confounds the generation of their parents, whose fear tends to brush aside the more positive attributes of the commons that is shared by their kids. We must always remember the words of the guy who essentially invented the Web, Tim Berners-Lee:

> *The Web is more a social creation than a technical one.*

The leap from anonymous socializing to named socializing is also an important element of local blogging communities. Sooner or later, these groups will start having meet-ups or other social gatherings, because that's what people with shared interests do. I've been to many blogger meet-ups, and the hugs are very real.

So anonymity isn't nearly the draw for the local Web as it is for the global Web, and this is just one of the differences between the two.

This is why the exciting new fields of word-of-mouth, viral and pull advertising are where to place your bets for the future. Rupert Murdoch is certainly learning this in the wake of his purchase of MySpace, and so far, they've not made any huge mistakes in trying to monetize the site. He knows that it is the permission of the users that determines the value of any cyber property, and especially where identities are attached to the zipcodes in the database.

Of all of the wonderment that is communications these days, nothing inspires me like the potential of the local Web. This is why my work with local media companies emphasizes the achievement of local scale through genuine service and not just the practice of mathematical formulas that reduce the Web to page views and stickiness.

The local Web is where the Web itself will find its real value propositions, and that's enough to make a guy want to stick around for awhile.

THE AMMUNITION BUSINESS

February 2, 2006

Many years ago, I saw a 30-minute drama about a slick televangelist who had an encounter with an angel in his dressing room. On the air, he railed against "the homosexuals" and "the abortionists," but the angel demanded that he "feed my sheep."

"But that's not my ministry," he replied.

To make a long story short, the man was profoundly moved by the angel and went on the air intending to tell the world about his encounter and the new call to care for the poor and afflicted. Once the camera was on, however, he reverted to his old self. (1)

Old habits and belief systems die hard, especially when there's profit to be made, and it's especially noticeable when the chips are down.

Gordon Borrell, the local online sales research guru, has a neat slide in his dog-and-pony show that speaks to the personal media revolution in a way that's both humorous and revealing. "The deer now have guns," the slide displays. We (the media) are in the business of hunting prey (the audience), and we need to be aware that our prey is now fully armed to do the same thing. It doesn't necessarily mean they're after us, but by remixing, rebundling or making their own media, they're able to attract some of the same eyeballs that we used to call our own. We've lost our exclusivity for content creation and distribution in the marketplace, and that's trouble for an institution that's used to having it all to itself. But all is not lost.

"So what do you do when the deer have guns," Gordon asks? "You get into the ammunition business."(2)

Stop right here and think about that statement. It's a profound truth and one that mainstream media companies are reluctant to embrace, because, well, "It's not my ministry." Moreover, few media executives really understand what it means.

It's not going to be enough in the years ahead to be a pure content provider, regardless of the distribution methods available, because market fragmentation isn't going to slow down. Moreover, in a fragmenting marketplace, there is no mass market anymore, so even the arena in which we've played our games all these years has been torn down.

Jeff Jarvis points this out in a recent blog post called, "The dinosaurs whine." It's about commentaries from three old-school journalists.

> They whined about the passing of what they thought was their captive mass audience. But they don't understand that the audience was never mass and never captive, and given a chance at choice, we took it. That is the natural order of media. They blame network executives and even the government for the decline of what they define as quality, important news. But the truth is that the public is going elsewhere to get news and these demititans' (little titans) definition of news did not always serve that public. (3)

Not only are we going elsewhere, but we're also making our own media. In a world where everybody is a content provider (the deer), the information needs of the local audience changes, because there's so much more stuff available to absorb now. The paradigm is reversed; the "mass" has shifted from demand to supply.

So how does a single media entity meet information needs in such an exploding scenario? The truth is it doesn't, but that's hard to admit. Some try to make the case that their information is somehow better or more important than what they see as the riffraff of the Web, but that foolish argument makes the dangerous and incorrect assumption that the audience needs to trust in that which has been proven untrustworthy. The reality is that they can make their own filtering systems now, bypassing the gates that professional media have "kept" all these years.

This is the ammunition business to which Borrell refers. If our content alone isn't sufficient to support our business needs and our filtering mechanisms aren't enough to ensure audience, then we need to be thinking about ways in which we can help users of all media in our communities do their own filtering. This is where the technology industry is moving, and if we're smart, we'll move with them.

It begins with paying close attention to RSS and how it can be used to effortlessly move an infinite assortment of special niche content from place to place and ultimately to users. What users need is help in winnowing the growing fire hose blast of disparate bits into forms they can assimilate and understand. This is one method of getting into the ammunition business, as Borrell notes. And who's in a better position to provide this kind of application than media companies?

The thing a lot of my contemporaries don't understand is that RSS is more than just a way to communicate news. Here are just a few samples of non-news RSS feeds that help people stay informed. This list was culled from the basement.org Website. (4)

- Airfare deals between cities you select
- Calendar of events
- Motivational quotes of the day
- Favorite comics
- Deals and more Deals
- TV Listings

As you can see, even the little syndicated niche content that, say, newspapers used to provide as part of their bundle is now available for user-filtering via RSS.

Another list to peruse is one provided by Michael Arrington of TechCrunch (5), an informative site that examines new companies and their role in the Web 2.0 scheme. This list is of companies created to offer interactive RSS aggregators that work in a relatively new programming language called Ajax.

- Eskobo
- favoor
- Google
- Goowy (Flash, not Ajax)
- HomePortals
- Microsoft Live
- Netvibes
- Pageflakes
- Protopage
- Wrickr
- Zoozio

Click on any of these, and you'll get an idea of where the growth is in the Web 2.0 world. This is where media companies need to be shifting resources, for our traditional business model hides the possibility of making money in an unbundled world. It's not just the content anymore; the money is in providing the application within which a variety of content is served.

Many of the new applications coming down the pike offer the ability for users to upload their own videos, and this is another space where local television stations need to be involved.

All of these things are "ammunition" that feed the disruptive innovation of Media 2.0. If they seem contrary to the core competency of local media, that's a good thing. What do you do when the deer have guns? Get into the ammunition business.

And by all means, get there first.

Knowledge of the local market is what separates broadcasters from all the outside companies already in the game, and that is a significant competitive advantage.

But moving into the new world isn't just another adventure in top-down media. The rules are very different, because the user — not the media company — is in charge, and that's the hardest thing for traditional media to understand or accept. This is producing some foolishness in the current unbundled mania with iTunes downloads of television programs. While you can purchase an episode of Lost for $1.99, you can only rent — for 24 hours — an episode of CSI or Survivor from the CBS Website for the same price. People will reject this idea, of course, but that won't stop other old media giants from trying to hang onto the power to play by the old rules.

This conflict is also being played out with Internet companies. Amazon, the daddy of the online book, CD and DVD industry is struggling with how to monetize digital downloads of video in a world where they — and the movie studios — make much more money by selling DVDs. Amazon is stuck in the middle, and as Rafat Ali of PaidContent.org reported recently, they're trying to offer a best-of-both-worlds service.

> *Variety* reports that the service might launch by end of April, and will have movies from indie studios, and at least two major studios.
>
> But the service might have some offline-DVD variant to it: one possible scenario is that an Amazon customer could stream a digital copy of a film for a fee and apply that charge as a credit toward the eventual purchase of the DVD. Basically, try-before-you-buy...
>
> Another plan is for a customer to buy a DVD; while waiting for it to arrive, he could stream the content over his computer.
>
> Bottomline: doing everything not to erode into the DVD revenues...as the story mentions: "When you go to a product page on the site, it will say all the variations about how you'd purchase that video — stream, buy or maybe a combination (of options)."

> I'm not sure the best-of-both-worlds approach will work in the medium to long term. (6)

This approach won't work long term, because customers will ultimately push all media companies into the unbundled, Media 2.0 world. Look at what's happened to music.

When former FCC Chairman Michael Powell made his important statement, "Application separation is the most important paradigm shift in the history of communications, and it will change things forever," (7) he was referring to the idea that what is being communicated (the content) no longer needs to be tied to a delivery mechanism (a television transmission, for example). But the reality is that the disconnect runs far deeper than that, and in a world where people can now manipulate their own unbundled, "separated" content, it behooves us all to invest in helping them do that.

"It's not my ministry" is a weak rationalization for keeping one's head in the sand.

THE WEB'S PARADOX OF POWER

April 6, 2005

L ong ago, I worked for a guy who studied power and influence in various communities around the U.S. and beyond. Where do you think he began his research when walking into a metropolitan area cold? How does one begin looking for the seats of power? He started with the executive director of the local United Way. The thesis is that the aristocracy of any community is directly tied to the community chest. "Noblesse oblige," the French used to say — nobility obligates. While it's easy to argue that enlightened self-interest is at work in this process, the reality is it's demonstrative of the concept of influence through giving.

Mystics and other spiritual teachers throughout the centuries — regardless of their cloth — have taught the same thing in many different ways. If you want to be tapped into the source of life, you must first align the outbound connection through serving the rest of humankind. So it is that through giving, we receive.

This understanding forms the paradox of power that so perplexes hierarchical Modernist thinkers, especially as it relates to the Internet.

In real life (IRL), there are formulas for getting to the top in any endeavor. If a banking company, for example, wants to be the top bank in the country, they can buy up enough other banks to make it to the top. Size is power, so the more the merrier. That position gives them clout.

Wal-Mart is another example. They're the top retailer, and that's based on their size. They're so big that they can actually influence (manipulate) prices.

In local television, power is determined by ratings. The more people that watch, the higher the advertising rates; the higher the ad rates, the more revenue; the more revenue, the more can be spent on projects and programs; and that translates to influence in the community. It's a circle.

Sometimes, IRL power is determined by one's connections, rather than one's size, although it's amazing how size influences connections. Nevertheless, IRL often assigns influence based just on one's friends. Associations with organizations produce this kind of potential influence, and so does your Alma Mater.

We've grown up in a mass marketing culture, where the one at the top disperses knowledge, information or whatever to the masses at his, her or its discretion. Power is determined by how many are buying what's being sold. This is true in economics; it's true in politics; and it's true in communications. We understand this world, and we've been trying to transfer it to the Web since we've known of its existence. It won't work, because power here is dispersed along the bottom.

In the pure URL world, there is no top or bottom. A URL is just a URL. Nobody's forced to do anything, because the usual forms of power don't work in a place that isn't governed by the two Cs of the IRL world, command and control. You can't buy your way to the top. You can't associate your way to the top. You can't force your model, killer application, or your system to the top.

And even where the rules of reach and frequency seem to apply, there's something else going on under the surface. It's the Web's paradox of power.

Technorati, the blog search engine, knows more about the blogosphere than anybody else, and they apply this paradox of power in determining rankings for blogs and information Websites. The key measurement for Technorati is inbound links. The assumption is simple: if you are consistently talking about things that are of interest to others, they (the others) will link to you. The more people do that, the greater your influence.

Take a look at this graph (*opposite*) prepared by Technorati founder, Dave Sifry. It ranks inbound links to mainstream media (MSM) and bloggers. The gray bars represent mainstream online news outlets. The black lines equal blogs. At first glance, the MSM is more influential, but some blogs are also well-placed. Remember, though, that this graph represents inbound links, not reach or frequency.

Here's where the paradox comes in. One doesn't find influence in the URL world without providing a service to others, for it is the linkers (the bottom) who provide the influence, not those receiving the links. Size doesn't matter. Only inbound links. In Sifry's graph, the *New York Times* online is the most influential. What makes them influential? The bloggers and others who are creating the links. This is not a measure of readership or revenue. It's a measure of other people thinking enough of what's being produced (one way or the other) to create a link to it.

The *New York Times* gives material freely to the bloggers, and the bloggers reward them with influence. This is why the people who run *The Times* should think very carefully before charging fees or otherwise locking up their content. This is why logical (Modernist) attempts to force demand by restricting access are playing a dangerous game with their online futures. And this is why online media companies need to make their archives freely available as well. Free is the operative word here. Influence is the currency.

Free online access to content is also good business, because money follows influence, even online.

MSM vs. Blogs — 3/05

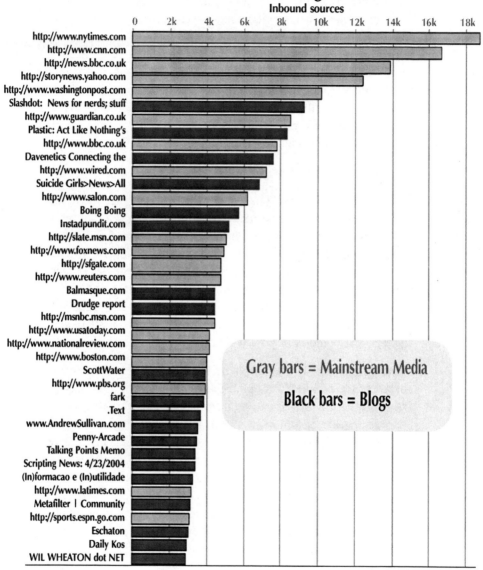

Inbound sources

Gray bars = Mainstream Media

Black bars = Blogs

In Greensboro, North Carolina, the *Greensboro News & Record* is currently involved in an effort to turn their media company into the public square in the community. It's a natural place for a newspaper to go. They want to be *the* "record" in the Greater Greensboro area, so they've launched a fascinating effort to embrace the local blogosphere and make them a part of the discussion that is news. Editor John Robinson may not know where the money's coming from in all of this, but he's betting it'll be there downstream. The paper is giving to the bloggers, and they are returning it with links and influence.

This is the paradox of power in the URL world.

Understanding this type of influence also provides insight into the overall workings of the new media world versus the world of mass marketing. That's because this influence originates naturally from what mass marketing views as the bottom, and it happens without any artificial prodding. Mass marketers employ strategies to feed their twin gods, reach and frequency, and those strategies all originate from the top. The influence of the Web can't be so managed. Different strategies are required, but it all begins with understanding the paradox of power.

There is a symbiotic relationship between the blogs and the mainstream press, and the Technorati graph illustrates it quite nicely. It's why the former will never replace the latter, and why the media business models of tomorrow will be based in strategies that will seem entirely opposed to our instincts and training. This is why MBAs often look at us as if we've completely lost touch with reality when talking about life in this world. The laws of economics aren't changing, but our ability to manage them most certainly is and will. Put another way, if hype and promotion are anathema to contemporary media consumers (and they are), then we need to be exploring a paradigm that is entirely the opposite.

Reach and frequency may, in fact, be the end, but the means to that simply has to change. Because if URL influence flows from the bottom up, as the Technorati stats reveal, then establishing an aggregated "mass audience" is actually out of our hands. In fact, the more we try to manage it, the further away it gets.

Moreover, it necessarily follows that this transition will take place at the local level, not at the networks, cable news channels or other national news operations. The "bottom" begins in our homes and offices and expands outward to our neighborhoods, communities, regions, states, etc. This is why we should be paying close attention to citizens media experiments in communities like Greensboro, North Carolina and Bluffton, South Carolina, where media companies are exploring these uncharted waters.

The news media has for too long been preoccupied with its own status and perceived importance. Life on a pedestal, however, produces the unintended consequence of separation from the masses. It's nice and neat and clean up there, but life is lived in a different place, and the view from up there is distorted anyway. Is it any wonder we're deemed irrelevant by many these days and that the growth of citizens media is so explosive?

We need to reinvent ourselves, and we need to do it in a hurry. It all begins at the bottom-most point of our outdated, worse than useless (worse because we still believe in it) hierarchy. If we can bring ourselves to help and support this media revolution, we'll wake up one day and find that we've actually helped ourselves too — and in ways we can't even begin to imagine today.

CONVENTION VERSUS THE INTERNET

January 22, 2005

The only thing worse than a square peg in a round hole is a square peg trying to get into a round hole.

Long ago, in one of my news director jobs, a young man showed up at the small market station and asked to speak with me. In the lobby, I was greeted by a fellow — tape in hand — who was just about the strangest looking job candidate I'd ever encountered. He was what Ichabod Crane would've seen when looking in the mirror — a neck four sizes too small for his collar, hooked nose, ears perpendicular to his head, and a mangled wad of hair on top.

"I've been traveling the country for the past year," he said, "talking to small market news directors about getting that first on-air reporting job out of college."

I invited him into my office, looked over his resume and tape, and told him the facts of life about working in a business that demands cosmetic perfection. He was stunned. All the way through school and through a yearlong interview process, no one had suggested that he had a face for radio.

He was a square peg trying to get into a round hole.

So it is in the war between convention and the Internet, and there is indeed a war underway. While the conflict is everywhere, the inability to see the real battle lines has created a significant structural barrier as old media companies struggle with infiltrating the new. Convention sees the surface, but the war is underneath. Square peg, meet round hole.

The debate between the mainstream media and the blogosphere is one highly visible example.

Convention believes that what has been will always be, while the Internet shoots from the hip in a blaze of entrepreneurial gunfire. Like a patient father, convention smiles at the imagination of these children, but when the pushing and shoving begins, it steps in with its infinite wisdom and a resounding, "Enough!" In doing so online, however, convention runs the square peg/round hole risk, because the structure here cannot and will not run from the top-down, regardless of who wants to be the father. The rules of convention can backfire badly, and this is precisely what's happening in the unseen nooks and crannies of New Media.

The guardians of convention are the lawyers of the land. Their lifeblood is codified rules that can be manipulated from the top, and whenever circumstances impose barriers to this, new rules are simply created to continue convention. The problem with convention's rules is that they don't apply online, because there is no control mechanism.

When CBS released its Memogate report, they did a smart thing. Along with the story of network action in the wake of the report, CBSNews.com also provided its users access to the entire 234-page report. This was presented in Adobe PDF format, a popular software for transmitting documents for printing. Bloggers and other Internet communicators dislike PDF, because the text in the format isn't easily copied for reproduction in other forms of media, especially those online. Nevertheless, it can be done, but there were still complaints from the blogosphere about the network choice of PDF. These were overshadowed, however, by the fact that CBS had released the entire report.

Bring in the lawyers. Two days later, the PDF file was replaced by one with Digital Rights Management restrictions enabled, which completely prevented copying any of the text electronically. This was a bad move by CBS. It infuriated the blogosphere and further alienated the same people who broke the original story that caused the network so much embarrassment in the first place. The network's lawyers responded that they did it to prevent anybody from making and distributing a bogus copy (or parody) of the document. This was an act of convention trying to wiggle its way into the round hole of the Internet.

From an Internet perspective — where the law of attraction rules — the action of the lawyers was almost laughable, but the CBS team of attorneys viewed it as a logical and rational response, because their world is top-down, command and control. Like other Modernist institutions, CBS is addicted to being right, and feeding their addiction has blinded them to what's really taking place in the world around them.

The Achilles' Heel of convention is its insistence that what has been will always be. This is what led *New York Times* columnist Bill Safire to suggest that bloggers are just waiting to become a part of the mainstream, which is where the money is found.

> Blogs will compete with op-ed columns for "views you can use," and the best will morph out of the pajama game to deliver serious analysis and fresh information, someday prospering with ads and subscriptions. The prospect of profit will bring bloggers in from the meanstream to the mainstream center of comment and local news coverage. (1)

The "prospect of profit" can never be a value proposition for the blog osphere, because it would be another square peg looking to get into a round hole. The currency of the blogosphere is passionate involvement and the sense of closure that comes with participation. Citizen journalism's great power is its voluntary involvement in the things that matter to its various denizens. Nothing kills passion like money, and while there certainly may be bloggers who make lots of money, they will then have to morph into the rules of convention and, therefore, lose the street creds earned within the very community in which they used to dwell. This is inevitable, and those who propose a prospering blogging community with ads and subscriptions are fooling themselves.

Convention demands control while the blogosphere rejects it. The disruptive innovations that permit an individual to be his or her own publisher — whether text or video — aren't what's fueling the citizen journalism revolution. It's the distribution system, one that has no top or bottom, and wherein audience is determined by the readers/viewers, not by the publisher or network. Moreover, the relationship between blog writer and blog reader is far different than that of editorial writer and newspaper consumer. Why? Because the readers of blogs aren't just reading. They're also judging and thinking and writing and linking. A viable blog doesn't broadcast. It a part of a conversation, and conversation is, well, free.

There's an important discussion underway about whether the Internet is a medium or a place. Convention understands and welcomes the former, but the latter is the actual reality. Cyberspace is still space, and the immutable laws are a little different here. A medium moves content from one place to another, usually outward. A space is where people gather and share the experience. Conversations are two-way in a space. A medium moves messages in one direction. This adds to the square peg/round hole problem.

Despite the arguments of those within the institution of the fourth estate, the role of the so-called "professional" press is the manufacture of consent. This was the dream of its founder, Walter Lippmann, who introduced the idea of an educated and elite class to control the uneducated masses 100 years ago. However, the role of the blogosphere is the deconstruction of that consent, with the resultant hope of establishing a more universal consent at street level. Square peg, meet round hole.

Convention's most dangerous trap is to seduce that which is new. Like the Borg of Star Trek, it boldly proclaims that resistance is futile and that assimilation is the only way. Convention must assimilate or be destroyed and replaced by something else. As Picasso said, "Every act of creation is first of all an act of destruction." That which is being destroyed — the fatted calf that went before —

doesn't want to let go, but that's exactly what's happening in this brave, new world of ours. This is why people like Mr. Safire, and those who rest comfortably within convention, can see only what has been.

PR guru and blogger, Steve Rubel, wrote of the "rock star" status of some bloggers.

> With interest in blogs rising, some bloggers are rapidly becoming celebrities. They're popping up in the press, attracting flocks of followers and, in some cases, even a roster of advertisers. And why not? They deserve it. After all, these "A-listers" can easily sway the opinions of thousands. (2)

This is convention trying to seduce a threat. Steve encourages companies to invest in endorsement deals and the like with bloggers, because it's smart business. Square peg, meet round hole.

In an article called "Blogger Backlash," *New York Press* writer Russ Smith notes the conflict between the mainstream press and bloggers:

> "The bloggers—"citizen journalists," pajama pundits, whatever you want to call them—are reaching millions of Americans, and while many will be co-opted by traditional media companies, it's a kick in the pants and skirts of the Beltway cocktail party crowd, whose precious words and broadcasts don't matter as much anymore." (3)

Note the assumption that bloggers will (of course) be "co-opted by traditional media companies." Assimilation. Resistance is futile.

George Simpson wrote for MediaDailyNews that blogging is a hobby that won't pay the rent, so Rubel's idea of payola to grab extra income is appealing. Simpson sees what's really happening.

> One of the things that make blogs appealing is that they have no rules. But no rules mean that they will never escape the shadow of doubt. (Not that having rules stopped payola in any other industry.) So let's not overreact to bloggers and understand that they are subject to the same corruption that infects every other medium. With one tiny exception: they are accountable to no one. (4)

In addressing media companies who are experimenting with citizen journalists, Poynter's Steve Outing writes that the idea of identifying your best citizen journalists and paying them as they continue contributing isn't a bad one. "But perhaps a better idea is to pay frequent contributors with goodies like t-shirts, caps, and coffee mugs — all emblazoned with the brand name of the Website, of course." This is smart, because it doesn't force the assimilation issue. It simply recognizes the contribution of everyday citizens and differentiates them from professional journalists. Once they get paid, they've been assimilated.

When discussing the Internet and the blogosphere with media people who are uninformed, the first question that's usually asked is, "Where's the money?" It's an understandable question, because we're so indoctrinated in the laws of mass marketing that nothing else is real or valuable. The top wants to be shown how the bottom will support its position. But this is the heart of the misunderstanding about the Internet in general and the blogosphere in particular. Certainly, there's money to be made online, but if we approach it only from convention, our minds will be closed to the infinite possibilities it offers.

Broadcasting needs to return to its roots in order to have a successful future, and I'm not talking about the business basics. In its infancy, the industry was driven by an entrepreneurial spirit that brought us innovation after innovation and built a model that lasted for 50 years. But the business rules and concepts that carried the industry are exactly what's killing it today, and the only way out of that is to get back to that entrepreneurial spirit. Invite the right-brainers around you; get out the whiteboards and zero base your company.

I often think of that young man who came to see me so long ago, and I wonder what happened to him. He's no doubt found a square hole for his gifts and skills, because life has a way of making that happen. So it is with all of us.

OVERCOMING FORMULA ADDICTION

November 15, 2004

You can find him in every engineering shop, a strange fellow tucked away in some corner who just doesn't seem to click with everybody else. His creativity begins "out there," where different drum beats beat. The story is told at a large hi-tech company in the South of a power problem with a new device that had stumped the best minds in the building. They reluctantly handed the widget to the guy with funny hair, who immediately retired to his corner of the shop. He didn't sleep for three days and emerged smiling with the problem solved.

What's most intriguing about this story is that he had found a way to bypass three-fourths of the processing steps that the engineers had deemed necessary to make the widget work, and it was this revelation that led to the solution. Impossible, they said with shaking heads. Impossible. The engineers were blocked by their own formulas.

As we look around us, there is without question a revolution underway in the information, media and entertainment worlds today. The revolution is a creative revolution — a revolt against the formulas that Modernist business logic demands — and when this tidal wave has swept over all, those still clinging to their formulas will find that these anchors have done nothing except take them to the bottom of the sea. This is especially true for the business of broadcasting and the people who work therein.

Despite all the wonderful inventions that logic has given us, the truth is logic and creativity cannot exist in the same space, for they are opposites. Where logic has dominion, creativity can only work within already defined parameters, and that is logic's downfall. For while life itself is often logical and ordered, chaos has equal footing, and attempts to manage life will always fail. The basic problem with any formula is that parts of it are based on as- sumptions from previously-stated axioms. This locks any formula to the past despite tangible evidence from the guy with the funny hair.

What is it about formulas that make them so seductive, even in what should be a creative environment? While there is a sense of safety that comes with something known, the truth is that we're all searching for what follows the equals sign. Two plus two is the problem. Four is the answer, and it is answers we seek. So hope is the real attraction — the source of the addiction — a hope that success and happiness lie just beyond the equals sign.

All of the institutions of the West promote this hope.

- Politics and government = laws and security
- Business = wages and products
- Religion = comfort and strength
- Education = knowledge and careers
- Media = information and entertainment
- Medicine = health and well-being
- Finance = resources and wealth

With addiction comes dependence — and that's just fine with the institutions — but ultimately, the dependence fails and the addict crashes and burns. And, like any other addiction, this one offers only the illusion of betterment. All around we see the failures of Modernist institutionalism. The blue smoke and mirrors are being revealed for what they really are — the false promise of hope beyond the equals sign.

Within each institution exist the formulas of its validity, a series of rules that it follows — primarily to assure its own future. Each serving its own best interests, the promises to the society as a whole take a back seat, and people aren't very happy about it. For the formulas are there to direct the masses in an endless cycle of promise and failure.

And so people are taking matters into their own hands, and technology is making it happen.

Broadcasters are stuck in their formula: *License + tower + mass audience = money*. This is a tried and true formula, but let's look at how it's under assault.

The license grants a station exclusive use of prescribed analog bandwidth for broadcasting a television signal. The government wants that bandwidth for other purposes, so the FCC is moving broadcasters to digital bandwidth and requiring a digital signal. This has already happened in several countries, but by moving the mandate for digital to 2009 in this country, the FCC is helping broadcasters cling to their old formula and thereby assisting in the death of broadcasting altogether. In another five years, digital communications will have advanced to the point where broadcasting a single signal will be irrelevant. WiFi, WiMax and yet to be created technologies all undercut the value of that one-to-many license. Broadcasting itself needs to be redefined for the license to retain its value.

The tower is an expensive tool that turns the license into a television signal. Usually found on the highest ground around, these things reach into the heavens to rain down their signals on the households the license allows them to serve. Two-thirds of U.S. households, however, now have cable to their homes, and the value of the license has been transferred to cable and satellite providers. This begs the question; do you really need a tower to be a broadcaster anymore?

The biggest chink in the armor of broadcasting's formula is the concept of mass marketing. The real value of beaming that signal over the community occurs when multiple households (many multiple households) tune in to watch something at the same time. When this happens, broadcasters can send commercial messages to those homes and get paid for the limited airtime. But mass marketing is going the way of the Wooly Mammoth, because technology is bringing to the surface the truth that there is no demand for unwanted messages. Fragmentation alone isn't the problem. Human nature is, and broadcasting — the penultimate mass marketing tool — needs to find another core competency.

If the three elements to the left of the equals sign are disintegrating, the conclusion of the formula must be as well. Yet broadcasters cling to the false promise of hope that their addiction demands.

Another example is a current discussion about Website design. At AD:TECH in New York, executives spoke of a new paradigm that Web publishers must acknowledge — the growing irrelevance of the home page. Washingtonpost.com CEO & Publisher Caroline Little noted that coming in through the home page is an old model and coming in sideways is the new method of arrival for most users. The panel agreed that every page is a home page. RSS and search (Google) enable users to bypass all the unwanted messages of the portal and go directly to what they're seeking. This is a terribly significant shift and one that publishers simply *must* accept, because it impacts design of the entire Website.

And yet, the highly-esteemed research firm, Jupiter Research, came out with a recent report giving publishers hints for fighting this. Here is Jupiter's marketing on the report.

> Heightened by the industry's focus on search, the Internet has come to be seen as an on-demand, "pull"-oriented, consumer-driven medium. But content presentation tactics actually work in driving user behavior—you can herd the sheep. (1)

Jupiter is playing to the formula addiction of the status quo, because there's a dollar sign attached to it. In so doing, they have to ignore the reality that people are sick and tired of being herded like sheep. This is the denial of formula addiction.

Video Weblogs (vlogs) form another opportunity for denial for broadcasters. This is the most dangerous denial, for these are the embryos of the new form of video content delivery. Anybody can do a vlog, and that's the blind spot that broadcasters can't (or won't) see. There is so much money attached to the status quo in terms of "professional" equipment and staffing that managers automatically dismiss competition from upstarts like Rocketboom in New York. This wonderfully creative vlog lives outside the broadcasting formula while meeting information needs of its youthful users, and broadcast companies need to pay attention.

We live in a remarkable time in human history. We've longed for the days when the "smartness quotient" of our culture would go up, and technology — including the Internet — is actually making that happen. But while we rejoice, we also tremble, for we miss the comfort and promise of the formulas of the status quo. Broadcasters, if you cannot rise to meet the challenge to overcome your addiction, you will lose it all.

Here are broadcasters' Twelve Steps to recovery from the addiction to formulas:

1. Admit that you're fighting a battle you cannot win. Surrender to the truth.
2. Come to believe that technology can restore you to profitability.
3. Make a decision to give creativity preeminence in your company for a season.
4. Make a fearless and searching inventory of your resources.
5. Bring in people — including your viewers — who've already experienced the transformation.
6. Become ready to admit the deficiencies of your formulas.
7. Ask everyone — including your investors — to remove the limitations of their addiction.

8. In whiteboard sessions, make a list of things that are possible with your resources.

9. Try to implement changes wherever possible, except where to do so would undercut your core competency.

10. Continue to search for creative solutions.

11. Improve your constant contact with trends in technology, so that you can adapt and adjust wherever possible.

12. Having had an awakening that formulas can be self-destructive, practice keeping creativity at the forefront, so as to avoid the seduction of transferring your addiction from one formula to another.

Don't wait. Begin this process today. The doorway to the new world is before you. All you have to do is open it.

BEYOND THE WORLD WIDE WEB

July 2, 2004

L ike most other news directors, I was an early user of the Inter-net. I took to email like a kid in a candy store, but it wasn't until I left the news business in 1998 that my real education began. I was President and CEO of an Internet company with a largely advertiser-driven business model. When we were invited into a hi-tech business incubator, one of our early investors boasted that we'd soon be worth $100 million. He was wrong, and I went broke.

Early attempts to exploit the Internet for business purposes — a.k.a. "the bubble" — mostly presumed a Modernist top-down model as the core competency. The ability to easily reach vast numbers of people meant that getting there first was the only re-quirement for success. This was a great mistake, for while it made many early speculators wealthy, it eventually ruined even more. This failure to understand its real core competency is the essen-tial lesson for all of us — and especially broadcasters — when pondering the Internet and the future.

The great mistake was an honest one, however, for no one had ever previously considered the full ramifications of a life form like the Internet. The Internet Society, for example, notes the "world-wide broadcasting capability" of the Net, so it's natural it would be viewed that way from a business perspective. The reality is that the Internet is much more than a broadcast delivery system, and that's where most people in the television world continue to miss it. Television is, after all, a genuine broadcast medium, and it's hard to shift your perspective when that's all you know. Trust me. It was a significant blind spot in the development my former company.

Here's a secret that those of us who work in the industry understand about the Internet, but most people don't: the Internet is not the World Wide Web. The Web is just a part of the Net. Once freed of this misperception, you are able to view a multimedia news product in a different light — that a monolithic Website is hardly the be-all-and-end-all that many suppose it to be today.

Tim Berners-Lee, the man credited with inventing the World Wide Web, views the difference between the Web and the Net this way:

> The Internet ('Net) is a network of networks. Basically it is made from computers and cables. What Vint Cerf and Bob Kahn (early Internet pioneers) did was to figure out how this could be used to send around little "packets" of information. As Vint points out, a packet is a bit like a postcard with a simple address on it. If you put the right address on a packet, and gave it to any computer which is connected as part of the Net, each computer would figure out which cable to send it down next so that it would get to its destination. That's what the Internet does. It delivers packets — anywhere in the world, normally well under a second.
>
> Lots of different sorts of programs use the Internet: electronic mail, for example, was around long before the global hypertext system I invented and called the World Wide Web ('Web). Now, videoconferencing and streamed audio channels are among other things which, like the Web, encode information in different ways and use different languages between computers ("protocols") to provide a service.
>
> The Web is an abstract (imaginary) space of information. On the Net, you find computers — on the Web, you find documents, sounds, videos... information. On the Net, the connections are cables between computers; on the Web, connections are hypertext

links. The Web exists because of programs which communicate between computers on the Net. The Web could not be without the Net. The Web made the net useful because people are really interested in information (not to mention knowledge and wisdom!) and don't really want to have know about computers and cables. (1)

This is why delivering news content via RSS (Really Simple Syndication) is revelatory of the Internet. The Web doesn't have to be involved — although it often is — because the technology is an Internet application. Until we can look beyond the Web, we're going to limit what's possible as providers of local news.

We owe a lot to early pioneers like Vint and Kahn, for their vision enabled what we have today. Four ground rules were critical to Kahn's early thinking. When you understand these, you understand the Internet just a little better.

1. Each distinct network would have to stand on its own and no internal changes could be required to any such network to connect it to the Internet.
2. Communications would be on a best effort basis. If a packet didn't make it to the final destination, it would shortly be retransmitted from the source.
3. Black boxes would be used to connect the networks; these would later be called gateways and routers. There would be no information retained by the gateways about the individual flows of packets passing through them, thereby keeping them simple and avoiding complicated adaptation and recovery from various failure modes.
4. There would be no global control at the operations level. (2)

That last ground rule confounds Modernist thought, because it reveals the Internet's lack of hierarchy. The Internet, although a network in name and geography, is a creature of the computer, not the traditional network of the television industry. This is why we all missed it on the original business model, because a computer network features two-directional communications. Everybody's equal, and that's why broadcasters (and many others) have such difficulty understanding its power. It is the communications medium of Postmodernism, which rejects hierarchical structures of all kinds, including the broadcast model.

Doc Searls, one of the authors of *The Cluetrain Manifesto*, understood all this long before most. In May of 1998, Doc offered a prophecy in the form an essay called, "There Is No Demand for Messages."

> The Web is not TV. Repeat after me: the Web is not TV. Excite, Lycos and Yahoo see themselves as the new TV networks. They may have newfangled services, but they make money the old fashioned way: by aggregating scarce access to dumb eyeballs. That model will fail once the Web starts meeting its promises:
>
> 1. the need to know; and
> 2. the need to buy.
>
> In economic terms, these are the only promises made by the Web. Neither of these are met by this year's "portals," last year's "push," or the original notion (circa what, 1995?) that all people really want is to surf through Web sites the way they click through TV channels...
>
> ...The main reason I got out of advertising and PR was this epiphany:
>
> *THERE IS NO DEMAND FOR MESSAGES*
>
> Let me see a show of hands: who here wants a message? Right: none. And who wants to shield themselves from messages they don't want? Exactly: everybody.
>
> TV advertising has negative demand. It subtracts value.
>
> The day will come, hopefully soon, when we will measure demand for advertising on a customer-by-customer basis, and not just by its indirect effects on large populations. When that happens, and direct vendor-customer conversations start adding serious value for both parties, that new conversation will disintermediate most media. Companies will drop advertising like a bad packet. (3)

That day is already upon us, and it's critical that broadcasters understand the hows and whys of it. The broadcast metrics of reach and frequency are bound for the grave. A study released this week by InsightExpress finds that people (with DVRs) are most inclined to view ads they have not seen before, and consequently are most likely to zap ads they've already seen. Joe Mandese of MediaDailyNews wrote, "it suggests that the economics of a business based on serving redundant commercial impressions to a mass audience in order to reach an impressionable few will no longer work in the future." This is the kind of thing Doc Searls prophesied over six years ago.

And so the issue once again is what do broadcasters do? I strongly recommend at least the following:

Embrace new media

Bring your employees up-to-speed on New Media, especially your newsroom. Hire people from the local technical school to come in and teach such things as Photoshop, HTML, Web slide show software, and other skills. Contrary to the way you might feel, technology is not your enemy.

Embrace Internet marketing

There are plenty of companies who'll send somebody to your station — in many cases free of charge — to do workshops with your sales and promotions departments. You'll not survive the New Media world without this knowledge, the lack of which produces an unspoken fear among sales people about the Internet.

Local, local, local

Your role as an information provider in your community is under attack from people who understand things you don't appreciate about the Internet. That includes your local paper and various search engine companies and others who are trying to build a market within yours. For you to survive, you're going to have to think of yourselves beyond traditional broadcast roles. Build your own searchable shopping and classifieds database. Don't stand by and let somebody else do it. This will have unimaginable value downstream. Thoughtfully develop local franchises and do whatever it takes to own them, for in the end, all that matters is local.

When our industry first confronted the Internet, I remember a lot of folks saying it was a way to expand our reach. History now reveals the silliness of that proposition. We need to think of it as a better way to reach and interact with those we already — or in many case used to — serve. The Internet buzzword is "conversations." There's no time like now to begin conversing with the people in your market. In that sense, a Website is but one tool in the vast toolbox offered by the Internet.

A Wolf in Aggregator Clothing

May 20, 2005

L ike most boys growing up in the world before toys were able to do the playing for us, my brothers and I spent a lot of time in the alley playing marbles. In addition to learning to be a competitor and a good sport, marbles first introduced me to the concept of categorizing. There were boulders and steelies and cat's eyes and peeries and aggies, to name a few.

Of all the marbles in my bag, I liked the peeries most, and soon I had a separate bag for them. And so began a process that would be with me for the rest of my life.

As human beings, we're natural collectors and compartmentalizers. We make our own judgments and build our own hierarchies. One of this; two of that. Our goal is to make sense of things. We blend this, that and the other to form the boundaries that define us and our views of everything. Institutions are there to help us with the process, but we're increasingly becoming aware that maybe they don't exactly have our best interests in mind. So we're striking out on our own, and our results are surprising, even to us.

We're becoming our own news media, making our own music and films, and challenging the authority formerly taken for granted in our modernist world. And nowhere is this more discernable than the way we organize and compartmentalize. We're actually writing our own encyclopedia and building our own communities.

This do-it-for-ourselves paradigm is a crucial point to understand, as newspapers and television stations move to assimilate the world of the blogosphere. The word is aggregation, and the business model is advertising via the old tried and true method of reach/frequency.

Lincoln Millstein, Senior VP and Director of Digital Media for Hearst Newspapers, summed it up at the Syndicate Conference in New York, as quoted by Rafat Ali of Paid Content: "The big money is being made by aggregators, so who wants to be one of 1,000 publishers? That's just nickels and cents...we want to play the role of the aggregator."

As logical as this seems, aggregation is actually a touch point between the worlds of Modernism and Postmodernism when it refers to citizens media. It's a place where the bottom up is changed to the top down, and it's a leap of faith to assume the bottom is interested.

The mainstream media views organizing information as their high calling. Even the term "mainstream" is itself revealing, for it conjures up a vision of a stream formed by many tributaries, all flowing to one gathering place. Streams can be organized and controlled with various gates and dams, and that's the perceived role of the press — to organize the flow of information in such a way that it's understandable. Along the way, there are ads to be served to a captive audience. The personal media revolution, however, tosses an enormous monkey wrench into the equation.

Technorati, the blog search engine, reported earlier this year that they're now tracking over 8 million blogs. The report added two important pieces of information: the blogosphere is doubling in size every 5 months and that a new blog is added to the mix every 2.2 seconds. Regardless of the number of blogs that have gone or will go dormant, these numbers still boggle the mind. As Linda Seebach, editor of the *Rocky Mountain News* in Denver noted recently at BlogNashville, "It's like trying to drink from a fire hose."

Anxiety over not being able to get one's arms around all that writing is one of the most common complaints that mainstream press people offer regarding the relevance of the personal media revolution. After all, if it can't be organized, what good is it?

Staci Kramer of PaidContent.org led a session on journalism at the BlogNashville conference and made the traditional observation that compiling viewpoints was one of journalism's roles. "It's fine to have 15 people giving all they know," she said, "but somebody has to synthesize all that."

If synthesizing is really necessary, the question becomes who will do it?

In his brilliant essay, "Ontology is Overrated," Clay Shirky writes of the difference between organizing information through categories and through search. Yahoo!'s Web directory, for example, is an elaborate system of categorization that is supposed to help people find what they're looking for, much in the way the Dewey Decimal System is supposed to help one find a book in the library. It runs into trouble, however, when the users' ideas of categories are different than what the Yahoo! creators envisioned. Google, on the other hand, takes an entirely different approach and organizes content based on a set of variables stated by the user, most of whom find this method of locating something far superior to any preset classification.

> It comes down, ultimately, to a question of philosophy. Does the world make sense or do we make sense of the world? If you believe the world makes sense, then anyone who tries to make sense of the world differently from you is presenting you with a situation that needs to be reconciled formally, because if you get it wrong, you're getting it wrong about the real world.
>
> If, on the other hand, you believe that we make sense of the world, if we are, from a bunch of different points of view, applying some kind of sense to the world, then you don't privilege one top level of sense-making over the other. What you do instead is you try to find ways that the individual sense-making can roll up to something which is of value in the aggregate, but...without a goal

of explicitly getting to or even closely matching some theoretically perfect view of the world. (1)

This is a crucial issue to resolve as people attempt to "make sense" of the blogosphere through the aggregating of its voices. Whether it's at the community level or through blog content or size of readership, aggregation provides a logical way to divide the wheat from the chaff, so to speak, and create a manageable consolidation of voices at different levels and in different categories. It's an advanced labeling system where the decision to label is determined by the aggregator. On the surface, this is an inevitable advancement of the many conversations that make up the blogosphere, but it also opens the door to new hierarchies in what is necessarily an anarchical structure. And, as with any hierarchy, somebody needs to be calling the shots.

In San Francisco, Cozmo Media CEO and self-described "serial entrepreneur" Alex Rowland is researching and writing about what he calls open and closed distribution systems. Closed distribution networks, he writes, are based on unidirectional communications, whereas open systems are based on bidirectional communications. This is the essence of the two-way conversation made possible through the Web and, especially, blogging.

> Common belief appears to be that "open" networks, while easier to scale, are actually less profitable and harder to defend than their "closed" counterparts. Much of this stems from the idea that the more valuable the content (ie. able to draw large audiences that will pay to consume it) the more likely the content owner is to turn to a closed distribution mechanism to deliver this valuable asset to consumers. (2)

The open network view was commonly expressed in the Web's bubble days in the saying, "The Web demands that it be free." As Rowland notes, free is easy to scale, which is why advertising was the core business model of the bubble. Unfortunately, the only people advertising in those days were other Web companies, so the whole thing collapsed. But, as we're learning these days, Web advertising is big money, so it wasn't the business model that was flawed. "Money follows eyeballs" will always be true.

> Open content encourages a great deal of specialization in what's produced. This specialization makes targeting specific demographics much easier than when your audience is huge and highly fragmented. Second, open networks encourage community and conversation, which can drive massive improvements in the contextualization of the media. I think if you combine these things, we'll find advertising that is orders of magnitude more efficient and, as such, a solid foundation for profitability amongst producers. (3)

But Rowland's thinking goes beyond the free versus paid argument and strikes at the core of the personal media revolution. An open, bidirectional network assures that the distance between the bottom and top is negligible, while closed networks assure command and control functionality, usually at the top. The Internet's real value is that it levels the playing field for everybody and transfers control to the end user, not the publisher.

Just like portal Websites of the past, an aggregator provides a starting point for users, and the extent to which that gateway is under the control of the user determines how open — and, therefore, successful — the aggregator will be. Aggregators that attempt to close what is an open architecture will, in the end, find themselves in the same predicament as AOL, with its shrinking subscriber base, because people will not accept the imprisonment of somebody else's structure once they've been exposed to doing it for themselves.

Rowland and Shirky are exploring different sides of the same coin, and it's important we pay attention. The Web remains a place that is counterintuitive to both our training and our logic. What the Web user views as freedom to choose, mainstream critics call an echo chamber. This meme comes from the belief that, if given the choice, people will only surround themselves with what they want to hear instead of what they need to hear. This is self-centered logic that usually comes from people who are currently providing what they think people "need" to hear, and they fear the whacking of their fatted calf. Moreover, there is no evidence whatsoever to prove that people can't or won't find what they "need" to hear on their own.

In the end, it comes down to your view of people and human nature. If you think people are stupid and require direction, then you'll tend towards hierarchies, organized categories and closed distribution. This was Walter Lippmann's view of people, and it is reflected in the "professional" press that he birthed. If, however, you believe people will generally get it right, if given the chance, then you'll be comfortable with all that a free, searchable and open system has to offer. This is vital as we attempt to innovate the business models of tomorrow, for if you can accept the latter position, the lust for aggregation being expressed by the institutional media looks short-sighted and foolish.

Regardless of what I did with them, those marbles of my youth were mine, and that sense of ownership is powerful beyond words. I could organize them in any form or fashion. I could make a bag of orange peeries and one of green peeries, if that's what I wanted to do. The sense of personal control that I first experienced with my marbles is at the heart of what's driving people to the Web today, and information aggregator tools that don't respect it won't be in the game for very long.

GOOGLE LIFTS ONLY GOOGLE

October 8, 2007

The aphorism "a rising tide lifts all boats" was made popular by John F. Kennedy when defending his tax cuts to fellow Democrats. His colleagues didn't like the fact that the cuts included the wealthy. In a June 1963 speech, Kennedy said, "As they say on my own Cape Cod, a rising tide lifts all the boats." He got the phrase from the letterhead of The New England Council, a chamber of commerce type organization and applied it to politics, but the phrase has been widely used to describe ebbs and flows in many other walks of life.

The concept is important to understanding what's really taking place with Internet advertising, because it reveals a significant weakness in the efforts of traditional media companies to transition to a Web-based business model. We see the money moving. We know we need to "be there." We try lots of things, but so far, the big revenue numbers have generally escaped us.

This is because we think that merely getting into the game will lift our boat and produce significant revenues. While there certainly is a rising tide effect, it's mostly illusionary, because this rising tide is actually caused, in large part, by the presence of another entity in the sea.

Ashkan Karbasfrooshan at HipMojo has taken revenue numbers for the first half of 2007 (1) from Google and overall ad numbers in a new report (2) from the Interactive Advertising Bureau (IAB) and come to the remarkable conclusion that Google now accounts for 40 percent of all Web advertising in the U.S. That's four of every ten online ad dollars in this country going to Google.

The caveat is that these numbers come from two different sources, so the belief that the IAB's figures include Google's actual reported numbers is an assumption. It's one, however, that I'm comfortable accepting in an effort to make a point.

Using Ashkan's calculations, Eric Shoenfeld at TechCrunch reveals that the real strength of Google is not in its ad share but in its growth. (3)

Google's share of 39.8 percent in the first half of 2007 compares to 34.6 percent in the first half of 2006, so its actual revenue growth is significantly outpacing that of all other Web companies combined. Google's revenues grew 45.7 percent year-over-year, compared to 26.5 percent for total online revenues. However, the total figure includes Google, so if you remove them, everybody else's growth is paltry in comparison.

Revenue Growth 1H06-1H07

> Overall = 26.5%
> Google = 45.7%
> Others = 15.4%

Google is like an enormous mountain rising up from the bottom of Lake Advertising, its mere presence raising the water level and giving the appearance of a rising tide that's lifting all the other boats. It's not. Google is a textbook disruptive innovation that's attacking the advertising industry. The more Madison Avenue tries to assert its paradigms, the more the people at Google smile, because they know that traditional advertising methods are insignificant (and ineffective) in the wide open world of the Web. This is something that traditional media companies — who live (and die) by hardcore reliance on the traditional methods of Madison Avenue — are unable to see, much less grasp.

Google's revenues — indeed, all search revenues — should not be included in IAB reports about Web advertising, because the two are completely unrelated. Moreover, including Google in the mix gives a false impression of the work the IAB represents — Madison Avenue's traditional models moved to the Web. The two are simply different species.

Jeff Jarvis notes that we shouldn't blame Google for leaving everybody else behind:

> Big, old media handed them this opportunity on a platter. Google was the one company that truly understood the economics of the open network. It understood that it could grow much bigger enabling than controlling. We in media should have followed that model. We should have asked WWGD. What would Google do? (4)

This whole business with the illusionary rising tide is driven by our mistaken belief that the disruption is one of new forms of media, and that has produced strategic errors in our response. We emphasize multi-platform distribution, but that does nothing to stop a hundred forms of Google. It's not about our output; it's about our input. The real disruption is in advertising, that which supports media.

This is so critical for us to understand as local media companies, because the Holy Grail in all of this is local advertising. Is Google Maps a local application? You bet it is, as are all forms of search. Is MySpace a local application? Absolutely! While its reach may be global, its use is local — a way for local young people to stay in touch with each other and share their lives.

Google begins the day with the assumption that people come to the Web, because they're looking for something. We begin the day with the assumption that people are looking for us. In our minds, we are the ones who control growth, because everything has to happen on what we view as our property. In the collective mind of Google, the people who make up the network that is the Web control the growth by their actions, and Google's ad mechanism doesn't care where that takes place. As the network grows, so grows Google. Not so for local media.

In our world, content drives consumers. In Google's world, content isn't nearly as important as behavior. As Jeff Jarvis noted, Google is simply an enabler of that behavior.

We must get our hands around what I call "the Local Web," because that's where our future lies. If we're serving the Local Web, its growth is our growth. The problem is that this requires extremely proactive efforts — not so much resources as plain old hard work. Our applications must feed that growth. We must build it assuming they will come.

This is strikingly different than most local Web strategies, which generally examine revenue sources and go after them with conventional reach/frequency methodologies. The situation simply demands that we do more, because if we don't do something quickly, local online advertising will default to the pureplays, most notably Google. Remember that the disruption is in advertising, not media, and as long as it continues without our efforts to offer alternatives, it won't make any sense for advertisers to put there money anywhere else.

As I've written previously, the media world views Google as a media company, while Google views itself as an advertising application. CEO Eric Schmidt gave a clear picture of that in an interview with *Wired Magazine*:

> Think of it (Google) first as an advertising system. Then as an end-user system — Google Apps. A third way to think of Google is as a giant supercomputer. And a fourth way is to think of it as a social phenomenon involving the company, the people, the brand, the mission, the values — all that kind of stuff. (5)

So in order to compete with Google at the local level, we also must become an advertising system. There are a variety of ways to go about this, but here are five things that are required for making it happen:

1. Define and identify the Local Web. This is job one for us, because the result will outline the market that we are trying to serve. Only until we know its scope and nuances will we be able identify how best to serve it. We must view ourselves as undergirding the whole infrastructure, for the Web is a world of user empowerment — the best position we can hope for is as *the* enabler of the Local Web.

2. Organize the Local Web. This is the real work, because this organization doesn't currently exist, and it won't happen by itself. It requires legwork, handshaking, and tons of research. The objective isn't to surround the Local Web in the conventional sense; it's more a sales challenge — to let everyone know that they are part of something more definable than "the Internet."

3. Provide tools to help it grow. While there already exist tools for any local business to use the Web to help their business, the reality is that the vast majority of merchants and companies know nothing about this. We cannot accomplish the mission without participation by local merchants, and that may mean actually building Websites — or ad widgets — for many people.

4. Serve it by enabling commerce across the network. Our mission is to help the business community use the Web to conduct business, and advertising is our tool. But this is not advertising as we know it, for the Web isn't so much about building brands as it is about direct sales and marketing. Hence, our sophisticated ad software will put people directly in the path of messages from merchants.

But perhaps a more important element here is that the enabling of commerce puts us in the business-to-business advertising world for the first time. This is a lucrative growth area in Web advertising and one in which we've not been invited to play, because our emphasis has always been on consumers.

5. Sell the concept to the community. This is perhaps the most difficult of all for traditional media companies, who are used

to having it the other way around. A television spot sale doesn't generally involve selling the medium, because the local ad community is familiar with the paradigm. The Web is so new that few people understand, much less participate in, this world. We must be proactive here, because to do nothing means that the efforts of the pureplays will reach local advertisers without any alternatives, and that would be suicidal.

I know I sound like a broken record on this, but these efforts should ideally involve all members of the traditional media in each community. It just makes sense for media players to attack this as a problem that impacts everybody and one that requires a combined approach. That is not likely to happen, however, so what's left is an incredible opportunity for one entity in each market.

The problems we face as institutional media are enormous, but they're made more difficult by factors that hide or disguise the real causes of the problems. In the end, we have two choices with Google. We can either let them have the local market and work with them to ensure that we get a piece. Or we can take the position that we can better serve the commerce needs of the Local Web at the local level and use our mass marketing reach to sidestep the encroachment of the all the pureplays.

One way or the other, the Local Web will be served.

LOCAL TV'S NEW DEADLINES

August 5, 2004

In the mid-70s, a developer in Milwaukee made plans for a downtown hotel and shopping center that would forever alter the skyline and the energy of the city. It was the cornerstone of a massive public/private sector project to revitalize the downtown area, and I found out about it many months before anybody else. I went to Indianapolis with the developer and shot film of a similar project there. Everything was embargoed until the developer was ready. Meanwhile, I did other research and prepared an in-depth package for our news (in those days, we didn't do "team" coverage).

In the news business, there's nothing quite like the rush of waiting for publication/broadcast. When the day arrived, nobody else knew about it, not even the two newspapers in town. We'd made the decision to break the story at 6 o'clock without any promotion, because we didn't want to tip the competition. I did a very brief teaser during our 5 o'clock show, and that was enough for one of the other stations in town to write a short report to lead their 6 o'clock program. It broke my heart, even though my report buried everybody. It was an enormous scoop and one that even prompted letters of praise from the newspaper business reporters, who were completely caught with their pants down.

258

But it was only a partial victory to me, because that other station was able to scoop my scoop.

When TV news shifted from a business of covering the news to one of managing audience flow, this fear of tipping competitors became the source of internal arguments between the news and promotion people. Sometimes we won. Usually, they won. Nevertheless, in every TV newsroom in America, news people still gather around a bank of monitors to compare their content with that of their competitors in a ritual that often determines how well the news director sleeps.

As deeply rooted as this practice may be, the truth is it is increasingly irrelevant in today's media environment. Worse, it is actually self-destructive, because it shields news people from the overriding reality of the post-mass market era — that people no longer want to wait until 6 o'clock to get the news. It's an "I want what I want when I want it" world, and technology is its servant. The news broadcasts may still be your bread and butter, but that simply cannot last, and those who aren't moving in another direction *right now* are risking everything. As marketing guru Seth Godin recently noted:

> Whenever you are faced with a situation where your competition is afraid to change but you can see the reality of the situation, you have a huge opportunity. This is the biggest growth and market share opportunity in at least a decade. (1)

The "situation" is that the marketplace is ripe for a local station to have the balls to break stories online — when they have them — and not wait until their allotted broadcast time. If not, the local paper will do it, and if not them, then somebody else will. If yours is the "live, local, latebreaking" brand, you'd certainly better be adopting that same slogan online. Otherwise, you're simply shooting yourself in the foot every time you wait until 6 o'clock to present the efforts of the day, because you're not telling the truth.

Until we begin respecting the power of the immediacy offered by the Web — and especially RSS — we'll be hopelessly left behind in the race to see who wins the local online news prize. Money follows eyeballs, and the eyeballs are abandoning broadcast in favor of the Internet at a speed that frightens every corporate broadcast executive on the planet. And yet, there isn't a single station that will put the full weight of its news operation into feeding this explosive growth market. Why not? Because we think it would be self-destructive to spill our goodies online and that people wouldn't watch our programs if we did. But is that really so?

- People already aren't watching our programs.
- There is zero evidence to support this belief.
- It is actually self-destructive to *not* adopt such a strategy.

Moreover, and regardless of what's going on around us, we seem to be the last to figure out that news is an ongoing conversation, not a program that appears when we say so. Old habits not only die hard; they can be dangerously deceptive.

The resistance in newsrooms to the immediacy offered by the Web is mystifying, especially because the industry itself pioneered and refined the concept of immediacy in big stories. If, in our judgment, a story justified it, we could turn out the resources and produce compelling content that made us all proud. Many of the most memorable moments from my career involved this type of coverage. The problem is that every story is a big story to somebody, and the Web presents a different form of deadline for all of us.

In the mid-80s, Steve Friedman brought NBC's Today back to prominence in the morning news race after nearly a decade of losing to ABC's Good Morning America. A brilliant television guy, Friedman told Electronic Media in 1986 that he used the concept of immediacy to do it.

> Aside from building familiarity with the viewers, the show itself has changed, he says, to a more active, "less reactive" program, with a "shift in emphasis from a review of the day before to what's happening now."
>
> "People are brought in as spectators to history, he says, explaining, in part, why the show is doing more and more live material. (2)

This "spectator to history" concept is the real core competency of the TV news industry, and it's why live coverage is as important as it is. Isn't it amazing, then, that the industry can't see the value of applying the same concept to its Internet strategy, especially since that's where its former audience is heading?

And that audience wants its news when *they* are able to receive it, not when news entities say it's ready, and increasingly, they want their news during the day and at the office. This was evident in the groundbreaking "State of the News Media 2004" report by The Project for Excellence in Journalism:

> What attracts people to online news? One appeal is convenience. Part of the rise in news consumption online is occurring at work, a place where in the past people generally did not have the time or means, or found it unacceptable to get news. A May 2003 study by the Online Publishers Association found that 62 percent of at-work Internet users visited a news site in a typical week.
>
> This, as online journalists are quick to point out, is essentially a new group of news consumers. Previously, most news consumption occurred largely at home, at morning and night. Sitting around the office reading the newspaper was frowned upon. Sitting in the office reading news on the computer apparently is not, or in any case is not forbidden.
>
> When people go online for news, they break down into three distinct groups, according to studies of the Pew Internet and American Life Project. About half go online to see what the latest headlines are. Indeed, many online news operations say their "prime time" is the period from 1 to 3 p.m., when people are returning to their jobs after lunch or a mid-day activity. About 30 percent pursue news online after they have encountered it while doing something else online (for instance, checking out information on a portal and seeing the news displayed on the home page), and the rest are pursuing information about a story they have already heard about from another media source. (3)

According to surveys, anywhere from half to 70 percent of those online get news there. That figure was much higher in a research project I helped develop for a broadcast group. And in that study, more than half said they planned to get more news online in the future.

The Internet brings with it new deadlines and new challenges for news people, and they are all driven around the reality that the user (formerly known as consumer) is in charge. Building an Internet strategy around this isn't as difficult as it might seem, but it begins with fundamental changes in our attitudes and approaches to the Internet. The attitude adjustment is this: We meet the news and information needs of our community wherever they are, and meeting those needs is far more important than beating the competition. Changes in our approach to the news include — but certainly aren't limited to — the following:

1. Challenge our newsrooms to view our Internet delivery systems as vital to our overall strategy and as important as any broadcast.

2. Make sure every member of the staff understands that they are as responsible for Web content as they are for broadcast content.

3. Provide training to encourage staffers to explore the many variations of multi-media storytelling.

4. Regularly break stories online and let the community know we're doing it.

5. Pay attention to our online competition. Create a bonus program that rewards news staffers for breaking stories online.

6. Promote the value of RSS as a delivery means for Internet news hounds in our community, including offering links to downloads of free RSS readers, like FeedReader. RSS, whether inside a browser or in stand-alone news aggregators, is the news dissemination vehicle of the future.

7. Involve our audience in what we're doing by encouraging story and blog comments, newsmaker chats, and discussion boards.

But the biggest change is one that has to occur internally with all TV (and other) news people. Our deadline clocks must be reset.

An ongoing story may have multiple deadlines throughout the day, and our obligation to online news consumers is to advance the story regularly. Perhaps one day broadcast news will evolve into something beyond the who, what, when, and where of the day — into something compelling and creative that can be referenced in online coverage throughout the day — a program that assumes (at least some) audience knowledge of the day's events before it begins.

Broadcast journalism's salvation lies beyond the box of the 6 o'clock news, and we need to get past our deeply-rooted beliefs and traditions in order to find it.

TV VIEWERS AND INTERNET USERS
ARE DIFFERENT ANIMALS

July 18, 2003

There's an old joke about the devil not wanting televangelists in hell. Billy Graham would get everybody saved. Oral Roberts would get everybody healed. And Pat Robertson would raise the money for air conditioning. I used to work for Pat and acknowledge the truth behind that joke. One year when I was there, we raised $246 million in contributions. This master fund-raiser taught me many things that I've applied in my life. One of my favorite quotes is, "If you want to catch trout, you've got to use trout bait."

To broadcasters, people are just people and everybody's a viewer. That presumption, I'm afraid, is leading the industry into a crisis as New Media continues to erode viewership. The industry has responded with Websites that ignore the essential truth that an Internet user is *not* a television viewer. The mindset that any broadcasting paradigm will work on the Internet is just, well, ignorant. Hence, the Web doesn't work for broadcasting, because if you want to catch trout, you've got to use trout bait.

In my work, I've studied volumes of research and talked to hundreds of Internet CEOs. I used to run an Internet company, and knowing my users was priority number one. So, for the sake of furthering the discussion about why I believe broadcasters are missing an important opportunity, here are some of the differences between TV viewers and Internet users. I sincerely hope that this will help lead to the creation of Internet trout bait for broadcasters.

Television is passive and the Internet is active. This is rule #1 in understanding the trout we're trying to catch, and I cannot possibly overstate its importance. The person with a hand on the mouse is absolutely in charge. You will not, can not overcome this reality. The instant you attempt to sidestep this truth, you've lost the user — and likely for a very long time. Internet users don't want to be held by the hand. They want to use what they've been taught, not sit through lectures they don't need. Nowhere is this truer than with local weather. Give me the forecast, but let me play with the toys you use.

Broadcasters are used to having it their way. They determine what people watch, when they watch it, the number of commercials they have to endure, and so forth. Broadcasters originally denied the influence of remote control devices only to learn that a great many people click the moment their program goes to a commercial break. I know many people who watch several programs at once by simply switching back and forth during commercials. The control an Internet user has is far, far greater than one equipped merely with a remote.

None of the fundamental assumptions of broadcasting apply with the Internet. It's a completely different communications medium. For example:

- All things to all people. The fundamental reality about broadcasting assumes that a single entity can provide programming that will serve the masses. It worked in the early days of TV, but the extent to which broadcasters cling to this belief in the 21st century amazes me. The Internet works on the basis of narrowcasting, but even the "casting" is erroneous thinking.

- Daypart programming. The Internet allows people to do what they want when they want it. And given the staggering numbers of people who access the Web on-the-job, it's critically important that information providers realize that "once a day" simply can't and won't work. The Internet is 24/7, something smart providers understand completely.

- Managing audience flow. The audience will manage itself, thank you very much. While I think it's possible to promote upcoming events, etc., it's dangerous to do so *during* the process of serving the user's entertainment or information wants and needs. Always remember rule #1. You, as a provider, are not in charge.

- Commercial interruptions. I was in broadcasting when we actually used this term. I like it, because it's honest. It speaks the truth about selling on TV. Programming is interrupted for commercials. Attempts to do this on the Internet are ultimately self-defeating, because of rule #1. I'm a strong supporter of Flash ads on the Web, but the extent to which they interrupt the user's experience is a massive turn-off. There are ways to use the technology to create wonderfully effective ads without interfering with the user's experience. The most important person a station should hire is the top Flash person in the market to work with the sales department in creating such ads.

- Homogeneity of product. What's slowly killing television news would kill Internet video news even quicker. Information providers simply must tailor their presentations to be hyper-local, and that includes a deep respect for the personality and tastes of the community being served.

- People follow people. This is a critical truth for broadcasters to understand. Given its nature and ability to reach mass audiences, broadcasting has done more to create and maintain celebrities than any medium ever created. It's been a symbiotic relationship since broadcasting first came on the scene, but the nature of the Internet means an information provider doesn't need celebrities to provide quality information to users. This is a bitter pill to swallow, but to Internet users, a quick and easy method of getting information is more important than developing a relationship with the people providing the information. I believe there will always be a place for storytellers in the video news business, but the days of the star anchor are surely numbered.

- More is better. Reach and frequency don't apply, no matter what your mind tells you. You don't need a mass audience to be successful. You merely need to help sponsors sell their products. In fact, the "more is better" mindset will actually block creative attempts to do business on the Web. This means an entirely new advertising paradigm, but that's the subject of another essay.

- Captive audience. This one directly relates to rule #1. Broadcasters' processes and procedures are built on the assumption that when a viewer is on their channel, they are — at least for the moment — theirs to serve. Nowhere is this more evident than when stations interrupt programming for news bulletins or weather events. The Internet offers ways to alert users without interrupting their experience, and news providers would be wise to accept that.

For the time being, Internet users are above-average in intelligence. The current television-programming trend of appealing to the lowest common denominator is a recipe for disaster on the Internet. Always remember than the mouse is far more powerful than the remote control.

For the next decade, I believe local TV stations are in the catbird's seat in terms of providing video information conduits via the Internet. People are still watching TV news, although in shrinking numbers. Use your station to drive people to your news Website, where you can build tomorrow's loyal audience. But this unique opportunity won't last forever. Video technology is such that a smart entrepreneur, with modest investment backing, could win the local Internet video news market and undercut the opportunity that exists for broadcasters.

The time for broadcasters to act is now. And never forget. If you want to catch trout, you've got to use trout bait.

Media 2.0
101

DVRs, YouTube, MySpace, Facebook, iGoogle. The Media 2.0 disruption has put Internet users firmly in charge of their own time and experiences. The essays in this section explore all aspects of the Media 2.0 realities and offer insight into how Media 2.0 can offer an opportunity for our brands to prosper in the days to come.

Media 2.0 is the name of our unit at Audience Research & Development, and it's aptly named. We live and work in Media 1.0, and Media 2.0 is what the reinvention is all about. But what is it? What are its rules, and how do we fit? The reader will find plenty of food for thought here, especially "The Remarkable Opportunities of Unbundled Media" and "It's Not the Same Game."

BEYOND PORTAL WEBSITES

September 7, 2004

The first time I ever heard the word "portal" was in the early
Star Trek episode, The City on the Edge of Forever. This
award-winning episode found the Enterprise crew on the "Time
Planet" standing before a portal called The Guardian of Forever.
"Time and place are ready to receive you," the portal spoke. "I am
a time portal. Through me the great race which once lived here
went to another age." (Story summary: Kirk, Spock and McCoy
end up on earth in the 1930s, Kirk falls in love with Joan Collins.
Saves her life. Alters history. Back through the portal. Returns.
Lets her die. Heartbroken.) (1) Portals have become central to science fiction, including the film, Stargate, and the television series
of the same name.

By definition, a portal is a doorway or a gate, and pre-bubble Internet business models adopted the concept as a logical way to
manage content. The World Wide Web itself was seen as one giant
portal, because of the linking ability built into the language of the
Web, HTML. Within the Web, it was natural to produce portal sites
to help people find things, but as so often is the case, greed set in.
Framing options available through HTML code made it possible

to keep users within the confines of the portal site, thereby validating its advertising business model through new metrics, such as page views, unique users and stickiness.

AOL is a giant portal (in ISP clothing) that offers users access to the Web through the AOL software. The early attractions for AOL were easy access to the Web, organization, interaction and the use of keywords to find things. We used to call AOL "Internet training wheels," because it really functioned as a Web within the Web. And while the AOL community taught a lot of us how to use the Web, there came a time when we could ride the bicycle ourselves, thank you very much.

Nearly every Website has portal functionality, because, well, it's just so darned logical to build it that way. Here's the thinking:

- An attractive home page to welcome users. For awhile there, we had the trend of Flash animation "pre" home pages. Go figure.
- The home page offers access to the content of the site through links. We call this "navigation."
- These links often lead to other portals, called "departments" — or something like that — and links to the content are found there.
- Therefore, the actual content of the site is usually two, three, four or more layers deep within the site.
- Content is then further broken into more than one page, so that the site will produce more clicks.

Portal sites are great for organizing and managing content, but the concept drags Modernist baggage into what is essentially a Postmodern entity. The concept presupposes a marketing mentality that is contrary to the nature of the Web — that everything is organized from the top-down. Technology is leveling playing fields everywhere, and no where is this more evident than with the Internet. Disruptive innovations are shattering the status quo, and portal Websites are becoming increasingly irrelevant for anything other than storage and maintenance.

Throughout our history, we've always managed knowledge and information from the top down. Whoever has the highest knowledge mountaintop wins. This notion is at the core of the current debate between so-called professional journalism and the citizen phenomenon of blogging. With millions of blogs, the argument goes, how is it possible to get a handle on what's being said? This presupposes the idea that the filtering all of that dialog is essential to an overall understanding, and that comes from the highest mountaintop belief.

The logical mind assumes the position that only a few items can occupy "top of mind" status, while the rest lie underneath in descending layers of importance. In that sense, the mind is a portal to knowledge, and managing all that knowledge becomes the task.

And so we produce TV station Websites that function the same way. We build top-down portals with only links to the important stuff on the home page. I once removed all of the design elements from the home page of a client's Website. When the colors and graphics and ads and promotional material was removed, the only thing left was links and perhaps a short paragraph on the top story. Try it sometime. You'll be amazed. There is no content on the home page of most supposedly "content" Websites.

Then, along came Google and changed everything. Like the Star Trek "Guardian," Google's portal works in two dimensions — horizontal and vertical — but the technology does more than just provide links. It's what they're linking to that's important and the way it has changed how consumers use the Web. A Google search takes the user inside the portals of others and straight to the content they seek. The company can track FedEx or UPS shipments simply by entering the tracking number and "FedEx" or "UPS" in the search bar. Up pops the page from the FedEx or UPS site with your information! Google didn't partner with either FedEx or UPS to provide this service. They didn't need to, and there's really nothing to stop them from spreading such services.

History may well judge Google's real contribution to be teaching people how to reroute themselves around all the top-down, portalesque Websites that clutter the Internet landscape. This is significant, because it's exposing the reality that a URL is just a URL, and that there are ways around the traffic lights we used to take for granted.

The logical mind views Websites as places where people go, regardless of the reason. As such, it makes sense to welcome them with some sort of home page, and then lead them through the process of finding what they're seeking. The problem with this is it makes an assumption about people that is simply incorrect — that people want to be led through the process of finding what they're seeking. This view of Websites also completely disregards the reality of the Internet. Contrary to the way it seems, a Website is not a destination. The Web browser that sits on an individual's computer is the destination. The truth is a Website doesn't actually exist until the browser on a user's desktop translates the coded language that's sitting on a server somewhere. All of the work takes place in a connection between the two computers, but it's displayed only on the user's desktop.

Most people view a browser as a vehicle that transports them from place to place along the information superhighway. Not true. You don't "go" anywhere. It all comes to you.

This isn't merely a semantic argument. It's key to understanding the media revolution underway, because the power to find and obtain what is being sought increasingly lies with the user today, not companies providing the information. It is purely bottom-up, and it's why RSS is such an important innovation. RSS brings the content being sought directly to the user's desktop, by-passing the portal Website that's hosting the content. And this direct connection between user and content will only grow downstream, because human nature — not some business model — is what's driving it. I want what I want when I want it, and technology is my servant. This is trouble for companies who base their Internet strategies on reach/frequency advertising models. A different mindset is required to make money, and it begins with understanding that today's Internet portal is on the desktop of the Internet user, not in some distant place under the command and control of somebody else.

Keeping in mind that a Website is not a TV station, there are four things we can do to better position ourselves for the long run.

1. We need to think narrowcasting, not broadcasting, and get out of the portal mindset. Perhaps we need more than one Website from which to offer our content. If we feel that local news is a reason for people to visit us on the Web, then perhaps we should think about doing a local news Website. Regardless, we need to get our content as high up into the site as possible, and that includes our home page. This is one of the beauties of blogs. No navigation is required. All the current content is right there on the blog page.

2. Remove all the cluttering navigation links, keep things clean and simple, and incorporate search prominently. Search is interactive and intuitive, and users find it terribly satisfying. People want to find things themselves, and our archives are vastly more important than we think.

3. Delve deeply into RSS. This technology is going to revolutionize the way news is delivered. It's already making waves, and most of the big Web publishers are making their material available via RSS. Every local news entity should do likewise. RSS is demonstrative of the true nature of the Internet. It "pulls" material from portal Websites and delivers it to the user's desktop. Marketeurs obsessed with push marketing have yet to discover how money can be made here, but that's inevitable. RSS is where people are going, and where the people are, there's money to be made. Some publishers are experimenting with delivering ads along with the news, and branded readers make it possible to deliver ads.

4. Actively and aggressively encourage our viewers and users to move forward with new technologies that bring what we can offer directly to them. This is a smart strategy for several reasons. One, it's where everything is going anyway, and

it positions us with a cutting-edge image. Two, it will move people away from our competitor's Web offerings while bringing them to ours. Finally, it will seal our commitment to the new reality in which we live.

As The Guardian of Forever noted, time and place are indeed ready to receive us. The future isn't nearly so frightening as we may think. All we need to do is step through the portal.

THE MATTER OF "GETTING IT"

September 15, 2005

In one of my previous lives, I was involved in a fundamentalist Christian group that many would probably consider a cult. We took pride in the belief that we shared some secret knowledge about the Bible, and this was often manifested in the use of a common phrase — *They just don't get it* — when applied to other people.

In the late 70s and early 80s, there was even an evangelical marketing campaign called, "I've got it." Billboards, posters and buttons all proclaimed this slogan as a way to suggest to others that maybe they didn't have it. As you can imagine, this didn't go over very well with the ecumenical crowd.

But times change, and people grow up. I've learned to be suspicious of that phrase now and many others, including my favorite, "There's no question about it." When I hear that these days, I immediately assume that there *is* a question about it.

So it's with some trepidation that I say that there's a lot of "not getting it" these days when it comes to new media and technology, especially with my friends in TV news. One reason we don't "get it" is our experience with the first go-around of the Internet. Who can forget the bubble days, when similar cult-like statements and promises were being made? We're justifiably apprehensive.

But where that apprehension blinds us to reality, there's a real problem. That's because even with all the overzealous projections, the bubble era foundation was solid. We're in the midst of the most significant communications shift in the history of humankind. You either believe this or you don't, and your behavior regarding it is determined by your belief.

Former FCC Chairman, Michael Powell, had his own terminology for the change. "Application separation," he said, "is the most important paradigm shift in the history of communications, and it will change things forever." (1) The essential nut of his statement is that one no longer needs to own the infrastructure in order to publish, distribute or broadcast content. This is turning the media world upside-down, and most of the traditional media response, I'm sorry, falls under the category of "they just don't get it."

It's turning the media world upside-down, because smart people now have their hands on the tools that used to be exclusively ours. They're innovating ways to communicate using those tools, and people are responding. Cumulatively, observers call these innovations Media 2.0. This is the new wine of media, and the initial response from traditional businesses has been to try and pour it into the old wineskins of Media 1.0.

This is no small thing. In the old, mass-marketing world, it was essential that all roads flow *from* the media entity, whereas the new model demands the opposite. The road now flows *to* the media entity. Local television seems the least capable of understanding this, for our brands are attached to transmitters that beam down on everybody. The only way we know how to make money is to attach ads to the roads that flow away from us and our brands.

So we're clueless when it comes to disruptive innovations that challenge our business assumptions. Our first response is to hope the disruption fails, so we misread and underestimate cues from the disruption. Any failure is magnified to prove the bigger point that everything's fine the way it is. It's the "baby with the bath water" syndrome that's so inherent in businesses confronting disruptive innovations.

In the following graphic, which is a re-worked version of an image from Borrell Associates and Harvard Business School, the Media 2.0 circle is encroaching on the Media 1.0 space. The area of displacement is viewed as a line of defense by mainstream media, so that's where energy and resources are concentrated. We're busy trying to recover lost territory, but the disruption is actually much bigger. And therein lies opportunity, not woe. The reality is the disruption wouldn't be disruptive unless there were possibilities there. We need to see it as our friend — a place where we can innovate — not as a threat.

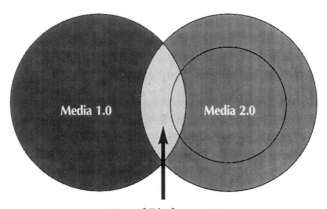

Area of Displacement

The circle of disruption threatens to overtake the business being disrupted.

What do we need to "get" before we can play in the new media world?

1. We are no longer a television station; we're a media company. This is the most fundamental of all the new truths about media, and it applies to any mass marketing entity, be it TV, radio or newspapers. It's crucial to understand, because it defines how we'll proceed. As long as we try to force all of our new business ventures through our brand, we limit not only our options but also our potential vision. And without a vision in this new world, we will surely perish.

The problem with our brand is that it is linked to an old media entity in a new media world. Our brands won't save us, because media brands don't translate to the Web without the systems, mass-marketing business models, and baggage of our real world operations. Think about it. We may still produce large, cumulative audiences, but viewing habits have changed so much that brand loyalty is irrelevant. It's a commoditized TV world in which we live; it's all the same. We even face irrelevancy in news, because the vast majority of people in any market simply don't watch local TV news anymore. Those audiences are in a free fall in most places and in general decline everywhere. If they stopped following our brand on-the-air, what makes us think they will fawn all over us online?

So what do we accomplish by driving our shrinking and aging audience to our branded sites on the Web? Not much, and this is why I advise clients to not put their future into a branded portal Website.

If we can view ourselves as media companies and not television stations, then we can use some of our resources to build revenue-generating businesses that go beyond our brands, and this is what will determine who wins and who loses down-the-road.

Google, for example, is exploding exponentially, because the company made the decision long ago that it would create the world's largest (searchable) directory of information. The company has little value beyond its database, but it is growing that database every minute of every day. What about local information? Google wants that, too, but we don't have to let them have it. Who will build the local database? There is absolutely nothing stopping a local media company from doing this, but a television station wouldn't even consider it.

This is just one example of how thinking of ourselves as media companies instead of TV stations opens our minds to possibilities to not only make money but also meet the information needs of the communities we serve.

2. Application separation works both ways. The more we deny and ignore the realities of the new world, and the more we consider it a threat, the less inclined we'll be to see that we can use the same technologies and energies to compete in areas where TV stations previously never could.

   Remember the case of Kodak. The company wasted energy and resources defending its film business against the disruptive innovation of digital photography. New management embraced the new technology, and now Kodak is clawing its way back to the top. But what about Polaroid?

   Which one are we? We need to embrace the tools of the personal media revolution and use them to our advantage. We're experts in many areas, but we need to point that expertise in a different direction. What holds us back is our belief that we're "professionals" and therefore either immune from the citizens media explosion or above it. As media companies instead of TV stations, however, we can free ourselves of both structural and inertia barriers.

3. The user is in control. It is impossible to do business in a world where streams must lead back to the local media company unless we first accept that we're no longer in charge. This is perhaps the most difficult thing for traditional media people to "get," because everything about it is counterintuitive to our instincts and training. The law of attraction is our only friend, and we must give up our belief that we can "market" (manipulate) our way out of the demands of the new world.

   As our audiences have shrunk, we've continued to talk only with those who are left behind, while ignoring those who've gone on to discover other ways of meeting their news and information needs. The problem for us is that these new forms are consumer-empowering. They're in charge; we aren't. While we may "get" this, we don't like it, because we don't know how to behave in such a paradigm.

But while we're in denial, we drift farther away from the people we so desperately need to generate revenue in an unbundled media world.

4. Transparency is the new currency. All our lives in the TV biz, we've pretended that our viewers don't know what goes on behind the scenes, nor do they know the tricks of our trade. The blogosphere, reality shows, and the popularity of insider media — especially that which targets the entertainment industry — have pulled back the curtain and revealed us for what we are. We cannot continue to shove slickness down our viewers' throats, nor can we operate in old ways when people can see that the emperor has no clothes.

   In terms of news, we also can't keep pretending that our audiences trust us the way they once did, nor can we even assume that we speak on their behalf anymore. Gallup measurements show media trust at an all-time low and headed downward.

   As Stephen Covey wrote, "You can't talk your way out of something you behaved your way into." (2) We need to learn that truth and adopt the paradigm of Media 2.0 — if you share your tools and your world with your users (viewers), they'll participate. This means getting off our pedestals and rubbing elbows with our communities. It also means the courage to be transparent, to stop hiding who we are and what we are from the people we're trying to serve.

5. It's not all or nothing. This is by far the biggest block to real progress in the face of the Media 2.0 disruption. We hear things like "mass marketing is dead" and we react negatively, in part, because we intuitively know that's simply not true. There will always be mass marketing approaches to business in our world — even if they're smaller in scale. What Umair Haque calls the "blockbuster" events necessary to create mass audiences are and will be fewer and farther between, and that should be a concern to any mass marketer.

Do we have to drop *all* mass marketing to succeed in a Media 2.0 world? I don't think so, but we do need to develop methods and models that work in an unbundled, individualized media world, and these are definitely at enmity with mass marketing practices. We can and we must learn them, however

We need to strike the words "always" and "never" from our language, because this is vastly more complex that simple black and white explanations would have us believe. That said, "getting it" includes a little willingness to explore extremes despite how we feel about them.

Elisabeth Kübler-Ross was an expert on loss, and she wrote an historic book about it called *On Death and Dying.* (3) In it, she opened our eyes to the realities of grieving. Psychologists have expanded the ideas of grieving to include such things as job loss, divorce, and even the empty nest syndrome. Grieving, she wrote, has five stages: denial, anger, bargaining, depression and acceptance. They don't necessarily follow one after the other, but they're all present on the road to acceptance.

And isn't acceptance what we really need now, as our old media models slip away? To the extent that we look the other way, bitch and moan, try to "work together with new media," or wax nostalgic in our own despondency, we're sitting ducks for others not tied to the past. Acceptance is what we need to shake the "don't get it" label and move forward with innovative models that meet the information needs of our communities and bring the roads of business opportunity back to us.

After all, we have a TV station in our arsenal. That gives us a huge advantage over anybody else.

THE REMARKABLE OPPORTUNITIES
OF UNBUNDLED MEDIA

November 1, 2005

What parent isn't familiar with the struggle to get little Johnny to eat those food items that taste a little different? These sorts of food wars have changed over the years, because our addiction to fast food has produced mouths and taste buds that have difficulty trusting anything that doesn't come in a wrapper. It's not just Brussels sprouts anymore. My then 13-year-old daughter once spit out a mouthful of homemade strawberry pie (imagine that), because the texture was unfamiliar and somehow threatening.

But we grow up, and we try things. We discover that our fears were silly.

This analogy is apropos to many things in life, and especially in the media world today. Unbundled media, for example, is an acquired taste, but once the palette has been sufficiently soaked in its broth, there is no going back. This is the great and deadly reality confronting all of the mainstream, for bundled media is all we know, and it's increasingly a Twinkie next to the strawberry pie of that which is unbundled.

Television newscasts and programs, CDs, the morning paper, cable TV tiers, magazines, books, movies — virtually every form of mass media comes already bundled. It's as much a part of our consumer society as keeping up with the Joneses. The bundle includes everything that makes up the whole, from the content to the ads. This is how we do things. "Drive people to the bundle" is the mantra of mass marketing, which then uses its part of the bundle to rifle unwanted messages this way and that.

But bundled media has a serious drawback, one that cannot be wished away. It takes time to consume anything prebundled, and time is a precious and valued commodity in today's world. We're working more, and we have less time to ourselves.

And so, driven by the very real demand of less time, we've begun the process of tasting that which is unbundled. We unbundle television shows by skipping the commercials with our DVRs. We unbundle CDs by downloading the songs we want. We unbundle the national media by subscribing to specific RSS feeds. The signs of a burgeoning unbundled media world are everywhere.

Viacom's Comedy Central cable channel is launching what they're calling a "broadband TV channel." Motherload will essentially be a Website offering unbundled TV media. Modeled after MTV's Overdrive (also Viacom), the site offers ad-supported two to eight minute clips in a slick Flash player. It'll be original content, along with some repurposed Comedy Central clips. The possibilities for this concept are endless, and Viacom is smart to be exploring here.

MSNBC is beginning to offer a same-day stream of NBC Nightly News. The video stream will be available at 10 pm ET each night after the last station on the West Coast has aired it.

ABC has inked a deal with Apple to provide same day, downloadable feeds of some of its programming, which can be played in the new Video iPod.

All of these are forms of unbundled media, and this is just the beginning. Unbundling will take place at the most basic levels, and technologies will flourish that assist people in rebundling according to their preferences.

Our response as media professionals has been to sigh and offer repurposed media items to the noisy crowd that used to be our consumers. This is a grave mistake, for it shortsightedly views the drift to unbundled media as a sideshow. It is not; it's the whole enchilada, and while we're busy toying with it, people we never imagined would be our competitors are grabbing market share. Can you say "Yahoo!"?

The problem is that while we're repurposing our content, the bulk of our attention is still focused on the creation of that which is bundled. That's where the money is, we convince ourselves, and so we don't ask the right questions.

Like what could we do differently in a world of unbundled media? As TV news people, for example, would we start our day thinking about how we're going to fill the hole of the evening newscast, and empower program producers to use our considerable resources to craft bundled programs? Or would we think about creating unbundled bits that could be repurposed in a bundled program and along the way be made available in their unbundled form.

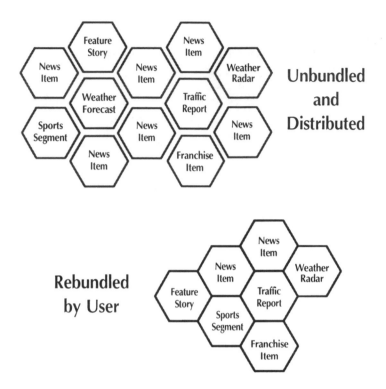

Perhaps it's time for those of us in local mainstream media to start thinking seriously about this unbundled thing. In so doing, we might actually discover that elusive business model that everybody's waiting for. The business model is not as far away as you might think. There are at least six ways we can make money in an unbundled media world, and only a couple of them are obvious. For purposes of discussion, an "item" is any unbundled piece of media, including advertisements, provided by the media company.

1. Ads in or around the items. This is the model that Viacom is using and the existing revenue model for most streaming media on information Websites. It's a simple matter to "attach" a commercial to an unbundled piece of content, and the only question is the length to which users will sit through such an attachment. The answer seems to depend on the

length of the video item, with seven to 12-seconds being optimum for a simple 90-second streaming clip.

The desire to be able to sell this type of advertising is moving print media companies into the online video business. It's also why the Associated Press is making such a concerted effort to provide video to members of the cooperative.

This is a logical move for media companies, but most are still simply repurposing what they already have in house. This may generate a healthy revenue stream, but it does little to move the company into a genuinely unbundled media strategy.

And we must learn that coupling a video story to a particular branded player is just another form of bundling. If people can't link directly to the video or play it with their own player or in an embedded window on their site, it's not unbundled media. We can force the file to play from our own servers, but beyond that, we're not participating in an unbundled media world. When we think we've unbundled something, we probably need to unbundle it some more. That's how deep this new paradigm is taking us.

2. Expand distribution channels and the number and type of items offered. In concert with attaching ads to unbundled items, the next logical step is to scale it by increasing not only the number of unbundled items being offered, but also

the type. This is typical mass market thinking, but it also applies in today's unbundled marketplace. Take a look, for example, at the RSS page of a typical television station Website and compare that with, for example, CNN or MSNBC. The station might offer news, weather and sports RSS feeds, but CNN provides 15 feeds and MSNBC 28, including five video feeds. If we're going to play in the unbundled world, we need to think beyond the boundaries of news, weather and sports.

3. Charge for some items. This is another obvious entry into the unbundled media world, but one that must be approached carefully. If there is some content niche your media company owns or other exclusive material you feel has value beyond what can be monetized through advertising, you may consider charging a subscriber fee of some sort. The jury is still out on *The New York Times* "Times Select" venture, for example, so there's not a lot of evidence out there on this one.

4. Ads as items. Assuming our unbundled media items are distributed via RSS, another way to make money in the unbundled world is to distribute advertisements *as items* in our distribution feeds.

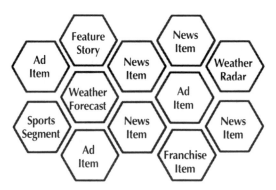

Online advertising is largely print advertising, and this has been the model for most forms of RSS advertising. Print ads "surround" content text, which is why advertisers resort to bells and whistles in order to attract attention. By distributing advertisements *as items*, we use more of a broadcasting ad model, in that the ads are a part of the stream of content. PaidContent.org has pioneered this kind of advertising, and it makes great sense in an unbundled media world.

The new video iPod has already encouraged the creation of infomercials that can be distributed via the Web, and this is another revenue opportunity for local media companies.

5. Helping users re-bundle. One of the most logical moves for local media companies in an unbundled media world is to get into the business of helping consumers rebundle content, regardless of its source. Branded RSS readers and local aggregators are the vehicles for this, with the media company serving ads in the software application being used to re-bundle distributed content.

   The *Los Angeles Times* provides its readers with a branded RSS reader, and "Nashville Is Talking" and "The Bay Area Is Talking" are examples of local aggregator sites.

6. Ad feeds. The greatest potential for local media companies in an unbundled world is the creation of new businesses that take advantage of the company's stature within the local advertising community. The sad reality, however, is that broadcasters and newspapers are so caught up trying to maintain bottom-line integrity that these opportunities are being delivered into the hands of non-media people.

   RSS is a way of life to those familiar with the unbundled world, while media companies view it only as a way to move their own content. In a world where all that we make is unbundled, it's much easier to see the opportunities beyond our broadcast towers or newspaper delivery people. This is why we need to start looking at how to use the unbundled technologies and systems to help commerce in the communities we serve.

   Since anything unbundled that the media company creates can be distributed and rebundled at the customer end, this opens the door for the development of an infinite number of local smart aggregator sites that can be developed. In the example below, we've created a smart health aggregator site that draws health content from many sources and distributes that content via RSS to anyone who wants it. Hence, when consumers are rebundling content items, they can include items from a brand new business operated and promoted by the media company.

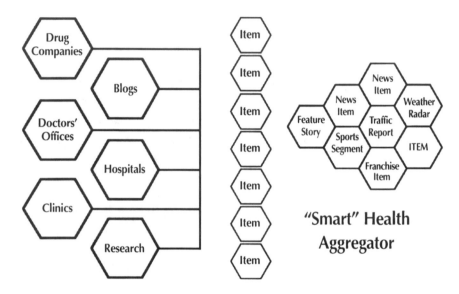

"Smart" Health Aggregator

RSS and distributed content have not gone unnoticed by the business community. Titleist, the golf equipment maker, offers RSS feeds for people interested in its products, and this model can be easily duplicated at the local retail level. Aggregating multiple retail business feeds is the natural business of local media companies, but somebody has to make the feeds available first. Whoever does that will have a significant advantage in the community. (See graphic, page 291.)

Of course, technology will one day bring those feeds directly to consumers, but don't underestimate the value of aggregating such feeds. People who can do this well will be producing the "sale paper" of tomorrow.

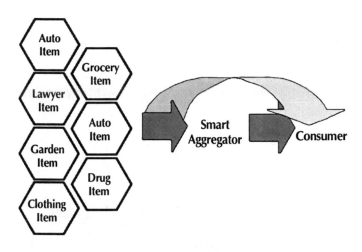

The business opportunities for unbundled media are truly remarkable, but in order for local media companies to take advantage of them, they must begin viewing themselves as more than one-dimensional deliverers of bundled media. For broadcasters, that means finding the courage to say to ourselves that our transmitter isn't our top business anymore. It's but one of many, and our internal systems and even our organizational charts should reflect that. Only then will we be able to truly reinvent ourselves for the future.

This is a tough sell for the industry, because our bread and butter, bundled models are still delivering significant revenues and will continue to do so for years to come. Those revenues, however, won't (can't) be enough to sustain real business growth, and so the only choice seems to be to cut costs. We keep missing the point that revenue isn't the problem; audience is the problem, and they're moving to the unbundled world.

And they're not coming back, either. After all, once you've acquired a taste for filet, a steady diet of hamburger doesn't cut it anymore.

THE UNBUNDLED NEWSROOM

November 9, 2005

My father worked in a furniture factory to support his family in the 1950s and early 1960s. I visited the place once as a child, but I didn't pay much attention to what he did, which was to stand in the same place for eight hours and make the same router cuts, on identical pieces of wood, over and over again. I was too busy looking at the enormous piles of sawdust and smelling the smells to notice that, further down the assembly line, workers put his pieces together with others to assemble nice furniture.

This is the model of all manufacturing. We make the pieces that fit with other pieces that make up the whole, and it's the model of making television news as well. We come to work and have a story meeting. We brainstorm and discuss. We go out and cover. Armed with sophisticated computer technology, producers take a little bit of this and a little bit of that to shape their programs. Orders are passed along to field units who take the pictures and make the sound bites that are later cut to fit the needs of the producer. Live trucks and reporters are dispatched to provide a sense of urgency for every story, all under the guidance and direction of the producer.

And so it goes, in the same endless, repeatable cycle that my father knew in the furniture factory. Occasionally, something new and exciting comes along, but eventually, we return to the same system of building our news programs.

We're good at it too, having made technology our servant. Every significant television news technological development of the past 50 years happened to assist command and control of what's known as "real time production" — the ability to make complex, live television programs in one, fell swoop. The thinking has always been that pre-produced television was simply too time-consuming and costly to apply to day-to-day news programs. Besides, the deliberate shift away from substance to one of shallow coverage of breaking news events made the idea of pre-production seem silly.

"People want to feel like they're participating in history," we said, and that gave us live, live, live. The 24-hour news model led the way.

But now we find that for all our expertise at producing real-time television, people aren't watching us anyway (major event exceptions noted), and we ought to be thinking about whether our assumptions still apply. Just because we can do something well doesn't mean that we should be doing it, especially when the evidence clearly shows a major shift in the way media is being consumed.

Time has become the principal currency in our culture, because we're working more hours and playing less. So technology is helping us unbundle media from its pre-packaged state, so that we can consume what we want, when we want it, and increasingly, where we want it. This is the real enemy of the status quo. So powerful is this paradigm shift that it has the potential to destroy the fundamental business model of mainstream media unless we begin to adapt to it instead of fighting it.

You can actually pet a porcupine by going *with* the flow of its spikes, so let's try that with this new world. Let's dismantle a day in the life of a contemporary newsroom and put it back together in the world of unbundled media.

We know that seven in ten people who visit news Websites do so during the day, and most RSS-delivered subscription feeds also take place during the day or in the earliest part of the day. The consumption of unbundled media, therefore, takes place in large part before people go to work and while they're at work. This becomes our new target, and that impacts our current methods and systems, because we're used to making something that is birthed at the end of the day.

There is a growing discussion over whether it's good for business or not to permit workers to get their news during the day, but the reality is that it's going to happen whether it does so on the worker's computer or on some other portable device. That's because technology isn't what's driving it; time is the engine that's pulling the change. We must not forget that, as we move forward with our new model.

So our essential mission is to first serve the information needs of our community throughout the day, and then to create programs that will summarize the news of the day. This means a fundamental change in our approach to the news, for the best way to meet the needs of people during the day is to create news in an unbundled form. No longer can we simply repurpose content that's created for a bundled program and distribute it elsewhere. On the contrary, our unbundled content is what should be repurposed to create our end-of-the-day summaries.

Of fundamental importance in this paradigm is the recognition that every moment of our day is committed to meeting the information needs of an audience in that moment. This is the reverse of our current thinking, and whoever reaches this point first in a competitive marketplace will be rewarded by people hungry for news and information — including those who used to make up our audiences.

An unbundled newsroom begins earlier in the day, and its systems are built around immediate publication via the Internet. That means field crews need tools for directly publishing to the Web, including text, stills, video, blogs, e-mail, cellphones, handhelds, and especially RSS. We need to see ourselves as pushing content at every turn in the creation and development of our journalism. Nothing is too insignificant to justify a departure from this goal.

A single story, therefore, contains elements for publication at various points.

1. We're pursuing this and why.
2. Here's what we're finding.
3. Here's what we've found.
4. Here's reaction.
5. Here's our finished product.

Think of these "points" as unbundled bits of media that we can distribute. We're dispatching a minimum of five elements on this story during the day in this model. That's five opportunities for a person to read, watch or listen and five opportunities for us to serve them an attached ad, assuming that's the revenue model we've chosen. Regardless, we're churning out a continuous stream of content choices for people in our community.

At each point of the story, we're also soliciting input from our audience in the form of comments and reactions. This can be incorporated later into our on-air daily summaries. All of these elements will be stored as part of our permanent record, so that they can be later called upon for use in long tail scenarios. We must never be fooled into thinking, however, that the permanent record is more important than meeting the information needs of people during the newsgathering process.

If we're going to make this happen, we have to drop our formality and move to a more authentic "voice." We're telling people what's happening in their community, not presenting a well-honed speech in front of an auditorium of thousands.

We need to treat every story as if it impacted everybody, because the reality is that it impacts somebody, and that's really the point of unbundled media. If somebody takes the time to read it, it's important to us. In a mass media, bundled world, we're trying to cast a net over as many people as possible, and that forms the basis of relevancy to us. But in an unbundled world, every single person matters. They are the ones in charge, not us. It's about relationships and conversation.

Since the industry hasn't demanded the technology to do this sort of thing (yet), we have to adopt the tools of the personal media revolution until it does. That means blogging software, FTP uploading, podcasting systems, small cameras, laptops, wireless broadband connections and a working knowledge of RSS distribution.

Our Websites will be transformed from petty marketing portals into interactive and customizable workspaces for users. Since everything we're making is RSS-enabled, we don't really care where people consume our content, and that includes places like myYahoo, myMSN, Live.com, Google's personalized homepage, or any of a hundred other Web-based or desktop RSS readers.

Since all of this material is RSS-enabled, we can tag it and rebundle it in any form we choose. If users can rebundle our content (which we want them to do), then we should take advantage of the same technologies and rebundle items for our own purposes.

Our broadcast news products are an example of our rebundling. Producers are tasked with the job of repurposing the content created throughout the day and serving it in a summarized form, and in so doing, transforming newscasts from staged platforms with an artificial sense of importance into real summaries of the news of the day. Anchors can become genuine guides in this process, instead of reading predictable intros and scripted interaction with reporters in the field. Gone is the artificial energy created by an obsession with unnecessary live shots. That's replaced by the drama of real stories that impact people and the satisfying sense of being informed.

Purists will argue that there is a need for compelling live news coverage during newscasts, and where that's justified, we should do it. Perhaps we need a bridge between the old and the new, and perhaps that should be some sort of hybrid newscast. The only thing that matters is that the end-of-day products not be driving the ship.

Just as our forefathers had to make adjustments when our culture moved from agricultural to technological, so we must make adjustments as media moves from a bundled to an unbundled paradigm. The consumer/user is now clearly in charge, and that means our world has been turned upside down. We'll surely not respond properly, if we choose to view things from an upright posture in this stand-on-your-head world. We must break our existing habits and structures in order to find something new that appeals to people and sustains revenue.

My father quit the furniture factory after his three sons left home. He went to work in the motor pool of the local police department. It was work he loved, hanging around with all those cops. Always something new. Never boring. Meanwhile, the factory automated and later was assimilated into a multinational company and eventually closed. People still need furniture, but the way it's made has changed. There's no longer a need for a guy standing in the same place, cutting the same piece of wood, over and over again.

It kind of seems appropriate, somehow.

NEWS AS A COMMODITY

August 13, 2007

In the world of business economics, few words frighten the market leader like "commoditization" or "commodification." In plain English, this means that the market for a unique, branded product that the leader produces is transformed into one that's based purely on price. It takes time, and competition is the cause, but over the lifetime of many products — especially those that cross the line from luxury to necessity — they become commoditized.

Consumers are usually the winners when products are commoditized, because the market produces lower prices. Recent examples would be generic pharmaceuticals and commodity silicon chips. Once you know that the active ingredient in Tylenol is acetaminophen, there's no need to pay more for the branded variety. When drug patents expire, the companies who held the patents usually alter them somewhat to produce, for example, a "timed-release" variation in an effort to maintain market share. This only works for so long.

In the silicon chip industry, there are specialized, highly-sophisticated chips, and there are chips that perform basic functions. The latter is a global market that is highly commoditized.

Sometimes, commoditized products become a part of other, bigger markets. For example, you don't see a lot of ads for gas stations anymore, because, well, gas is gas, or so it is with consumers. While not a true commodity (crude oil has avoided commoditization), things other than brand are at play in consumer decisions. Purists may argue, but this is a form of commodification.

In my younger days, the petroleum companies battled over the airwaves, trying to convince consumers that their gas was better, cleaner or somehow made your car run more efficiently than the station on the opposite corner. Does anybody else remember Pure's old "Be Sure with Pure" slogan?

Nowadays, people make decisions based on the price sign, which side of the street it's on, or what's inside the convenience store.

Qwik Trip makes a great iced coffee. Who cares about the gas? Gas is now a part of the convenience store industry.

To fight all this — to delay the inevitable — a whole manual of strategies and tactics exists, whereby the market leader attempts to crush competition and protect the company's investment. Branding is a big part of that, and so companies spend millions to convince the public that their brand of what's becoming commoditized is better than the other versions. Ultimately, though, the choice belongs to the consumer, and usually price becomes the paramount consideration.

In the world of media, products used to be divided into categories: newspapers, magazines, television, radio, etc., but the personal media revolution (a term coined by J. D. Lasica in his book *Darknet, Hollywood's War Against the Digital Generation*) is eliminating the infrastructure and distribution mechanisms that make each of these unique. Not only is the digital generation taking advantage of this to create their own media companies, but the incumbent companies are using technology to transform themselves as well.

The *Washington Post*'s online division has not only been running videos for many years, but their video journalists have actually won National Press Photographers Association news video awards. The

AP is now becoming more video-centric, spreading video news to newspapers through the country. Most major newspaper companies — seeing the handwriting on the wall — have adopted video strategies. Online ad revenue growth is predicted to come from video, so everybody's a TV station now.

Content management systems for television station Websites were originally text-oriented, because that's what the early iterations of the Web could handle. Spellcheck suddenly became an essential tool for TV newsrooms, as stations began to compete in the print world of newspapers.

Dan Mason, president of CBS radio division, told Jack Myers recently, "In the near future, every radio station will have the ability to become a TV station. We will see Webcasts and Webisodes. There's no reason we can't have our own Webcast shows with talent (in the same way Imus was simulcast on MSNBC). Radios will soon be developed with TV screens. The terrestrial radio medium will evolve and occupy more share of the digital space." (1)

In TNS Media Intelligence's "StrADegy: Advertising In The Digital Age" report, President-CEO Steven Fredericks argues that in the future, "Content is defined not by its old media name, but by its core property: text, video and audio. All content, clarified and freed, can be distributed via any converged technology." (2)

The world of blogs, video blogs and other forms of citizens media is exploding, and media companies are frantically trying to get in on the action. Anybody can do video. Anybody can create text. Anybody can make audio. Media scarcity has been turned on its head. The only real scarcity that matters today is the attention of the people formerly known as the audience in the decaying mass marketing paradigm.

The point is that media itself is being commoditized and, along with it, the content it provides. This is a key fruit of the personal media revolution, and already the economics of media are shifting in response. No longer can news content alone carry the burden of supporting the specialized infrastructures and distribution models of media of the past. No longer is "news" sufficient to justify subscriber fees or high dollar ad models, because consumers are increasingly deciding that it's all the same.

The *New York Times'* decision to drop its Times Select subscription service is a direct response to the commoditization of news. It was a tactical error in the first place to create such a foolish venture — a quick revenue fix that cost them in the long run. We must never forget that revenue isn't about revenue with public companies; it's about revenue growth, and there was no way a subscription service was going to grow revenue in an era of commoditized news and information. Moreover, Times Select cost the paper dearly in its need to be a top-dog news authority, because its "voice" — its unique positions on issues — was kept behind a pay wall.

Last year, CNN dropped its pay-to-view service in favor of an ad-supported model, because it wasn't producing the kind of revenue growth they had hoped it would produce.

But both of these organizations — and every company in the professional news business — are fighting commoditization, because the whole world of media is morphing into one, giant glob of sameness, and it's hard to convince people you're special when they think everybody's the same. This is the breakdown of Media 1.0. This is what's destroying the foundation upon which our businesses have been built.

The idea that "the people" are in charge is the most difficult bridge to cross for media people who are used to having it their way. It is at the core of Media 2.0, and it needs to impact everything we do from here on out. Aggregation and context are king now, because that glob of sameness is a puzzle to many consumers. Information has always been like that, but the tools for filtering it are now in the hands of the people.

Brand matters, and it matters more than ever, but what does that brand stand for? If it's "we're special" or "we're unique," it's not going to work. The audience is in charge and they will determine your brand based on performance, not promotion. Promotion is a Media 1.0 concept; the Law of Attraction is what works in today's marketplace. Attraction is the defining dynamic of influence in our increasingly postmodern culture, and it is 180 degrees from what mainstream media companies currently practice.

Here's part of my essay, "The Power of Attraction," that was published three years ago:

> In life, there is intended influence and unintended influence. The former is the work of, among others, journalists, entertainers, PR flacks, advertisers, politicians and all sorts of bullies. The latter is that which resonates within, a picture that inspires, the voice of a friend, human touch, a laugh, a right word spoken in time of need. The line between them cannot be deliberately bridged, for the right to be unintentionally influenced belongs to the individual, and that is powerfully enabled by the Internet.

The net allows people to determine nearly every influence in their lives, although most people don't yet use it that way. It's just a matter of time, however, because the technology to do so is advancing in both sophistication and ease of use.

This is extremely important for people in the media business to understand, because news in a postmodern world isn't a product and, therefore, not a commodity. It's a conversation.

Doc Searls, one of the authors of *The Cluetrain Manifesto* and the creator of the phrase "markets are conversations" has this to say about the concept of news as a commodity:

> The Net revolution has always been about radically improving the connections between demand and supply, and about equipping profusions on both sides of the relationship — while reducing intermediary costs and frictions in the direction of zero.
>
> As a term for describing this development, "commoditization" is a misleading failure. Roles are changing far more than "content" — a term which itself misleads by reducing the informing of people to deliverable commodities. People still need to inform other people. More ways to do that will emerge. There will be business models there. Supply and demand will find each other. We

need to figure out how to make new and better money with new and better roles. Advertising will still be part of that picture, but it won't fund the whole thing. (3)

I certainly don't disagree with Doc, but there's an important distinction between what he's saying and the theme expressed here. News as a product is very much a part of the Media 1.0 world and the economics thereof, and I don't believe that mass media and mass marketing will ever completely go away. It's a part of human nature to use a crowd to draw attention to oneself.

It's actually likely that new masses will be created through the tribal aspects of Postmodernism (note Jeff Jarvis's excellent analysis of new Pew research "the emergence of media tribes") (4) and that those will be advertiser-supported. However, the growing of revenue through the scarcity of content in a mass marketing, one-to-many paradigm is surely bound for extinction. In many ways, it's already vanished, replaced by a nostalgic illusion. Media companies, therefore, who are able to successfully detach themselves from this illusion will survive and thrive in the new world, but those who can't will become mere shadows of their former selves.

When confronted with this, many ask who will function as the fourth estate when this happens? The people will, because the fourth estate is more than the institutional press.

First Amendment press freedoms apply to everybody, and we cannot, as a culture, allow this to be redefined by changing the meaning of its words. The earliest dictionary that can be applied to early American documents is Webster's 1828 classic. Note carefully, the appropriate definition of the word "press" as used in the First Amendment:

> The art or business of printing and publishing. A free press is a great blessing to a free people; a licentious press is a curse to society. (5)

So "the press" is a business or an art, which opens the door to include anybody. This doesn't sit well with the status quo, but it does paint a picture appropriate to today.

The role of professional news and information in a Media 2.0 context is just beginning to be defined and articulated, and it will certainly have to play by the rules of engagement, beginning with Dan Gillmor's discovery that "the readers (audience) know more than I do." This moves it to conversation status, and the Web's ability to facilitate that. We already know, for example, that the professional press is often the conversation starter, and that ought to be deemed worthwhile in Doc's supply-and-demand chain.

This is all very unsettling for people who are trying to figure out the new while managing the old. We must fix the car while driving it at the same time.

Like changes in culture, changes in media aren't all or nothing, and we can't let ourselves lose sight of that. If it were so, video really would have killed the radio star. Postmodernism doesn't "negate" modernism anymore than news as a conversation completely obliterates news as a product. The business problem, therefore, is one of evolving to amphibian status — the ability to live and breathe both under the water and above it.

We can do this, but it begins with the courage and the willingness to try.

IT's NOT THE SAME GAME

January 8, 2008

During the Vietnam War, I was stationed at a long-range navigation base in the Philippines with 15 other guys. Our beacon was used by the B-52s to guide them as they bombed North Vietnam. It was considered "isolated duty," and we had a lot of free time on our hands, especially during the rainy season. We played poker and a wonderful game called Euchre, a trump game where the jack of trumps is the highest-ranked card and the jack of the other same colored suit is the second highest.

Euchre is only popular in pockets around the states, so we had to teach it to newcomers who joined us on the base. One guy, a fellow from New Jersey named McDowell, said, "Oh, this is like Hi, Lo, Jack and Game." Actually, the games had little in common except the use of trump, so we set him straight.

"No, there may be similarities, but that's a different game. This is Euchre."

A few years ago, I was delivering my new media message to a group of media executives led by a man with great vision and skill. His history and thinking, however, was all based in the Media 1.0, mass marketing paradigm, so his disconnect with the Media 2.0 concept was along these lines:

"No matter how you slice it, Terry, it's still the same game."

He was referring to the assembling of audience, whether en masse or by grouping fragments. This has long been the central framework for advertising, and it is in this area that media companies have considerable expertise. But is it true? Is the revenue challenge for media companies today one of understanding new rules for the same game, or is it a new game altogether?

As we said to the newcomers back in the Philippines, "There may be similarities, but it's not the same game."

Late last year, Jeremy Allaire, founder/CEO of Brightcove and one of the brightest minds in technology, wrote in his predictions for 2008 that nothing about the Internet changes the fundamentals of media, adding that "value is created by controlling the content or controlling access to the audience."

"Media companies with established brands and new start-ups," he continued, "will continue to build successful branded destinations so they can control the access to audiences." (1)

This is quite a statement, and one that bears close examination in light of disruptions to mass media, disintermediation, unbundling and the escalating fragmentation of all forms of media. The key fundamental that has shifted is that the pyramid is upside-down. The people formerly known as the audience are now in charge. Access to the audience, therefore, is what's restricted today, not access to the content.

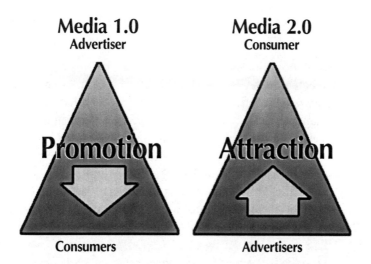

It's the opposite of mass marketing. Consider the soapbox image of a guy above a crowd pitching his message, the preacher at the pulpit, the anchor at the news desk, or the full page ad in the paper. These are all one-way messages from the source to the crowd. The Web, however, makes the opposite possible. The consumer is on the soapbox facing a sea of messages. The mission now is to make those available in an easy-to-access form.

We're in an "unmarketing" era now, one wherein attraction is the key to value creation, not promotion. The days of the captive audience are gone forever, and how do you "control access to content," when your content is either being commodified or replaced by that which isn't controlled? In an era of attraction as the key to growth, more attention — and resources — must be given to product creation, not marketing. What we say about what we create was important in a top-down paradigm, but it's mostly meaningless in a world where users are in charge.

So the assumption that controlling access to content is still a valid business model in today's disruptive environment is problematic, at best, and more likely, dead in the water altogether. There are three issues to consider:

First of all, the "branded destinations" spoken of aren't unique in the architecture of the Web, and this is a problem. It doesn't matter how many people "visit," how long they stay, or what's available through any particular URL, the Web considers them all the same, what I call pixels on a page. Therefore, any system of control is fragmented to the nth degree. Cable changed the value proposition of broadcasting, and the Web does the same to cable. We can spin things with HDTV and other things like specialized content, etc., but the dynamic is the same as what drug companies encounter when patents expire on their products. "Time-released" becomes the selling point, not the product itself. But people — who are driven by price — go for the new generic. Same with content creators. No matter how we spin it, it's just another pixel on the page in the architecture of the Web.

So from a structural perspective, the media value proposition is lessened, because the eyeballs necessary to earn from that "value" have thousands, if not millions, of other choices. Moreover, as content becomes more and more commodified, it gets harder to identify any of it as "special."

Secondly, the assumption requires a belief that this "content" has sufficient qualities to compel the eyeballs in the first place. This, too, is a problem, because the creators of professional content have known — even before people starting unbundling things for themselves — that it was getting harder and harder to produce profitable demand. There were many factors at play here, but the one that the creators least wish to discuss is that content built on previous success — that is to say content based on research and history — does not necessarily lead to audience growth. And without growth, the fundamentals are meaningless. Hollywood, the record companies and the rest of the copyright industry are largely victims of the crap they've been producing for years. But crap is easy — and it can be profitable.

It is into this paradigm that J. D. Lasica's "personal media revolution" has blossomed, people educating and entertaining themselves with technology's help. Nokia is predicting that in just five years, this type of "media" will account for one-fourth of all entertainment in the U.S.

The value of YouTube has never been in the distributing of the kinds of content described in media accounts of alleged pirating; it has always been about growing communities who are entertaining themselves. Professional video creators can scoff at and discount this all they wish, but eyeballs viewing this type of content are eyeballs that once needed the restraints of those creating value through restricted access.

Thirdly, and perhaps most importantly, this assumption dismisses the contemporary reality that advertisers — the people who funded the assumption in its earlier times — don't need the content anymore in order to do business. Advertising *is* content in Media 2.0, and where money is spent by advertisers in creating their own content, it is not being spent on supporting the content of Jeremy's "branded destinations." Some advertisers are actually becoming their own media companies, and this challenges the assumptions of traditional media.

The problem may not be that the value proposition of media is changing as much as the definition of media itself, which is why companies must proceed down simultaneous strategic paths — monetizing their "content" as best they can but also moving to become portfolio companies by innovating in the worlds of advertising and Media 2.0.

So "media" is not the same game as it was in the old world, and the most dangerous move any media company can make today is to operate as though it's simply a matter of rules changes. It's not. It's a new game, and the rules aren't so much about gathering audience (en masse or fragmented) as they are about two significant value creation opportunities:

1. Helping the people formerly known as the audience do their own thing. The rise of personal media is a significant opportunity for local media companies, because in producing

their own forms of media, people are demonstrating a desire to do what we do and know what we know. If nothing else, we can teach them, but by enabling this — actually helping the process — we are in a better position to organize and aggregate its output in a variety of new businesses.

At a conference of leading edge technical types — pioneers, if you will, of personal media — I asked 500 people if anyone would be interested in a subscription service of raw video that they could use as they wished. Every hand in the place shot up.

There is a market for people creating their own newscasts or creating videos from archival material that's currently just sitting in vaults across the country. This is money waiting to be made.

2. Helping the people formerly known as advertisers do business. The aggregator of the messages is the opportunity here. I wrote about this three years ago in "The Economy of Unbundled Advertising," and it's still a valid business proposition for local media.

Letting people search for the messages they want is clearly one of the paths before us, and it will spawn a whole new form of attraction-based advertising, which will enable commerce in our communities and return local media to a key role therein.

There are business and governmental issues in a world where the "top" is occupied by everyday people. How does one grow a business, for example, when access to the mass is restricted? We'll figure that out. The real meaning of branding will be the foundation of new approaches, for the need to stand out in a crowd of other messages is the real challenge. We're already developing primitive solutions through, for example, search engine optimization.

What about civil defense? How will we get the word out to people in times of emergencies? We'll figure that out, too. Just as we do now, messages of local, regional, national or global concern could be assigned a priority.

And the warning for media companies is serious. We can either participate in the new game, or we will have to deal with increasing irrelevance, because somebody else — most likely the Internet pureplay companies — will do it instead.

SECTION VI

Advertising/ Marketing

The business of media is advertising, but it is all driven by mass market theory and practice. The Web isn't just another mass marketing medium, and this confounds people trying to make money online. Local advertising dollars are currently being gobbled by Google and other Internet pureplays, and this should not be. This section explores how advertising and marketing has been and continues to be changed by the realities of life in a Web-based media world. It contains some of the most often quoted essays in the book, but I continue to run into people who simply cannot get their heads around the ideas contained in them. This section will challenge you more than the rest, especially "Selling Against Ourselves" and "The Economy of Unbundled Advertising."

313

TO BRAND OR NOT TO BRAND

APRIL 24, 2007

My daughter graduates from college next month with a degree in marketing and is rightly asking the question, "What do I do now?" Marketing is a catch-all term these days that includes lots of careers, but mostly, it's about selling. The Internet is impacting selling in ways we're just beginning to understand, so it is to my daughter and all her fellow students everywhere that this essay is dedicated.

Any business executive who's ever written a business plan knows all about core competencies and their relationship to customers. Media core competencies are generally built around some form of editorial content, whether it's the form or style of the content, the people writing it, a particular perspective, or the manner in which it's distributed. Some would say that media *is* content; more so than the vehicles used to move the content.

The Media 1.0 world of mass marketing is all about core competencies, and the farther down the mass marketing stream we've gone, the more we've viewed media products as property.

The term "brand" or "branding" has its origins in a property paradigm. The most obvious example is the wild west world of the cattlemen who marked their stock for identification, although the idea of branding property — even humans — goes back centuries. One of the fundamental concepts of branding, therefore, is the statement that "this is mine," which is certainly an aspect of contemporary branding, too. And as long as media content is property, there's a need to mark it accordingly.

In the marketing world of today, brands are more subconscious and include characteristics such as the emotions and qualities that "connect" a product, company, individual, or service with customers. So branding is associated with the building of relationships.

This is the kind of stuff my daughter and her classmates just learned.

In this context, there are important assumptions that underlie the relationship-building, the most significant being the sense of control that accompanies a long list of strategies and tactics that companies use to build relationships. We build those relationships the way we want to build them, or more precisely, we have the power to build relationships the way we want them. Another assumption is that research alone can correctly speak for customers in the relationship-building process. And then there's the notion that brand management is the straightest path to prosperity, that you can talk your way into business success. A brand is a one-way statement of the value — to the customer — of the product, company, individual or service. That value, however, is what we say it is. A company's brand or brands still state "this is mine."

This is incredibly important stuff in the world of Media 1.0, for that is the home of one-directional media. Without attention to brands here, those businesses who function herein would collapse and disappear, for this is the world of an infinite number of inbound signals for customers. Without a way to cut through all that clutter — and be both consciously and subconsciously considered — media companies especially would die on the vine. Branding is absolutely mission-critical in the world of mass media and mass marketing, especially in this day and age.

The problem is that the mass media and mass marketing world — with its tenets and laws — is being disrupted from every possible end.

- It's possible now to separate content from the form in which it's presented, and that has the potential to strip that "property" from its brand. Media is also being fragmented by the choices available to customers, and in many of these cases, "free" is a tactic that's being employed to pull eyeballs from point A to point B.
- Media content is being disintermediated — the era of the middle man is disappearing, as technology enables customers to get their content (and never forget that they think it's "theirs") straight from the source or a convenient aggregator of that source material.
- Media is being disrupted by the personal media revolution — J.D. Lasica's term for describing the explosion of what tradition media companies call "user-generated content." People making their own media — or tweaking the content of others — means more choices for eyeballs that used to "belong" to the mass marketing world.
- Mass marketing is most disrupted by how people are using technology to remove unwanted advertising from their content. This is not only gutting the core business model of media companies, but it's also destroying their ability to self-promote.

Moreover, people are now able to obtain — with specificity — those items of content that they want to view/read/listen to and chuck the rest. In the words of the Wicked Witch of the West, "What a world! What a world!"

So what does this do to all that business school stuff that my daughter just learned? It doesn't render it irrelevant, but it does demand a rethinking of those assumptions that underlie media's core competencies and the marketing thereof.

Let's look at branding first.

Mark Effron is a smart guy and a former news executive with MSNBC, among a long list of other news management positions. He writes in the April edition of the RTNDA Communicator that for media companies to be successful, everything needs to be under one brand.

"You should have one brand on the air, on the Internet, on digital channels, on cell phones, on PDAs," he wrote. "That's what you are selling: your integrated identity. To have the station called one thing and the Website another is cause for confusion for consumers who already are bombarded with too many brand names and concepts to keep straight." (1)

This is classic Media 1.0 thinking and completely correct, if the media world — Web included — was only about mass marketing. The problem is it isn't, and this has led countless media execs down a path of wasted time and resources with strategies that do nothing but extend their brands. At AR&D, we counsel clients that brand extension is an important part of being a local media company today, but that limiting ourselves to only brand-extension strategies is ultimately self-destructive.

Witness the case of MTV. In April of 2006, Wayne Friedman wrote for MediaPost's TV Watch that MTV had come up with a new metric for advertising across all its platforms — transference.

> "In a multi-platform world, the brand is a signpost to guide consumers," Colleen Fahey Rush, executive vice president of MTVN Research told Mediaweek. "That consumers are more likely to transfer the positive feelings they have for these signposts to the client validates what we've been doing with our non-linear platforms." (2)

Wayne went on to note that this idea is exactly what marketers want ("They'd rather consumers not do too much digging. Just remember all those good feelings—even though a product might actually be worse now than years ago."). (3)

Ms. Rush's argument appears completely logical, and it is from a mass marketing perspective. But here's the thing: consumers also transfer bad feelings they have for these signposts. It's called baggage, and even baggage that's good offline can actually be bad online. MTV, to use Rush's own company, is a cable network. That's its first identity. It used to play music videos (hence, the name "Music Television"), but now it's mostly shows and adventures that involve young people, many of which are titillating and not the stuff of which certain parents would approve. It's owned by Viacom, a media company with lots of baggage, too.

The point is that pushing brands online also carries downsides, the biggest one being that if you can be anything you want online, why limit yourself to your brand? Going in as MTV, therefore, brings everything that MTV is with it, and while this has advantages for old school marketers, it deliberately limits the universe in which the company can play. It also limits creativity and opportunity.

Fast-forward to April of this year and an announcement from MTV of yet another new strategy. This time it involves the creation of "thousands" of Websites from which the network will do business with advertisers and engage with more than just their viewers (they hope).

> "People tend to find content on the Internet through thousands of front doors as opposed to one," said Mika Salmi, the new digital president of MTV Networks…"In some ways we're in a better position than most media companies are — we're where people want to be."
>
> MTV Networks' new strategy is part of an effort by Viacom to reach a wider audience that is spending as much time on the Internet and on video games as watching television, and no longer cares when or where programming is shown.
>
> It aims to build Web sites related to every personality and aspect of its shows, hoping to catch viewers wherever they happen to be on the Internet and on mobile phones, Salmi said in an interview. (4)

So much for brand "transference" and the mass marketing need to assemble people under one roof.

MTV has discovered a great truth about Media 2.0, and one that strikes at the center of any media company's business model — that edge competencies can deliver more and targeted audiences than the company's core competency. The idea of edge competencies was first developed by new media economic guru Umair Haque and it's now a part of the lexicon of contemporary new media thinking. The idea is that the discovery of one's edge competencies — and the creation of niche businesses built around the edge — is a much more natural fit for the Web than that which can only be built around the core.

This is not the kind of stuff my daughter and her classmates learned in school, and yet it's the path to prosperity in the world of Media 2.0.

So let's look at a few of the edge competencies of every local media company.

1. The sales staff. This is a huge edge competency, and one that gives local companies a competitive advantage over the Internet pureplays like Google and Yahoo. We have feet on the street, and those feet are attached to people who have real relationships with purveyors of commerce within our communities. If we can bring ourselves to view this as a separate company that helps enable commerce within the community, we'll be better able to explore business models to that end.

2. News department beats. Every market has special information niches that are built on the unique attributes of the community. Local media companies exploit these niches as beats or special assignments that bind themselves to the essence of the community. Even where these aren't unique, we still divide content into subsections like weather, sports, crime stories, government stories, etc. These are the edge competencies of local media, and they are a perfect starting point for the creation of Media 2.0 businesses.

3. Production and engineering. If we can bring ourselves to expand the skill sets of each of these departments, we'll find

business opportunities therein. Advertisers without a local Web presence can be accommodated by an edge competency that allows us to create Web sites for such businesses. Technical questions and programming assistance also could be hallmarks of our edge, assuming we can see the wisdom of bringing such expertise in-house.

4. Other local programming. Many local media companies produce material that is not under the purview of the news department, and these, too, are edge competencies. We need to be free to exploit these in ways similar to the new MTV strategy. Don't think of the host(s), for example, only as a part of the whole; consider the host(s) as a separate franchise.

This is moving everything away from the core, which is essential edge marketing. From there, you can apply whatever rules you wish, but always remember the viral nature of the Web. One of the essential teachings of Umair Haque is that money is better spent on product than marketing in the upside-down world of the Web. People will find and help you promote what you offer but only if it meets their standards for usability and quality.

Of course, the beauty of local Media 1.0 companies who play in this space is that they have at their disposal a dynamic tool to jumpstart new businesses the old-fashioned way. This is another competitive advantage we have over the Internet pureplays.

All of this new thinking is what marketing students everywhere will face as they move from student to employee in the real world. The beauty of young minds, however, is that they are unencumbered by predisposition and experience. Their intuition hasn't been colored by years of plugging away in the rules of Media 1.0. They will be free to create, and that's just another reason we all should be viewing this as the most exciting time in communications history.

SELLING AGAINST OURSELVES

June 27, 2006

Rounding upwards has been around since people first started estimating. When I hung around with evangelical Christian ministries, we used to call it "evangelically speaking." When standing in front of 501 people, the evangelist would always say, "Looks like we've got nearly a thousand people here tonight." If the rules of math permitted selecting a higher number, you can always count on the evangelist to do so. It's good for his faith.

Of course, this isn't the sole purview of church people. Ask any march organizer how many people showed up, and they'll always stretch things — and often more than a bit. This is why smart reporters will always go to the police for their estimate, because it's usually closer to reality.

Rounding upwards is precisely the problem local television affiliates have as they seek to build online business models. The industry is so accustomed to its own spin that it becomes suddenly dysfunctional in the face of something different. And, to really make money off the Web's disruptive influences, stations must eventually sell against themselves and all that rounding. That's a tough pill to swallow, when your bread and butter is based on such.

But if we don't sell against ourselves, the ad industry will do it for us. Already, there are rumblings in the form of a down upfront season. According to Merrill Lynch, the slowdown caused by digital and multi-platform elements in deals was expected, but the principal reason for the drop was haggling over price. This is just the beginning, because more and more advertisers are taking a very close look at what they've been getting for what they've been paying.

Two years ago, Kathy Sharpe of Sharpe Partners in New York made the proclamation that the advertising industry was in denial. In a guest commentary for MediaPost, Sharpe wrote that the whole industry was based on intricate myths, and it wasn't so much that its foundation was cracking as it was that there never was a "real" foundation in the first place, "just a series of shared beliefs, like a religion or a culture."

> Did Nielsen ever offer more than a gross proxy for the real television audience? No, but that was okay, as long as that stand-in was big and growing (and the one with the most buying power). Were media planners ever blind to the implications of magazines inflating circulation numbers with cheap subscription drives? Even in the days of the two-martini lunch, everyone knew that the value of the impression had to decline. It's just that nobody much cared to do anything about it. Certainly, nobody from the agencies would; and even advertisers blithely ignored it because there was no alternative to TV other than print. (1)

But the Web has changed everything for advertisers, because its value proposition to advertisers is precise measurement. And what television station account executive wants to make the case with advertisers that he's been selling blue smoke and mirrors all those years? Yet, that's exactly the pitch to be made in selling the Web over broadcast. Ask any competent Web sales executive, and they'll smile at the notion.

While the ad industry is still primarily tilted in the direction of Kathy Sharpe's intricate myths, they're now beginning to ask the right questions. Like a fish flopping around out of water, industry trade publications are filled with "try this" and "try that," and industry observers are so filled with lashing out or defending the myths that the fish actually leaps off the ground from time-to-time. This writhing is not only necessary but it's helpful, as the industry tries to get its footing in the new world.

But in the process, one can truly say that neither the media industry nor the ad industry really knows what its doing, and the tendency still is to remain with the old model. This is why the banner ad game — whether it's rich media or otherwise — is built upon the cost-per-thousand impressions (CPM) game. The problem here is that this game was created (and priced) based upon the myths that Ms. Sharpe rightly points out everybody knew were blue smoke and mirrors anyway. The Internet, however, doesn't produce such hocus pocus; the numbers here are real, and nobody knows how to act. The reality is that if we're going to play the CPM game with the Internet, then there must first come an acknowledgement that an online CPM has a greater value than any other CPM, because the advertiser will get real numbers instead of somebody's self-serving estimate.

Why pay a $500 CPM for a television ad that estimates the thousand people when an online ad will honestly deliver those thousand people? It makes no sense. There's the argument that the thousand people the TV ad reaches are different than the thousand people the online ad reaches, and there's certainly truth to that. But it begs a whole series of other questions about which thousand the advertiser would rather reach, and the Interactive Advertising Bureau (IAB) is right there with compelling arguments that are increasingly resonating with advertisers.

One day — and sooner than you might think — online ads will command greater CPMs than elsewhere, and that will do more to remove the blinking, whirling, disruptive (un)creative that passes for ads these days than any industry efforts to do so. And the important thing for broadcasters to recognize is that this will happen regardless of their efforts to slow it down, and unless they get involved in accelerating the event, the bulk of those nice ad dollars will go to smart companies from outside their markets.

So the idea of selling against ourselves doesn't offer us much of a choice. We either do it, or we watch others take the money. There is a way to do it, however, that is tried and true in the business world, for media isn't the only industry that's ever faced this kind of disruption. It requires courageous leadership, and a willingness to think beyond the quarterly report, for overcoming the vast shifting of audiences currently underway requires a longer runway than many are willing to provide.

Clayton Christensen is one of the leading thinkers on the subject of disruptive innovations that influence markets. His books, *The Innovator's Dilemma* and *The Innovator's Solution* are the standards for what to do — and what not to do — in the world of business disruptions. In an interview two years ago with Gartner Business Fellow Howard Dresner, Christensen was asked how companies can match up against disruptive innovators. His answer reveals the formula:

> To catch up against disruptors, incumbents must be prepared to set up subsidiaries and give them autonomy to kill their parents. There are a few examples in recent times. HP used to sell its inkjets through its laserjet business but it wasn't very successful. They then set up an independent organization in Vancouver to kill its laserjet business.
>
> Surprisingly, they discovered the inkjet business took off without cannibalizing the laserjet business and they remain as the dominant printer company. (2)

So the smart thing for broadcasters to do is set up autonomous Web businesses and let them do their thing, even to the point of killing the parents, if that's necessary. Along the way, these businesses would be free to sell against the blue smoke and mirrors that is the heart and soul of the parents' business model.

In order to get this started, broadcasters must begin talking to people who don't watch them anymore. Follow this thread from Dresner's interview with Christensen:

> *Dresner*: Would you say a company's install base of customers is another inhibitor of innovation?

Christensen: That's right. A customer will never lead you to develop a product which that customer cannot use.

Dresner: So sustaining innovation of course can keep a company viable for many, many years, but listening only to the customer base, for the long term, could in fact be quite damaging.

Christensen: That's right. In fact, if you're looking to start a new-growth business, very often, the most important customers to understand, are non-customers. Because if you figure out why it is they're not customers, and then bring an innovation that allows them now to become customers, that's what growth comes from.

Dresner: For an existing company with an installed base, how would you suggest they simultaneously serve the installed base, while trying to invest in future growth businesses? How do you do that? What's the right structure?

Christensen: If the organization or the business unit charged with serving the installed base is also asked to go after non-customers with the more affordable, simpler product, they can't do it. Because the business models are so different, and small customers with the lower priced product — it's not an attractive financial — it doesn't solve the financial goals of an established business unit. Almost always, this new game begins before the old game ends. If you somehow create a strong economic incentive for the management of the existing business unit to go after the new disruptive opportunity, you take your eye off the main profit and cash engine of the company, and you stumble very quickly. And yet, while that is still going, you've got to get your foothold in the new market. And that's why it's just really important to set up a separate unit. (3)

No company has gone through a more massive restructuring in recent years than Kodak. Disrupted by digital photography, the company fought the disruption rather than embracing it, and it nearly cost them everything. It wasn't until new, more courageous management was brought in (from the outside) that the company was able to right the ship and reassert itself in the world of photography.

In January 2004, the company laid off 20% of its workforce (15,000 people). Its net income had fallen to $19 million, or 7 cents per share, compared with $113 million, or 39 cents per share, in the same period the previous year. In May of this year, Kodak president Antonio Perez announced another restructuring that gave its various units autonomy but also expected more from them. Pay close attention to what he said in the press release (emphasis mine):

> "We will hold the businesses more directly accountable for their results. *Kodak is now a digital company, and these actions are required to support our digital business model.*"
>
> "As a result of the rapid and effective actions we have taken over the past two years to restructure our manufacturing assets, we can increasingly assign responsibility for manufacturing to the business units that the production facilities support," Perez noted. "In one sense, *this marks the last break with the 'economy of scale' manufacturing model that served our company so well for more than 120 years.* In a digital age, we need to make decisions faster and better, and these changes will enable that." (4)

So Kodak is now functioning free of a business model that sustained the company for 120 years. Its stock price is above $23, and while the company still has a way to go to overcome mistakes made in the face of the digital disruption, it is clearly better positioned today.

2006 is turning out to be *the* critical year for broadcasters to make forays into the digital (Internet) world. It's not just about extending our brands into this new pond; it's about whole new ways of doing business. There is only trouble ahead if we don't see the value of selling against ourselves. In terms of revenue, 2006 is not delivering what's normally expected of an Olympics and election year, and that means 2007 will be a year of shake-outs the likes of which the industry has never seen.

Who will survive and who won't? It'll largely be based on who has the courage to back away from speaking evangelistically and sell against themselves.

THE CONVERGENCE ADVERTISING TRAP

March 10, 2005

In our culture, when a salesperson doesn't like the term he or she has to deal with, a new one is often created as a substitute. This is a common practice in the automobile industry, where the guy in the slick clothes would much rather sell you a "dealer demonstrator" than a "used" car. After all, it's higher on the food chain, right? There's also "pre-owned," "like new" and "almost new," but they're still — regardless of the softer language — just plain, old used cars.

This is practiced in all areas of buying and selling, but most often when the product being sold is, well, lesser than the sales guy would like it to be. Wouldn't you rather buy from a "scratch and dent" sale that from one of damaged goods? And of course, a trained salesperson would rather move you to a brand new washer and dryer than burden you with that dented model.

So it is in the television world, and especially where salespeople are forced to sell the Internet. What TV salesperson can get excited about commissions on a five-dollar online cost-per-thousand (CPM) rate, when they could be spending their time selling $500 CPMs? Thus was born the "convergence advertising" model — a

327

concept that blends on-air and online ads into what appears to be a win-win for TV stations.

Here's how it works: A station's Website has a section on, let's say, health. This section provides the latest in health news, links and stories from the station's health reporter. The station puts together a deal to sell "sponsorships" of the section to health care providers in the community, but the deal also contains on-air ads. Hence, the station gets to charge whatever it likes, and the pitch to the sponsors is that it's a TV buy built around an Internet element. The on-air ads are intended to drive traffic to the health section, so everybody appears to win.

It's hard to disagree with the logic of using an Internet promotion to drive TV sales — especially in these days of sharp business downturns — but the concept of convergence advertising is, at best, a bridge between television advertising and Internet advertising. Stations that use these tools to create the notion that they are into Internet advertising are fooling themselves, because convergence advertising isn't Internet advertising — it's TV advertising wrapped in a URL. Moreover, those stations who engage in this type of advertising exclusively are less inclined to look beyond their dying business model and dip their toes in the pool of pure Internet revenue.

This is a very dangerous position, because it keeps local television in a continued state of denial and ignorance. As long as stations believe that convergence advertising is the holy grail of Internet revenue, there is no incentive to learn of the new world. Moreover, this model keeps stations locked into the portal Website concept and the belief that their brand transfers to the Web in the same way it does in the real world. These beliefs have been proven to be untrue, so by placing resources in bundles of convergence deals, stations continue to drift into the bog of missed opportunities instead of moving into the new reality.

For the past two years, Richard Sullivan has been tracking Internet sales efforts among TV stations as "The TV Guru." He publishes a weekly newsletter with case studies of Web sales programs in the local TV industry. The newsletter goes out to TV stations — and others — who wish to keep track of the business of making money off the Internet.

"I've not kept any particular stats on this," he says, "but as I review my 200 plus Case Histories, all but a very few of the contests, promotions, etc. that I report on have some sort of on-air element as well." He notes that, in many cases, the Internet component is in "support" of a larger on-air presence. "Most sponsored promotions," he adds, "have a corresponding on-air buy to create an overall convergence package. Rarely have I found a stand-alone Internet promotion." (1)

But Sullivan also notes that stations are starting to build more interactive features into their online promotions. "For example," he notes, "contests increasingly require online entry. These entry forms include links back to the sponsor or sometimes sponsor coupons. More and more, sponsor links are provided, no doubt because more local businesses now maintain a Web presence."(2)

Gordon Borrell's company studies local online revenue for the newspaper industry, although he's increasingly including local online broadcast properties as well. He's quick to point out that while there's good money in convergence packages, "too many newspapers and TV stations view the Internet as a packaged sale, period, end of story."

For broadcasters, convergence ad packages present a two-sided coin, according to Borrell. On the one hand, they can and do pull dollars from newspaper, Yellow Pages or direct mail markets, but these deals keep local stations working with their same, limited group of advertisers. "In any market," he says, "the vast majority of businesses can't afford a broadcast-online combo buy, but they can afford online-only advertising. And they're buying it. So a TV station has an opportunity to use this new medium to grab new customers."(3)

"Convergence packages are good," he continues, "but stations that rely solely on using the Internet to sell more broadcast advertising will wind up being more vulnerable to advertising downturns than those who use the Internet to insulate their station's revenue streams with a whole new set of customers." (4)

The newspaper industry offers an excellent example of what can happen when media companies try to exist by blending their core distribution vehicle with the Web. Newspapers built Web-based classifieds, but only as an adjunct to the print version. Buying a classified newspaper ad a few years ago meant "you get the Internet with that." What was billed as adding value to a classified ad has blown up in the face of the industry, because smart entrepreneurs saw that the Internet was different. CraigsList now threatens to completely destroy what used to be a significant part of a newspaper's revenue. Where CraigsList isn't doing it, the Monster.com's and eBays of the Web are piling on.

New England based newspaper consultant George Dratelis says the industry is currently in love with bundled deals that revolve around digitizing ads and creating a browse/search area in the marketplace. "There was considerable concern in the industry," he says, "about taking 'print ads' and posting them online, but the focus now has shifted from the visual to the deconstruction of the contents of the ad in order to make all advertising carried in the paper searchable." (5)

As a result, Dratelis thinks much of the industry is still stuck in an effort to save its existing model rather than fully explore other options. "The business model has varied from upsells to package deals which are most prevalent now," he says. "The key issue remains the fact that the advertiser gets an Internet component to their ad buy without fully being sold on the value of the Internet piece itself."(6)

So what should local TV stations be doing? The problem isn't revenue; it's audience. Fix the problem and the revenue will take care of itself.

The future begins with understanding and accepting that a local station is more than just a local station; it's a local media company, or better yet, a local multimedia company. This may seem like splitting semantic hairs, but it's actually the new model for any local media business. If the television station's business model — which is based on a mass marketing core competency — is all that drives the company, it will ultimately find itself gasping for air like a fish at the bottom of a pond that's slowly draining. Any local media company's business model will be advertiser-driven, but that's where the similarity between the old and the new ends.

Tim Hanlon, Senior Vice President/Director, Emerging Contacts for Starcom MediaVest Group — and one of most most forward-thinking people in the advertising world — looks at the new.

> The news department at NBC5 Chicago (WMAQ-TV) shouldn't think of themselves just as four-times-a-day newscasts but as a 24-hour news service across multiple touchpoints: linear, on-demand, online, wireless, digital multicast — whatever. The target audiences, then, are less about Nielsen ratings, but the total exposure package via ratings, VOD sessions, tuning data, click data — whatever.
>
> Separating stuff into traditional delivery buckets probably becomes futile over time, especially as younger news consumers — with Internet/ on-demand/consumer control-type expectations — look for news differently than their parents or grandparents. (7)

But why stop there? Media companies — especially at the local level — also need to look at diversifying in order to grow revenues, and the Internet provides a fertile field for non-traditional revenue models. Paid local search is a great example. Stations can acquire a software license and outsource sales to build and operate a viable local paid search site. The longer the ownership, the greater the multiples, so such a project can be very profitable. But the real secret to its success lies in the television station's ability to promote the business using its core competency — mass marketing reach. This places a different kind of value on ad availabilities and gives a local multimedia company with a television "wing" a considerable competitive advantage over, let's say, a newspaper.

Reliance on convergence ad models poses a significant inertia barrier to progress. At best, they are a bridge to tomorrow, but even that can be a dangerous assumption. For the idea of a bridge is illusionary. There is no standing still when it comes to the sweeping changes around us. We're either on one side or the other.

We're either inventing new names for the same old used cars, or we're adding a line of boats to the inventory.

THE ECONOMY OF
UNBUNDLED ADVERTISING

January 3, 2006

My two brothers and I grew up in a small, two-bedroom bungalow in Grand Rapids, Michigan. We didn't have much, and back in the 1950s, there wasn't much on television to remind us of that. TV families always seemed to have enough, but abundance wasn't the norm. Lucy and Desi lived in an apartment, as did The Honeymooners. The Cleavers and the Nelsons lived in nice neighborhoods, but they were hardly extravagant. You don't miss much when you don't know what you don't have.

We bought our food at the A&P store and did all of our clothes (and toy) shopping via the Sears Roebuck catalog. We had little need for advertising; the catalog was our window on the retail world. We let our fingers do the walking, and whether it was shoes or a model airplane, mom and dad ordered what we needed. Ours was a typical post-war family, and mass marketing specialists were just beginning to refine the craft of manipulation for profit. How times have changed.

One of the big questions that I'm asked as I talk about unbundled media and the collapse of the mass market is where will people go for consumer information in an unbundled world? Despite the downsides of excesses, conventional thinking goes, surrounding ourselves with messages at least keeps us informed about where to buy what, to say nothing of helping us find new goods and services available. If newspapers shut down and network TV goes out of business, how will our economy be served?

These kinds of questions arise from a belief in the artificial dependence that exists between messenger and consumer in a hierarchical culture. This illusion views consumers as an enemy to be conquered, because even if the consumer doesn't *want* the marketer, he or she *needs* the marketer. Even the word "consumer" suggests — to borrow from Doc Searls — a passive open mouth that's crapping cash for the merchant and, let's not forget, the marketer.

The language of mass marketing is all about warfare. We "target" this; we "launch" a thrust here; we "attack" and "saturate." It's all so exciting. Ries and Trout called their seminal book *Positioning: The Battle for Your Mind* — a battle with victory being sales.

But the advertising industry forgot to ask people for permission to play war games in their minds, and now things like DVRs and the Internet are enabling people to simply shut the door. Nobody wants to be targeted. Nobody wants to be positioned. Nobody wants to be manipulated. The consumer is now the one with the power, and people with goods and services to sell need to start thinking of them again as customers.

New media economic genius Umair Haque has written extensively about the differences between what works in the mass marketing world (the blockbuster) with what works in the Media 2.0 paradigm (the snowball). In the blockbuster concept, he notes, attention has the highest value and therefore commands the most dollars, because attention is a scarcity that can only be overcome with a significant marketing budget. In the new world, however, where the customer is at the controls, attention isn't the scarcity, because the customer is already providing it — quality snowballs are where the new scarcity exists, and that's why the value shifts from attention to production. This has profound implications for television, because its core competency is the providing of attention.

In the following illustration, for example, the business must pay either employees or an agency (or often both) to determine how best to reach a consumer with a message about its product. Huge dollars are spent buying the attention required to reach a mass audience, wherein the business believes (scientifically, of course) that their customer will be among the many. This is inefficient at both ends of the equation, and the only way the business knows its message is getting through is by sales figures. This process has been governing most buying and selling during the last century.

But now we've entered the world of unbundled media, where people download individual songs instead of buying CDs, watch programs when and where they want (without the commercials), and read news stories or snippets of stories via the World Wide Web instead of going out to the driveway every morning. Movie-going is down; music radio is falling fast; and you can now watch Lost on your Video iPod instead of Wednesday night on ABC. The mass audience is disappearing and with it, and the economy it supports.

If unbundled media is where we're headed, then unbundled advertising must necessarily follow. This is a scary concept, however, for there is no command and control mechanism or manipulable infrastructure in the unbundled world. The upside, though, is that it costs very little to participate. All that's necessary is the release of what I call "ad pieces" into the seeming chaos of the Internet, where other businesses will take those pieces and reassemble them when summoned by customers who are trading their scarcity for information they actually want.

Ad pieces don't have to be slick, finished ads. Think of them as parts of a conversation with customers.

What appears to the traditional marketer as the swirling vortex of a black hole is actually a highly efficient machine that sorts and filters based on product, service, price point, location, and a whole host of variables determined by the customer and/or his liaisons with all those pieces — aggregators. In the illustration below, the customer has at least three options in acquiring knowledge: search, dumb aggregators (where aggregation is strictly a software solution) and smart aggregators (where human "editing" enters the picture).

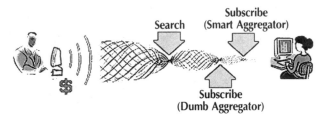

An advertiser can influence positioning with search results by paying for it. This is how Google makes its money, but it's essentially mass marketing, because the advertiser's message is placed in front of lots of eyeballs. Similarly, an advertiser could buy positioning in a dumb aggregator. After all, any software can be "instructed" to give precedence to the highest bidder.

But a smart aggregator is a different animal altogether, and it's here where potential customers will increasingly provide their scarcity while the unbundled media world is exploding. With options expanding exponentially, people will turn to each other (as they always have) for advice on purchasing decisions. New businesses — perhaps subscriber-driven — will flourish based on their ability to cull the wheat from the chaff and meet the needs of their customers. Buying influence here may ultimately be acceptable, but the price tag for the smart aggregator will be transparency, and that may negatively impact customer appeal. In all things Media 2.0, we must never forget that the customer is in complete control.

The software generating the ad pieces is a simple content management system (CMS) that publishes an xml file via RSS. Aggregator businesses that make their money by satisfying customers, will gather and sort all ad pieces and publish an aggregated RSS feed to be viewed by customers or other filtering aggregators. A business that wishes to sell its goods or services need only release updated ad pieces into the system. This could be hourly, daily, weekly, monthly, or whatever. The business is able to precisely control its message and get an accurate count of potential customers at the other end, but it can't influence the process by throwing money at it.

Along the way, merchants can be very specific both in terms of time and merchandise they're offering without spending a lot of money. A jeweler, for example, may come across a great deal on bracelets that can be offered at a discount on one weekend. This jeweler would then release ad pieces detailing pricing and including photos or perhaps video, which would then be "found" by smart aggregators on a constant search for jewelry deals for their customers.

This potentially levels the playing field for smaller businesses and offers considerable economic incentive for the production of quality products and services at reasonable prices. You won't be able to buy your way to business success in this paradigm. Leave your blue smoke and mirrors at the door when entering the world of unbundled media.

Let's examine, for another example, the automobile industry in this model. Automotive advertising accounts for the largest chunk of local television's revenue, whether it comes from dealers, regional associations or manufacturers. I once worked for a station that had turned its newscasts into programs with five commercial breaks, so that the five big auto dealers in town could each have exclusivity in an ad pod. This is the extent to which local TV will protect those big ad dollars.

Like everything else, the auto industry is going through big changes. CSM Worldwide, the leading provider of market intelligence and forecasting to the automotive industry, warns in its latest Automotive Production Barometer of a "difficult transition across many facets of the industry" in this country as it evolves from the traditional "Big 3" to the "New 6" that will include Toyota, Honda and Nissan.

Smaller suburban dealers are disappearing, largely because the cost of per-vehicle advertising for them is more than 50 percent above the national average, according to Borrell Associates, a Virginia-based research and consulting firm that tracks local Internet advertising. Many of Borrell's clients are newspapers, who are staring at 24 straight months of declines in auto advertising.

The industry is shifting ad dollars to the Internet, in part, because car buyers are doing research online before walking into a dealership. This has implications for all media, because automotive is such an important ad category. Borrell:

> By 2009, newspapers will lose 11 percent in total auto ad revenue while online media will more than double theirs. And while total new vehicle ad spending will grow from $36.5 billion this year to $47.6 billion by 2009, only cable, radio and online will see gains in their shares of this market. (1)

Unbundled advertising in this space would have a dramatic impact on all trends, because it runs on creativity and business smarts and not on the muscle created by huge ad dollars. It levels the playing field and would reduce the customer acquisition costs for smaller dealers as well as large. Autotrader.com, Vehix and other search applications may allow buyers to drift through the inventory of dealers in town, but a smart aggregator is much more current and tailored to the needs of the customer today.

The "smart" in the aggregator would be directing customers to the best deals and inventories moment-by-moment from information provided as often as the dealers wished to provide it. A suburban dealer, for example, could offer a special deal of a particular vehicle *that afternoon* and reasonably expect that potential customers would see it. The smart aggregator provides a direct conduit to people in the market for cars in that community, and all that's required of the dealer is attention to releasing ad pieces into cyberspace for use by a hundred forms of new media.

Does the technology for this exist today? Absolutely. Does the system exist? Not yet, but it's simply a matter of time. Meanwhile, the people formerly known as customers continue to redefine all markets through new habits that exploit the power of the Internet. According to a holiday shopping study by Nielsen//NetRatings, Goldman, Sachs & Co., and Harris Interactive, "consumers" spent 27 percent of their holiday budgets online at e-commerce sites this year—up from 16 percent in 2002. Was this the result of mass marketing telling people what to do, or did people come to this decision on their own? The answer to that question is one that few in the status quo wish to explore.

In many ways, the Web takes me back to my childhood and the days of the "Wish Book" we used to get in the mail a few times a year. It's much more efficient, of course, and it isn't restricted to Kenmore appliances and Craftsman tools.

Reading it in the bathroom only requires a wireless laptop. My mom and dad would've loved that.

RETHINKING NEWS PROMOS

January 26, 2005

"It's not even safe to walk to your car in daylight anymore," the local anchor announced as we watched surveillance video of an assailant with a box cutter chasing a woman in a mall parking lot. Welcome to the world of news "teases."

The video was certainly compelling and the story interesting, but it had nothing to do with whether it was safe for "me" to walk to "my" car in daylight. This ridiculous conclusion was part of the station's prime-time promotion of its late newscast, where it's deemed necessary to relate upcoming stories with the viewers at home by focusing attention on how it might effect them. It was textbook "tease" or "topical promotion" writing, and, delivered with just the right air of concern, it was enough to scare the crap out of anybody.

And we wonder why our country is driven by fear these days.

So it is in the world of local news, where the content itself is supposed to be governed by ethics, but anything goes in the name of driving people into the tent. Despite considerable evidence that this practice is abhorred by viewers and that it's actually turning people away from news programs, it's still considered a fundamental necessity in the "how to" book of local news. Moreover, the manipulative language has become an essential part of the newscast itself, as we attempt to "drive" viewers from one segment to another.

In my 1998 essay, "The Lizard on America's Shoulder," I wrote about the history of this.

> Experiments with attention-getting concepts to maintain market share began, and thus was born the news consultant. What "worked" anywhere was winnowed from that which didn't "work" and was spread from city to city. The exploitation of base human emotion, disguised by words like "compelling," dramatic," or "interesting" became the draw. When the Nielsen company created meters to put in viewers' homes that directly measured viewing habits, these resourceful "experts" came upon a whole new way of doing things. Almost overnight, local television news was transformed into the business of managing audience flow, and along with it, I believe, came a sad disrespect of things once sacred.
>
> Of paramount importance in this paradigm is the development of stories that attract, so that promotional announcements cleverly placed in, say, prime time would compel viewers to stay and watch. At the expense of that which was important, news managers suddenly found themselves devoting considerable time, effort and resources into finding and developing offbeat, titillating and sensational items for the promo boys to use. And now, only a mist separates all of television news from up-front exploiters like Jerry Springer.

The managing of audience flow is now clearly the business of television and television news. Nobody cares about image anymore. It's how you get a viewer from point A to point B. This is an archaic and dangerous practice in our new world, a hole that stations have dug for themselves by repetition of something that has been disrespecting and insulting the intelligence of TV viewers for too long.

It begins with the false notion that audiences can be managed. The idea gives business managers a sense of importance in controlling their own destiny, and it's built the careers of many. But let's think about it for a minute. In Postmodern America, the consumer is increasingly in charge of their own experience. Disruptive innovations in technology have turned the idea of passive participation into something that belongs in a museum. As Rishad Tobaccowala of Starcom Mediavest Group says, we've entered an empowered era in which humans are God, because technology allows them to be godlike. "How will you engage God?" he asks. Well, you certainly don't try to "manage" Him.

It's just not a top-down world anymore, and we can't see that we've been a part of its destruction. Consider the language we use. We're trying to "drive" viewers. Who wants to be driven? We're "teasing" viewers. Who wants to be teased? We're "compelling" viewers. Who wants to be compelled? And we manipulate viewers as if we think they don't know they're being manipulated. Guess what? They see through it and the evidence is everywhere.

I had the opportunity to examine Nielsen diaries on behalf of a major-market client last year. While stations live and die based on Nielsen ratings, you'd be surprised at how few make the effort to actually read the dairies. They offer far more than viewing preferences. They're a window into the worlds of individual viewers and their families alike — little stories that help paint an overall picture. As such, they provide a wonderful context within which to view change.

Over and over again, people wrote in the comments section of these diaries how much they disliked news teases. Not only did these people freely note how much they hated the practice, they were also quite accurate in their understanding of what was going on. They know what we're doing, and they think it's silly. We're not fooling anybody, except perhaps ourselves.

You can get the same kind of feedback by interviewing former news watchers. The industry doesn't do much of that, preferring instead to focus on existing news viewers. This gives station groups and researchers a slanted view of what's really taking place.

The greatest evidence of the public's distaste for the practice is that they're turning away in droves. When people fast-forward ads with their TiVos, do we honestly think they're pausing to watch the upcoming news announcements? When TiVo says users regularly skip commercials, they're referring to *all* promotional announcements. Tobaccowala's new "God" wants nothing to do with wasting time.

Christopher Schroeder, former head of *Washington Post* Interactive, noted in a recent essay that people these days "don't want to be told what to do, think about, or enjoy."

> For traditional media and distribution channels to embrace the power of the individual, it will take some significant rethinking about how they do business, how they will make services available when the individual is the aggregator, what their cost structures and perks are, and what life is like in an anti-monopolist world. In a word, it will take innovation, and innovation across the board — from product and services to business models to mind-sets. (1)

But before we can get to any of that innovative thinking, we've got to first stop digging the hole in which we find ourselves.

Promotion "experts" and consultants will no doubt argue with this thesis, but their argument begins with the notion that they can prove that cleverly written teases will "move" people from one daypart to the next. This hides a more important question: just because we can, does that mean we should?

And what's their evidence that it works? Nielsen in-home meters.

These devices were introduced in the mid 1970s and are now available in 56 markets in the U.S. They automatically record and store minute-by-minute tuning records for channel, time of day, and duration of tuning. Hence, managers in metered markets can get direct feedback in terms of what works in delivering or turning away viewers. Meters, the argument goes, scientifically measure viewer behavior, and you can't argue with that. The problem, of course, is that meters tell you nothing about people who are no longer viewers.

The same practices can be found in non-metered markets. News consultants, stations groups with metered and non-metered markets and managers with metered market experience have spread the emphasis on managing audience flow throughout all 250 markets. They can't get the immediate feedback that comes from Nielsen meters in markets that don't have them, but that doesn't stop the topical promotion juggernaut. And budding producers in smaller markets who covet the big money of bigger markets learn quickly that the one who can deliver the best in terms of this kind of promotional announcement will get the good jobs. Everybody does it, because, well, that's the way it's done.

Before meters, stations depended on what were called "image" and "proof-of-performance" promotions to build their audiences. The stronger the station's image in the market, the more likely that station would have the top newscasts. The closest they came to topical promotions was a little 60-second headline presentation during prime time.

In the early days, images were developed in the minds of the audience, and it wasn't always what a station said that mattered. It was more what stations did. Soon, however, stations began experimenting with various types of slogans and images in an effort to bring self-determination into the picture. After all, the ability to "plant" an image in the minds of consumers is the core of mass marketing trickery.

And at most stations now, image promotion has taken a back seat to topical promotion, and that has likely contributed to the overall decline in news viewing.

That's because, in reality, a station's or industry's image isn't necessarily determined by the efforts of the station or the industry. The less stations talk about image, the more likely a default image emerges — one selected by the audience — and that's exactly what's happening to broadcasting today.

An image rests in the mind of the viewer, and that is determined by many factors, including likes and dislikes, habits, and so forth, and the public image of television news is pretty bad these days. A station's insistence on the kinds of topical promotions noted above leaves an impression with viewers that sticks. When everybody does it, the subsequent image is widespread and highly negative. It is precisely this "image" that is turning people away.

"I hate these stupid ads. I've complained about these stupid ads. Nobody cares what I think. I'm going elsewhere." They have weighed us in the scale of usefulness and found us wanting. They're exercising their right to look elsewhere, and we're left holding the bag.

And as much as we'd like to blame our audience travails on technology and competition, the truth is we've not done much to help. Embracing the power of the individual begins with what we do on-the-air, so that's where we need to begin. Common sense needs another chance in broadcasting, and that means giving up on a few things that we've perhaps come to believe are absolutes.

We need to do a real gut check, and make the effort to listen to what people who've gone away are telling us. They're tired of our bullshit. They're tired of being scared. They're tired of being insulted and disrespected. And they're tired of being taken for granted. Then, we need the courage to act accordingly.

It's difficult to imagine a world of television news without hyperbole, because it would be such a jolt. Perhaps it's just a matter of degrees. Regardless, something needs to be done, because our hype is killing us.

THE VALUE OF LOCAL SEARCH

July 20, 2004

I have a nice balcony/lanai at my second-floor apartment. It's snuggled up next to a giant sycamore tree, and we enjoy being outside. Bugs are a problem, though, and I had often thought of putting up screening. However, the floor is slatted, along with the railing, so it wouldn't keep *all* of them out. Several people in the complex had indeed put up screening, so the idea was always on my mind. One day, I walked past one of these apartments, and the lady of the house was on the porch. So I asked, "Does the screening really keep the bugs out?"

"No," was her reply, "but it sure does keep my cat in."

This is a lesson in perception. If you're always thinking bugs, a porch screen has but one function. So it is with TV people, I've come to believe.

Item: ESPN.com is running ads touting their new "myESPN" *local* pages where you can find everything about your favorite college and pro teams. It's really very cool and designed to not only keep me on ESPN.com, but take me deeper inside their site for stories (and those contextual ads based on my zip code).

Item: Google has created a wonderful *local* search function that allows users to let their mouse do the walking instead of their fingers. It's already pretty good, but it will get better and better. Local search is *the* hot thing in terms of advertising.

Item: Topix.net has built an online news aggregator that functions as a *local* news search engine. The business model is suspect, because RSS can do the same thing without all the extraneous marketing and links that come with a Website.

Item: Google is developing a new feature that will allow users to search for audio and video files on the Web. AOL bought Singingfish.com last year to provide the same kind of service. Based on Google's success with local search, one must presume the future ability to search for *local* news clips in a similar manner.

Item: Print directories, such as the Yellow Pages, see their business models buckling under the weight of online search and are offering their resources to companies who provide them to online publishers in the form of *local* search.

This is just the beginning, as the world of marketing discovers the efficiency with which the Internet can connect local buyers with local merchants, and it's a huge threat to local content publishers, like television stations. Most of the people who run local media Internet outlets are either drunk or asleep (or both), and as every day goes by, they abdicate a little more of their piece of the local Internet pie to outsiders. Google hasn't entered the local search business blindly. It sees the handwriting on the wall. Broadcasters can't see it, because, well, they're too busy being broadcasters. They view the porch screen only one way.

The value proposition of any television station is its ability to provide eyeballs for advertising. As that ability diminishes through ever-shrinking ratings, the ad community is responding with an increasingly open mind about alternatives, and the primary one is online. TV's value proposition doesn't work on the Internet, because the medium isn't passive, so in order for a local television station to survive in the not-so-distant future, it must redefine its value proposition to one where the principal purpose is multimedia and interactive. Television is a part of the multimedia future, but it's only one part. So we must begin with a white board session asking three questions:

1. What *can* we do online?
2. How can we make money online?
3. What can we do to help local advertisers online?

According to the Kelsey Group, online directory lookups could surpass print directory lookups within the next three years. And a study by Kelsey and BizRate.com shows about 25% of all Web searches are searches for local businesses close to consumers' home or workplace. Chuck Davis, President and CEO of BizRate.com said, "Consumers are increasingly using search for shopping related queries. In fact, over a third (36%) of all search activity is now shopping-based, defined as using search functionality to look for a merchant, research a purchase or make an online purchase. We expect to see shopping searches continue to increase."(1)

Poynter's Rich Gordon spells out the consequences: "Could local search be as much of a threat to newspapers — and in some advertising categories, local TV — as online classified services have been? I think it's certainly possible. Leaving out classifieds, a newspaper's business model revolves around connecting local buyers to local merchants." (2)

A report last week by Borrell Associates puts it plainly:

> We are strongly encouraging our local media clients to jump on board the Paid Search bandwagon. Options are the Google AdSense or Yahoo! Overture programs; private label vendors such as PlanetDiscover, FindWhat, Interchange, PremierGuide, Approxi-MATCH and Kanoodle; or hedging your bets by creating non-exclusive agreements with multiple partners. Whatever you do, get into the game now.

…The real action in local search is in getting national advertisers and small service-oriented businesses that don't advertise in newspapers or on TV stations.

…We are estimating that the Google program (alone) boosts online revenue of newspaper and TV sites by 2% to 10%.(3)

Meanwhile, a report this week by Nielsen//NetRatings suggests the demand for search advertising is growing far more quickly than the supply of available advertising spots. That'll lead to higher prices, which the report says would mean only the deepest pockets could afford to put their ads near the best keywords.

The resources noted by Borrell all offer simple local search solutions — like the kind employed by the *Sacramento Bee* in launching sacramento.com this year.

This is a one-stop local search page. The main search is powered by PremierGuide's software using the SureWest print Yellow Pages directory. PremierGuide offers a plug-n-play solution for this, depending on whether it has a business arrangement with a Yellow Pages provider. It allows the *Bee* to "feature" certain businesses in the rankings (based on what they pay) and sell contextual ads alongside the search results. Here's what a search for "restaurants" produces:

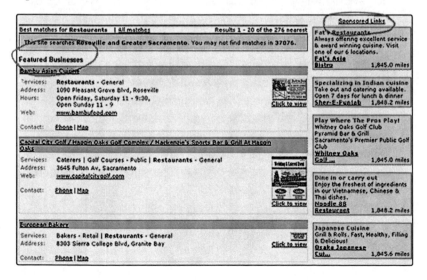

The other niche searches on the main page come from Classified Ventures, LLC, an organization developed in the mid-90s by newspaper companies to provide online classified services. The automotive search goes through cars.com, the apartment search through apartments.com, and the home search through homefinder.com. Classifieds inputted by The Bee's users wind up on the massive databases maintained by Classified Ventures.

Local TV stations who use, for example, Worldnow to provide their Websites don't have the luxury of Classified Ventures. Worldnow has cut deals with existing (and well-known) search providers like autotrader.com, match.com, and the Yellow Pages. Searches that begin on the TV station sites go directly to these providers. All these arrangements do is provide them customers. They do nothing for the TV stations except give the appearance of providing a service.

There is no value in hosting a path to somebody else's application without compensation. Moreover, why should a user opt to go through your portal to get to cars.com or apartments.com or match.com when he or she can simply go directly there? Somebody looking for cars, for example, isn't likely to do so simply by being routed through your site. They will go directly to the source, and your arrangement with an auto search provider will have virtually no value to you. All you're doing is providing traffic for the content site.

The same is true with local search. Bringing Google or Yahoo or even that similar to the *Sacramento Bee* to your Website provides only a short term solution. The answer is to build your own local search database and reap the rewards downstream. There are financial gains beyond just advertising that can also be realized. Since the beginning of TV, stations have made commercials for local advertisers, and they need to do the same with Web-based advertising.

In a thoughtful piece on the value of local search, Gus Venditto of InternetNews.com wrote:

> The first impact is sure to be Web development for small business. Right now, it's estimated by the Kelsey Group and ConStat's Local Commerce Monitor that only 48 percent of small businesses who advertise have a Web site. Lester Chu, vice president of marketing and strategic planning at Verizon, believes that 60 percent of all businesses don't have a Web site.
>
> Today, many of those Web-unaware businesses are able to keep their online base covered by buying listings through the Yellow Page directories. For a few extra dollars, 1.4 million businesses who advertise in print Yellow Pages have the option of buying on-line listings that appear at SuperPages, Yahoo and other portals. And if it weren't for Google, all local businesses would compete on a level playing field, because they would all have an equal chance to buy their way into the same online directories.
>
> Google's impact could be seismic because it will rank the pages, and that will re-define the meaning of a good retail location. A small store on a remote side street can build more foot traffic with a good Web site than it could with a busy corner location. All the lower-rent store needs is a better education in the intricacies of search engine rankings.(4)
>
> A smart local TV station will build simple Websites for local advertisers and host them on their server. This would increase the value of the station's property and cement the relationship with local advertisers. Stations also need to develop rich media ads for their advertisers, but nothing will bring in the revenue like local search. A local merchant directory has unlimited value, but only to the company that owns it.

The days of the monolithic local television station Website are numbered. They're all built on the portal model, with a home page and links to material deeper within the site. That model is being rewritten by people who don't want to be forced to go here just to get to there. RSS and search are enabling people to have it their way, and who knows what's to come downstream? News will always have value, but even its value is changing as disruptive innovations permit just about anybody to get into the news business. A television station will always have its place in the media spectrum, but developing an online brand that includes content beyond news and entertainment is the key to downstream profitability.

And it might just keep the bugs out along with keeping the cat in.

THE CHALLENGE OF ADVERTISING

October 22, 2003

In the earliest days of television, the programs were nothing more than radio shows in front of a camera. Dramas were done live, just as they were on radio. There were variety shows, comedy shows, game shows and news/information programs. The medium was new, and all anybody knew was radio, so it was natural that the transition to TV would produce similar programs. And radio programs were sponsored, so commercial messages found their way into the television mix, too. The new medium took what it could from the film and radio industries and put it together to become television.

There has been a similar, albeit accelerated, evolution as the Internet has grown, only this transition has been from the print industry to the World Wide Web. We took the best we had from newspapers and magazines and mixed it together with a little interactivity to make the early Net. As bandwidth problems were overcome, the Internet welcomed various elements of radio, television and film, and now we have a brand new medium. It's still largely text-driven, but that's only because text is easy, requires little bandwidth, and is ideally suited to the unique ability of the medium to store, sort and present.

There is a growing sense now, however, that the Internet is much more than text with pictures, and that television of the future will run through an Internet-enabled computer.

This presents a rather large conundrum for Madison Avenue as it figures out how to sell goods and services via the new medium. Clearly, conventional print-style ads don't work. Like many other people, I ran a little company with an advertising business model during the bubble years of the Internet. After 28 years in television, I knew the value of eyeballs, so we built a site that not only recruited users but also kept them. Before we finally gave up on the business model, we were getting a million page views a month, and we were second only to ebay in our ability to keep people on the site. But all those eyeballs were meaningless, because banner advertising simply didn't work.

The latest thing that has the advertising industry all a-twitter is broadband (read: television) ads that are run adjacent to video clips on the Internet. Microsoft and NBC have put together a little deal wherein the network will provide news video to MSN as part of Microsoft's foray into the new world of Internet TV. Video on the Net is nothing new, but the entry of a third partner into this deal is. Starcom MediaVest Group (SMG), a big Los Angeles ad agency, has structured what the ad industry calls an "upfront" buy for MSN Video. It's a first for the Internet. The plan calls for the sale of 15 seconds of commercial video time for every five to six minutes of streaming-video news content, and it has all of Madison Avenue salivating. The deal allows MSN to present the video free-of-charge to consumers, something that will bring in those eyeballs. TV commercials? On the Internet? Oh my, this MUST be the future!

Or not.

The Internet is not TV, not at all. And those TV executives who roll the dice on this as the ultimate solution to the problem of how to make money off their Internet properties are risking more than their careers. Much as those programmers of yesteryear, we're taking what we know and mixing it into this new medium, but what we're failing to see is that the Internet is not a medium of mass marketing, and traditional methods of advertising just don't work very well. In an environment where the user has complete control, he will not long suffer an interrupted experience, and we need to be very careful in presuming that he will.

Starcom, MSN and NBC are reported to have done their homework on the Internet TV ads. A 6-minute story will be divided into two 3-minute segments with a 15-second ad in the middle. My money says they'll discover users leaving during the commercials. Why? Because the Internet isn't TV! Television is a medium that speaks to a passive mass audience. The Internet is an active, one-to-one medium with the user in charge. These ads will have only limited, short-term success. The more producers try to "hide the good stuff" until after the little commercial, the more users will abandon the concept altogether.

The idea of running TV commercials has some short-term merit. It's an easy, familiar sell for TV salespeople, and it will bring in local revenue. In the long run, however, media Web outlets are going to have to look at what's really working.

"Return on involvement" is a new buzzword, created by agencies that are developing metrics to measure how involved a user is with their ad experience on the Internet. This concept fits beautifully into a Postmodern world, where mass audience is passé and users/viewers/readers/listeners have an escalating number of choices. And involvement in media goes beyond simply a mindset. Postmodernism is the Age of Participation, and that is extending into the world of advertising through creative, interactive concepts that couldn't have been imagined just a few years ago. The simple fact is that this interactive advertising works, and it especially works with the Postmodern crowd. This group builds its core values around its experiences, and anything that produces an involved experience is going to click with Postmoderns, including advertising.

A key component of General Electric's "Imagination at Work" brand makeover earlier this year (GE used to be "We bring good things to life") was a breakthrough Internet ad called "The Pen." Similar to the old Etch-A-Sketch game, the ad featured the text tagline "All Ideas Start With a Sketch. What's Yours?" next to a virtual felt-tip marker pen. The ad caused large numbers of users to doodle out illustrations that were then e-mailed to co-workers, friends and relatives in a viral blitz that even GE didn't see coming. "Pen" was so popular that it sprung up on sites frequented by Web developers, animators and others throughout the creative community. The click-through rate on "Pen" was three times higher than the average click-through for banner ads, and the viral send-along component had a 28% higher e-mail opening rate. The ad was so successful than GE is planning another one in January of 2004.

The interactive nature of this ad is credited with its success, but there's something else that bears observation. There was no sales pitch whatsoever associated with the ad. It was pure branding. There was no "call for the close." Users didn't have to pay any price whatsoever for making a sketch. This is brand advertising in a Postmodern world.

Similarly, Orbitz is touting the success of its interactive pop-under ad campaigns that feature a plethora of games such as miniature golf (I'm addicted), Dunk the Punk, All-Star Home Run, Pilot the Blimp, Catch the Firefly and others. The facts that these are those awful pop-unders and that they include an automatic click-through doesn't seem to stop people from using them and doing so over and over and over. Consumers are spending staggering amounts of time playing the games, while simultaneously driving travel sales and building the Orbitz brand. The average playing time for these ads is 5 minutes, but some of the reports about how long people play them are mind-boggling.

One user clicked 930 times in a 1.8-hour time span on the "All-Star Home Run" pop-under. Another player spent 30 hours on "Pilot the Blimp." Each person who clicks on the "Belly Flop" does so an average of seven times, and nobody dunks the punk just once.

The Onion and Salon both employ ad strategies that involve viewing a full-page ad prior to accessing content. Salon requires the user navigate through an ad that usually involves several pages, but Onion includes an option to skip the ad — something that makes the intrusion tolerable, because the choice to watch is with the user.

On-demand advertising is a Postmodern, digital concept that flies in the face of conventional "commercial interruption" thinking. The idea is simple: People will seek out advertising when they're in need of purchasing something. It's the sale paper concept delivered in ones and zeros. Cox Cable's Freezone experiment in San Diego has been a raging success, according to a study by the folks at Frank N. Magid Associates. Freezone is a series of on-demand advertiser videos. According to Magid, each unique viewer spends approximately 25.5 minutes per week viewing advertiser content.

From a Postmodern perspective, this is extremely significant, for on-demand advertising on TV fits the Pomo mindset perfectly. Regardless of the cultural framework, people will always have to make purchases, but Pomos turn away from traditional sales techniques that disrupt the experiences they choose. In an on-demand, digital video environment, people can make their own choices about which ads to view, and, as the Magid study suggests, the advertisers who get there first will have a significant leg up in a Postmodern world.

AdAge shocked the publishing world last week, when it gave its annual "Magazine of the Year" award to Conde Nast upstart *Lucky Magazine*. This is significant, because the magazine is really nothing more than a catalog dressed up as a magazine. Its appeal is to young female readers, but there are no articles about health, relationships or career advice. In giving the award, AdAge wrote: "...The culture warriors in the audience can start hand-wringing, if they haven't already. But since its late 2000 launch, Conde Nast Publications' *Lucky* has invented a genre, made its influence visible elsewhere — seen any eye-candy product pages in magazines lately? — and, not least, delighted marketers and readers." *Lucky* is a classic Postmodern publication, an honest, in-your-face advertising vehicle that doesn't try to disguise itself as something else.

Local online ad spending is growing at a staggering rate this year, according to a new report by Borrell Associates. While Internet ad revenues are growing overall at 15 percent, local spending is growing at a rate of 26 percent. There is a fresh energy in the air that Internet advertising can and will work and, for the first time, this energy is being felt at the local level. Yet many (if not most) local media Web properties are ill-prepared to dip their net into this growing revenue pond.

Here are five things you can do immediately to position your Web property for revenue growth.

1. Register your users. This is a small price for people to pay to have free access to your content, but it opens significant future doors to you. You can't provide targeted ads unless you know a little about who's using your site. Registration doesn't have to be an arduous task. Keep it simple. Get their email address, gender, age, and zip code. A first name is nice, if you want to provide a personalized service. Make it public that you've weighed the options and decided to keep your content free and that all you're asking in return is that they register.

2. Hire the top Flash artist in your market and begin designing interactive games for your local clients. Providing this service will give you a significant competitive advantage in trying to woo those local online ad dollars to your Website.

3. Bring EyeWonder to your table in providing streaming video content and ads. EyeWonder leads the pack in terms of playerless video streaming, something that is critical if you're going to get into running TV ads online. Why? Because there's no waiting for downloads with playerless streaming, so the interruption to the user's experience is decreased.

4. Make sure your Web design can accommodate the various ad types and sizes that are being developed. Simple banner

advertising is the horse & buggy of Internet advertising, and your site needs to be structured to reflect new sizes. There are approximately 45 new models out there, and the industry is crying for standardization. Don't expect that to come for awhile.

5. Learn the language of rich media. This is the medium for online messages, and you need to know it like you know television. Explore DoubleClick's new DART Motif software for serving and tracking ads. Developed by DoubleClick and Macromedia, the makers of Flash, it is the new model for rich media advertising.

While the institution of advertising desperately clings to norms and standards, there are a lot of very talented people in the trenches who recognize what's really going on. These people vent their frustration on various blogs and bulletin boards, which make for fascinating reading for a person like me. Here's a recent example from Mediapost's Online Spin:

> ...Sooner, but probably later, the ad community is going wake up and realize that (online) advertising is becoming a lot more about "farming" than "hunting." Attacking viewers with online ads doesn't acknowledge their control of the space. We have to develop relevant, entertaining, informative content that answers the unasked questions — the questions consumers need answered before they act. Build it. Let consumers know it's there. Show them some respect. And if what you have to say is worth their time, they'll let you know by visiting regularly...

In so doing, the industry will recognize that the Internet isn't a newspaper, a magazine, a radio or a television station. It's a whole new medium. We can mix the best from the old world to prime the pump of the new, but eventually, the medium will define itself.

And if you have eyes to see, that's happening with each passing day.

The Business of Media

My nearly 30 years in media gave me a wealth of experiences, memories both pleasant and painful, and a deep understanding of what life is really like for media people. "The Defensive Newsroom" is by far the most read and passed around essay I've ever written. I think it strikes a resonant chord with most media people, because we go to work these days fearing unemployment. This section also contains my ode to Charles Dickens, a remake of his classic "A Christmas Carol," which was actually made into an audio podcast by blogger Hugh Brackett.

THE FUTURE IS NICHE MEDIA

July 2, 2007

I grew up in a little house in a working class neighborhood of Grand Rapids, Michigan. The C&O railroad tracks ran on the other side of a field that bordered our backyard and created a nice dividing line between neighborhoods. They went to a different school "over there," so I really experienced firsthand the boyhood curiosity about life on "the other side of the tracks."

This enchantment with looking upwards is one of the things that fascinates me most about life. It is the fruit of capitalism, the bait that's dangled in front of the have-nots as an incentive to work hard, obey the laws, and get ahead. Information about people who live on the other side of the tracks can be quite newsworthy to many of those who live on this side, and likely, to some who live over there, too.

But it's not information that's newsworthy to others — perhaps not even most.

And this is precisely the problem with news organizations who carry the editorial burden of determining what is important to most. It's foolish to think that a single news agency, regardless of its size, can adequately be all things to all people, and yet this is precisely what takes place at every daily editorial meeting in every contemporary newsroom. It's at the core of the disruption being caused by the personal media revolution, for people who feel their interests and needs are not being sufficiently fed are taking matters into their own hands on many levels.

The case of Paris Hilton and her trouble with the law in Los Angeles County is a textbook example of this that bears examination, for it reveals much about the state of contemporary journalism in America. When MSNBC anchor Mika Brzezinski declined on-the-air to read a Paris Hilton lead story the day after she was released (a popular video now on YouTube), Mika became the darling of many in the news business — a hero standing up for integrity and news judgment. That the event was a running joke throughout that morning news program is brushed aside by those who want to give her a Peabody or some other distinguished journalism award.

To lead with Paris or not, that is the question.

I'm not what you'd call a Paris Hilton "fan," but I have been deeply intrigued by her life in the month of June 2007. My interest is in her as a person, not a celebrity, for I'm a student of human nature, and here was a fascinating human nature story: someone from the other side of the tracks having everything taken away, albeit for a short season, and I was most curious about how it impacted her, all judgments about her behavior aside.

It's not every day that a person of such "position" is stripped of that position and placed in a situation of extreme conflict. I found the whole mess to be a great study in class bias from every conceivable angle, but most of my curiosity was directed at Paris, the woman herself. All that I knew of her was a media creation, but that boyhood curiosity was still there, so I followed the story.

This is the chief reason why I was so incredibly disappointed in the shallow, mind-numbing, infantile and idiotic "interview" done by Larry King with Ms. Hilton on the second night of her freedom. King proved (once again) that he is inept beyond words in the ability to ask anything resembling a probing question or to follow-up anything that isn't scripted. Ever glued to his written questions and their predispositions, he doesn't pay attention to what's taking place in front of him. He is a caricature, at best, and no matter how provocative the subject, he always defaults to vapid and insipid irrelevancy.

Some are speculating that King was given a list of areas to talk about as a condition for the interview, but this gives him too much credit. Paris Hilton came with pages of things she had written in jail, so she was clearly prepared to talk about what was of interest to me.

I'm not alone in my beliefs about King. Here's a part of what Jack Myers wrote about King's interview with what he calls "the most recognizable person in the world:"

> ...You could almost hear the groans of CNN executives as the King of Non Sequiturs failed to ask obvious follow-up questions, repeated irrelevant questions multiple times, pursued a line of questioning on the impact of attention deficit disorder, and neglected issues that might have generated some actual emotion from Paris.
> Early in the interview Paris commented that she had "a new outlook on life." Later she added that being in jail had "changed my life forever." King never asked what new outlook or how had it changed her life. When Paris said "I've been immature and made mistakes but I've learned from them," King's follow-up question was about friends Paris had "gotten rid of." When she talked, several times, about her work, King never asked what her companies did and what her role is. When she complained "There's so much more to me than what people think," King asked "Did you write a lot [in prison]?"...(1)

Sure, there were lots of "hard" questions to ask and statements she made that needed challenging, but I'm more concerned that an opportunity to probe a unique event like this was completely missed.

Cynics will respond that this was exactly what Paris and her "handlers" wanted, but I don't think so. I think she wanted to be unedited and live, yes, but I sensed a young woman who'd been through something traumatic (for her, but why does that matter?) wanting and willing to talk about it. I was ready to listen. The enormous audience was ready to listen. Our conduit to Ms. Hilton, however, was either unwilling or incapable of it.

And that, my friends, is a much bigger problem for all of journalism than we think.

For the treatment of this story by the press all along has been yet another exercise in journalistic malfeasance — a lesson in how the coverage of the voyeuristic periphery — the "game," if you will (she's here, she's there, she's in, she's out) — leaves everyone dissatisfied and disenchanted. Who got the interview, in the eyes of the press, was a vastly bigger story than the one of a privileged young woman in confinement for 23 days and how that affected her life.

Stories today are colored by the people telling them. That's a simple fact, for in today's world, the storyteller is as important as the story. Those with live programs make their personalities a part of "the show," so I guess Paris chose the path with the least personality. But in so doing, we all lost, and *that's* the problem.

I'll have to wait for the book to judge for myself now, but a book doesn't provide the non-verbal communication that would come from a good interview so soon after the event. That's gone forever.

In its zeal to be all things to all people, the news business regularly churns out a shallowness that, by default, hides everything. In the same way that "general assignment" reporters can't possibly compete with those assigned a specific beat, we probe the simple and turn away from the complex, and niche journalism is its inevitable fruit. We watch as niche specialists grab attention and try desperately to wrestle it away from them. It's a losing battle, because the best we can do is Larry King and a veritable legion of self-promoting "celebrity interviewers."

In the case of Paris Hilton, the entertainment press rose to the occasion. TMZ.com clearly had the inside track on the who, what, why, where, and so forth, and they are now a leader in the hugely important world of entertainment reporting. TMZ.com, I should add, is basically a blog with hundreds, if not thousands, of professional and amateur contributors. The Paris Hilton story, to them and their niche, was the equivalent of Hurricane Katrina (a news blockbuster), and they made the best of it. Good for them.

The *Los Angeles Times* deserves props for its investigation into the sentence that Ms. Hilton received. This story never got the overall coverage it deserved, because the special interest crowd demanded their usual 15 minutes, and the *Times'* discovery didn't fit the paradigm that Paris Hilton was getting special treatment. It was too deep, you might say.

And so, we're hung up on the "value" of the story to us (um, did NBC offer a million bucks for the interview or not?) and not the story itself. It's all about the ratings, baby. How sad and pathetic have we become?

We look around us and we see the explosion of people doing media for themselves, and we're astonished that they're doing this without us. People are telling us why, but we don't want to listen.

Earlier this year, *Wired Magazine* got into a public spat with bloggers over a story they were pursuing about Michael Arrington, the founder of TechCrunch and a very influential fellow in the world of Internet start-ups. Two of the people they chose to interview, Jason Calacanis and Dave Winer, both refused a traditional interview and wanted instead to be interviewed via email. That way, they could post the entire interview if they were taken out-of-context, something both felt was a distinct possibility.

Here's a part of what I wrote then:

> It's all about control, folks, not facts.
>
> Think about your own life as a journalist. How comfortable would you be if everyone you interviewed was able to publish the raw interview in some form? You wouldn't, because *you're* the one telling "the story." It's *your* story, right? (Did you see/read *my* story last night?) You need the ability to interject quotes as you see fit in telling "the story," because "the story" is what you say it is.
>
> This is why this whole business of defending the professional press in the wake of the personal media revolution is so problematic. The rules simply have changed. The deer have guns.

Neither Calacanis nor Winer were quoted in the subsequent *Wired* article, which led Jeff Jarvis to wonder "whether they're trying to send a message: i.e., we're in charge here."

No group is more aware of this than professional athletes, many of whom are turning to or already using the Internet as a way to bypass what they view as biased filters and speak directly to fans. Boston Red Sox pitcher Curt Schilling's 38pitches.com is there specifically because Schilling doesn't trust the press to present him fairly. Same with Kobe Bryant's kb24.com. Tiger Woods announced the birth of his baby girl and Mark Cuban discussed his colonoscopy on their own Websites rather than in the press.

The best we can do — as exemplified by Mike Wise in *The Washington Post* — is make fun of it.

> Frankly, it's a godsend the Internet was invented just the last decade. How many more of us would have no career prospects had blogs been around, say, 200 years ago?
>
> Lewis and Clark: "Wassup Y'all. We're in Montana. Man, they could use a 7-11 around here. Uh-oh. Blackfeet tribe across the river! Gotta jet."
>
> Babe Ruth: "Hit No. 700 today. Ate 12 hot dogs. Met a nice girl on the train. You seen my socks?"
>
> Ali with a blog wouldn't have needed Cosell to tell him, "You're very truculent today, Muhammad." Bundini Brown could have merely typed, "Frazier's be-hind will be mine by Round 9" into a laptop and that would be it. End of Howard. (2)

And that's precisely the point for Mr. Wise and for all of us in the world of news. It isn't about the story; it's about us and our careers and our fame and our fortune. It's about furthering the establishment, and this is precisely why people are taking things into their own hands. The audience is dissatisfied, but we are unable to turn away from fostering that dissatisfaction.

The personal media revolution and its inexpensive tools are enabling people to cover what's important to them for themselves. Another significant event the last week in June should give everybody in the all-things-to-everybody crowd a severe case of the spine chills.

This time, it was the technical community, not the entertainment world, and the event was the long-awaited sale of Apple's iPhone. We saw live "witness reporting" from lines of purchasers who'd gathered to buy one of the coveted phones. Multiple live streams were available, and this has profound ramifications for contemporary journalism.

Duncan Riley of TechCrunch has tagged this phenomenon "event-streaming," and it's something that bears watching.

> Thousands of people who were not lining up for an iPhone, be that because they simply weren't interested in doing so or as in my case were unable to due to geography, experienced the highs and lows of iPhone day vicariously through live streams. (3)

Is this not the essence of live coverage of a newsworthy event? To be eyewitnesses for those who can't be there?

Jeff Jarvis sees this as huge, because the infrastructure to enable more common use of this is already being built. And I guarantee you, it's not being done by the news industry itself.

> The infrastructural challenge in this is that we, the audience, won't necessarily know where to find what's going on. For a time, there will be portals for live — UStream et al — but it's already hard to find out what's happening there. Portals don't work. So I imagine that news organizations will need to devote people to combing all the live video to see what's happening out in the world. The real value will then be alerting all the rest of us that something is going on now so we can watch on the Internet ... or perhaps on our iPhones. (4)

While I agree with Jeff that this is a challenge for news organizations, the truth is it's more than that. A whole new world of media is springing up around us, people informing themselves and their tribes as a part of the personal media revolution. Traditional professional journalism is really at odds with this, because the ability of groups to do it increasingly shines a light on the shallowness of the all-things-to-all-people paradigm. If I'm interested in the iPhone, I will trust the group that's covering it for themselves. If I'm interested in Paris Hilton, I will trust the group that's covering entertainment in the same way.

The morning news may be able to send a crew to cover the line outside the Apple store, and show producers can stack Paris Hilton "coverage" where they think it ought to be in their shows. But in both cases, the surface is all that can be scratched, and people intuitively know there is so much more. Consider similar treatments for just about everything "in the news," and you begin to understand the source power of the personal media revolution. It isn't at all about amateurs stealing thunder (or jobs) from professionals; it's about the soul of journalism itself — the story.

Jeff's right when he says that "finding out what's happening" is the real challenge ahead, and that's why aggregators are so important to the future of media. What we have today is nothing compared to what entrepreneurs are bringing us in the months and years ahead.

And the real challenge for us as existing local media companies is coming to terms with the basic issues of our communities and dedicating resources to "own" them as niche properties. If not, I'm convinced the people will do it for themselves and leave us out of it completely. Meanwhile, we need to be organizing the local Web and building the local infrastructure to enable the personal media revolution in our communities.

This is where our future will be.

2007: THE BATTLE
FOR LOCAL SUPREMACY

December 13, 2006

2006 was a year that media historians will view as the tipping point for all media companies in the face of powerful disruptive innovations that are pulling the rug out from under both the theories and practices of mass media and mass marketing. From the music industry to television, everything is unbundled now, and a whole new form of media economics called "The Long Tail" is being developed.

Look at any crowd in any city, and it seems every other person has white wires dangling from their ears. Who ever heard of an iPod just five years ago? TiVo, YouTube, Slingbox, and a hundred other new technologies are, as Jeff Jarvis says, "exploding TV."

The Personal Media Revolution — a phrase coined by J. D. Lasica in his book *Darknet* — flooded the Internet with new forms of expression in 2006. On YouTube alone, Funtwo's rocking rendition of Pachelbel's Canon in D has been viewed more than 12 million times; an obscure band, OkGo, found fame with geeky dance videos shot with one camera, and two guys in white lab coats turned us all on to what can be done with Mentos and Diet

Coke. These videos reached "mass," but the real strength of YouTube is the enormous social network built around all of the lesser-viewed personal videos.

The number of people blogging doubled and then doubled again in 2006. Bloggers added video clout, and now we have a new genre, vloggers. Rocketboom made news twice: first when they auctioned off advertising on eBay and then when Amanda Congden left for greener pastures. The hilarious, albeit obscene social commentator ZeFrank is the new darling of vloggers, and he's likely to end up in Hollywood.

And while all of this was going on, local media companies watched their stock prices plummet and scrambled to create plans to offset the audience erosion left in the wake of the very real business disruption caused by all these new innovations. When the networks began exploring different distribution vehicles for their content, it sent an unmistakable message to local media companies that their value would never again be what it was. And this has set the stage for what I believe will be the big media story of 2007 — a rediscovery of what is meant by the word "community," and especially as it relates to more than just geography. This story is one of three trends I see for the coming year, and it will unfold in a hundred different places. It might not get the publicity that network-level strategies and tactics get, but the salvation of local media lies in its ability to meet the information needs of the people it serves, and those people — the people formerly known as the audience, as Jay Rosen calls them — are increasingly an online community.

In his 1999 book *Weaving the Web*, Tim Berners-Lee — the man who invented the World Wide Web — stated that the Web "is more a social creation than a technical one." (1) This simple truth forms the core of Media 2.0, but it continues to baffle local media companies, because we tend to view the business disruption as purely technological — a way to extend our core competency. In so doing, we haven't been able to see that limiting ourselves to our "brand" online hands the keys to the local Internet community over to smart outside players, who are doing a better job of meeting the information needs of the community than we will ever do trying to be a Media 1.0 company in a Media 2.0 world.

2007 will be *the* turning point year in the struggle for local supremacy, and those who do not address it immediately will find themselves being nothing more than content creators feeding the same companies that have descended upon us to pull money from our local markets. Not everyone will survive a shift in media power from content companies to those who aggregate content, and while I suspect we might see attempts by mainstream media companies to fight it, the two need each other.

And make no mistake, this is all about money, serious money.

Nobody understands online ad spending like Gordon Borrell. His company is at the forefront of gathering and tracking data about who's spending what where. A lot of people look at his numbers with skepticism, because the dollars seem so high, but this is contempt prior to investigation and guarantees inaction. In recent years, Borrell has been pointing to a shift in online ad spending that will bring local more in line with national. In order for that to happen, local online spending will have to explode, and the reality is that local media companies just aren't equipped — from either a knowledge or technology standpoint — to compete with the Googles and Yahoos of the world for those ad dollars.

According to Borrell, the local-national split for all advertising in all media is 53% local, 47% national. Online, that split is 30% local and 70% national. Online parity will likely not come soon, but in some key online local advertising sectors, it's gone way past the 50–50 mark. Automotive, a key category for broadcasters, is one of them. Here's Borrell:

> The Internet has provided dealers the ability to reach other markets efficiently. For instance, car dealers are realizing that buyers can expand their online search options to "100 miles from ZIP Code 12345" and find them, so they're willing to spend more on "local" online advertising programs like Cars.com that has the potential to reach car buyers well outside their traditional market boundaries. We've heard many stories of people driving hundreds

of miles to buy the exact car they want at the best price they can find. By year-end 2006, the split for auto advertising in terms of online spending was 68-32 local vs. national. (2)

This ability of local advertisers to reach customers outside their typical market is a significant factor that is completely overlooked by local media companies who are busy trying to do the same old thing with the Internet that they do with their legacy platforms.

> We know of a tiny company in North Carolina that made lightbulbs to supply regional businesses, suddenly picking up contracts for Las Vegas hotels (which have a boatload of lights!) via his Internet advertising, and a small diner in Virginia that has a small shop that sells peanuts and hams, suddenly picking up orders from Asia because of their online marketing. (3)

Borrell also sees a war erupting next year between local broadcasters and newspapers, because without political ad money, it's going to be a tough year.

> Both face no-growth years for their core products but exciting growth prospects from online ad sales. TV wants a piece of classifieds, newspapers want a piece of TV advertising, especially automotive. Nearly one-third of newspaper sites feature streaming video, and many have begun selling preroll. I also expect a lot of raiding. The demand for online managers, especially in sales, will have TV stations raiding newspapers, a fertile ground of pre-trained and competitor savvy Web workers. (4)

The prize in the local online ad revenue war will go to the company that takes a Media 2.0 approach to information online. This company may or may not use their brand in the effort, for the Internet is simply bigger than media companies think, and I agree with Gordon that there will be an enormous demand for people with new skills and new talents in the coming year, not only in sales, but also in production and technology. We simply cannot expect people from within the incumbency to drive our response to the disruption, and this is a fact for all businesses, not just local TV. More and more local media companies are beginning to realize that we can't plan our own way out of the conundrum.

And when we finally get serious about all this, we're going to be surprised at what we find — that a new community has grown up around us, one that Doc Searls and David Weinberger say resembles the old "commons" concept, a place owned by no one, where people could come and go as they pleased, play, gather, and do business. This is a word we never use in contemporary culture, because its roots are very old. The understanding, however, is key to our online future success, and the most important discovery is that this is a very real community.

It's hard for us in media to see this, because our view of the world is one of danger at every turn, a bad guy behind every bush, corruption in high places, death and destruction, and man's inhumanity to man. When we examine the Web, we report only the dark side, because, well, that's our niche.

I've been writing for years about the postmodern concept of tribes, and how technology has enabled us to pick and choose our own tribes beyond geographic limitations. But human beings need to connect on a physical level, so the joining of people with similar interests — though these "connections" have been made in a world of seeming anonymity — is a very powerful thing. I've witnessed this in every place where I've been fortunate enough to be a part of first-time blogger meet-ups. People from all walks of life that "know" each other only by reputation or online interaction form immediate and lasting bonds when they actually meet in person.

This discovery (or rediscovery) of community is an eye-opening experience for local media executives, because we've grown to believe that the Internet is technology used by people and not a place where a new kind of community has gathered. Once you have this revelation, you will not approach people online in the same way, and I believe we're going to see more and more of this in 2007 as media companies — driven by business economics — push further into the world of the commons.

The online community doesn't drive the "real-life" community, not yet anyway. But it is occurring here and there, and the phenomenon will continue to gather strength in 2007. We can sit by and let others create the platforms for this, or we can drive its growth ourselves.

A key to any local media company's online efforts is increasingly its ability to adapt and be flexible, and that brings me to the second major trend that I see coming in 2007 — internal and external pressures to bring creation, control and maintenance of a local media company's Website into the operation of the local media company instead of farming out the responsibility to third-party providers.

Third-party television Website companies — and the ad networks that come with them — have served the industry well. Ten years ago, it was cost-prohibitive and too complex for everybody to build and run their own high quality Website, so we wouldn't be nearly as far along the Internet content road as we are without the efforts of of these companies.

Yet, everywhere I go, I encounter a troubling issue with television stations: "They're unresponsive to our needs," is something I hear all the time, especially from the people actually doing the local online legwork. This may or may not be true, but the perception certainly exists, and it makes for a significant inertia barrier, because it can become a built-in excuse for news not to do news and sales not to do sales.

But third-party sites are also increasingly bad strategy in the same way that farming out the presentation and distribution of our on-air content would be. They work well when plans are static, but we're in a competitive world now that cannot abide static plans. As Rishad Tobaccowala says, we need to be "flexible, adaptive, fleet-of-foot, and open-minded." This requires control of our own destiny, and we just don't have that if somebody else is leading our efforts.

It's unfair to paint all third-party Web providers with the same brush, because they are not all created equal. And I've found a great willingness on their part to explore flexibility with their clients. They have to do this, or they risk irrelevance themselves. However it happens, 2007 will be a year when television stations assume greater and greater control of their own online futures, and that will mean running their own Websites to one extent or the other.

Finally, the most visible and obvious online media story of 2007 will be the shift of the Internet's center away from text and towards video. The Web is extremely efficient at delivering text, so it will always be a core component. But it will increasingly be sharing the stage with video, and I think this will become even more so in 2007. A lot of seemingly disparate events are coming together to provide genuine video convergence, and this will greatly impact local broadcasters. Again, we will have a choice: bury ourselves in the value of high definition or explore the reality that the quality play has limited potential.

YouTube is offering a new service now that allows people to upload directly from a Web camera. This seems insignificant to those of us who value production and presentation, but the concept will be a new driver of the Personal Media Revolution. The company has to work out a lot of kinks in the system, but when they do (and they will), YouTube's value as the conduit for unbundled video items will skyrocket. The applications for local news and information aggregation are staggering, and once again, we find an Internet pure play company out-thinking and out-maneuvering the mainstream.

There are and will always be bandwidth issues when it comes to streaming audio or video, but those are technical limitations only. I've heard engineers dismiss new thinking based on the belief that the video compression of today will be the same tomorrow, and it keeps us from exploring possibilities. 2006 saw a dramatic rise in the use of Flash for video, and that will continue.

A more video-centric Web ought to help us, because that's our medium. However, we need to shift our language on the Web to that which is also video-centric. We don't make "pages;" we make channels. YouTube has figured this out. Why can't we?

2007 is likely to be a very bad year for local media companies financially, and this is most unfortunate, because it's a time when we really need to be investing, not cutting expenses. We'll see more bankruptcies next year, more efforts to take companies private, more lay-offs, and more churning in the rank and file. While nothing is certain, the one thing we can count on is change. We're in a season of change, and it's going to be that way for a very long time.

As executives and employees in the volatile world of local media, we can't control the events that are rocking our world, but we do have control over our reaction. We can knee-jerk what's happening, or we can rise above it and look to an absolutely amazing future in serving our communities in ways we never thought possible. Our success clearly lies in embracing the word "local" more than the word "media," for this is our lifeboat in the storm of change.

We must not give it up, regardless of the cost.

THE TRANSPARENCY MARKETPLACE

August 7, 2006

When the flamboyant American Basketball Association (ABA) merged with the National Basketball Association in 1976, the deal brought with it more than new teams in new cities. The ABA was a running, gunning and highly entertaining form of professional basketball, so the merger brought with it the 3-point shot and returned the slam dunk to the game. In the end, the NBA still played basketball, but it did so with different rules, rules that ultimately led to its current freewheeling style.

So it is with media companies in the face of the Media 2.0 disruption. So-called mainstream media will ultimately merge with the disruption and adopt its new rules or be swallowed up by it entirely. And high on the list of new rules is an entirely different approach to advertising, one that relies on empirical proof of performance instead of sample-based methodologies. This is what smart ad executives mean when they refer to "transparency" — precision in a world formerly dominated by blue smoke and mirrors.

A mainstream media executive recently said to me, "Terry, it's all the same game, whether there actually is mass or a perception of mass, it's still about offering those people to advertisers." Well, it is, but it isn't. Among other things, what's different is that the disruption relies on precise measurement of those people, whereas the business model of the mainstream has always relied on scientific estimates. This is not a semantic argument, nor is the eventual embracing of the measurement disruption optional.

The other element of transparent measurement is direct proof-of-performance through clicking on links. This is the foundation of Google's strength — delivering predisposed customers to businesses online. It's not about fancy, award-winning 30-second commercials; it's about the measurable ability to put customers in the showroom, and it's raising eyebrows everywhere. It's cheap, efficient and gaining reliability for the people who pay, and that spells trouble for those who count on the continued big budgets of reach-frequency estimates.

In dealing with television station groups, I often hear "None of this stuff matters, Terry, because we live in the world of Nielsen. If it doesn't have a Nielsen number, we don't care about it."

But it is Nielsen's world that is most threatened by the transparency paradigm, and this is something few people wish to honestly discuss. Billions of dollars are at stake through traditional sample-based methodologies, and a collapse here could have wide-ranging implications for the whole economy. When Nielsen announced earlier this year that it would begin providing television ratings for commercials this fall, the whole industry trembled. And now it appears a delay is likely.

Joe Mandese, editor of MediaDailyNews told readers of a hasty gathering of "all sides" in the commercial ratings concept in an effort to halt or slow down the Nielsen plan. Alan Wurtzel, president of research and media development at NBC (and one of researching's most amazing spin doctors) told Mandese, "I don't think there's anyone out there who thinks that Nielsen has a full grip on this. We need to find a forum in which the industry can get together and start to deal with some of these details."

One of the chief problems surrounding the new ratings is that the commercial ratings are processed by using a relatively shaky system for identifying when the commercial minutes actually air. That system, Nielsen's Monitor-Plus service, was designed as a competitive advertising monitory system, which apparently does not have the same level of detail or rigor as the systems Nielsen uses to compile and process TV ratings. (1)

But there are others — especially leading edge thinkers in the advertising world — that think even Nielsen's process of TV ratings cannot possibly provide accurate measurements in today's fragmented marketplace. One of them is Tim Hanlon, senior vice president of Ventures for Denuo, the media futures consulting practice of Publicis Groupe.

It's very difficult for me to believe that a sample-based methodology over 10,000 homes as a representation of the entire country can accurately measure what's really happening over hundreds of media possibilities. We have such a myriad of choices including hundreds of hours of video-on-demand, and the variability of each individual's habits just seems infinite. So a 10,000-person sample, people-metered or not, is still sample-based methodology.

With all due respect, Nielsen can barely keep up with the today of television let alone tomorrow. It's pretty clear that these announcements are an endless game of catch-up. I'm not saying the Emperor has no clothes, but it's beginning to look like a strip tease. (2)

What Hanlon and others see coming from the advertising side of the relationship is a question that must be answered sooner or later. Even in its most primitive forms, broadband video provides far more data than advertisers ever got before, and the question is "why can't we do this with television?" The question, says Hanlon, is rhetorical in nature, but it must be answered. "These people are driving the intellectual curiosity," he said, "and there's an expectation that all media needs to be similarly proven."

My belief is that television becomes a series of data points for people like us to measure and discern instead of just a simple

Nielsen rating for program or commercial. We need to be much more sophisticated, and our online people get that, but our television and print buyers don't, because they're still stuck with a heritage of crude data points that are accepted with a smile, a wink and a nod.

It is amazing to me that the billions of dollars in advertising hinge on such crude metrics and data points for all forms of traditional media. (3)

Hanlon points out that advertising data is becoming more sophisticated "by the week" and that the existing system isn't transforming fast enough. The four billion dollar ad machine known as Google is creating the future, and "they didn't ask Madison Avenue for permission to do it."

More evidence that the transparency provided by technology is completely disrupting the TV ad game came recently from a group of big players. Nine major television advertisers, including Wal-Mart, Microsoft and Toyota, are funding a project to create an online auction for television spots. They've hired eBay to create the application and are hoping to avoid the costly network "upfront" by using this as a way to buy advertising availabilities. $50 million has been committed to the project, and listen to what Ann Bybee, corporate manager, Lexus Advertising, Brand and Product Strategy has to say about it.

> To be effective in the future our processes must embrace the advancements in technology and the benefits of our digital world. (4)

Jeff Jarvis, whose popular Buzzmachine blog offers a cutting edge view of all things media, calls it "a pipe dream for marketers and a nightmare for the networks."

> The creators of the new e-Media Exchange are making noises about this not being the end of TV upfront. But it is. This is the end of control by scarcity. TV time is just more advertising now, and the days of raising rates even as audience shrank are over. Now the market will set the price. Watch out, Hollywood. (5)

A third consideration in the "Nielsen is everything" paradigm is that new metrics are being developed by third-party Internet companies that will provide even more data points for ad execs to consider. As television moves more consistently to TV over IP or IPTV, these metrics will play a role in ad rates, but they are invisible to most mainstream media companies today, because they have no bearing in the old circulation or ratings models.

Chief among these new metrics is the ability to measure inbound links to a Website, which most consider a way to assign "influence" to a content provider, whether that's a blog or a traditional media site. Since this element is a major consideration in Google page ranking — and Google is *the* source of search traffic — everyone who does media business via the Web should be involved in encouraging links. Very few mainstream sites do this, however, because the operators are still living in old models of doing business, where reach is more important than links. Every mainstream media company should have on its staff an expert in search engine optimization and not rely on a third-party to help with this important element in Media 2.0.

The transparency marketplace is going to get more and more active over the next five to ten years, and during this time we'll likely see combinations of measurement and impression-based data move to the forefront in the setting of advertising rates. Consumers who are interested in ads will be able to dig deeper and perhaps even make a purchase of items like CDs and DVDs.

Technology is making possible — with remarkable accuracy — the ability to deliver the right message to the right audience at the right time. There will likely be wars with viewers over this, because one of the most important elements of the Media 2.0 world is that the people formerly known as consumers are in charge, and unwanted messages — which means most mass marketing ads — run the risk of producing exactly the opposite of the desired effect. Is it possible to do permission-based mass marketing? Television's old assumption that the audience provides the permission because the programming is free is just one of many that are being challenged by new media.

Hanlon, who cut his teeth in the television business, has some important words of wisdom for people in the industry:

> If I run a TV station, and I'm at least smart enough to understand that I'm not just one linear channel, I'm exposed to great examples as to why I need more sophisticated measurement data. Nielsen doesn't measure HDTV, for example, because the number of people using it isn't big enough for their methodology. But in very high-end homes, do you mean they don't exist? HD Net doesn't exist? People watching the World Cup aren't real?
>
> In a multicasting environment, the difference between a .5 and a hash mark ain't going to cut it anymore. Companies like Atlas, Doubleclick, and LightningCast are introducing new forms of measurement, and I should be looking at that data as a "holy shit" event. TV people should be asking the same questions about why this isn't available for broadcasting.
>
> I would urge anybody in the TV business to be *very* focused on what happens with broadband video. Data expectations are high and we're getting comfortable there. If a TV station person starts to get comfortable with that, they'll be well prepared for anything that comes down the television pike. Whether Nielsen is the place for that development remains to be seen. History isn't on their side, because innovation is coming from the edges, not the incumbents. Stations, agencies and Nielsen are a part of the incumbency. (6)

In the end, if the Media 2.0 opportunities are targeted to what the advertisers want, then they will have value and great value. The quality of the targeted audiences is likely higher on line than it is in the broadcast world, but ad rates are much lower. This is the key to watch as the transparency marketplace evolves. Will it ever provide the same kinds of revenue levels to which mainstream players are accustomed through a methodical game of lay-ups and 2-point shots?

That is the multi-billion dollar question.

INVESTING IN A LOCAL FUTURE

March 27, 2006

One of the basics of business history is to start small and scale upwards. All of the great franchisers of the late 20th century practiced this. The name of the game was turning a profit in one community before moving on to others. The speed with which the franchises spread was based on the need for volume in a world of small margins, but the brilliance of people like Ray Kroc and Sam Walton was formed in a deep understanding of customer needs — something they gained by being up close and personal.

In so doing, each developed an appreciation for servicing (or creating?) the wants and needs of their neighbors. This meeting of a local human demand has been the cornerstone of business development since the beginning. It's interesting, too, to note that when the discount store phenomenon began in the 60s, it did so in a climate of local laws that prohibited outside discount stores in the name of protecting local businesses. How far we've come.

So we shouldn't be surprised, as we move from Media 1.0 businesses to the wild west of Media 2.0, that the concept of the importance of geography is extremely rare. This is especially true when looking at how venture capitalists work in the digital age and where their money is going to help build the new world. These smart people are exploiting the lack of walls — geographic or otherwise — that the Internet enables, which means profitable scale can be achieved more quickly than building Wal-Marts in expanding circles around Rogers, Arkansas. MySpace, for example, redefines the idea of community, and there's little need for a geographic base with YouTube or NetVibes or Pandora or a hundred other 2.0 start-ups. And yet, the biggest of the digital big boys, Google and Yahoo!, are now working to reposition (at least a part of) themselves as companies with geographically local value, which has turned the old franchising model upside down.

Google has begun placing local ads on their mapping application, which means people who use it to get directions are now going to encounter billboards along their digital trek. Yahoo! has begun offering local news items aggregated from the RSS feeds of local media companies as a new, local service for their users. This remarkable ability for a single, outside entity to better serve the information needs of geographically disparate people than the media companies in those geographic regions is a sad commentary on the ingenuity of local entrepreneurs and the investment community that serves them.

From a distance, it seems that this is the way the big VCs and their money want it to be. By continually supporting only those business models that attract large numbers quickly, they are forcing basic top-down (1.0) laws on those of us who see greater value at the local level. So while the Web and all that it offers is moving to a one-to-one or bottom-up paradigm, the world of the dollar continues to draw its influence and power from the top-down. This is beyond ironic, especially with venture capitalists who tout Media 2.0 applications.

It's also not healthy for our economy or our culture, because as the Googles and YouTubes of the world continue to grow, they do so at the expense of local communities. Every advertising dollar spent on Google Local, for example, is money taken from the local community and transferred elsewhere. That's just fine with the investors of those companies, of course; it's the American way. But our unbridled support of this means fewer choices in a world that these investors proclaim as one of more.

In the venture capitalist world, no one is more visible, transparent and open than Fred Wilson. He operates an important blog and is the Managing Partner of two venture capital firms, Flatiron Partners and Union Square Ventures. He's based in New York and is widely quoted by my colleagues throughout the media observation world. I've been reading his blog for several months, and his is an important voice in the Media 2.0 space.

In an email exchange over the weekend, I asked Fred why VCs seem to avoid local investments.

> I have had numerous discussions with people doing local stuff like New West, Fresno Famous, Buffalo Rising, the stuff going on in Charlotte, Northern Virginia, Philly, etc.
> And I have encouraged all of them to come see me when they have a model that can scale to a real business.

The truth is that most of these services don't yet have more traffic than my blog, which is shocking to me, but that's where it's at today.

> I think we are going to cross the chasm soon, and people will start using the Web for local news instead of or as a compliment to the home town paper.
> But the geeks are the first to adopt this stuff, whether its blogging, online commerce, PayPal, eBay, digital downloading, YouTube, etc, etc.
> So until the soccer moms, plumbers, and grandfathers start going online with the gusto of the geeks, we'll have to wait for these opportunities to turn into venture plays. (1)

The examples Fred lists above generally attempt to deliver hyper-local news and information using a reach/frequency business model. This is why he expresses surprise that his own blog delivers bigger numbers. But local attempts to capture ad dollars this way — even those that involve the local citizens media community — are competing with other local portals in a never-ending quest for eyeballs. Their competitors have two advantages. One, they have deeper pockets, and, two, they have mainstream media outlets with which to promote their online activities, so it is an extremely difficult, uphill climb to capture market share.

Meanwhile, everybody misses the point of slick 2.0 applications elsewhere pulling ad dollars from businesses more interested in doing business than propping up what used to be the only ad game in town. This should be viewed as a significant challenge to media companies and local investors across the country, because there is significantly more at stake than meets the eye. As that ad money drifts outside the local community, it will impact more than just the media businesses located there. Big cities don't build stadiums to make professional sports team owners happy; they do so, because a local pro sports team means far more to the community than ticket sales. Same with local advertising dollars.

No one sees this better than Gordon Borrell, whose research and consulting business is based on counting local ad dollars spent online. One service he provides is a precise analysis of the local online ad business, and the volume of dollars being spent usually astounds executives of local media companies, most of whom are getting only a very small slice of the pie. Many simply refuse to believe the numbers, while others look at their sales managers with that unmistakable "you're not doing your job" look, and neither of them know what to do. And in my business, I find that when eyes are finally opened, local media companies find themselves at a significant disadvantage, because they have neither the resources nor the time to try and capture that which has been lost. That they will continue to lose even more is still not enough to force such investments.

Borrell poses an important question when he speaks with local media companies. "Will," he asks, "the online advertising pie ever reach the local/national parity that's found with advertising overall?" (2)

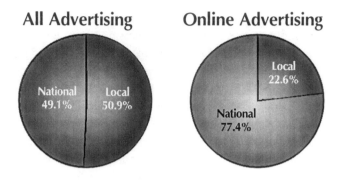

All Advertising

National 49.1% Local 50.9%

Online Advertising

Local 22.6%

National 77.4%

Like Borrell, I believe parity is possible — but not without three important things happening first.

One, local media companies simply must move forward with Media 2.0 concepts that offer real value to the communities they serve. This is a difficult proposition, because a.) most existing media companies don't understand the space and b.) they're too busy defending themselves against the disruption to see the value of embracing it. While existing 2.0 applications have proven that geography isn't a barrier to entry, the reality is that every community has an identity and values that cannot be duplicated from without. It's simply a matter of applying technology properly. Unlike a Wal-Mart Supercenter moving into the neighborhood, barriers to entry in this space make it possible for anybody to compete without spending a fortune.

Two, the local advertising community needs to be brought up to speed on what's possible locally in the 2.0 space, and that doesn't mean spending more on some local media company's portal Website. This is the biggest roadblock to breaking the stranglehold that well-funded outside entities have on those local ad dollars. Inexcusable local advertiser ignorance is bliss to those who are sucking ad dollars away from local communities. And there's a catch-22 with this one that moves the ignorance into the category of deliberate. Ad agencies have a lot to lose in a world that doesn't respect middlemen or their role in the economy, so they don't really want to learn. These companies will disappear as an advertising factor downstream unless they, too, find a way to embrace the disruption.

Three, the VC community needs to see the potential in Borrell's reaching of advertising parity and help fund local online businesses that may or may not be affiliated with public media companies. Outside investment capital isn't encumbered by quarterly bottom line demands, and local media companies are helpless to invest the resources necessary to create local 2.0 applications. As Fred noted, hyperlocal efforts to date aren't "real" businesses yet, and the big VCs are more interested in duplicating that which already works than trying to build things that might. So the job falls to local investors and entrepreneurs, but so far, that's not happening. Everybody, it seems, wants the big score.

The reality is that there are likely many more cumulative local ad dollars that one can obtain with an old-fashioned strategy of applying the franchise model to New Media than by spending lots up front to build a new, global start-up. The technology is there to do so; it's just a matter of the right entrepreneurs and the right investors finding each other.

NEW METRICS AND PRINCIPLES

March 5, 2006

On a recent flight from Nashville to Los Angeles, I had the misfortune of sitting near a two-year-old boy who was traveling
with his father. The boy was completely out of control and spent
most of his waking hours screaming "no" or "mine" and carrying on
like he was all that mattered in the universe. This is the curse of
a child determined to be the center of attention (or is the curse for
those who are nearby?), and it got me to thinking about how all
of us who've been a part of mass media have employed similar
strategies.

After all, attention in a crowd goes to the one who screams the
loudest.

This is a core principle of mass marketing and, of course, one of
the reasons people are rushing to get seats at the back of the plane
to escape all the screaming. We smile at our cleverness in dis-
guising the screaming, but it's still noise. The triumph of personal
technology over mass technology (Glenn Reynolds's marvelous
phrase) has given people peace from all the screaming, despite the
insistence by the status quo that all it's really done is increase the
noise by adding voices to the discussion. That's not true, but I digress.

The failure of mass marketing is occurring on two levels. One, it's just harder to draw a crowd these days, and without a crowd, you have no "mass" into which to cast your messages. Despite empirical and anecdotal evidence to the contrary, the marketing world still insists that old metrics of reach and frequency are the pathway to success, and this is problematic in today's ever-fragmenting media world. Reach and frequency still count, but they share the road with lots of other things.

Today's "attention markets," as Umair Haque calls them, are places like Digg or YouTube, user-generated destinations that carry a hip and counterculture flavor, where people go to escape the screaming and do their own thing. Media 1.0 attempts to create their own or assimilate these (or others) will ultimately fail, because they'll drag the screaming along with them.

But if you can bring yourself to back away from the crowd and the noise, you'll find a second significant (and undiscussed) failure of mass marketing. We — those of us who use mass marketing — have been sucked into believing the hype associated with our own screaming. This is perhaps the greater failure of mass marketing, because it's left us vulnerable to circling the wagons around false claims — claims that the people increasingly see through as self-serving and, to be blunt, bullshit.

Consider the television news industry. If you talk to people who don't watch the news anymore, you'll discover that this hype is one of the big reasons people have walked away. We regularly raise the stakes for viewers on some stories to the life or death level, and they know both intellectually and intuitively that it isn't true. But in declaring it so, we fall into the trap of believing our own hype. We convince ourselves that the story lives up to the tease, and that, folks, is very rarely the case.

This isn't just the case with TV news. It's everywhere. We're so awash in hyperbole that the only people really to trust are those we choose to be members of our own postmodern tribes — friends, sometimes family, acquaintances, references from friends, people who've "been there, done that," and others that we encounter in our day-to-day lives. This is the success of the Diggs and the *Clue-trains* of the Media 2.0 space, but it's basic Postmodernism.

And since they know that our messages tilt towards bullshit, guess what? There's an inherent element of bullshit in our brands, those bastions of faith upon which mass marketing are built. What is branding anyway, except a marketing metaphor borrowed from the cattle industry of centuries gone by. Why "brand" my cattle? So I can find them in a crowd.

"I want my headache to go away," Rishad Tobaccowala of Publicus told the recent OPA Global Forum in London, "I don't want a relationship with Tylenol." This is a significant statement of new media speak, and it strikes at the very heart of mass marketing. For with all the money spent on the Tylenol brand, a great many people today buy plain old acetaminophen, the generic name for the drug.

In fact, the generic drug industry is growing at a double-digit pace. According to Generic Pharmaceutical Association statistics,

- Generic medicines account for 53% of all prescriptions dispensed in the United States.
- Of the top five U.S. pharmaceutical companies, based on the number of prescriptions dispensed, four are generic companies.
- U.S. brand pharmaceutical sales for 2004: $217 billion. U.S. generic pharmaceutical sales: $18.1 billion. (1)

These numbers say nothing about the over-the-counter branded versus generic business.

The success of the generic versus the brand is complex, but there are clearly a couple of factors worth noting that are important to this discussion. One, cost is significant factor in the choice between branded and generic. This concept can be expanded to include other forms of currency as it relates to media, most notably time. Two, one must assume a certain high level of knowledge on the part of drug customers in choosing generics over brands. While there are likely some people who'll stand in the headache remedy aisle of Wal-Mart holding a bottle of Tylenol in one hand and the company's "Equate" generic in the other who'll say, "Nope, it's not the same," the truth is most people know the only difference is in the packaging — the brand.

This is important when we hear over and over again that "the news is all the same," and we hear that because it's true. As Michael Rosenblum so wonderfully puts it regarding television news, "It's a guy with a box over his shoulder."

And so technology is allowing people to escape the screaming, and what's the response for companies that need to do business with running customers? It certainly isn't to scream louder. What's needed is a new metaphor to replace the old one, and new metrics upon which to place value in a world of unbundled media. The value will be there, because access to eyeballs (or eardrums) will always have value. But those eyeballs are scattered, knowledgeable, hip to our ways, and highly suspicious. This requires a completely counterintuitive set of metrics and principles.

In offering the list below, a caveat: this isn't an "all-or-nothing" proposition. Mass marketing and branding and all that goes with it isn't going away completely. There will always be a need for differentiating yourself from your competitors. It's just not the only game in town anymore, and the disruption of avoiding the screaming is something we need to embrace instead of fighting. So how can we restructure value for advertisers and ourselves in the marketplace of conversation?

1. Respect. This basic rule of life is cited in the Biblical mandate to "give and it shall be given unto you" or "as you wish to be treated, treat others." I cannot possibly overstate the value of this principle in determining the long-term health of any business, media or otherwise. (Points to the business that does away with automatic telephone answering systems first.) We need to find a way to measure this through a combination of other metrics and principles, because its value is utmost in the minds of the running masses.

2. Genericize. We need the courage to see that even our best "brands" can have baggage, and it usually comes from the hype associated with the brand. Dragging the brand into everything we do, therefore, places unnecessary obstacles in the paths of creatively meeting information and entertainment needs that are out there. We need the willingness to genericize ourselves in some of our work in order to overcome those barriers. We also need a way to measure the effectiveness of the effort.

3. Fluidity. This is a measurement of our ability to have our products and services read and viewed beyond our control. It's the opposite of the mass marketing notion of stickiness that is so much a part of portalesque Web design. If we want people to stay (so that we can make money) we'll do things that will actually push people out the door. So fluidity is a key metric in the Media 2.0 paradigm. Remember, they're running from our screaming.

4. Influence. Technorati is providing this through measuring inbound links to various information Websites. It's a sound method of determining which voices are providing leadership in the conversations that are news these days. The top sites generally belong to traditional media companies, whose role is evolving from final say to conversation starter in the Media 2.0 world. There is nothing artificial about this metric, which is why it has such value.

5. Trust. Trust networks are like amoebas that move and shift based upon the shifting values and beliefs of the trusters. Built upon the postmodern model of tribes, they're tough to get a handle on, but again Technorati is making an attempt by calculating the changing "favorites" lists of influencers within their universe. This is also a clever way for people to access new thinking within their sphere of interest, and it has great value.

6. Transparency. In hiding behind our hype, we've painted ourselves into a corner of mystery and intrigue that people increasingly see as suspicious and often hilariously

self-serving. We must discipline ourselves to come out into the light and speak in human terms and with a human voice. We also need a way to quantify this, so that value can be assigned.

7. Credibility and reliability. Based on their adherence to professional codes and traditions, media companies falsely assume they are automatically granted these two sides of the same artificial coin. People don't care about any of this, because media companies have generally hidden behind them instead of living them, and the result is a public that doesn't trust anything we/they say.

    Reliability and credibility, however, are hugely important concepts from which people choose sources, and we need to be open about what they mean, and demonstrate our adherence to the principles day in and day out. The problem with these two ideas, however, is that they cannot exist external to a point-of-view or argument. This was the dream of 19th century journalism reformers who were really after a sterile environment in which to sell advertising. It's nonsense, and people — especially informed people — increasingly see through it.

    That's why, if we're going to claim reliability and credibility, they must be defined beyond some unattainable ideal, which brings us back to the previous principle, transparency.

8. Listen and Link. These are from the fertile mind of Jeff Jarvis, but I think they're overlooked in terms of real value. If, for example, you have a sponsor who's recognized the value of what you're doing and wants to be associated, there is no reason such a sponsor shouldn't be attached somehow in the referential linking that you do. It doesn't have to be intrusive, but if my link provides you with influence, it is reasonable to suggest that real value is attached to that link. We need ways to do this and measure it.

If the father on that Nashville to L.A. flight had quieted his two-year old, everybody around him would've been more comfortable, and isn't that what we're all seeking as we look to the future and the Media 2.0 world (and beyond)? It isn't about us, about clawing our way to the top regardless of what that does to anybody else. But it isn't about some unrealistic utopian "can't we all just get along" notion either, for the nearby passengers on the plane (myself included) also had a responsibility to a father who was obviously in over his head. We could have made the experience better for him and ourselves.

In his new book, *Get Back In The Box*, Doug Rushkoff writes, "The Internet is not a technological or even a media phenomenon; it is a social phenomenon. And in this sense, interactivity has changed everything." (2) So media success in the new world will largely be measured socially, and one hopes that we all will learn a little more about ourselves and each other in the process.

That would make the flight called life a little better, and who could ask for anything more?

THE DEFENSIVE NEWSROOM

October 15, 2003

The ugly confrontation during game 3 of the Red Sox/Yankees championship series has been dissected and analyzed a thousand times, but nobody did a better job that day than ESPN baseball analyst, Harold Reynolds. For those who missed all this, the fight broke out when Red Sox batter, Manny Ramirez, angrily approached Yankees pitcher, Roger Clemens. Ramirez thought Clemens was trying to hit him with a pitch in retaliation for an incident the previous inning when Red Sox pitcher, Pedro Martinez, hit the Yankees' Karim Garcia with a pitch. That's the way it goes in baseball. If your pitcher hits my guy, my pitcher's going to hit your guy. That the pitch Clemens threw wasn't really close to Ramirez was irrelevant, as Reynolds brilliantly pointed out. The real issue was that Ramirez was expecting Clemens to throw at him. Reynolds showed videotape of the previous pitches to Ramirez, each of which was out over the plate. With each pitch — and for just a brief instant — Ramirez was seen leaning backwards as the ball approached the plate. He was, indeed, expecting to get hit.

The point is if you're expecting to get hit, it alters your behavior, and this goes way beyond the baseball diamond. It's a universal truth in human relations. It's really about fear, and it has a lot to do with the current state of affairs in local television around the country. Fear has become the dominant influence in newsrooms everywhere, and it's one of the reasons viewers are turning away.

I know an award-winning TV News photographer who shot some rather dramatic video of a search and rescue operation but declined to tell his station, because he was afraid of losing his job over it. It seems the young man had taken his company vehicle on a personal R&R trip, and while he was there, shot the footage involving the search for a drowning victim from his market. It was the lead story on all the stations the next day, but no one had any actual footage from the scene. This photographer struggled with the decision, but in the end, his need for a paycheck came out on top. He was afraid of the repercussions of violating a company policy on personal use of a company vehicle. He had seen too many people get fired for violating other rules. He had a family to support.

This would never have happened in the newsrooms of yesteryear, not because we were any more magnanimous than the managers of today, but because getting the story was always the top priority. Everything else, including the rules and regulations of the company, took a back seat to the mission of covering the news. In my day, this photographer would've been rewarded for the footage, even while being reminded that he'd violated policy during the process of obtaining it. Fear of getting hit by the pitch was never a part of coming to work in those days. Of course, people got fired, but it took a series of major screw-ups for it to happen. There was a M*A*S*H-like esprit de corps that existed, for our common enemy was the clock, not the management of the TV station.

I believe that the fear-based culture that exists in many TV newsrooms today is directly connected to declining viewership, because a defensive business can't respond to change.

Four years ago, the newspaper industry had a come-to-Jesus meeting about where the business was heading. They created The Readership Institute and gave it a 5-year mission to research and report on ways to increase readership. The ground-breaking research by the Institute in 2000-2001 was a multipart "Impact" study of 100 daily U.S. newspapers. One of the key components of this research was the culture of a newsroom.

> Newspaper readership has continued to decline for three decades despite extensive research into reader issues and many reader-growth activities at newspapers across the country. So from the outset of the Impact Study, the Readership Institute felt there must be an internal, organizational factor at play that was keeping newspapers from doing the things they knew they should do. The hypothesis was that culture would be linked ultimately to readership.
>
> This, in fact, proved to be the case. Impact research shows that newspapers with constructive cultures tend also to have higher readership. The finding echoes results from hundreds of studies in other businesses that link the culture of the workplace to employee satisfaction, customer satisfaction and business outcomes, such as profitability and shareholder returns. (1)

If that's true for newspapers, it is equally true for TV news departments.

The Impact study defined "culture" as the shared beliefs and values that shape employees' thinking and behaviors — or more colloquially, "the way we do things around here." About 5,500 employees at all levels in news, advertising, circulation and marketing at 90 newspapers completed three surveys to diagnose the prevalent operating culture at their newspaper and its effect on people and the business. They found that cultures could be divided into two types: constructive and defensive and that over 80% of the newspapers in the study group were functioning in defensive cultures.

> Constructive cultures tend to be outward-looking and responsive to market and technological changes. They expect achievement at both the individual and the group level. Collaboration and coordination across departments are not optional — it is how they operate. In businesses generally, those with a constructive culture deliver superior long-term performance and more satisfied customers and employees.
>
> In contrast, defensive cultures resist change. People are expected to focus on how well they are doing, as opposed to how

well the group or the organization — or customer — is doing.
They tend to operate in departmental silos. (2)

The study went on to define three types of defensive cultures found
at the newspapers.

> Aggressive Defensive. The primary behavioral style in these
> newsroom is perfectionistic, because people are expected to
> approach tasks in forceful ways to protect their status and
> security. "People feel they must avoid all mistakes, keep
> track of everything and work long hours to meet narrow ob-
> jectives." It is a classic stress creator. The secondary behav-
> ioral style is "oppositional," wherein confrontation is the
> norm. It is a culture that focuses on avoiding mistakes rather
> than making improvements.
>
> Passive Defensive. Here, people do what it takes to please others
> and avoid interpersonal conflict. Rules, procedures and or-
> ders are followed without question. Jobs are narrowly de-
> fined and supervision is intense. "Managers rarely catch
> employees doing things right, but never miss when they do
> things wrong."
>
> Passive/Aggressive Defensive. This is a combination of both of
> the above. (3)

Is any of this beginning to sound familiar?

Constructive cultures, on the other hand, encourage workers to
reach their potential, resulting in high levels of achievement, job
satisfaction, sales growth, and service quality. They are human-
istic in their approach to people, and the emphasis on achievement
generates excellence and problem-solving.

The Institute also asked those 5,500 employees to define their ideal
work culture, which produced significant gaps between the existing culture and the ideal. The biggest things lacking in the newsrooms?

- Giving positive rewards to others
- Encouraging others

- Helping others to develop
- Enjoyment of work
- Opportunity to think in unique and independent ways
- Maintaining personal integrity (4)

Fear is a corroding thread that reaches out far beyond the news-room in which it exists. It touches everything with which it comes into contact, and that includes the audience of a television news show. If our newspaper brethren can safely conclude that defensive newsroom cultures turn away readers, why can't we see that it does the same thing to television news viewers? People who consistently come to work in fear of their jobs simply cannot do a good job of reporting and presenting the news.

There's an old adage that newsrooms take on the personalities of their news directors, so news managers must bear much of the blame for a defensive culture. However, I know many news directors who regularly fear for their jobs as well, so compassion for newsroom employees must also extend to the managers. Who's really to blame? Well, we all are, but assigning blame isn't going to fix the problem. Besides, it's another defensive trait.

Each of us must decide — at one level or another — that we're simply not going to accept working in a defensive culture. Regardless of your place in the newsroom pecking order, you can make a choice that today will be different. What can you do? Here are some ideas:

1. The clock is your only enemy. This is the universal truth of television news and what makes our business so different from anybody else's.
2. Emphasize what was done well over what was done poorly. Do this with yourself and with everybody around you. You'll never overcome a negative mindset by dwelling on negatives. It's a waste of energy. Congratulate yourself and those around you — even in things that seem minuscule — and you'll be amazed at how much different it will be when you come to work the next day. Don't dwell on mistakes; not yours; not the other guy's. The clock doesn't care.

3. Always thank your co-workers before you go home at night. No matter how "good" you are, it takes an enormous team effort to get anybody's work on the air. Everybody's important, and so much of our business requires that little "extra" or "above and beyond" that we tend to take it for granted when somebody takes a risk to get the job done. We need those risks and nothing will produce them like an environment of appreciation.

4. Expand your responsibilities to include those around you. Always ask where you can help somebody else. This seems so obvious, but it's amazing how many people in newsrooms won't go beyond their own cubicles in pulling together the daily product. A newsroom is a living entity with a real enemy. I am my brother's keeper.

5. Your boss is not responsible for your happiness. We're not victims of bad bosses or bad general managers or bad corporations. We're victims of the way we react to them. No matter how lousy a manager you have to work for, your misery is your choice. If you give the power of your happiness over to somebody, anybody else, you'll always be living for them.

6. Stop comparing yourself and your work to others — especially those across the street. Your audience isn't watching them. They're watching *you*.

The last few years have witnessed an escalating animosity between management and labor and a general disrespect for co-workers in the local news business. This is demonstrated over and over on Internet bulletin boards such as the Watercooler and Newsblues. It's beyond sad. It's tragic, and I believe it can be directly attributed to the defensive cultures of most modern TV newsrooms. Like our friends in the newspaper world, we need to address this, because competing in a fragmented, Postmodern world demands that we be able to quickly respond to change.

That's hard to do when you're expecting to get hit by the pitch.

BEYOND RSS AGGREGATORS

December 31, 2003

I grew up in the 1950s, when science fiction was just beginning to play with robots, the most famous of which was Gort from the 1951 classic, "The Day The Earth Stood Still." Robots went bad a lot in those days, especially the ones in Superman, but the idea that machines would one day serve our needs was something we dreamed about. Who wouldn't want one like Rosie from The Jetsons? I think we fantasize about these things for many reasons, but a lot of it comes from the belief that technology can and should be harnessed to serve mankind.

We've certainly seen a proliferation of gadgets and gizmos in recent years that accomplish the task quite well, and nowhere is this truer than in the way we communicate. Even such a marvelous invention as the telephone seems clunky by today's standards, and who wants to retrieve a wet newspaper from the lawn, when the same thing is available — in living color — on the World Wide Web.

But the newest thing to aid in being well-informed is a dandy little item known as a news aggregator. You'll hear a lot about these in the years to come, and I predict this will be the primary method of news delivery worldwide within the next 5 years.

A news aggregator is essentially a robot that communicates with the Internet and finds the news you ask it to find. Current aggregators provide text-only, but I think that will ultimately change to include multimedia content.

News aggregators take advantage of a technology that's been around since 1997 called RSS. RSS stands for Rich Site Summary or Real (or Really) Simple Syndication, depending on whom you ask. It's used to syndicate news content or any kind of text subject matter that is regularly updated. It speaks in the Internet dialect of Extensible Markup Language (XML), and here's how it works. Let's say I'm the *New York Times*, and I want to make my editorial content available to as many people as possible, so I create an XML version of each story's first 30 words and publish it on my Website (software does this automatically). Then, let's say that you are interested in news from the *New York Times*, so you obtain a simple — and in many cases, free — piece of software called a news aggregator. You give it the address of my XML file and, voila! Every time I load a new story, your news aggregator alerts you that it's there. You are automatically informed every time a new story posts on my Website. You can read — on your desktop — the first 30 words or so and decide if you want to click on a link to read more.

You don't have to scan *all* of the news from my site. Yahoo, for example, has a host of RSS feeds available, through which you can be very specific about the types of news stories sent to your news aggregator. This will no doubt be further refined as the technology develops.

As a regular consumer of news, I can tell you that there's nothing quite like my simple little news aggregator. The news comes to me instead of me going to it. It's very robotesque and enormously time saving for me, to say nothing of what it's done in terms of broadening the scope of my information reach. I keep track of many news outlets and blogs this way. It's simply a marvelous technology for news.

This concept is built on what FCC Chairman Michael Powell calls the "most powerful paradigm shift" in communications history — the fact that applications aren't woven into delivery infrastructures anymore. What he's saying is that anybody can be a phone company now with a simple application, just as anybody can be their own newspaper or TV station with a high speed Internet connection. One doesn't need to own the delivery system in order to be a player, and Powell views that as a major threat to the status quo. He told the San Jose Mercury editorial board, "Now to be a phone company, you don't have to weave tightly the voice service into the infrastructure. You can ride it on top of the infrastructure. So if you're a Vonage, you own no infrastructure. You own no trucks. You roll to no one's house. They turn voice into an application and shoot it across one of these platforms. And, suddenly, you're in business.

> And that's why if you're the music industry, you're scared. And if you're the television studio, movie industry, you're scared. And if you're an incumbent infrastructure carrier, you'd better be scared. Because this application separation is the most important paradigm shift in the history of communications, and will change things forever.

Riding atop the infrastructure, the aggregator concept will be moving forward on two fronts, I believe, because of the economics involved and consumer demand.

The first front is video, or multimedia in the vernacular of the Web. AOL's decision late last year to purchase SingingFish.com, the Internet's first multimedia search engine company, was made, in part, to keep Google from gaining an advantage in this developing market. SingingFish has indexed more than nine million audio and video streams and powers the multimedia search engines on several big Websites. Content categories include movies, news, sports, music, radio, TV, and "other," which often refers to adult content. AOL recognizes the demand and has responded accordingly.

Video search is going to be huge in the years to come, as news video on demand (NVOD) services develop.

While we're on the subject, Google already functions as a form of an aggregator. Google news gathers stories from various sites it has tagged and gathers them together for users to pick and choose from a newspaper-like page. It doesn't really stretch the imagination to see the value of providing this kind of service for multimedia news. Google News offers users the ability to receive emails on stories or subjects of interest to them, thereby providing a watchdog service that is continually scanning the Web and, in a sense, duplicating the functionality of a separate news aggregator. It's a terrific service, but I'd prefer to do this myself rather than hand it over to a profit-motivated third party.

Google's wants advertising impressions and aggressively pursues them by bypassing entry pages from a variety of Websites in order to serve the search needs of Google users. This has not gone unnoticed by the businesses they're searching. They like the traffic Google gives them but are scratching their heads over whether it might not be an overall liability. By employing a site's own technology, for example, Google is able to provide a simple text search for nearly anything, and that includes content deep inside a company's Website. Late last year, Google launched a service wherein users can track FedEx or UPS shipments simply by entering the tracking number and "FedEx" or "UPS" in the search bar. Up pops the page from the FedEx or UPS site with your information! This is great for the consumer but not necessarily so for FedEx or UPS. Google didn't partner with either FedEx or UPS to provide this service. They didn't need to, and there's really nothing to stop them from spreading such services. That could be a problem for news organizations that would prefer to have users visit several pages on their Websites.

While it's true that a client side news aggregator does the same thing, the choice on what goes out to the aggregator rests completely with the company providing the content, not a third party search firm. I think this will be increasingly important in a VNOD world, because it'll determine how many and whose commercials I have to watch.

The biggest advantage news aggregators have is that the user can determine what sites are searched and have that delivered, unfiltered, right to their desktop. That includes keeping up with certain writers, in addition to various subjects and news sources. Search engines like Google have a lot of muscle, but the Postmodern Internet tends to reject any kind of Modernist manipulation in favor of freedom of choice for the user. This is why my money is with the new aggregators of the future.

The second front on which I think we'll see this develop is in the advertising of goods and services. While Madison Avenue is all a-twitter over who can be the sneakiest in creating clever marketing in a changing culture, the industry seems to have lost sight of the reality that consumers really want and need advertising. Let's face it; we all make consumer decisions based on advertising, whether it's the big sale at the mall or the rebate from Chevrolet. We need to know these things, so advertising will always be with us.

But like everything else Postmodern, people want some say in what's delivered to their advertising plate. For example, there are certain TV ads that automatically force a channel change with me. It's not that I'm offended by *all* commercials — some are downright entertaining — but I'm mightily turned off by some. I believe the idea that anybody with the right amount of cash can interrupt my life to sell me something is dead, or at least dying. I can put up a "No Trespassing" sign to deter door-to-door salesmen. The phone company offers me technology to screen telemarketers. Junk mail goes automatically in the dumpster, and one day somebody will come up with a workable solution to spam. Why? Because we want a little privacy, thank you very much, and we don't think we should have to put up with constant sales pitches. Why is it any different with other communications' media, including television?

Some day, a smart entrepreneur is going to develop a multimedia ad Website built on RSS that allows people to decide whether they want to view a new advertisement for a product or service that interests them. Moreover, I think it's likely that one day most, if not all, Websites will serve ads based on user preferences and not just demographics or psychographics.

If you run a news Website and don't offer your content to users via RSS, you need to make that priority one for 2004. You want your XML address in your users' aggregators and not your competitors.

If you're a news consumer and don't have a news aggregator on your desktop, you're missing a powerful New Media robot that'll serve your information needs better than you can imagine.

Is TV News Giving Away the Future?

May 1, 2003

My mother always cut the apple pie into six pieces, so I grew up with an appetite for a fairly hefty slice of pie. There were five of us in the family, and the extra piece went to Dad's lunch bucket. It took me a long time to understand the nasty looks from the people at church when I put two pieces on my plate at the newcomer's potluck. I couldn't quite figure out why they made the slices so small in the first place.

This explains why I have a fairly simple understanding of the FCC's relaxation of ownership rules. What I don't understand is why TV station groups don't recognize and act upon the ultimate futility of the strategy of buying up more pieces of the pie. A better metaphor would be the purchase of more deck space on the Titanic.

For the past 3 years, the UCLA Center for Communication Policy has conducted tracking research about the changing media landscape in the U.S. The findings are chilling, especially for television and television news. Here are the basic, irrefutable facts:

- Internet use continues to grow rapidly.
- As Internet use grows, television viewing goes down.

- People with both in the home now use the Internet as much as they use TV.
- Broadband is growing rapidly.
- People with broadband spend even more time on the Internet and less watching TV.
- These trends are more acute with children, young people and experienced Internet users.
- And, among Internet users, the Net has become their most significant source of information.

Despite this obvious movement away from television and to the Internet (especially among young people), TV stations and their owners continue to ignore that they have the wherewithal to actually bridge the two mediums. But they don't understand the Internet and are frustrated by attempts to employ broadcast sales strategies in a medium that rejects the very nature of passive participation. They gave up years ago, and now the world of local television station Websites is dominated by two companies, Internet Broadcasting Systems (IBS) and Worldnow.

The formula is simple. These companies provide co-ownership Websites for the stations. The stations drive traffic to the sites through their broadcasts. The "network" type effect created by these companies is attractive to some advertisers. The groups and the networks split the revenues and costs, with the financial specifics varying among the member groups.

It seems like a magnificent business win–win. According to Broadcasting & Cable, IBS revenues grew from $27 million in 2001 to $42 million last year and a projected $58 million this year. The company was profitable for the first time in the fourth quarter of 2002 and expects to build on that in the year ahead.

In a time of downsizing, Internet networking seems like a no-brainer for TV stations and groups, but I believe the partnership is based on false assumptions and the promise of something for nothing for the stations.

- False Assumptions: You can be a TV station and not do TV on the Internet.
- You can't make substantial revenue from the Internet.
- The broadcasting mindset of "all things to all people" works on the Internet.
- Cluttered portal sites are what users want.
- Advertisers will accept banner advertising.
- Users can't see through the shallowness and sameness of these sites.

The underlying truth is that these networks exist for the benefit of the networks, not the TV stations or their ownership groups. And it's a double whammy for station groups who've put cash into equity positions with these networks. To object, therefore, is seen as shooting oneself in the foot. However, the truth is that the wound was inflicted when the deal was signed in the first place.

Television stations are obsessed with recruiting young viewers, yet they gave away their access to young people when they signed on with these networks. Who could blame them? The promise was easy money. The promise hasn't changed, but the price certainly has.

It's not too late for local TV to get back the years they've given away, but they must act quickly. If your deal with an Internet network can't be broken, buy another domain and get busy doing TV News on the Web! You need to do this, because if you don't, somebody else will.

Ten recommendations to consider:

1. Always remember, users are in charge. You are not. Respect them. Empower them. Steer clear of manipulation of any kind. Internet users can see right through it.
2. The narrower the focus, the greater the likelihood for success. In other words, get out of the mindset of "broadcasting'.

Trying to be all things to all people is self-destructive. Resist it. Portals don't work. Forget links to the network or anywhere else. Keep it very simple and serve that niche will all your might. Forget all the "live, local, late breaking" hype (for now).

3. Think young and postmodern. Don't shy away from points of view. Don't feel everything needs to be explained, make sense, or have a reason.

4. The most important person you can hire is a creative Flash programmer, somebody who can bring ads to life.

5. From the beginning, design it to be advertiser-friendly. Sell sponsorships that give the advertiser exclusive exposure on a rotating, user-by-user basis. Let's say Bill Heard Chevrolet is a sponsor. Depending on where they are in the "rotation," when a user hits during their "turn," the only advertiser that user is exposed to is Bill Heard Chevrolet. Create Flash ad pieces that compliment the user experience and give him options for more. All the skins (the frames around media players) and backgrounds have a Bill Heard influence. In other words, the entire user experience changes, based on which sponsor is in the rotation. Use your Flash master to create games and other interactivity for the sponsor.

6. Install the Groopz or some other interactive chat software in the sales offices of the station and your advertisers. When somebody hits the interactive request for more info, a sales professional can talk to them in real time. This is power, because you're delivering customers directly to their business!

7. The guts of the site would be an interactive machine with pizzazz. Stack thumbnail-sized, playerless versions of stories on one side. Users could play them with a click or move them to the main player to view in a larger size or full screen. Select the company that provides your video streaming based on the quality and speed they can provide.

8. Provide nothing about your TV personalities. Personality doesn't drive the Internet. Information does. Anchors represent elite authority, something young (postmodernist)

people reject. This doesn't mean they can't or won't identify with point-of-view anchors and reporters. They just don't accept the idea of traditional authority figures.

9. Provide interactive weather tools. You've spent all those years teaching about the weather. It's time to let your viewers/ users use what they've been taught.

10. Don't be afraid to compete with yourself. Get over the "bastard child" view of the Internet. It's got the people you want, and unlike your broadcast facility, the audience is growing. Break stories there. Sell it, sell it, sell it. Adjust your thinking to the current reality and create a synergy that'll show the entire community you can meet their information needs regardless of the forum they select.

Thus far, the FCC's decision has spoken only to those who view it as the death knell for modern journalism and the diversity of opinion. Frankly, I think that's grossly overstated, and I hope media owners can rise above the weeping and gnashing of teeth to see a future that's actually quite the opposite of the rhetoric.

It's not about carving up a single pie. It's about firing up the oven of the Internet and baking a few more.

THE FUTURE IS MULTIMEDIA

January 26, 2004

Much to the dismay of friends and advisors, I was always much more the grasshopper than the ant when I was young. I played my banjo and sang on TV while my classmates all went off to do their studies. Of course, the draft board didn't have an exemption for banjo players, so I wound up in the service when Lyndon Johnson ordered troop buildups in Vietnam. You'd think I would've learned.

But most of my TV news career was the same way. Settle down? Nah. The adventure of new markets and new challenges drove me. I was a "fixer" news director, not a maintainer. And when I retired in 1998, with no 401k, little cash tucked away, and the business I used to love changing rapidly, I found myself needing to nurture my inner ant and quickly learn some new tricks.

Today, as a grown-up grasshopper-cum-ant, I can clearly see what old Aesop meant when he wrote of the wisdom of preparing for days of necessity. And as I survey the television news landscape these days, I find a lot of floundering grasshoppers (a few ants too!) who are stuck in desperate situations, taking pay cuts with longer hours, and working with no sense of where they're going — probably wondering why they ever got into "the biz" in the first place.

So it is with change, especially the type that pulls the rug right out from underneath you. My heart goes out to these people, and it is to them that this missive is really addressed.

That cliff you're running towards is life, post-broadcasting. The whole idea of mass marketing is being turned on its ear, and the handwriting on the wall is saying you've invested your entire self in a dying industry. As a friend of mine puts it, it's like being drawn to the tar pits by those who enthusiastically shout, "Hey, c'mon. There's food here." Extinction, thy name is mass media.

Ad people are just starting to get it. Kathy Sharpe of Sharpe Partners in New York wrote an op-ed piece for MediaDailyNews smacking her contemporaries for living in denial. "This is a serious and angry denial involving high-paid executives and threatened litigation, and just about everyone scrambling for cover. But it's still denial, a massive group-think to figure out how to fix the ratings, replace Nielsen, punish Nielsen, or just find out why — specifically — men aren't watching TV anymore."

Ms. Sharpe added that the entire TV ad industry was based on rather elaborate myths and that people are beginning to discover that the foundation isn't just crumbling; it was never there in the first place. But she offers hope through the Internet.

"Despite the best efforts of a few misguided media folks to market it as the proxy for TV, the Internet really is the stand-in for the next generation of TV. It is viewer-controlled, interactive, and thus completely responsive to reality. It is what TV viewers are doing today — already — and in a far more thorough scale." (1)

This post-mass media threat is real not only to broadcasters but print journalists as well, despite the pronouncements of those like Toronto Star publisher, John Honderich. "More and more newspapers are becoming the sole mass medium," he told the Advertising Club of Toronto recently, "particularly for advertising, as television becomes more and more fragmented." This is a shallow and self-serving observation, for even Mr. Honderich knows the preferences of young people, preferences they won't give up when they get older and replace his subscriber base. (2)

My children are the last generation that will know what it's like to wash newsprint ink from their hands. David Card of New York-based Jupiter Research says the future of newspapers is multimedia. "Printed newspapers are not going away in our lifetime," Card told the *Minneapolis Star Tribune*. "But I doubt that a lot of young people who grew up on TV and the Internet are going to retreat to the printed newspaper as they settle into middle age." (3)

Card is right. The future for news people of every hue is a world called multimedia that exists in the interactive conduit we now call the Internet. It may look a lot like TV, but with the user in control, all of the rules are different, and a variety of multimedia skills are absolutely essential for those who will work therein.

The definition of "multimedia" depends on who's writing it, but it's generally thought of as a communication that uses a combination of different media, including text, spoken audio, music, images, animation and video. A newscast is a form of multimedia presentation, with it's audio, video, music and graphics, but in the new world, the multiple specialities of the control room required for real-time broadcasting are reduced to a computer with a single operator — you. It means a modified skill set for journalists, but one that offers unlimited creative possibilities in communicating their stories to people.

In a multimedia environment, the story — and how it's communicated — is all that matters. We don't care about a reporter's walkin', talkin', shuckin' and jivin' stand up. In fact, we could go through the whole story without seeing what the reporter looks like. Some things may be best presented solely as text. Perhaps a slide show with music will do for others. As I've previously written, the days of celebrity anchors are numbered. Along with that will go the media's obsession with personality and presentation over content. Young people will stop going to school only because they "want to be on TV," and we might actually see a return to journalism as a trade for those wishing to make a difference instead of a profession of elite celebrities who don't want to get their hands dirty.

We'll never again be "filling time," because time (rightly) belongs to those with whom we are attempting to communicate. The clock will remain a constant enemy in a competitive environment, but the deadline will be how quickly we can get the story to the people, not one arbitrarily based on the time of day.

In a multimedia news world, there are many ways to tell stories or portions of stories, and we should be welcoming this instead of ignoring it or running from it. The rush of "the story" remains exactly the same as it was in a mass-media world; the only differences are immediacy, form and format. Frankly, it's an environment that would bring me to work every day with a smile on my face.

For existing news people — and I'm specifically referring to those in TV News — you have two choices. Carry on and begin looking for what you really want to do for a living downstream or begin developing the skill set you'll need in the new world. For those who choose the latter, here are 10 recommendations.

1. Learn the Internet. This is the field of play for multimedia news, and the only way to learn it is to use it — and not just for boredom reduction. It means leaving the safe training wheels of AOL's closed environment, and learning the idiosyncrasies of, for example, Google. Find out who really knows how to search in your shop and spend a little time with them. Explore news sites, and not just those in the US. Don't give up on this until you've become a sophisticated and proficient user.

2. Get involved in the community of bloggers. Pick a subject of interest to you and start exploring. Use your Google knowledge to find directories or individual blogs. Whatever your hobby or interest, you'll find bloggers writing about it. Blogging is interactive, so interact. This is important, because it'll begin opening your mind to the realities of what's happening on "the streets" of the World Wide Web.

3. Get yourself an RSS news aggregator. I cannot overstate this in terms of importance. RSS and variances thereof are the news distribution vehicles of the future. They are so, because the user can pick and choose what news he or she wishes to view and where it comes from. The new world isn't about single points "broadcasting" to large audiences. It's the pyramid turned upside down, where the guy at the bottom has the power of choice. RSS is simply a technology he or she can use to exercise that power. You need to be a part of it to fully understand how your work will get to the end user in the years to come.

4. Learn digital, non-linear editing. If it means coming in on weekends or staying late, learn it, learn it, learn it. The reason for this is simple: storytelling in the world of multi-media — whether it's video, a slideshow, animation, music or effects — is assembled in a form of digital — mostly non-linear — editing. If you can learn an Avid, you can handle anything the multimedia world throws at you. I'm not talking about mastering individual technologies. That will come later. What you need now is a foundational understanding.

5. Put the camera on your shoulder. Better yet, if you can find one, get behind the wheels of a Sony PD-170 or similar camera. This will be a tool of tomorrow's journalist. The days of 2-person crews are on the wane. The economics don't make sense anymore and neither does the restrictive nature of split functions in the newsgathering process. We've always known that the person looking through the viewfinder (and editing the story) generally has a better grasp of how to put the finished product together than the writer, and this is no longer an issue in the world of the Video Journalist (VJ). Where the idea of the "one-man band" seemed insulting just a few years ago, it's now recognized (at least in Europe) as a better way to do electronic news gathering.

6. Learn HTML and Photoshop. Take courses at the local technical institute or make friends with a Web developer and ask

for some one-on-one training, even if it costs you money or a few beers. Technology has advanced to where you can create Web pages without knowing html, but being able to write your own code gives you a head start over those who can't. And while there are many photo editing software applications on the market, Photoshop is the choice of nearly everybody in the Web world. If you can use Photoshop, you can use any picture editor. Photoshop comes with a little gem called "Image Ready" that will make animated graphics for you. Learn that and you're on your way to making better stories for a multimedia environment.

7. Learn PowerPoint. This may seem silly, but producing a nice PowerPoint presentation is an essential part of life in a multimedia world. It's a great way to make a graphically rich, controlled presentation to an audience, whether it's in a boardroom, on a projector, or via the Web. But beyond that, PowerPoint teaches you how to think in ways to illustrate a story with still or animated graphics. It's elementary compared to other technologies, but show me somebody who can make PowerPoint sing, and I'll show you a multimedia producer.

8. Get to know your station's Webmaster and spend time with him/her. This person should be the most Net-savvy member of your station's staff, and you can and should take the time to do a little brain-picking with such an individual. Only the Webmaster will know ALL of your Internet capabilities and shortcomings, and this is a person you need to know. Ask if you can spend time watching, and don't be afraid to ask questions. You're not looking to replace him or her. You're just seeking helpful knowledge. Be a sponge.

9. Be proactive in getting your stuff online. Few stations even understand, much less use, all that they could be doing online. Most stations are a part of either the IBS or Worldnow networks, and content is generated through the use of templates and often with strict guidelines. There's room for creativity, but it's usually considered on a case-by-case business, something that defeats the immediacy that the Web

can provide. Get to know your station's limits and be a little pushy when it comes to getting your stuff front and center. The day is rapidly approaching when our beloved "resume tapes" will be presented online and consist of more than just a few standups and a few stories. You're going to want to show off all that you've learned, and the best way is to get it on your station's Website.

10. Expand your personal network to include multimedia players. Get to know others that are producing nice multimedia news. Chances are you'll find these people at the bigger newspapers, because they are ahead of TV stations in the online multimedia race. I continue to stress that a station's biggest competition downstream is not the other stations in town but the local paper. Cruise the Internet and look at papers that are deep into this. Get on Dirck Halstead's mailing list for The Digital Journalist. These people will be in demand for a long time to come, and becoming a part of the circle is certainly a good idea for any young TV journalist trying to prepare for the future.

There's no time like the present to give some of your grasshopper time to your inner ant. It seems laborious, but it's actually fun, and investing in tomorrow has never been more important than it is today. And I can promise you one thing. You'll like yourself better in the morning.

SEARCHING FOR THE BOTTOM

February 15, 2005

Our world is filled with tops and bottoms. When you're on the bottom, your quest is to get to the top. When you're on top, your quest is to stay there, lest you fall, and we've known all our lives that gravity is an omnipresent, natural force that threatens to take us to the bottom. We're obsessed with tops and bottoms. We want to be top dog, because the view is incredible, but the way to get there is through the bottom line. Top is up, and that's good. Bottom is down, and that's bad. Without one, the other doesn't exist. Up, down, top, bottom. These are terms and concepts that we logically use to make sense of many aspects of life.

Our modernist minds are obsessed with measuring everything, because it gives us a sense of control. This is especially important in business, and the television industry is doing a lot of it these days.

Right now, television managers are looking for the bottom, because we're in a revenue free fall. The bottom is usually discovered by cutting costs, but the quest to discover the bottom has the whole industry distracted from what's really taking place. By instinct and training, managers believe that once they find the bottom, they can — sooner or later — manage their way back to profitability. This is a dangerous illusion these days, because all the rules have changed.

Television is desperate for revenue, but revenue isn't the problem. The problem is audience. Solve that problem and the revenue will follow, but we'll never solve that problem as long as our attention is focused on revenue. It's the business model itself that's flawed and under attack. We're not just in a business downturn.

Few industries have been ravaged by disruptive innovations like the home photography business. Polaroid is gone and Eastman Kodak is going through staggering changes, but now there's a light at the tunnel for them. The research firm IDC reported a few weeks ago that Kodak had taken the top spot in U.S. digital camera sales in 2004, a key achievement for the company's new efforts. Sales of point-and-shoot cameras were up 66%, placing it ahead of perennial winner Sony Corporation and prompting an in-depth report in *Time Magazine* called "Getting Kodak To Focus." (1)

Kodak's biggest challenge was this: How could it generate sufficient profit from digital sales and cut costs fast enough to offset the precipitous decline of its primary source of profit? Kodak CEO Daniel Carp brought in Antonio Perez from Hewlett-Packard in 2003 and set about the task of fixing their very broken business.

> "People think our challenge in becoming digital is that we don't understand the technology," says Perez. "They're absolutely, terribly wrong. We have technology coming out of our ears." What the company didn't have was focus. (2)

Perez provided one, organizing the company around three areas and selling off divisions that split their focus.

> "I guess, as a legacy from a very rich, very successful company, [Kodak's management] was sloppier than we wanted it to be," says Perez. "We were looking for accountability. We organized the company so it was very clear who was responsible for what." Perez also had to find the right people to — as Carp puts it — 'teach' Kodak about the brave new world it was entering. Many have come

from outside — including seven of the 10 most recently appointed senior managers." (3)

Pierre Schaeffer, director of business strategy for Kodak's digital and film imaging business, wants everybody to be aware that they're blazing new trails in the world of home photography. "We're involved in a really exciting transition," he said. "Regardless of the outcome — and hopefully, we're playing it for the best — the moments we're going through now will be making the textbooks."

Broadcasting needs to take a close look at those textbooks, because its focus is all wrong as the digital revolution similarly eats away at its foundation. Cutting costs, raising rates and stunting left and right to maintain a revenue picture that resembles what used to be won't work, because the problem isn't revenue; it's the audience, and this is where our focus needs to be.

Like the legacy companies of the photography industry, we're clinging to a method of doing business that's dragging us into a bottomless pit. We're wasting our time trying to right the ship, when what we really need to do is find another boat.

Here are just a few of the lessons we can learn from Kodak.

1. We must break free from denial. This was Kodak's biggest problem as the digital revolution was building. Business denial is usually accompanied by arrogance, so a little humility would also help.
2. Our legacy culture is strangling us. We need freedom and room to roam. We need to find an entrepreneurial spirit and create, not sit back in the comfort of a culture destined for the tombs.
3. Ossified managers need to find other employment. We need energy and fresh air, not people stuck in rigidly conventional patterns of behavior, habits or beliefs.
4. We must find the courage to go on a major diet. Our real competitors — those who are taking advantage of the low

cost of entry into our space — are lean and mean, and we must get there too. Fat is killing us. Not only does it drag us down (to the bottom), it also keeps us from taking risks and moving quickly.

5. We need to carefully define who our competitors really are. We're not just competing with other broadcasters; we've got a boatload of new kids on the block. Cable, DVRs, Web companies, bloggers, podcasters — these are our new competition. We own the video news niche in our markets today, but that's likely not to be the case tomorrow unless we move quickly. We must view anybody who occupies the local news, information and entertainment space as our competitors.

6. We need to stop leaning on our brands. Kodak's brand didn't save it during their free fall, and ours won't either. The new world is all about consumer empowerment, not who can "manage" their brand best. People are quite hip to mass market manipulation these days. The age of promotion is giving away to the age of attraction, and brand means less than service in the new world.

7. We need to break our addiction to high margins and the easy fixes they bring. It's going to take a lot of hard work, but the reward will be there. Instead of one stream of high margin revenue, we need to be thinking of multiple, smaller streams to make up the difference.

Regardless of how we do it, the starting point is the people in the communities we serve. What are their entertainment and information needs and how can we best fill them? The problem is not revenue. It's the audience. They're not coming back to the old way of doing things. In fact, they've been telling us that for years, but our search to find the bottom has turned a deaf ear to their pleadings.

The road to profitability means a new vision and a new skillset. "We're a television station" used to be top dog. But he's tired and weary now, and gravity is beginning to take over. The new top dog is something like "we're a multimedia company and we also have a television station." He's fresh and new and ready to go.

So let's forget about the bottom and get busy.

A BROADCASTER'S CHRISTMAS CAROL

December 13, 2004

A gust of wind swirled around the trees in front of old Ebenezer Broadcaster's hilltop house this cold December night, scattering snow from the branches like an invisible broom sweeping dust from the attic. The large evergreen at the corner bent in the gale and rerouted the gust over the valley and its inhabitants. It was Christmas Eve.

It was a peaceful and starlit night throughout the land, and the little ones dreamt of the next morning with its joy and gifts — all except the little ones at the cottage of Bob Gadget. Gadget had worked as an engineer for Ebenezer for 30 years, but this Christmas, he feared for his job and, along with it, his ability to care for his crippled son, Tiny New. Rather than buy gifts, he was saving what little money he had for the inevitability of Broadcaster's axe.

Ebenezer was a second generation Broadcaster, having built his empire from a small AM radio station his father owned in the 50s. With a penchant for squeezing every last penny from a dollar, Ebenezer Broadcaster had a reputation as a hostile and difficult employer. He boasted that many celebrities had come through his television stations on their way up the ladder, but the truth is he never paid anybody enough money to want to stick around.

"Humbug," he would say on the matter. "I just did my part in helping their careers move along."

Earlier in the evening, Ebenezer had been enjoying his holiday brandy, when a vision appeared to him warning of visits by three Ghosts during the night. Dismissing the apparition as too much booze, he went to bed as usual. However, his fitful sleep was interrupted when the clock struck midnight, and he bolted upright in bed as a strange presence rattled chains while emitting a comfortable but frightening warmth. The Ghost was small in stature, and a broad smile never left its face.

"Are you the Spirit, sir, whose coming was foretold to me?" asked Ebenezer.

"I am."

The voice was soft and gentle. Singularly low, as if instead of being so close beside him, it were at a distance.

"Who and what are you?" Ebenezer demanded.

"I am the Ghost of Broadcasting Past."

"Long Past?" inquired Ebenezer, observant of its dwarfish stature.

"No. Your past. Now, come. Let us look and observe."

Suddenly, Ebenezer Broadcaster was pulled into a vortex of sight and sound — familiar yet unfamiliar. The tunnel was lined with all sorts of money — floating cash, loose change, profit, credit scores, check books, and an endless sea of balanced budgets. He reached for a $100 bill, but it slipped through his fingers. Laughter and merriment echoed from every direction, and he was aware of a profound sense of power as they flew along on their journey.

"A journey to where?" he wondered.

The Ghost turned to the left and suddenly they were aboard a cruise ship with hundreds of old associates and clients.

"I never thought the Broadcasters would ever spend their money on something like this," said a stout fellow holding a martini.

"Their money?" replied his companion. "Hell, it's *our* money they're spending. They've got us by the balls, they do. If we want to reach our customers, we're a slave to their outrageous rates."

With a sudden yank, the Ghost pulled Ebenezer heavenward, and they were soon floating over the city. Tucked in an envelope of warmth, it seemed they were immune to the cold night air. Every home had an antenna attached to the chimney, and inside smiling faces were everywhere as families gathered around their television sets to enjoy the programming Ebenezer's station provided. It was good and all was well, but in an instant Ebenezer was back in his bed. With its toothy smile, the Ghost stood before him and announced that another Spirit would soon knock.

Then, Ebenezer Broadcaster was alone.

In mid-snore, he was again awakened as the clock struck one. A stream of light from the next room beckoned, and Ebenezer reluctantly investigated, discovering a giant Phantom surrounded by a floating field of electronic gadgetry and wires that filled the room. The Ghost of Broadcasting Present was pleasant and young, and she carried a torch shaped like a computer screen. When the Ghost turned to the left, the floating field turned with her. When she turned to the right, the floating field followed. It was most strange indeed.

First the Ghost of Broadcasting Present showed Ebenezer the people of the town in all their merriment on Christmas morning. As they watched the townspeople, the Ghost sprinkled good cheer on them from her computer and the people rejoiced. As Ebenezer looked around each home, he noticed that no one was watching television. The set still stood in the corner of the living room, but youngsters played video games and DVDs, while older people watched cable niche channels like HGTV and The Food Channel, each in their own room. How awful, he thought.

Computers were evident in other rooms of the homes, and people sat typing and drawing and reading and watching. There was only a scattering of antennas on the chimneys of the homes.

A bone shivering chill swept over Ebenezer's body as he considered the scene before him, and he felt a want that was unfamiliar.

"What's happened to my business?" he inquired of the Spirit. "You cannot represent the present, Ghost. Where are the people watching television? What about Nielsen? What about my clients?"

"You seek the past in what is now," the Ghost replied.

"Humbug," Broadcaster muttered. "This is nonsense! My spreadsheet still shows profit."

Off they flew to the northeast corner of the valley and entered the home of Ebenezer's most loyal employee, Bob Gadget. Electronic machines sizzled and swirled in every corner of the cold house, and Bob himself was busy in front of a computer. As he pecked at the keyboard, the Ghost led Broadcaster to read the screen. Gadget was making an entry to his blog — forecasting doom for the industry he'd served for 30 years and gathering links from like-minded bloggers who were searching for ways to calm their unemployment fears.

"Rebellion," Ebenezer cried. "My own trusted employee is rebelling against me."

"You've given him no choice," answered the Spirit. "He must protect his family, including Tiny New Gadget."

In the living room, the Gadget family was gathered around the TV watching a Seinfeld rerun between the commercials.

"At least these are loyal to me," Ebenezer thought, but the Spirit directed his attention to the empty floor beneath the Christmas tree.

Suddenly, Ebenezer Broadcaster was alone once again, and he trembled for perhaps the first time in his life.

The clock struck two, and he awoke to a room filled with a terrible sense of foreboding and dread. Before him stood a third Spirit — this one ghastly and misshapen.

The Phantom slowly, gravely, silently approached. When it came, Ebenezer bent down upon his knee; for in the very air through which this Spirit moved, it seemed to scatter gloom and mystery.

It was shrouded in a deep black garment, which concealed its head, its face, its form, and left nothing of it visible save one outstretched hand. But for this it would have been difficult to detach its figure from the night, and separate it from the darkness by which it was surrounded.

He felt that it was tall and stately when it came beside him, and that its mysterious presence filled him with a solemn dread. He knew no more, for the Spirit neither spoke nor moved.

"I am in the presence of the Ghost of Broadcasting Yet To Come," said Ebenezer.

The Spirit answered not, but pointed onward with its hand.

"You are about to show me shadows of the things that have not happened, but will happen in the time before us," Broadcaster pursued. "Is that so, Spirit?"

The upper portion of the garment was contracted for an instant in its folds, as if the Spirit had inclined its head. That was the only answer he received.

The city appeared before Broadcaster as if it sprang up around him, and the Ghost's hand directed Ebenezer to listen to the conversation of several groups of men in the streets. They spoke of the death of a man and a funeral that no one planned to attend.

"He died a fool," said a fellow with a moustache and glasses. "The old coot just couldn't accept change."

"He also died broke," added another. "He never knew what hit him, because he wouldn't listen to anybody."

Ebenezer stared into the black emptiness of the Phantom's hooded face and said, "They're talking about me. Is it not so?"

Suddenly, they were above Broadcaster's old television station. It was a shadow of its former self, its windows broken and its walls covered with the utterings of vandals armed with spray paint. Equipment racks had been ransacked and anything of value removed. The parking lot stood empty. The tower was broken in half, and its transmitter was covered in overgrowth and wires. The cold wind whistled through the buildings of Broadcaster's once proud station.

"This, this cannot be," Ebenezer cried.

Over the city they flew, and joy and merriment was all the Ghost could reveal. Life went on. The people were entertained. The people were informed. Gone was any trace of a TV antenna. Inside the homes, the people entertained themselves with a variety of gadgetry. Elaborate menus of content drifted before his eyes, along with acronyms he didn't recognize. VOD, DVR, iPod and PSP. There were no television sets, only flat screens, laptops and handheld units — some connected by wires,others not.

Broadcaster's thoughts turned to his own sense of worthlessness. All this time, he had believed the people of the town couldn't live without him. Yet, here they were doing just fine despite the loss of the TV station.

Once again, he found himself inside the dwelling of Bob Gadget. The family home had been transformed into a sprawling mansion, the splendor of which overwhelmed Ebenezer. Laughter and joy filled the house, and prosperity flowed from every room. Bob's son, Tiny New, was the center of attention, and cash fell from his pocket as Bob lifted him into the air and set him in a special chair.

"It's all been worth it, my family," Bob announced as he raised his glass in a toast. "While that old bastard Ebenezer Broadcaster wasted away the hours counting on the immortality of his spreadsheets, we've explored the many new ways of doing what he used to do. Mass marketing died when the Internet was born, and media is now all about consumer choice.

"Our company has gone public, and thanks to our Tiny New Gadget here, we've come to a place where we can enjoy the fruits of life's many blessings."

And Ebenezer found himself in a graveyard, alone with the Phantom. Before him stood a tombstone that read

Here lies the body of Ebenezer Broadcaster.

He dug the hole in which he is now buried.

The scales fell from his eyes and he realized what the Ghost of Broadcasting Yet to Come was telling him, so he asked, "Are these the shadows of the things that Will be, or are they shadows of the things that May be only?"

He begged the Spirit to assure him that if he changed his ways, this would not be his end, but the Ghost did not answer. He threw himself at the Spirit's feet and pleaded saying, "I will honor New Media in my heart, and try to keep up with changes. I will live in the Past, the Present, and the Future. The Spirits of all Three shall strive within me, and I will spend what the Future requires."

Ebenezer watched frightfully as the Ghost began to shrink until it melted away into nothing more than a bedpost.

As the sun broke through the window, Ebenezer Broadcaster awoke with a stretch and a smile. He was also on a mission, and there was no time like the present to get started. He made his way to the mall and burst into the door buster sales to buy this gift and that. He turned his car northeastward to the home of Bob Gadget and his family.

When Gadget opened the door, old Ebenezer smiled and announced, "Ho, ho, ho. Merry Christmas to you and your family."

He handed out gifts to one and all, put his arm around Bob, and said, "Let's you and I sit down and talk on Monday about what's going on in the business and what we can do together to prepare for the Future."

And Tiny New raced to Ebenezer and squeezed his leg.

"God bless us all," he proclaimed, "each and every one of us."

WHEN SUPPLY EXCEEDS DEMAND

September 27, 2004

When CNN shut down its Spanish language news Website last month, the press release said it wasn't making money and that they were relaunching CNNenEspañol.com as an information site, focusing on scheduling, programming and anchors. The company said it wasn't giving up entirely on the concept and would try again "when financial conditions for interactive companies improve and new business models emerge." This is corporate-speak for "We don't have a clue why it isn't working."

This mystery — how media companies are supposed to make serious money online — is behind most of the shaking heads in the television industry today as broadcasters look to the Internet to make up for shrinking revenues.

In so doing, many discover that the Modernist business absolute known as supply and demand — a law as old as (mass) marketing itself — is working against them.

The logic of the law of supply and demand is simple and pure, and it determines the prices of goods and services in a free economy. When the supply exceeds demand, the thinking goes, prices will be low. But when demand exceeds supply, prices go up. And so business people try to balance the two, and most of the laws and rules of business are based on supply and demand.

The business world likes the law of supply and demand, because it provides companies with a modicum of control in a mass marketing paradigm. They can raise demand through advertising and public relations, and they can limit supply by reducing manufacturing. Hence, supply and demand form a control panel, the knobs of which businesses tweak and manipulate to make a profit. For all our talk about "the market" setting this, that or the other thing, the truth is that the law of supply and demand is why God made MBAs.

But along comes that rascal, the Internet, and messes everything up. The law of supply and demand may be immutable, but in the Internet's networked economy, the ability of businesses to manipulate it vanishes. This poses great difficulties for institutional Modernism, and it's at the bottom of why CNN has decided to wait for "new business models" to emerge. Supply is out of control. There are just too many information options for Internet users these days, regardless of their language preference (and if you can't find it in your language, you can translate it for free!). It's the supply side of the law that's gone to seed, and the real question CNN and many others are asking is, "How can we control it."

We can't. Starcom's Rashad Tobaccowala said it best: "2004 ushers in an empowered era in which humans are God, because technology allows them to be godlike. How will you engage God?" Indeed. (1)

And yet, this hasn't stopped some companies from trying to force new wine into old wineskins, and there's a sub-cultural discussion underway about this that's highly relevant as we look at the future and try to form workable business models for a Postmodern world. These kinds of discussions are taking place in the blogs and forums traversed by the advance guard of the new age — the techies.

One illustration is in the UK, where *The Sun* recently cut back on its online content, because they felt it was hurting their core business. BrandRepublic wrote:

> News Group Newspapers, the division of News International that oversees The Sun and the News of the World, has discovered that about 90,000 readers a day (5% of their total) were looking at the Sun Online rather than buying the newspaper. The fear of cannibalisation of newspapers by their online products is one that has posed a conundrum for publishers, but The Sun is first newspaper to cut back. The Observer reported that ... most of the editorial will be cut back to only show story samples, to encourage people to go out and buy the newspaper. (2)

This circle-the-wagons mentality will backfire, because Internet users will simply go elsewhere to meet their information needs. The content of The Sun just isn't compelling enough to move people back to buying the paper.

Subscription models are another attempt to limit supply and justify price. Restrict access, the thinking goes, and the content has more value. The *Wall Street Journal* is the model for this, but its reader base is unique and quite willing to pay for access to the online content. This is true of most publications that are considered essential in the business world, where the cost is reimbursed or can be written off.

Elaborate site registration processes also restrict access to content, and the question in the techie community is whether that's deliberate. John Dvorak, *PC Magazine* writer and techie guru, thinks it is.

> I have to conclude that the typical newspaper in this country does not want you going on its Web site, and deliberately creates a barrier in order to prove to the shareholders that the Web is losing them money. It's a feeble attempt to emphasize the printed version of the paper at the Web site's expense. The Web seems to be just something that newspaper people feel they have to do because everyone else is doing it.

When you peruse the Web sites of newspaper publishing associations, it's almost as if they are reluctant to even discuss what's going on. There are few studies, no hard numbers that I can find, and no information on best practices. And when it comes to running one of these sites, it always appears to be part of a very expensive content management scheme that has to hurt profits. You get the sense that the more popular a publication becomes online, the more money it must be losing, hence the barriers. Maybe it's time to change the model. (3)

Media companies that require in-depth registrations say they use the information to help provide contextual advertising, but the reality is that the on site behavior of users alone is sufficient for contextual advertising to be effective. Simple site registration, where users are only asked to provide zip code, gender and age, is much less intrusive and also provides rich data for contextual advertising.

But the prize for the most absurd attempt to restrict access to content goes to Patrick Kenealy, CEO, International Data Group (IDG) and publisher of InfoWorld, a popular and important techie magazine. Kenealy doesn't think it's right that money-making businesses should be able to link to his content without him getting a cut. While this may sound terribly logical to business types, it's actually a blatant example of shooting oneself in the Internet foot. By restricting simple links to his content, he's closing himself off to the very audience he wishes to reach.

We're talking about straight links here. Nothing more. One of the beauties of the Web is that writers can link to source material from which they quote or reference. Mr. Kenealy thinks that's fine, unless, for example, the writer is selling advertising on his or her site. Here's the way he justified it in "Technology Marketing":

> IDG has become concerned by "deep linking for profit," where money-making entities use our content to sell advertising, sell sales leads or build direct marketing lists. Here's our version 1.0 policy: Outsiders who use our content to gather registration data must share that data with us. Outsiders who use our content to sell advertising must share revenues with us. Outsiders who use interaction with our content to create sales leads for sale to third parties

must share revenues with us. Outsiders who use our content must respect our privacy policies. (4)

The result is that unless and until a Website has a formal arrangement with IDG, links from that site to IDG content produce this:

> We regret that we can not satisfy this specific content request because it originates from a source that is not authorized to redistribute our material. Please access all of our rich store of technical knowledge directly by clicking on any of the following links. (5)

The source of the link, however, is not "redistributing" the IDG material, but simply providing a link to IDG's own page. Mr. Kenealy is blocking access to his own free content from people predisposed to read it, and he's doing it on the misguided principle that supply and demand can be manipulated online. In building a wall around himself, he's isolating his company from the very people it is intended to serve.

If this view was extended to include all Websites, there would be no Google. In fact, there would be no Web, which is, after all, an elaborate series of hyperlinks. This would probably be fine, however, with those who lament the loss of control over supply and demand. The *Cluetrain Manifesto*'s thesis #7 is "Hyperlinks subvert hierarchy." But in the business world, hierarchy produces command and control, and so there is enmity between institutional business and the Web.

Blogger Anil Dash put it this way in an open letter to Mr. Kenealy:

> Patrick, it's well within your rights to ask people not to link to your stuff, or to do so conditionally. But it reflects a grave misunderstanding of the market you're in. Learn from iTunes, not from the RIAA. Ask your writers and your advertisers what they'd prefer. I bet they're not looking to be walled off from the Web. (6)

Dash is correct in identifying this as a copyright issue. Copyright is, after all, an important knob on the control panel of supply and demand. And this fear of others making a profit off of "my" content has also led to another sad, albeit humorous trend — disabling the user's right-click functionality by using Javascript code. Right clicking on a page in Windows opens a simple menu of actions, among those included are copy and view-source functions, which techies use to, well, copy images and source code. When sites disable this, the process usually produces a pop-up pronouncing the site's copyright ownership.

Again, what appears to be smart business turns out to be counterproductive. Here's the way Rosemarie Wise puts it in an article in SitePoint.com:

> Anyone who's determined to copy your content or code will do so regardless of his or her ability to bring up a browser context menu. If they want your source code then it's as simple as selecting "view source" from the main menu. Article text can be highlighted and copied, images and media presentations can be retrieved from the cache, and streaming media can be recorded.
>
> Disabling right-click will only make people more determined to learn exactly what it is you're hiding. And this could end up being counter-productive, as your images and source code attract unwanted attention. Not only that, but you can only disable right-click on browsers that have JavaScript enabled: a visitor only has to turn off JavaScript in their browser's options to be able to ignore the script altogether! (7)

As Internet ad spending continues to rachet upwards with double-digit certainty, more and more people are beginning to realize that there's money to be made online — even considerable money. However, the time, energy and resources we spend trying to "protect" ourselves from a supply-rich market would be much better spent looking for ways to capitalize as the market moves forward.

Restricting content is exactly the opposite of what we should be doing, for it's foolish to assume a limited capacity for information in a Postmodern world and arrogant to assume our content commands more attention than anybody else's. The law of supply and demand online is a paradox, and owning a bigger share of the supply is a more likely path to profit.

Doc Searls, one of the authors of *The Cluetrain Manifesto* and a visionary marketer, says the biggest mistake people make in applying the law of supply and demand to the Internet is an assumption that it's just another distribution vehicle.

> Face the fact that the Net isn't yet another medium for pumping "content" from a few producers to countless consumers. Instead, it's an environment — a very real marketplace — where the demand side has the power to supply. The consumers of yesterday are now full-power customers, plus something much more important: they are *participants*. They participate in the form of product advice, personal involvement, and by creating new inventions and businesses of their own. You either embrace that participation, or risk being shoved aside by it. (8)

The Internet simply isn't the easy money tree that we all hoped it would be 10 years ago. It takes work to make money — sometimes lots of work. The payoffs, however, can be spectacular.

TECHNOLOGY IS NOT THE ENEMY

September 29, 2003

M y heart was first broken in the 7th grade. Her name was Linda, and everything was going along fine until a boy named Steve moved into our neighborhood. He turned Linda's head, as it were, and the rest is history. His blonde hair disrupted my courting. I didn't know how to react. The more I tried to make him look bad in her eyes, the more wonderful he became. I lost, and not so much because he was the better guy. His entry into my space turned me into a defensive, conniving twerp. Ah, the stuff of youth.

In the business world, competition comes from many places, but the most deadly is called a "disruptive innovation" or "disruptive technology." Disruptive technology was first described in a 1997 business best-seller, *Innovator's Dilemma*, by Clayton Christensen. It's basically a treatise on how new technologies can disrupt core business, and makes the case that how companies deal with disruptive technology determines their survival or failure, whether they get the girl or not.

A good case in point today would be the photography industry. In a recent report, Peter Conti, Jr., a partner in the research firm,

Borrell Associates, said of Kodak, "How did Kodak react to digital photography, and then when they did get involved? It was to support their core business, but they couldn't separate what was a new, fast-growing business from their core business. They spent a fortune trying to save their core business. Today, Kodak is not the largest seller of digital cameras, by a long shot. They weren't paying attention. They tried to put in digital developing kiosks, and you were supposed to go in with your digital disks and print out your own photos, but that was trying to prop up a dying business. It didn't allow Kodak to look ahead to new business." (1)

And worse than Kodak is bankrupt Polaroid.

This is a critical lesson for broadcasters today, who find themselves caught in a similar vortex. Disruptive technologies abound in the media world, and broadcasters who cling to the belief that their age-old business models will carry them through the 21st century are the Polaroids of tomorrow. The refusal of some television executives to accept as inevitable the need to change is a slow form of suicide. The death threat is real and imminent.

Leonard Sweet, the cultural historian and Postmodernism guru, says, "The word is out: Reinvent yourself for the 21st century or die!" Kodak has made sweeping (and painful) changes through restructuring and reinventing its business model. They're counting on their brand to bring them back to market dominance, and one hopes they'll ultimately succeed.

And for broadcasters to succeed, I believe we need to reinvent ourselves as multimedia distribution and production companies. The creation and transmission of video, formerly the sole purview of TV, is now spread over a wide variety of technologies. (Even television production itself has changed — what used to require many people can now be done by one.) Video production houses have become multimedia production houses, yet broadcasters themselves cling to video production alone. How does a TV station's sales department sell online advertising when it has no mechanism with which to produce the online creative? The Internet is the best hope for TV stations, but most don't truly understand it and run from it as a result.

And the biggest online competition a TV station faces downstream is not the other guy across town with the antenna. It's the local newspaper. Incoming Associated Press chief, Tom Curley, says the A.P. will be working hard to turn newspapers into broadcasters by providing video for them to use online. "It's not my decision," Curley said. "It's a marketplace reality. I've heard from publishers of 30,000-circulation newspapers who believe they have to have video for their Websites. That's an indication of a profound change." (2)

Video News On Demand (VNOD) will be the way people get their video news in a Postmodern world. The news wars of the 21st century will be online, and TV stations who're content to provide text-only news services to their constituencies are giving up ground to smart print counterparts, who're more experienced with the Web and see where it's really going.

Dirck Halstead's Platypus Movement is equipping newspaper reporters and photographers to create local video for their employers, as video journalism bridges the divide between TV and print. The consummate photojournalist, Halstead writes, "We are trying to look for a way to create leverage to make our storytelling appeal to an ever-changing marketplace. We are using some of these new tools and skills to give us a higher place to stand so that we can exert that leverage." (3) He conducts popular workshops twice a year, and the work of his protégés is beginning to show up on newspaper sites throughout the country.

By denying the reality of the Internet, TV stations are abdicating their position as the purveyors of video news in the community. This is a death sentence for local television, because local news is the only video niche that cannot be filled from afar. And disruptive technologies may even change that! In some big markets, cable companies have had success doing local news, and I think the next player in this game will be satellite TV. The economics make sense, for video journalism is a lot less expensive to create these days than many think.

It's time for broadcasters to stage an all-out war against their newspaper counterparts. The theater of operations for this war is online. Like broadcasters, newspapers are caught in the disruptive technology of the Internet. Traditionally, 70% of newspaper revenue came from classified advertising, which is its New Media Achilles' heel. An October 2002 study by Borrell Associates reveals newspapers had lost a combined $5.4 billion in recruitment revenues in the previous 18 months. That's a 40% loss. Online job sites like Monster.com have transformed the recruitment services industry, and the best newspapers can do is include them on their Websites. "Classified Ventures" is a business formed in 1997 by an alliance of newspaper companies to create online classifieds, including Cars.com and Apartments.com. But all this has done is to shift what used to be a high-margin business to a low-margin business, and it's cutting into newspaper profits.

Broadcast Internet networks, such as IBS and Worldnow, have deals with some online classified providers like CareerBuilder.com, but these offerings are treated as tabs that get lost on a row of site links. I've yet to come across a television Website that uses the word "Classifieds." That makes no sense, because the online niche is there for the taking.

Auction sites, like eBay are the New Media form of buy-and-sell newspaper classifieds, but nobody is pursuing doing this at the local level. Using the technology of companies like ePier, it's easy to set up a completely hands-off form of classifieds online, then feed those sections to targeted advertisers with a variety of other technologies. Rather than charging people to post ads, stations could take a commission off of items sold, all without hands-on management.

Event auctions, where the Website auctions items provided by advertisers in trade for advertising, are being used successfully by newspapers and some radio stations to generate new ad revenue, introduce new advertisers, motivate staffs, increase walk-in traffic for sponsors, and, most importantly, take dollars from competitors. Television has yet to discover this method of revenue, because it doesn't fit into a reach/frequency, broadcasting mindset.

How sad.

Broadcast owners who ascribe the loss of business over the past few years solely to the economy haven't fully accepted the reality of disruptive innovations. The Borrell newspaper study says disruption impacts established industries in three phases: "In the first phase, both the traditional business and the disruptive business grow without disturbing each other. The second phase is characterized by a slowdown of the traditional business, and the third sees the traditional business enter precipitous decline while the new, disruptive business begins to erode the traditional business' core customers." Disruptive technologies have impacted broadcasting companies at varying speeds, but those in or approaching Phase III are in serious trouble.

WB Network chairman and CEO Jamie Kellner said recently that technology was becoming the enemy of broadcasting in the same way the Internet has been an enemy to the recording industry. He's talking about the disruptive technology of Digital Video Recorders (DVRs), like TiVo, where users can and do skip commercials. Here is an executive who has chosen to fight the disruptive innovation instead of finding creative solutions to work with it. It's Phase I thinking. As such, he's risking his entire network, because DVR industry growth continues unabated.

The Postmodern World doesn't care about any of this, of course, for it's simply the next stage in the evolution of Western culture. But Pomos *are* the customers of tomorrow, and anybody wishing to do business in the new millennium needs to understand where they are and what they're all about. They want their Internet. They want their DVRs. They want and demand choice, not to sit back passively as television continues along the path of same-o, same-o.

Technology is *not* the enemy of broadcasting. It's the friend who will take us back to more favorable revenue positions, if we'll just pay attention to what it's saying. Who knows? Perhaps if I'd welcomed Steve to the neighborhood instead of trying to run him off, all three of us would've become friends, and Linda and I would still be together today.

TERRY'S TRIBE

It's a daunting task to identify one's own "tribe," for it is constantly evolving. Mine consists of family, friends, co-workers and the following list of those who influence my thinking. One common denominator of all of them, ironically, is that they do not consider themselves influential, and I find that fascinating. You'll also notice that there's really only one person here from the world of traditional media, and I think that's reflected in my overall writing. The answers to the current media conundrum lie outside the industries of local media, and my association with these outstanding people helps shape my vision.

Dan Gillmor
Author, blogger, creator of the concept of "citizens media"
http://citmedia.org/

Michael Rosenblum
Photojournalist, blogger, Father of the VJ Movement
http://www.rosenblumtv.com/

Dirck Halstead
Photojournalist, Editor of *The Digital Journalist*,
Founder of the Platypus Movement
http://www.digitaljournalist.org/

Gordon Borrell
Web researcher specializing in local revenue,
CEO Borrell Associates
http://www.borrellassociates.com

Dave Morgan
Founder Real Media and Tacoda,
Web advertising guru specializing in behavioral targeting
http://www.tacoda.com/about/executive.php#dMorgan

Jarvis Coffin
CEO Burst Media, Web advertising guru, innovator
http://www.burstmedia.com

Harry Hayes
CEO Sausage Software, innovator,
expert in Flash and streaming video
http://www.sausage.com

Chris Pirillo
Blogger, creator/host of Gnomdex, innovator,
podcaster, new media and gadget expert, funnyman
http://chris.pirillo.com/

J. D. Lasica
Social media innovator, author, original thinker,
coined the phrase "personal media revolution"
http://www.jdlasica.com/aboutjd.html

Doc Searls
Author, *The Cluetrain Manifesto*, Harvard fellow,
blogger, speaker, creative thinker
http://blogs.law.harvard.edu/doc/

John Dewey
Philosopher, psychologist, education reformer
http://en.wikipedia.org/wiki/John_Dewey

David Weinberger
Author, *The Cluetrain Manifesto* and other important
books, blogger, Harvard fellow, speaker
http://www.hyperorg.com/blogger/

Dave Winer
Innovator, inventor, cultural
observer, original thinker, blogger
http://www.scripting.com/

Diane Mermigas
Writer, journalist specializing in new media, speaker
http://blogs.mediapost.com/on_media/

Jay Rosen
Journalist, innovator, NYU professor, media and press critic
http://journalism.nyu.edu/pubzone/weblogs/pressthink/

Jeff Jarvis
Blogger, columnist, journalist, CUNY professor
http://www.buzzmachine.com

Bill Wilson
Founder, Alcoholics Anonymous
http://en.wikipedia.org/wiki/Bill_W.

John Battelle
Founder/Chairman/CEO Federated Media, author, blogger
http://battellemedia.com/

Jerry Gumbert
President & CEO Audience Research & Development, best friend
http://www.ar-d.com/index.aspx?id=innovation_gumbert

Steve Rubel
Digital marketer, blogger, senior vice
president in Edelman's me2revolution
http://www.micropersuasion.com/

Chris Anderson
Editor of *Wired*, author of *The Long Tail*,
innovative new media thinker
http://www.thelongtail.com/

Umair Haque
Director of the Havas Media Lab,
consultant, economist, new media thinker, innovator
http://discussionleader.hbsp.com/haque/

Leonard Sweet
Theologian, author, futurist, cultural historian
http://www.leonardsweet.com/

Michael Arrington
Writer, editor of TechCrunch and owner of the
TechCrunch Network of blog and podcasting sites.
http://www.techcrunch.com/about-michael-arrington/

Mark Glaser
Journalist, critic, facilitator, New Media expert
http://www.pbs.org/mediashift/

Christopher Lasch
Historian, moralist, social critic, author
http://en.wikipedia.org/wiki/Christopher_Lasch

Abraham Zaleznik
Konosuke Matsushita Professor of Leadership,
Emeritus at the Harvard Business School
*http://drfd.hbs.edu/fit/public/facultyInfo.do
?facInfo=ovr&facEmId=azaleznik*

Richard Adams
Best-selling author, creator of the
concept of "The Unbroken Web"
http://en.wikipedia.org/wiki/Richard_Adams_(author)

Howard Reingold
Author *Smart Mobs* and other books, UC Berkeley and
Stanford University professor, original thinker
http://www.rheingold.com/

Hugh MacLeod
Cartoonist, blogger on how the Web affects
marketing and advertising
http://www.gapingvoid.com/

Craig Newmark
Founder Craigslist
http://www.craigslist.com

David Sifry
Founder, CEO Technorati
http://www.technorati.com

Drazen Pantic
Independent media pioneer, founder of Opennet
http://www.thenation.com/directory/bios/drazen_pantic

Joe Mandese
Editor Mediapost
http://blogs.mediapost.com/mdn_commentary/?cat=65

Rafat Ali
Founder ContentNext, including PaidContent.org, innovator
http://www.contentnext.com/

Mike Sechrist
Broadcaster, innovator, consultant, blogger
http://www.mikesechrist.com/

Robert Scoble
Tech geek blogger, cutting edge innovator
http://scobleizer.com/

Rishad Tobaccowala
Media innovator, president of SMG Next, an
idea incubator within Starcom MediaVest Group
http://www.smvgroup.com/news.asp?pr=1380

ENDNOTES

THE PUBLIC JOURNAL

1.
Arrington, Michael. "Super Panel at Davos: The Future of Mobile Technology." Tech Crunch. http://www.techcrunch.com/2008/01/25/super-panel-at-davos-the-future-of-mobile-technology/. Retrieved 25 January 2008.

2.
Picard, Robert. "Commercialism and Newspaper Quality." *Newspaper Research Journal*: Vol. 25, No. 1 (2004): 54-65. http://www.poynter.org/resource /63500/picard.pdf Retrieved 25 January 2008.

3.
Bucks, Simon. "Blue Sky Thinking." *Press Gazette*. 25 May 2007. http://www.pressgazette.co.uk/story.asp?storycode=37741 Retrieved 25 January 2008.

4.
Sarno, David. "Ledger's Death A Window Into Speed Reporting." Post on *Los Angeles Times* Entertainment Blog. 22 January 2008. 5:48 AM PT. http://latimesblogs.latimes.com/Webscout/2008/01/title.html Retrieved 25 January 2008.

5.
Scoble, Robert, and Jarvis, Jeff. "Davos08: Metavideo with Scoble." Video Post on Buzzmachine.com Blog. 25 January 2008. 3:46 AM Local Time. http://www.buzzmachine.com/2008/01/25/davos08-metavideo-with-scoble/. Retrieved 25 January 2008.

THE ON-DEMAND TRAP

1.
Jarvis, Jeff. "Everybody's a Network, Continued." Post on buzzmachine.com Blog. 22 May 2006. 8:17 PM Local Time. http://www.buzzmachine.com /2006/05/22/everybodys-a-network-continued/ Retrieved 21 May 2006.

2.
Hagel, John. "ABC and the Future of Media." Post on Edge Perspectives Blog. 11 April 2006. http://edgeperspectives.typepad.com/edge_perspectives/2006/04 /abc_and_the_fut.html Retrieved 21 May 2006.

3.
Prewitt, Edward, and Christensen, Clayton. "Disruption Is Good; Ignoring It Is Bad." *CIO Magazine*. 07 May 2001. http://www.cio.com.au/index.php ?id=1918308937 Retrieved 21 May 2006.

THE REAL THREAT TO LOCAL BROADCASTERS

1.
Borrell, Gordon. "What Local Media Web Sites Earn." April 2006. http://www.borrellassociates.com/Reports.aspx Retrieved 21 May 2006.

2.
Borrell, Gordon. "What Local Media Web Sites Earn." April 2006. http://www.borrellassociates.com/Reports.aspx Retrieved 21 May 2006.

3.
Calacanis, Jason. "BloggingOhio.com: Our First Local Blog." 17 April 2006. 5:33 AM Local Time. http://www.calacanis.com/2006/04/17/bloggingohio-com-our-first-local-blog/#c1167718 Retrieved 21 May 2006.

4.
Kaye, Kate. "Backfence Expands, Weblogs Join Local Ranks." ClickZ. 19 April 2006. http://www.clickz.com/showPage.html?page=3599896 Retrieved 21 May 2006.

STATIONS MUST EMBRACE PERSONAL MEDIA TOOLS

1.
Lasica, J. D. *Darknet: Hollywood's War Against the Digital Generation.* Hoboken: Wiley, 2005.

CHAOS AT THE DOOR

1.
Cairns, Adam. Comment on "Student to Panel: 'What's In It For Me?'", a post on The Pomo Blog. Comment made 19 June 2005. Post made 18 June 2005. 9:00 AM Local Time. http://www.thepomoblog.com/archive/student-to-panel-whats-in-it-for-me/ Retrieved 19 June 2005.

2.
Trippi, Joe. "Bottom-up Is Turning Everything Upside Down." MSNBC column. 20 October 2004. http://www.msnbc.msn.com/id/6291414/ Retrieved 28 February 2008.

3.
Reinhardt, Hazel. Personal Interview.

THE DEVALUATION OF INFORMATION

1.
Glaser, Mark. "Pay or Free? Newspaper Archives Not Ready For Open Web …Yet." Online Journalism Review. 1 February 2005. http://www.ojr.org/ojr/stories/050201/ Retrieved 19 February 2005.

CHAOS IN THE FEEDBACK LOOP

1.
Nachison, Andrew. Director, Media Center of American Press Institute. http://www.mediacenter.org/content/7057.cfm. Retrieved 23 February 2008.

NEWS IS A PROCESS, NOT A FINISHED PRODUCT

1.
Mohler, Bob. TMZ Celebrity News Blog. http://www.tmz.com.

2.
Tarquini, Milissa. "Blasting the Myth of the Fold." Post on Boxes and Arrows Blog. 24 July 2007. http://www.boxesandarrows.com/view/blasting-the-myth-of Retrieved 6 November 2007.

3.
Kennedy, Dan. "Plugged in, Tuned Out." Commonwealth Magazine. Fall 2007. http://www.massinc.org/index.php?id=652&pub_id=2188&bypass=1 Retrieved 6 November 2007.

4.
Searls, Doc. "Future to Newspapers: Jump in the River." Post on Personal
Blog. 19 October 2007. http://blogs.law.harvard.edu/doc/2007/10/19/future-to-
newspapers-jump-in-the-river/ Retrieved 6 November 2007.

VOYEURISM: JOURNALISM'S 21ST CENTURY CRISIS

1.
Covey, Stephen. *The 7 Habits of Highly Effective People.* New York:
Nightingale-Conant Corp. 1994.

2.
Lasch, Christopher. "Journalism, Publicity, and the Lost Art of Argument."
1990. Excerpted in Media Studies Journal, Volume 9, no. 1. Winter 1995.

3.
Mommy Bloggers Group Blog. http://www.mommybloggers.com/ Accessed 23
February 2008.

4.
Trusted Opinion Home page. http://www.trustedopinion.com/ Accessed 23
February 2008.

TRUSTING THE AUDIENCE AND THE READERS

1.
Aptheker, Herbert. "Walter Lippman and Democracy." Excerpted from History
and Reality. New York: Cameron and Associates, 1955.

2.
Jarvis, Jeff. Personal Blog. http://www.buzzmachine.com. Accessed 23
February 2008.

3.
Searls, Doc. "Saving the Net." Linux Journal. 16 November 2005.
http://www.linuxjournal.com/article/8673 Retrieved 25 November 2005.

ARGUMENT VERSUS OBJECTIVITY

1.
The Holy Bible. Luke 1:1-4. New Living Translation.

2.
8 July 1865. The *New York Herald.* Archived online at http://www.law
.umkc.edu/faculty/projects/ftrials/lincolnconspiracy/herald78.html. Retrieved 28
February 2008.

3.

8 July 1865. The *New York Herald*. Archived online at http://www.law
.umkc.edu/faculty/projects/ftrials/lincolnconspiracy/herald78.html. Retrieved 28
February 2008.

4.

Lippman, Walter. *The Phantom Public*. New York: Harcourt, Brace, 1925.

5.

Dewey, John. *John Dewey Responds*. New York: Arinety, 1950.

6.

Lasch, Christopher. *The Revolt of the Elites: And the Betrayal of Democracy*.
New York: W.W. Norton & Company, 1996.

7.

Dunlop, Tim. "If You Build It, They Will Come." Essay for the Evatt
Foundation. http://evatt.org.au/publications/papers/91.html Retrieved 02
December 2003.

8.

Sommer, Allison Kaplan. "The Journey of a News Item." Post on Personal
Blog. 12 November 2003. 9:12 PM Local Time.
http://allisonkaplansommer.blogmosis.com
/history/017968.html Retrieved 02 December 2003.

THE CHANGING FACE(S) OF LOCAL NEWS

1.
Sechrist, Mike. Personal Interview.

2.
Sechrist, Mike. Personal Interview.

THE NEW PUBLIC RELATIONS

1.
Bernays, Edward. "The Engineering of Consent." Quoted in Annals of the
American Academy of Political and Social Science, March 1947 edition.

2.
Bernays, Edward. *Propaganda*. New York: Horace Liveright, 1928.

3.
Krawiec, Richard. "Dealing with the Media: Advice From A Journalist."
November 1990 issue of "The Animals' Agenda."

4.
Locke, Christopher. Levine, Rick. Searls, Doc. Weinberger, David. *The Cluetrain Mainfesto*. New York: Perseus Books, 1999.

5.
Scoble, Robert. "The Corporate Weblog Manifesto." Post on Scobleizer: Microsoft Geek Blogger Blog. 26 February 2003. 11:43 PM Local Time. http://scoble.Weblogs.com/2003/02/26.html Retrieved 21 March 2004.

NEWS IS A CONVERSATION

1.
Locke, Christopher. Levine, Rick. Searls, Doc. Weinberger, David. *The Cluetrain Manifesto*. New York: Perseus Books, 1999.

2.
Gillmor, Dan. Personal Interview.

THE JEWEL OF THE ELITES

1.
Wycliffe, John. "John Wycliffe Quotes." http://thinkexist.com/quotes/john_wycliffe/ Retrieved 24 February 2008.

2.
Wikipedia article on John Wycliffe. http://en.wikipedia.org/wiki/John_Wycliffe Retrieved 24 February 2008.

3.
Boyd, Stowe. "Jay Rosen (and Others) on Blogs Meet the Mainstream." Post on Corante Blog. 01 October 2005. http://getreal.corante.com/archives/2005/10/01/jay_rosen_and_others_on_blogs _meet_the_mainstream.php Retrieved 01 October 2005.

4.
Rosen, Jay. Personal interview.

REINVENTING NEWS FOR THE 21ST CENTURY

1.
Walker, Bob. "Turn On. Tune In. Download." *The New York Times*. 21 September 2003.

THE DEMOGRAPHIC CANDLE

1.
Ehrenreich, Barbara. *Nickel and Dimed: On Not Getting By in America*. New York: Henry Holt and Company, 2001.

THE UNOBVIOUS RESULT OF THE WEB

1.
Bennett, Richard. "The Stupid Campaign." Post on The Great American Blog. 29 January 2004. 1:41 AM Local Time.
http://bennett.com/blog/index.php/archives/2004/01/29/the-stupid-campaign/ Retrieved 31 January 2004.

2.
Pope Pius XII. Papal encyclical. *Divino Afflante Spiritu.* September 30, 1943. Archived online at http://www.vatican.va/holy_father/pius_xii/encyclicals/ documents/hf_p-xii_enc_30091943_divino-afflante-spiritu_en.html. Retrieved 01 March 2008.

3.
Lurie, Peter. "Why the Web Will Win the Culture Wars for the Left: Deconstructing Hyperlinks." 15 April 2003.
http://www.ctheory.net/text_file.asp?pick=380 Retrieved 01 March 2008.

4.
Lurie, Peter. "Why the Web Will Win the Culture Wars for the Left: Deconstructing Hyperlinks." 15 April 2003.
http://www.ctheory.net/text_file.asp?pick=380 Retrieved 01 March 2008.

RIGHT BRAIN RENAISSANCE

1.
Dewey, John. *John Dewey Responds*. New York: Arinety, 1950.

2.
Lippman, Walter. *The Phantom Public*. New York: Harcourt, Brace, 1925.

POSTMODERNISM'S MOST IMPORTANT GIFT

1.
Stein, Ben. "The Gloomsayers Should Look Up." *New York Times.* 21 October 2007.

2.

Watts, Alan. Quotation from a speech. Partial sound file online at
http://www.hetnieuwenederland.org/download/philosophy/Alan%20Watts
/Seeing%20Through%20the%20Net%20I.mp3. Retrieved 18 October 2007.

2008: EMBRACING THE (REAL) WEB

1.

Nokia. Press release datelined in Espoo, Finland. 03 December 2007. Archived
online at http://www.nokia.com/A4136001?newsid=1172517. Retrieved 01
March 2008.

2.

Lazarus, David. "Free News Online Will Cost Journalism Dearly."
26 December 2007. The Los Angeles Times.
http://www.latimes.com/business/la-fi-lazarus26dec26,1,2276712,full.column
Retrieved 27 December 2007.

3.

Lazarus, David. "Free News Online Will Cost Journalism Dearly." 26
December 2007. The Los Angeles Times. http://www.latimes.com/business/la-
fi-lazarus26dec26,1,2276712,full.column Retrieved 27 December 2007.

4.

Wikipedia entry on Static Web pages.
http://cn.wikipedia.org/wiki/Static_Web_page Retrieved 01 March 2008.

5.

Wikipedia entry on The Semantic Web.
http://en.wikipedia.org/wiki/Semantic_Web Retrieved 01 March 2008.

LINKS — THE CURRENCY OF THE MACHINE

1.

Kelly, Kevin. "We Are the Web." *Wired*. August 2005 issue.
http://www.wired.com/wired/archive/13.08/tech.html
Retrieved 16 March 2007.

2.

Kelly, Kevin. "We Are the Web." *Wired*. August 2005 issue.
http://www.wired.com/wired/archive/13.08/tech.html
Retrieved 16 March 2007.

460

3.
Kelly, Kevin. "We Are the Web." *Wired.* August 2005 issue.
http://www.wired.com/wired/archive/13.08/tech.html
Retrieved 16 March 2007.

THE LOCAL WEB

1.
Duran, Marcelo. "Papers Hope to Profit From Online Partnerships." January
2007. http://www.newsandtech.com/issues/2007/01-07/nt/01-07_yahoo
_deal.htm Retrieved 19 January 2007.

THE AMMUNITION BUSINESS

1.
This occurred in a television drama that aired sometime in the early 1980's.
Extensive efforts to find a reference to it, in order to cite it, have not proven
fruitful at this time.

2.
Borrell, Gordon. In-person conference, late 2004. Nashville.

3.
Jarvis, Jeff. "The Dinosaurs Whine." Post on buzzmachine.com Blog.
31 January 2006. 1:14 PM Local Time.
http://www.buzzmachine.com/2006/01/31/the-dinosaurs-whine/
Retrieved 01 February 2006.

4.
Ziade, Richard. "Taking RSS Beyond Headlines." Post on basement.org Blog.
23 January 2006. 2:57 PM Local Time.
http://www.basement.org/2006/01/taking_rss_beyond_headlines_pa.html
Retrieved 31 January 2006.

5.
Arrington, Michael. "This Week's New Ajax Homepage." TechCrunch. 25
January 2006. http://www.techcrunch.com/2006/01/25/yes-this-weeks-ajax-
homepage/ Retrieved 01 March 2008.

6.
Ali, Rafat. "Amazon Plans Movie Downloads." Post on PaidContent.org Blog.
26 January 2006. 8:02 PM PST. http://www.paidcontent.org/entry/amazon-
plans-movie-downloads-might-start-april-end Retrieved 01 February 2006.

7.
Powell, Michael. 2003 interview with the *San Jose Mercury News.*

THE WEB'S PARADOX OF POWER

Graphs are from the Technorati.com site's blog statistics.

CONVENTION VERSUS THE INTERNET

1.
Safire, William. "The Depressed Press." *New York Times*. 17 January 2005.

2.
Rubel, Steve. "Would You Buy A Car From This Blogger?" Post on iMedia Connection Blog. 19 January 2005. http://www.imediaconnection.com /content/4930.asp Retrieved 19 January 2005.

3.
Smith, Russ. "Blogger Backlash: The Strange Career of the Pajama Pundit." *New York Press*. http://www.nypress.com/18/3/news&columns/rsmith.cfm Retrieved 19 January 2005.

4.
Simpson, George. "This Opinion Brought to You By Our Sponsors." Post on MediaDailyNews Blog. 19 January 2005. 10:04 PM ET. http://publications.mediapost.com/index.cfm?fuseaction=Articles.showArticle &art_aid=26503 Retrieved 19 January 2005.

OVERCOMING FORMULA ADDICTION

1.
Card, David. "Home Page Tactics for Information Sites." Jupiter Research Vision Report. Jupiter Research. 26 September 2004. http://www.jupiterresearch.com/bin/item.pl/research:vision/63/id=95649/ Retrieved 12 November 2004.

BEYOND THE WORLD WIDE WEB

1.
Berners-Lee, Tim. Cited by Griffiths, R.T. "The History of the Internet, Chapter Two." Last updated 11 October 2002. http://www.let.leidenuniv.nl/history/ivh/chap2.htm Retrieved 17 May 2005.

2.
Kahn, Bob. "IP Designed Neutrality." Cited in ARPANET 1970s history archive. http://www.cybertelecom.org/notes/internet_history70s.htm Retrieved 24 February 2008.

3.
Searls, Doc. "There Is No Demand for Messages." Web Informant #112.
26 May 1998. http://www.strom.com/awards/112.html
Retrieved 24 February 2008.

A WOLF IN AGGREGATOR CLOTHING

1.
Shirky, Clay. "Ontology is Overrated." Personal Homepage. 2005.
http://www.shirky.com/writings/ontology_overrated.html
Retrieved 24 February 2008.

2.
Rowland, Alex. "Open vs. Closed Distribution." Post on Democracy in Media
Blog. 10 May 2005. http://democracyinmedia.typepad.com/my_Weblog
/2005/05/open_vs_closed_.html Retrieved 17 May 2005.

3.
Rowland, Alex. "Open vs. Closed Distribution." Post on Democracy in Media
Blog. 10 May 2005.
http://democracyinmedia.typepad.com/my_Weblog/2005/05/open_vs
closed.html Retrieved 17 May 2005.

GOOGLE LIFTS ONLY GOOGLE

1.
Karbasfrooshan, Ashkan. "Google's Shock and Awe." Post on WatchMojo
Blog. 05 October 2007. http://watchmojo.com/Web/blog/?p=2149
Retrieved 05 October 2007.

2.
Interactive Advertising Bureau Report. Available online in PDF format at
http://www.iab.net/resources/adrevenue/pdf/IAB_PwC%202007Q2.pdf.
Retrieved 05 October 2007.

3.
Schonfeld, Erick. "Google's Share of Online Ads Hits 40 Percent." Post on
Tech Crunch Blog. http://www.techcrunch.com/2007/10/05/googles-share-of-
us-online-ads-hits-40-percent/ Retrieved 05 October 2007.

4.
Jarvis, Jeff. "The Real Media Consolidaton: Google." Post on
buzzmachine.com Blog. 06 October 2007. 1:08 PM Local Time.
http://www.buzzmachine.com/2007/10/06/the-real-media-consolidation-google/
Retrieved 06 October 2007.

5.
Vogelstein, Fred. "As Google Challenges Viacom and Microsoft, Its CEO Feels Lucky." *Wired*. 09 April 2007.
http://www.wired.com/techbiz/people/news/2007/04/mag_schmidt_qa
?currentPage=1 Retrieved 24 February 2008.

LOCAL TV'S NEW DEADLINES

1.
Godin, Seth. "Not Sure Which Is More Surprising." Post on Personal Blog.
30 July 2004. http://sethgodin.typepad.com/seths_blog/2004/07/not_sure
which.html Retrieved 02 August 2004.

2.
Friedman, Steve. Quoted in *Electronic Media*. Issue of 31 March 1986.

3.
The Project for Excellence in Journalism. State of the News Media 2004.
Archived online at http://www.stateofthemedia.org/2004/.
Retrieved 24 February 2008.

BEYOND PORTAL WEBSITES

1.
Wikipedia article on Star Trek episode, "The City on the Edge of Forever."
http://en.wikipedia.org/wiki/The_City_on_the_Edge_of_Forever
Retrieved 24 February 2008.

THE MATTER OF "GETTING IT"

1.
Powell, Michael. "The Powell Pulpit." 29 December 2003 issue of the *San Jose Mercury News*.

2.
Covey, Stephen. *The 7 Habits of Highly Effective People*. New York:
Nightingale-Conant Corp. 1994.

3.
Kübler-Ross, Elisabeth. *On Death and Dying*. New York: Touchstone, 1973.

NEWS AS A COMMODITY

1.
Myers, Jack. "Every Radio Station Can Become A TV Station." Commentary on Media Village TV Buzz Site. 8 August 2007. http://www.mediavillage.com /jmr/2007/08/08/jmr-08-08-07/ Retrieved 10 August 2007.

2.
Mandese, Joe. "Audio Kills the Radio Noir." MediaDailyNews. 13 August 2007. http://publications.mediapost.com/index.cfm?fuseaction=Articles.san &s=65528&Nid=33193&p=222600 Retrieved 17 March 2008.

3.
Searls, Doc. "Looking Toward Life Beyond Advertising." Post on Personal Blog. 09 August 2007. http://blogs.law.harvard.edu/doc/2007/08/09/looking-toward-life-beyond-advertising/ Retrieved 10 August 2007.

4.
The analysis referenced can be located at http://www.buzzmachine.com/2007 /08/11/the-emergence-of-media-tribes/.

5.
American Dictionary of the English Language. 1828 Noah Webster edition.

IT'S NOT THE SAME GAME

1.
Allaire, Jeremy. "Internet TV Platforms Come of Age." http://www.brightcove.com /about_brightcove/perspectives/internet-tv-platforms.cfm
Retrieved 05 January 2008.

TO BRAND OR NOT TO BRAND

1.
Effron, Mark. *RTNDA Communicator.* April 2007 edition.

2.
Crupi, Anthony. "MTV Networks Coins New Sales Metric For the Upfront." 03 April 2006. http://www.mediaweek.com/mw/news/recent_display.jsp?vnu _content_id=1002275778 Retrieved 25 February 2008.

3.
Crupi, Anthony. "MTV Networks Coins New Sales Metric For The Upfront." 03 April 2006. http://www.mediaweek.com/mw/news/recent_display.jsp?vnu _content_id=1002275778 Retrieved 25 February 2008.

4.

Li, Kenneth. "MTV Networks Embraces Web Chaos to Regain Viewers."
06 March 2007. http://www.reuters.com/article/internetNews
/idUSN0237821720070306?pageNumber=1 Retrieved 25 February 2008.

SELLING AGAINST OURSELVES

1.

Sharpe, Kathy. Commentary for MediaDailyNews. 14 January 2004.
http://publications.mediapost.com/index.cfm?fuseaction=Articles
.showArticle&art_aid=6470 Retrieved 24 June 2006.

2.

Christensen, Clayton. Personal Interview with Howard Dresner conducted on
26 June 2004. Archived online at http://www.gartner.com/research/fellows
/asset_93329_1176.jsp. Retrieved 02 March 2008.

3.

Christensen, Clayton. Personal Interview with Howard Dresner conducted on
26 June 2004. Archived online at http://www.gartner.com/research/fellows
/asset_93329_1176.jsp. Retrieved 02 March 2008.

4.

Kodak official press release. 05 May 2006. Archived online at
http://www.kodaknexpress.co.za/live/index.php?Item_ID=406.
Retrieved 24 June 2006.

THE CONVERGENCE ADVERTISING TRAP

1.
Sullivan, Richard. Personal interview.

2.
Sullivan, Richard. Personal interview.

3.
Borrell, Gordon. Personal interview.

4.
Borrell, Gordon. Personal interview.

5.
Dratelis, George. Personal interview.

6.
Dratelis, George. Personal interview.

THE ECONOMY OF UNBUNDLED ADVERTISING

1.
Borrell, Gordon. "2005 Online Automotive Advertising." A Special Report for Suburban Newspapers of America. Borrell Associates, September 2005.

RETHINKING NEWS PROMOS

1.
Schroeder, Christopher. *Media Magazine.* July 2005 edition. http://publications .mediapost.com/index.cfm?fuseaction=Articles.showArticle&art_aid=31454 Retrieved 17 March 2008.

THE VALUE OF LOCAL SEARCH

1.
Davis, Chuck. "Local Search Now 25% of Internet Commercial Activity" 11 February 2004. Press Release from The Kelsey Group and BizRate.com

2.
Gordon, Rich. Post on Poytner Online. 29 June 2004. 1:48 PM Local Time. Retrieved 02 March 2008 via search engine.

3.
Borrell Associations Client Memo on "Paid Search." 14 July 2004.

4.
Venditto, Gus. "Closing the Last Mile Gap: Local Search." Commentary on InternetNews.com site. 02 April 2004. http://www.internetnews.com /commentary/article.php/3335441 Retrieved 17 July 2004.

THE FUTURE IS NICHE MEDIA

1.
Myers, Jack. "Paris Hilton: World's Most Recognizable Person." Post on TV Board Blog. 11:00 AM Local Time. 29 June 2007. http://blogs.mediapost .com/tv_board/?p=109 Retrieved 30 June 2007.

2.
Wise, Mike. "Getting Blogged Down in the Details." *Washington Post.* 23 June 2007. http://www.washingtonpost.com/wp-dyn/content/article/2007/06 /22/AR2007062201886.html Retrieved 30 June 2007.

3.
Riley, Duncan. "Eventstreaming: The Seed of a Revolution." Post at TechCrunch Blog. 30 June 2007. http://www.techcrunch.com/2007/06/30/eventstreaming-the-seed-of-a-revolution/ Retrieved 01 July 2007.

4.
Jarvis, Jeff. "iPhone and the Future of News." Post on buzzmachine.com Blog. 01 July 2007. 9:25 AM Local Time. http://www.buzzmachine.com/2007/07 /01/iphone-and-the-future-of-news/ Retrieved 01 July 2007.

2007: THE BATTLE FOR LOCAL SUPREMACY

1.
Berners-Lee, Tim. *Weaving the Web.* New York: HarperCollins, 1999.

2.
Borrell, Gordon. Personal Interview.

3.
Borrell, Gordon. Personal Interview.

4.
Borrell, Gordon. Personal Interview.

THE TRANSPARENCY MARKETPLACE

1.
Mandese, Joe. "Buyers, Sellers Put Brakes on Nielsen's Commercial Ratings." MediaDailyNews Post. 04 August 2006. 8:00 AM EST. http://publications .mediapost.com/index.cfm?fuseaction=Articles.showArticle&art_aid=46406 Retrieved 01 March 2008.

2.
Hanlon, Tim. Personal Interview.

3.
Hanlon, Tim. Personal Interview.

4.
Bybee, Ann. "Auctions for TV Ad Time." Broadcasting & Cable. 04 August 2007. http://www.broadcastingcable.com/article/CA6359637.html ?title=Article&spacedesc=news Retrieved 17 March 2008.

5.
Jarvis, Jeff. "Exploding TV: Commercial Auction." Post on buzzmachine.com Blog. 04 August 2006. 8:26 AM Local Time. http://www.buzzmachine.com /2006/08/04/exploding-tv-commercial-auction/ Retrieved 06 August 2006.
6.
Hanlon, Tim. Personal Interview.

INVESTING IN A LOCAL FUTURE
1.
Personal e-mail exchange.

2.
Borrell, Gordon. In-person question.

NEW METRICS AND PRINCIPLES
1.
General Pharmaceutical Association official publication. http://www.gphaonline .org/Content/NavigationMenu/AboutGenerics/Statistics/Statistics.htm Retrieved 02 March 2008.

2.
Rushkoff, Doug. *Get Back in the Box.* New York: HarperCollins, 2005.

THE DEFENSIVE NEWSROOM
1.
The Impact Study. The Readership Institute. January 2001. http://www.readership .org/culture_management/culture/insideculture.asp Retrieved 10 October 2003.

2.
The Impact Study. The Readership Institute. January 2001. http://www.readership .org/culture_management/culture/insideculture.asp Retrieved 10 October 2003.

3.
The Impact Study. The Readership Institute. January 2001. http://www.readership .org/culture_management/culture/insideculture.asp Retrieved 10 October 2003.

4.
The Impact Study. The Readership Institute. January 2001. http://www.readership .org/culture_management/culture/insideculture.asp Retrieved 10 October 2003.

THE FUTURE IS MULTIMEDIA

1.
Sharpe, Kathy. "The Reality? Consumers Have Already Replaced Nielsen For Us." Commentary for MediaDailyNews. 14 January 2004. http://publications .mediapost.com/index.cfm?fuseaction=Articles.showArticle&art_aid=6470 Retrieved 23 January 2004.

2.
Honderich, John. Comments made in person.

SEARCHING FOR THE BOTTOM

1.
Kher, Unmesh. "Getting Kodak to Focus." *Time Magazine*. 07 February 2005. http://www.time.com/time/insidebiz/article/0,9171,1025191,00.html Retrieved 02 March 2008.

2.
Kher, Unmesh. "Getting Kodak to Focus." *Time Magazine*. 07 February 2005. http://www.time.com/time/insidebiz/article/0,9171,1025191,00.html Retrieved 02 March 2008.

3.
Kher, Unmesh. "Getting Kodak to Focus." *Time Magazine*. 07 February 2005. http://www.time.com/time/insidebiz/article/0,9171,1025191,00.html Retrieved 02 March 2008.

A BROADCASTER'S CHRISTMAS CAROL

This entire story is an obvious take-off on the classic by Charles Dickens, "A Christmas Carol."

WHEN SUPPLY EXCEEDS DEMAND

1.
Tobaccowala, Rashad. In person to DoubleClick 2004 Insight Conference.

2.
Editors Weblog Archives. http://wef.blogs.com/editors/2004/09/index.html Retrieved 02 March 2008.

3.
Dvorak, John C. "Registration? For What?" Column for PCMAG. 05 October 2004. http://www.pcmag.com/article2/0,1759,1646213,00.asp Retrieved 02 March 2008.

4.
Kenealy, Patrick. Quoted in "Technology Marketing."

5.
IDG Website Message to Inbound Links.

6.
Dash, Anil. "Why Does Patrick Kenealy Not Get the Web?" Post on personal blog. 14 July 2003. 1:32 PM Local Time. http://www.dashes.com/anil/2003/07/why-does-patric.html Retrieved 02 March 2008.

7.
Wise, Rosemarie. "Don't Disable Right Click!" Post on SitePoint.
11 May 2002. http://www.sitepoint.com/article/dont-disable-right-click Retrieved 02 March 2008.

8.
Locke, Christopher. Levine, Rick. Searls, Doc. Weinberger, David. *The Cluetrain Mainfesto*. New York: Perseus Books, 1999.

TECHNOLOGY IS NOT THE ENEMY

1.
Borrell Associates report.

2.
Linck, Michele. "New CEO Envisions A More Essential AP." *Sioux City Journal*. Archived online at http://www.siouxcityjournal.com/articles/2003/09/26/news/local/a3f05dc87aa1fdf686256dad000f097e.txt. Retrieved 02 March 2008.

3.
Halstead, Dirck. "The Platypus Papers." Archived online at http://dirckhalstead.org/platypus/platypus.html. Retrieved 02 March 2008.

Index

478

O

V

Vancouver—324
Vanity Fair—39
VCs—385-6, 389
Vehix—338
Venditto,Gus—351, 466
Veni—47
Ventures—380
Verizon—17, 31, 351
Verizon Wireless—31
Viacom—284, 286, 318
Viacom's Comedy Central—284
Vici—47
Video—3, 31, 45-6, 88, 117-8,
     127, 137, 152, 158, 182, 190,
     196-7, 199, 219-20, 231, 241,
     287-8, 295, 300, 304, 310,
     337, 340, 354, 371, 376, 398,
     405, 416, 418, 442-3
     business—31, 44, 121, 267
     news—44-5, 117-20, 158, 300,
          443
     niche—23, 424
     people—127
     portals—120
     stories—123, 287
Video iPod—284
Video Journalist, *see* VJ
Video News on Demand, *see*
     VNOD
Video-on-demand, *see* VOD
Video Post—452
Video Weblogs—238
Vietnam—414
     bombed North—305
Vietnam War—305
Viewers—29, 46, 51, 60, 74, 86,
     92-3, 95-6, 106, 109, 120, 124,
     131, 137-8, 150-1, 155-6, 238,
     260, 264, 267, 274, 281, 318,
     340-2, 344-5, 382, 391, 398
Vint Cerf—241-2
Virginia—373
VJ (Video Journalist)—viii, 30, 44-
     5, 86-9, 116-20, 152, 299, 418
     independent—45
VJ concept—87-9, 118

VJ Movement—446
VNOD (Video News on Demand)—
     45, 117, 119-21, 406, 443
VNRs—103-4
VOD (Video-on-demand)—14, 45,
     119, 331, 380, 431
Vonage—405
Vulgate—163
Volunteers—162
Voyeurism—viii, 57, 59, 455
Voyeuristic information—59-61,
     63-4

W

Wal-Mart—195, 223, 381, 393
Wal-Mart Supercenter—388
Walker, Bob—150
Walkman—197
Wall Street Journal—39, 205, 436
Walt Disney—82
Walton, Sam—384
War—46, 65, 70, 75, 82, 100, 105,
     162, 165, 229, 382, 443
Washington—31, 79, 107, 116
Washington Post—17, 37, 40, 299,
     367, 466
Washington Post Interactive—343
Watercooler—402
WB Network—445
Wealth—27, 88, 129, 235, 361
Weather—144, 285, 287-8, 319,
     413
Weather Forecast— 286
Weather Radar—286, 290
Web—ix, 4, 8-10, 21, 26, 28, 36-7,
     43, 45-6, 51, 53, 55, 62, 83,
     107, 113, 127, 138, 146, 157,
     160-1, 163-5, 175, 182-3, 187-
     90, 192-4, 196-201, 203-4,
     208, 210-5, 218-9, 223, 226,
     237, 240-4, 248-51, 253-4,
     256-7, 259-60, 262, 264-7,
     270-4, 279, 289, 294, 300,
     307-8, 313, 317-22, 328-30,
     339, 347-8, 351, 356, 358, 371,
     374, 376, 382, 385-6, 405-6,

     411, 418-9, 424, 436-8, 443,
     447, 450, 458-61, 467, 470
     businesses—42, 62
     autonomous—324
     companies—249, 253, 424
     global—214
     live—55-6
     local—210, 214-5, 320, 369
     publishers—274
     sites—243, 318, 320, 351, 436
     tiered—193
     video-centric—376
Web-based Video—120
Web Informant—462
Web-site—233, 273
     local media company's
          portal—388
Web Works—ix, 187
Webcams—45-6
Webcasts—300
Webisodes—300
Weblogs—16, 43, 77, 130, 165,
     170, 462
     helped pioneer—113
Weblogs Join Local Ranks—453
Webmaster—419
     station's—419
Websites—16, 18, 37, 45, 68, 99,
     131-2, 152, 182, 189, 237,
     245, 264, 271, 273-4, 284,
     296, 317-8, 347, 350-1, 358,
     367, 376, 382, 404-6, 408,
     438, 443-4
Website's—204
Webspeak—166
Webster—303
Webster, Noah—464
Weinberger, David—107, 113,
     146, 169-70, 374, 448, 457,
     470
Weirdos—156, 162, 166
Weiss, Steven—83
West—116, 182, 235, 316
West Coast—17, 284
What
     Local Media Web Sites Earn—
          453
     works—155
Whoosh—180

488

Printed in the United States
106670LV00003B/61-498/P